WOMEN, GENDER, AND HEALTH

Susan L. Smith and Nancy Tomes, Series Editors

Unlikely Entrepreneurs

Catholic Sisters and the Hospital Marketplace,
1865–1925

BARBRA MANN WALL

THE OHIO STATE UNIVERSITY PRESS
Columbus

Copyright © 2005 by The Ohio State University Press.
All rights reserved.

Library of Congress Cataloging-in-Publication Data

Wall, Barbra Mann.
　Unlikely entrepreneurs : Catholic sisters and the hospital marketplace, 1865–1925 / Barbra Mann Wall.
　　p. cm.—(Women, gender, and health)
　Includes bibliographical references and index.
　　ISBN 0-8142-0993-9 (cloth : alk. paper)—ISBN 0-8142-9071-X (CD-Rom)
　　1. Catholic hospitals—United States—Administration—History—19th century. 2. Catholic hospitals—United States—Administration—History—20th century. 3. Monasticism and religious orders for women—United States—History—19th century. 4. Monasticism and religious orders for women—United States—History—20th century. 5. Pastoral medicine—Catholic Church—History—19th century. 6. Pastoral medicine—Catholic Church—History—20th century.
　　[DNLM: 1. Hospitals, Religious—history—United States. 2. Catholicism—United States. 3. History, 19th Century—United States. 4. History, 20th Century—United States. 5. Hospitals, Religious—economics—United States.] I. Title. II. Series.
　　RA975.C37W34 2005
　　362.11'068-dc22
　　　　　　　　　　　　　　　　　　　　　　　　　2004030005

Paper (ISBN: 978-0-8142-5141-6)
Cover design by Jay Bastian
Type set in Adobe Caslon

For Robyn

Contents

List of Abbreviations	ix
List of Illustrations	x
List of Tables	xi
Preface	xii
Acknowledgments	xvi
Introduction	1

PART ONE:
EARLY BACKGROUND OF CATHOLIC SISTERS IN HEALTH CARE

1. Catholic Sisters in the Hospital Marketplace: The Genesis	13
2. "All the Advantages of a Religious Life": Religion, Gender, and New Public Roles	35

PART TWO:
HOSPITAL ESTABLISHMENTS IN THE MIDWEST, TEXAS, AND UTAH

3. "Not the Traditional Institution": Catholic Sisters in the Hospital Marketplace, 1853–1880	51
4. "An Institution for the Community and Not Narrowly Sectarian": Catholic Hospitals, 1880–1925	74
5. "Debts Are Our Only Wealth": Financing and Marketing Catholic Hospitals	102

PART THREE:
RELIGION, GENDER, AND AUTONOMY IN CATHOLIC HOSPITALS

6. "Our Heels Are Praying Very Hard All Day":
   Nursing in Catholic Hospitals   129

7. Power Sharing: Business Negotiations in Catholic Hospitals   148

8. Addressing the Times: Nuns and the Standardization
   Movement   166

   Conclusion   186

   Epilogue   192

   Notes   197

   Bibliography   237

   Index   257

List of Abbreviations

ACSJC-SL	Archives, Congregation of the Sisters of St. Joseph of Carondelet, St. Louis Province, St. Louis, Missouri
ACSJC-SP	Archives, Congregation of the Sisters of St. Joseph of Carondelet, St. Paul Province, St. Paul, Minnesota
AMIW	Archives, Motherhouse of the Incarnate Word, San Antonio, Texas
ASMW	Sisters of Providence Archives, Saint Mary-of-the-Woods, Indiana
CSC	Archives, Congregation of the Sisters of the Holy Cross, Saint Mary's, Notre Dame, Indiana
LSPC	Letters of Mother Saint Pierre Cinquin, translated by Sister Kathleen Garvey
RBSR	*Remark Book, Santa Rosa Infirmary,* San Antonio, Texas
RBSJ	*Remark Book, St. Joseph's Infirmary,* Fort Worth, Texas
ABSJH-SB	*Archives Book, St. Joseph's Hospital,* South Bend, Indiana
ABHCH	*Archives Book, Holy Cross Hospital, 1875–1920,* Salt Lake City, Utah
HCHRB	*Holy Cross Hospital Record Book, 1875–July 1920,* Salt Lake City, Utah
HCHBAA	*Holy Cross Hospital, Salt Lake City, Utah, Budgets and Annual Accounts from 1892 to Date*
"Annals-C"	"Annals," St. Mary's Infirmary, Cairo, Illinois
ABSMI	*Archives Book, St. Mary's Infirmary,* Cairo, Illinois
MDU	Manuscript Division, University of Utah Libraries, Salt Lake City, Utah
MPH	Marillac Provincial House, Daughters of Charity of St. Vincent de Paul, St. Louis, Missouri
UNDA	University of Notre Dame Archives, Notre Dame, Indiana

List of Illustrations

1.1	"The Sister"	14
1.2	Catholic Sisters in the Spanish-American War	22
1.3	Mother Angela Gillespie, CSC	25
1.4	Mother St. Pierre Cinquin, CCVI	28
2.1	Sister Lydia Clifford, CSC	38
2.2	Civil War Nurse Sister Paula Casey, CSC, and others, Santa Rosa Infirmary	45
3.1	Santa Rosa Infirmary	58
3.2	Holy Cross Hospital, 1875	61
4.1	Sisters of St. Joseph of Carondelet at St. Joseph's Hospital	79
4.2	Operating Room, St. Joseph's Hospital	80
4.3	St. Mary's Hospital, Minneapolis	83
4.4	Holy Cross Hospital with chapel	87
4.5	St. Joseph's Infirmary, Fort Worth, Texas	97
5.1	Private room, Holy Cross Hospital	105
5.2	Advertisement, St. Mary's Hospital	119
5.3	Entrance, Holy Cross Hospital	121
5.4	Interior, Holy Cross Hospital chapel	122
6.1	Horse-drawn ambulance	143
7.1	Nursing staff, Holy Cross Hospital	152
7.2	Graduating nurses, Sisters of Charity of the Incarnate Word	158
8.1	Meeting of the Catholic Hospital Association, St. Paul	169
8.2	Sisters of the Holy Cross and Poor Sisters of St. Francis Seraph	170
8.3	Holy Cross Hospital Pharmacy	173
8.4	Fifth Floor "Scientific Department"	175
8.5	Operating Room, Santa Rosa Infirmary	177
8.6	Early graduates of Santa Rosa Training School for Nurses	179

List of Tables

1.1	Ethnic Background of the Sisters of Charity of the Incarnate Word	30
2.1	Selected Work Histories	39
4.1	Hospitals, Churches, and Other Institutions	77
4.2	Personnel, St. Joseph's Hospital	81
4.3	Personnel, Holy Cross Hospital	89
4.4	Hospital Census Data	101
5.1	Financial Statistics, St. Joseph's Hospital	113
5.2	Income Comparisons	115
5.3	Expenditure Comparisons	117
5.4	Annual Accounts, Holy Cross Hospital, St. Mary's Hospital	124

Preface

This book analyzes Catholic sisters as entrepreneurs in hospital development in the late nineteenth and early twentieth centuries, in the full context of the social, cultural, economic, and medical history of the time. Historical argument is used to highlight the fundamental thesis that sisters created hospitals where a specific, socially beneficial type of care could be provided and purchased. This approach constructs and interprets the history of Catholic health-care institutions, the sisters who founded them, and the complex forces involved as they attempted to negotiate in the medical marketplace in the late nineteenth and early twentieth centuries.

The book shows the interaction between women's religious roles and broader economic roles of creating viable health-care institutions by exploring how boundaries and norms about health care are created in a market-oriented society. When immigrant nuns came to the United States in the late nineteenth century, they encountered a market economy that structured the way they developed their hospitals. Sisters enthusiastically engaged in this market as "entrepreneurs," but they used a set of tools and understandings that were counter to the market. Their entrepreneurship was not to expand earnings but rather to advance Catholic spirituality.

The sisters' story is important for several reasons. First, it illuminates the interplay between religious and secular institutions and the place of that interplay in American social history. Second, the history of nuns' work in health care in the United States illustrates the fundamentally gendered story of hospital foundations and what was to become the nursing profession. Third, it deepens understanding of the evolutionary development of consumerism by demonstrating how seemingly opposite topics such as commercialized exchange and spirituality can be interwoven. Last, the economic milieu in which the sisters found themselves, and the way they seized opportunities offered by the market economy to build health-care institutions and services, is a vital and thus far missing element in the history of the American health-care system.

The book comes at a crucial time in contemporary health-care debates. Hospitals were and still are places where both curing and death occur, and hence, places of important work.[1] In 2003, spending for health care in the United States reached $1.7 trillion, or 15.3 percent of the gross domestic product. Hospital care expenditures totaled $515.9 billion, representing one-third of total national health spending.[2] Furthermore, although the Catholic Church is one of the country's largest private suppliers of health services, sisters' attendance has been markedly diminished. As a result, Catholic hospitals barely resemble their predecessors of the late nineteenth and early twentieth centuries when the nuns' presence dominated. Health-care institutions that nuns have continued to manage have become increasingly bureaucratized and professionalized. What has been gained with these evolutionary changes? What has been lost? In the modern health-care climate, with the influences of national corporations, federal laws, spiraling costs, managed care, and medical practices that rely increasingly less on human judgments and increasingly more on technological innovations, the "modern" hospital setting reflects a dim memory of the institutions of the past. What issues will influence how government officials, managed-care providers, and other health-care planners respond to these changes? Who will provide hospital care as the sisters depart, and how will costs be met? Who will receive care, and who will be denied quality health services? This historical research informs these debates.

My background as a trained historian and nurse will enrich historical perspective. The methodology has involved seeking and evaluating evidence in primary sources that are located in sisters' archives, many of which have not been made public before. These include nuns' constitutions; official community records called "annals"; in-house circular letters; correspondence among sisters, clergy, and medical authorities; hospital chronicles and ledgers; prayer books, spiritual formation guides; sermons; and religious retreat records. While much of sisters' in-house correspondence reveals important aspects of their work, they often were written with a need to explain accomplishments to superiors. While attemping to present the sisters in as favorable a light as possible, they do not show evidence of any neglect in duties, which in all probability occurred. However, when viewed within the larger body of available evidence, indications of resistance sometimes show through. Other primary sources include minutes of nurses' and physicians' meetings; annual reports; account books; census reports; secular, diocesan, and ethnic newspapers; photographs; early city and medical directories; nineteenth- and early-twentieth-century trade journals; Catholic directories; and records of the Catholic Health Association (formerly the Catholic Hospital Association). Secondary sources have included religious, labor, and women's histories; nursing and medical histories; sisters' congregational histories; journals; and scholarship on nineteenth- and twentieth-century immigration. To respect confidentiality, patients' names have been changed.

To trace the evolution of women's entrepreneurial roles in Catholic hospital development, I have followed a chronological and thematic format. The book is divided into three parts. Part I provides early background information necessary to gain a picture of who these women were, where they came from, why they came, and what kind of lives they led. Chapter 1 provides an overview of the beginnings of Catholic hospital care in the United States. Using gender, religion, and ethnicity as integrating themes, chapter 2 examines how religious vocations were the means by which nuns could have opportunities to participate in hospital enterprises. The structure, organization, and politics of the Catholic Church provide additional context.

Part II draws from literature on the history of medicine to examine the sisters' hospital establishment in the Midwest, Texas, and Utah. Here the focus is on the hospital-building period. In the areas of financial support, purposes, patients, nursing care, and medical staff appointments, Catholic hospitals do not fit the model of non-Catholic voluntary hospitals, although as in other hospitals, ambiguities persisted. Chapter 3 examines the origins and growth of sisters' hospitals from 1853 to 1880. As a basis of comparison, successful and unsuccessful hospital ventures are analyzed. Chapter 4 focuses on hospital growth from 1880 to 1925. Growth of surgery was an industry, and it supplied income to hospitals across the United States. Nuns worked to attract surgeons and often expanded their facilities not only to provide the best available medical and surgical care to patients but also to meet physicians' and surgeons' demands. Chapter 5 examines sisters' financing and marketing strategies that they used to stay competitive in the expanding hospital field. Their marketing campaigns presented their institutions to the public by focusing on their service roles, their identification with scientific practices, and the sisters' distinct religious and gender identities.

However, one cannot understand Catholic hospitals in marketplace terms alone. Part III considers three important issues related to religion, gender, and autonomy: nuns' beliefs about illness and healing, their negotiations for power in their hospitals, and the tensions created by standardization and professionalization. Chapter 6 analyzes historical meanings of health and disease in the Catholic tradition. It was these formulations of meaning that underlay nuns' hospital establishment. Chapter 7 considers how religious, economic, and social boundaries altered the authority within Catholic hospitals run by women religious. In considering power relations, the relationships between medical men and sister-administrators and their negotiation strategies are analyzed using a framework by James C. Scott.[3] Chapter 8 shows twentieth-century changes in Catholic hospitals by exploring the impact of hospital standardization and the professionalization of nursing. The study ends in 1925, ten years after the Catholic Hospital Association formed to bring Catholic hospitals in the United States and Canada into compliance with national standards. By then, the Catholic Hospital Association and the hospitals under its watch had grown in power and influence. The conclusion ties the organizing themes together and assesses the overall significance of Catholic hospitals in the late nineteenth and early twentieth centuries. An epilogue examines the current state of the hospitals represented in this book.

Acknowledgments

I am indebted to many people and institutions for providing me with support. With a deep sense of gratitude and respect, I acknowledge the sisters and archivists of the women's religious congregations: Sisters Campion Kuhn, CSC; Kathryn Callahan, CSC; Georgia Costin, CSC; and Julie McGuire, CSC, of the Sisters of the Holy Cross in Notre Dame, Indiana, along with Carolynn Landgrebe; Sisters Mary Kraft, CSJ, and Charlene Sullivan, CSJ, of the St. Paul, Minnesota, and St. Louis, Missouri, provinces of the Sisters of St. Joseph of Carondelet; Sister Francisca Eiken, CCVI, of the Sisters of Charity of the Incarnate Word in San Antonio, Texas; and Sister Eileen A. Kelley, SP, of the Sisters of Providence of Saint Mary-of-the-Woods in Terre Haute, Indiana. The personnel of the Hesburgh Memorial Library at the University of Notre Dame, particularly Charlotte Ames and the staff in the university archives, helped me identify the many sources in American Catholic history. I am also grateful to the Daughters of Charity of St. Vincent de Paul, Marillac Provincial House, St. Louis, Missouri, who provided a copy of Mother Xavier Clark's "Instructions for the Care of the Sick," and to Christopher J. Kauffman, who recommended this rich source. Thanks also to Stan Larson and Walter Jones in the Special Collections Department, Manuscript Division, University of Utah Libraries, Salt Lake City, Utah; the staff at the Utah State Historical Society, Salt Lake City, Utah; personnel at the Catholic Archives of Texas, Austin, Texas; Chris Floerke and Dolores B. Olivarez at the University of Texas Institute of Texan Cultures at San Antonio; Jean Denham at the Memorial Hospital Archives, South Bend, Indiana; and the Indiana Center Province Archives, Notre Dame, Indiana.

The project was shaped by the intellectually stimulating environment at the University of Notre Dame. The history department offered continued support through all my endeavors. Christopher Hamlin was the best advisor and mentor anyone could ever have. Besides sharing his expertise, he always was encouraging, enthusiastic, and available, and it was a pleasure to be his student. I have also benefited from the guidance of R. Scott Appleby, Gail Bederman, and Suellen Hoy, all of whom shared their time and their wealth of knowledge.

I also extend a special thank-you to Susan Strasser, Philip Scranton, and Roger Horowitz who organized a conference sponsored by the Center for the History of Business, Technology, and Society at the Hagley Museum and Library in 2001. Entitled Commodifying Everything: Consumption and the Capitalist Enterprise, this conference brought together scholars from multiple disciplines. I especially want to thank Keith Wailoo for his comments on my paper presentation and for helping me to see that nuns' charitable and economic roles did not have to be mutually exclusive. I acknowledge Routledge for their permission to use excerpts from my chapter in the book that resulted from this conference: "Healthcare as Product: Catholic Sisters Confront Charity and the Hospital Marketplace, 1865–1925," which appeared in *Commodifying Everything: Relationships of the Market* (Routledge: © 2003), 143–68, ed. Susan Strasser, reproduced with permission of Routledge/Taylor & Francis Books, Inc.

This book reflects discussions at other scholarly conferences and sessions. I have learned much from comments by Christopher J. Kauffman, Ronald L. Numbers, Sister Mary Denis Maher, Sister Mary Oates, Conevery Bolton Valencius, and the Women's Studies Brown Bag group at Purdue University.

Excerpts of other articles have been revised and incorporated here, and I am grateful for permission to use these materials: "The Pin-Striped Habit: Balancing Charity and Business in Catholic Hospitals, 1865–1915," which appeared in *Nursing Research* 51, no. 1 (© 2002): 50–58, reproduced with permission of Lippincott, Williams, and Wilkins; "Science and Ritual: The Hospital as Medical and Sacred Space, 1865–1925," which appeared in *Nursing History Review* 11 (© 2003): 51–68, reproduced with permission from Springer Publishing Company, Inc., New York 10012; " 'We Might As Well Burn It': Catholic Sister-Nurses and Hospital Control, 1865–1930," which appeared in *US Catholic Historian* 20, no. 1 (©2002): 21–39, reproduced with permission from the University of Notre Dame Press; with Elaine Sorensen Marshall: "Religion, Gender, and Autonomy: A Comparison of Two Religious Women's Groups in Nursing and Hospitals in the Late Nineteenth and Early Twentieth Centuries," which appeared in *Advances in Nursing Science* 22, no. 1 (© 1999): 1–13, 18–22, reproduced with permission from Lippincott, Williams, and Wilkins; and with Sioban Nelson, " 'Our Heels Are

Praying Very Hard All Day,'" which appeared in *Holistic Nursing Practice* 17, no. 6 (© 2003): 320–28, reproduced with permission from Lippincott, Williams, and Wilkins.

Several sources provided financial support. As a graduate student, the history department at Notre Dame was generous in granting me fellowships and travel funds for research trips. Early manuscript preparation and research were supported by grants and/or fellowships from the Irish American Cultural Institute in Baltimore, Maryland; the Cushwa Center for the Study of American Catholicism at the University of Notre Dame; the Center for Nursing Historical Inquiry at the University of Virginia School of Nursing; the American Association for the History of Nursing; and Purdue University.

I owe a great debt to those colleagues who have given freely of their time, expertise, and unfailing support. I never would have undertaken a history project without the initial suggestion and mentorship of JoAnn G. Widerquist at Saint Mary's College in Notre Dame, Indiana. I was encouraged at the University of Notre Dame by Dorothy Pratt, Nicole Mishe Gothelf, Kathleen Sprows Cummings, Jane Hannon, and Estelle McNair. I also want to acknowledge Joan Lynaugh and Barbara Brodie for their support of my desire to merge historical study with nursing; the editors from The Ohio State University Press; and Sioban Nelson and Heather Munro Prescott, reviewers of this book, for their important comments and suggestions that influenced my thinking and interpretations.

Although too numerous to name, I want to thank colleagues at Purdue University School of Nursing. Lynn Holland's editorial assistance was invaluable. The final stages of the manuscript preparation would have been indefinitely delayed if it had not been possible to at least partially limit my academic responsibilities. Julie Cowan Novak and Linda Augustin Simunek allowed me that time, and Taunya Rapisarda and other colleagues willingly stepped in to cover for me whenever I needed help.

My final comments are for friends and family. Cynthia Cantwell and Kathy Yayboke deserve recognition for their friendship and the encouragement they extended over many years. I acknowledge the love, guidance, and tireless support of my parents, Billy and Jean Mann, and Debra Mann, my sister and great friend. My son, Austin, has given me more delight than he will ever know. His wonderful sense of humor has helped me through writer's block, computer panics, and numerous frozen dinners. Most of all, I want to thank my husband, Robyn. He has been the best supporter, friend, and critic, and his expert editorial marks can be seen throughout the book. Without him, it would not have been completed, and to him it is dedicated.

Introduction

In 1877, Sister Lidwina Butler sat in the dimly lit steerage compartment of a trans-Atlantic sailing vessel, her thoughts no doubt shifting between the Ireland she left behind and the New World she would soon embrace. Few in this last great wave of Irish emigrants could have foreseen that this youthful nun would one day become the administrator of a major Catholic hospital. And certainly most American citizens, many of whom viewed the Irish as the dregs of society, would not have imagined her ascension to such a challenging and respected position. Although Sister Lidwina's personal story was in no way unique—many other European- and American-born women were equally as successful—it is used now to personify the personal, spiritual, and business journeys of Catholic women who helped to establish the modern hospital system in the United States.

Sister Lidwina was one of the ubiquitous Irish nuns whom religious orders entrusted with hospital administration.[1] Born Annette Butler in County Kilkenny in 1850, she received her education from the Sisters of Loreto in Rathfarnum, where girls from upper- and middle-class families received a high-quality education. After her mother died when she was a girl, Annette had to manage the large household. In 1876, she joined the Congregation of the Sisters of the Holy Cross. When she made her final profession of vows in 1879, she was given the name Sister M. Lidwina. Her household management skills were early training for the executive tasks she would later undertake in two different hospitals in the United States. Following assignments in the infirmary and dormitory at the motherhouse in Notre Dame, Indiana, she became superior of St. Lawrence Hospital in Ogden, Utah, and later served in this same capacity for eighteen years at Holy Cross Hospital in Salt Lake

City.[2] The hospital underwent tremendous growth under her direction. She set admission policies, protected the hospitals' assets, and promoted it to the press and general public. She controlled equipment purchases, nursing assignments, and billing procedures. Sister Lidwina was known as a straightforward woman who could be quite formidable, and she often would exercise those personal traits in her role of approving all medical staff admissions and dismissals.

This illustration shows an important aspect of a woman's religious vocation: the entrepreneurial task of building an enormous health-care empire. Sister Lidwina built a large institution and controlled not only its personnel but also its finances. Another aspect of a religious vocation for Catholic women included the service-oriented role, although initially it was not clear what each nun's specific work would be. Sisters were frontline nurses during wartime and in hospitals across the United States. They provided care for physical sustenance, but equally important, they also tended the dying, giving spiritual care and saving souls.

In this book, the hospital activities of three orders of Catholic nuns are explored. Each has a long history in health care, and each was chosen because of different geographic locations and historical missions. The examination centers on the Sisters of St. Joseph of Carondelet from St. Paul, Minnesota; the Sisters of Charity of the Incarnate Word from San Antonio, Texas; and the Sisters of the Holy Cross from Notre Dame, Indiana. Each group embodied the issues of gender, religion, and ethnicity that animated the move westward. The book details sisters' establishment of hospitals during a key transitional period: from 1865, when Catholic hospitals first experienced significant growth as community-based, religious institutions, to 1925, when they transformed to expensive, modern hospitals of science and technology. Much of hospital history tends to focus on large eastern institutions in New York, Boston, and Philadelphia, but this book centers on the more numerous smaller hospitals in the Midwest and Trans-Mississippi West where gender roles, religion, economics, and local political independence and power were contested issues with distinct histories from eastern hospitals. Seven representative hospitals in Indiana, Texas, Minnesota, Utah, and Illinois have been chosen for study, with references to other hospitals and women's religious orders for comparison purposes. Significantly, in these areas nuns strengthened their influence among a growing, diverse population.

Between 1865 and 1925, the three congregations operated and owned more than forty hospitals in the Midwest and Trans-Mississippi West. They included general hospitals as well as facilities for mining, marine, and railroad patients who did not have women at home to care for them. Sisters also established orphanages, often in the same building as the hospital; homes for the elderly; and specialized hospitals. They staffed military hospitals, hospital ships, and "pesthouses" for people with contagious diseases such as smallpox. The sisters took large financial risks, and their institutions were not always successful. Still, today Catholic hospitals have become major actors in the medical marketplace. They are the largest single group of the nation's not-for-profit hospitals in the United States, thus warranting a voice in any historical examination of hospitals.[3]

In exploring Catholic hospitals' historical roots, the following questions are examined: How did Catholic sisters, many of whom were immigrants, become heads of major health-care institutions and compete successfully in the vast hospital industry by the early twentieth century? How could women, who took vows of poverty, carry out this huge feat? How did they negotiate through an emerging consumer market? What beliefs and attitudes did they hold which justified their actions? What were the interrelationships of gender, religion, ethnicity, class, power, and control within Catholic hospitals? How did nuns' health care translate into a distinct type of nursing? What was the influence of geographic region? To answer these questions, I rely on the methods of social and cultural history, seeking to understand the development of Catholic hospitals as a women's movement. By offering a new comprehension of nuns' roles in hospital establishment, this book begins to fill a void in the history of women, religion, labor, medicine, and nursing.

A major theme is that in the Midwest, Texas, and Utah, Catholic sisters engaged in cross-denominational and contracting work by which they could create hospitals where a specific, socially beneficial type of care could be provided and purchased. In Catholic hospitals, sister-nurses were spiritual agents. They dedicated themselves to their "purity of intention" and selfless service, and their religious devotion permeated their hospitals.[4] In describing the history of nuns' activities, I also argue that they shaped the experiences of illness, suffering, dying, and healing in distinct ways. Although the idea of the contemporary hospital is based upon the assumption that the human organism can be understood and treated through a reductionist concept of disease as a set of physiological and biochemical processes, the actors in this book would not have accepted this definition. For nuns, disease was seen not only in biological terms but also within a spiritual framework. Out of the tragedy of human suffering could come spiritual enlightenment, even spiritual salvation. Thus, from a new perspective, the book examines not only secular but also sacred influences on health care that have not been considered in consumer literature.

Gender is another integrating theme. These were single women who lived in a communal relationship with other women. Within the Catholic community, they were held in high esteem. They also were businesswomen who were actively engaged in hospital building and marketing, tasks that society believed at the time was men's work. Though biographies of Catholic ecclesiastical leaders and histories of Catholic social welfare movements recognize bishops and priests as the driving force behind Catholic charities,[5] it was nuns who built, financed, and administered most of the Catholic hospitals in the United States. Provision of health-care services that blended sacred and entrepreneurial motives was not a new idea in frontier areas.[6] What was novel about nuns' work was its multicultural emphasis, the contractual nature of the work, and the opportunity patients had to receive care in the proximity of religious women. In the process, sisters established bonds with patients, local governments, industrial companies, medical schools, and church authorities. In these interactions, gender-defined conflicts occurred between women and men, particularly friction between sister-administrators, physicians, and prelates over the issue of authority. These confrontations are analyzed throughout the book.

Ethnic values were also significant to the sisters. The book examines the entrants to religious congregations, including the many immigrants who composed much of the labor force in Catholic hospitals, and how they worked their way through the peculiar American capitalistic system. For example, the three orders featured in this book attracted many Irish women who subsequently became nurses and hospital administrators.[7] As immigrants during and after the Irish Famine or as daughters of immigrants, they strongly emphasized economic security. With a solid sense of self, they took decisive action on issues that they deemed important.[8] This characteristic would prove extremely useful as nuns negotiated new boundaries in the expanding hospital field. Furthermore, each of the three orders had French foundations, which significantly affected their spirituality and how they lived their lives. What abided for the women was a combination of traditions that emphasized a search for holiness through prayer and meditation, a life of discipline and self-abnegation, and action through service.

From 1866 to 1926, Catholic sisters established nearly five hundred hospitals in the United States.[9] In 1800, however, the hospital was insignificant to health care. Medical and nursing practices were considered the moral responsibility of families and neighborhoods. In the late nineteenth and early twentieth centuries, as society became increasingly industrialized and mobile and as medical practices grew in their sophistication and complexity, the notion that responsible families and caring communities "took care of their own" became more difficult to apply. The result was a gradual shift toward the professionalization of health-care practices that eventually included the development of a full and competitive commercial market for medical services. Medical care was no longer simply a societal function but, instead, had become a commodity to be purchased.[10] In this environment, Catholic sisters fused healing services with market activities, leading to tensions between the notion of caring and business practices. But there was no dichotomy between religious charity and marketplace roles for nuns. Their hospital activities reveal complex relationships that include an interaction of gender, ethnicity, religion, and economic realities.

The woman-centered entrepreneurship of Catholic sisters had a distinctive effect on the character of today's American health-care institutions. Nuns created hospitals much more similar to the modern hospital of fee-paying patients than the traditional nineteenth-century voluntary hospital. While they accepted much of the redefinition of hospital care and nursing that began in the late nineteenth century with the rise of capital- and science-intensive medicine, they subtly incorporated this redefinition into a concept of hospital care that remained distinctly Catholic; that is, it conformed with Catholic values and a sacramental worldview as defined by the Council of Trent.

The role that women have played in shaping the modern hospital has scarcely been documented. The focus on sister-nurses is a means to recover their centrality for a medical history, which has been defined by doctors; for a Catholic history, which has marginalized nuns; and for women's history, which does not quite know what to make of them. Women's historians have recognized the importance of evangelical Protestantism as a motivating factor for many women, encouraging them to enter the public domain and to develop new "bonds of sisterhood."[11] However, there have been few comparable studies on American Catholic women who became major players in a vast industry.

Lately, a number of scholars have written histories of Catholic sisters with careful attention to historical criticism and method and have avoided edification problems of early histories, although their main focus has not been on nursing sisters.[12] Christopher Kauffman's extensive religious history of Catholic health care has centered on sister-nurses, but it is not intended to be a gender analysis.[13] Sioban Nelson's book on nineteenth-century nuns in health care in Britain, Australia, and the United States brings sisters to the forefront of nursing and is a broad study, as well.[14] Bernadette McCauley examines sisters in New York and the complex relationships with the head of the Catholic Church there.[15] This study will build on these works to provide yet another view of nuns by evaluating the relationship among their religious worldviews, their practices, and how they shaped health care in the United States. Using gender, religion, ethnicity, and economics as thematic frames to examine the hospital movement provides a more nuanced understanding of the multiple perspectives that contributed to its development and growth.

The study also builds on earlier social and cultural histories of the modern hospital. The history of hospitals in the United States is largely a story of Eastern institutions founded and administered by men.[16] A more recent history by Guenter Risse has examined hospitals from pre-Christian times to the present, but it is not intended to be a comprehensive history of Catholic hospitals. While it shows the profound changes of Catholic hospital organization and management in Buffalo, New York, between 1954 and 1974, it does not posit these changes in the context of the late nineteenth and early twentieth centuries, when Catholic hospitals first emerged as community institutions and transformed to modern medical facilities.[17]

The book provides a complex study of how and why people participate in a market economy. In the late nineteenth century, nuns developed their hospitals as service-providing institutions within a capitalist economic system. Between 1865 and 1925, both Catholic and non-Catholic hospitals changed from primarily charitable institutions to modern medical facilities that served increasing numbers of paying middle-class patients. To obtain funding, sisters had to seek out constituencies of patients, and they worked with mine and railroad owners, government agencies, and the general public to do so. This study supports Rosemary Stevens's analysis of hospitals as both charities and businesses.[18] Although Stevens argued that hospitals developed a consumer orientation in the 1920s, findings reveal that Catholic hospitals' unique funding strategies necessarily demanded an earlier market orientation. Like other hospital owners, Catholic sisters saw their facilities as charities serving the community, even though they tried to maximize their earnings. At the same time, nuns viewed themselves as stewards of the hospital revenues, which were to be reinvested in the church's mission of evangelization and service to the needy.

This book also informs us more about women's work, particularly women's roles in the marketplace. Nursing literature seldom examines women as entrepreneurs competing in a changing market, nor are there many articles on religious women who defy the stereotype of passive nuns merely bowing to the wishes of the church hierarchy. This book attempts to fill these gaps. In addition, much of nursing history has involved the study of an articulate elite group of women.[19] By studying nuns as nurses and hospital administrators, we see another history, one that predates the well-known tradition established by Florence Nightingale. Most important, a historical perspective of sisters' work can provide increased understandings of women's access to social and economic authority.

The claim that Catholic sisters shaped hospital development in distinct ways requires addressing a number of discrete issues. First, although they were successful administrators and nurses, as Catholic nuns they had to remain within the ecclesiastical boundaries of their church. Women's religious orders grew out of what seemed to be a restricted environment after the Council of Trent, which met in three intermittent sessions between 1545 and 1563.[20] In sixteenth-century Europe, papal authority spoke in a clear and unwavering voice that Catholic nuns refrain from social activism and maintain strict enclosure. This position had been issued in the text *Pericoloso* in 1298 and reinforced by the bishops at Trent.[21] Furthermore, Trent had established a management model that required women's religious orders to be subject to male governance, and women's communities in the nineteenth century still followed this model. Hence, sisters had to deal with polarized tensions between their desires to establish new institutions and pressures to stay within hierarchical boundaries. In the late nineteenth century, nuns took major steps to establish more control over their work, thereby actively resisting interference from local dioceses. One manifestation was that they acquired autonomy and ownership of their hospitals. As they developed strategies to attain independence, however, they had to do so without alienating church and medical authorities.

A second important issue to address involves the influence of church and societal gender expectations on sisters' activities. Like other nineteenth-century women, nuns worked within the boundaries of traditional gender ideology. This invites new questions about Catholic sisters: How did their gender identity affect the way they created nursing institutions? How did it influence their understanding of saintliness, self-abnegation, salvation? How did it modify their relationships with those outside their orders, both Catholic and non-Catholic, male and female? This book challenges the prevailing view of the subordinate role that women played in late–nineteenth- and early-twentieth-century American hospitals. Determining the ways women negotiated their roles within gender-based traditions of both church and society is central to understanding sisters' influence in the hospital field.

Third, it is important not only to understand Catholic sisters in terms of how they negotiated gender roles but also to understand their particular roles as nuns. Women could balance the increasing power of the clergy through an alternative source of spiritual equality by entering a religious order.[22] This brought nuns increased respect and status. As they gained authority within the Catholic Church, sisters found a particular value in nursing. In that position, they discovered a sacramental role independent of the male priesthood. Hospitals were places of critical health situations that sometimes led to death; hence, they were sites of important sacramental power. Roles related to salvation could be played out. Particularly in their hospitals, then, sisters could obtain independent roles by being centrally involved in important sacramental occasions that involved mediation in sickness and death.

This book challenges paradigms that equate service and caretaking primarily with weakness and subordination. Although sisters took vows of poverty, chastity, and obedience, their ethos of service did not, in fact, make them weak or subordinate. And herein lies a paradox as one tries to understand sisters' missions. Many women who shared the zeal for progress, expertise, and optimism held by others of the Progressive Era typically saw obedience and service as retreats from power. Ironically, these very characteristics were routes to prestige and autonomy for nuns. Their obedience and deference earned them, within their church and society, a position of status and respect, which served them well in the management of large hospitals.

Fourth, the concept of entrepreneurship is used to interpret the meaning of sisters' work. It involves organizing, managing, and assuming the risks of a business or firm. Nuns oversaw budgets that totaled hundreds of thousands of dollars, purchased land and buildings, obtained financial backing for the construction of new buildings, and made other equally important financial decisions. They advertised and competed for clients and won approval of the medical community. Their hospitals were, first, manifestations of religious and charitable ideals. At the same time, sisters were attuned enough to the marketplace to adopt business strategies that allowed their institutions to grow and thrive.

Entrepreneurship also includes undertaking an endeavor that has long-term goals of growth. The point is not that growth occurred in women's religious communities, but that "to grow" was essential to their identities. Just as business firms must grow or yield to the competition, similar dynamics occurred within congregations of Catholic sisters. For practical and religious reasons, nuns made a powerful push toward expanding their communities, serving more people, and building more hospitals. Through this process, the career opportunities of community members could be realized as well.

And nuns' congregations did grow. In the seventeenth century, women established dozens of uncloistered religious communities, many in France where more than eighty were founded between 1630 and 1720.[23] Among these groups were the Sisters of St. Joseph and the Order of the Incarnate Word and Blessed Sacrament. Another growth period occurred in the nineteenth century when thousands of teaching and nursing congregations, including the Sisters of the Holy Cross, developed in France, Ireland, England, Germany, Australia, New Zealand, and the United States. The number of sisters in all congregations rose in the United States from 1,344 in 1850 to more than forty thousand by 1900.[24]

A fifth issue is the way in which nuns maintained nonsubordinate relationships with doctors. Control over revenues and admissions were negotiated issues in Catholic hospitals in the late nineteenth and early twentieth centuries. Although sisters cooperated with doctors in the provision of new kinds of surgery and yielded to their authority on medical treatment, nuns maintained a unique hierarchy and kept control over their hospitals' administrative and nursing affairs. What resulted was a relationship between sisters and physicians that was based on complementary interests.

Last, sisters' relationship with physicians requires us to rethink the role of professionalism within this context. Here I depart from the professionalization theorist Andrew Abbott, who describes a system of professions whereby a group achieves status through turf battles; that is, professions grow when a niche develops. Abbott suggests that one way turf battles are resolved is by creating subsidiary professions that have their own sphere as long as they admit their subordinate status.[25] Abbott places nursing within this circumscribed environment, arguing that it is subordinated under medicine.[26] However, where Catholic nuns were concerned, the appearance of subsidiary status was not a matter of carving off territory but rather one of recognizing the value of acquiescing in some ways to maintain autonomy in others. Thus, sisters found ways to do what they wanted. Conflicts became a matter of negotiation, not between subordinates, as Abbott would have us believe, but between parties of equal power. These nuns provide examples of women who created new roles for themselves without violating hierarchical boundaries within which they lived and worked. Yet, they took control of their destinies and gained a place for themselves in church and society. This translated into increased influence for them, and their stature enabled them to accomplish the tasks they deemed important.

Part 1

Early Background of Catholic Sisters in Health Care

1

Catholic Sisters in the Hospital Marketplace:

THE GENESIS

> Went on board of hospital boat 'Red Rover' for the first time with a message to our captain. Saw some of our wounded and sick. All seemed to be doing well. Found that some 'Sisters of Charity' were stationed on the boat and all the patients spoke very high of their patience and self-denial.[1]
>
> John Gordon Morrison
> July 20, 1862

In 1862, John Gordon Morrison, an Irish immigrant serving with the Thirtieth New York Volunteer Infantry, had been assigned to the USS *Carondelet* in the western theater of the war when, following an engagement with the Confederate ship *Arkansas* on the Mississippi River, he "put the last shot in her." Several of the sick and wounded from that battle were taken to the USS *Red Rover*, the navy's first hospital ship. After his visit to the ship, Morrison recorded the above note in his diary. The nuns he encountered actually were the Sisters of the Holy Cross, and they were among over five hundred Roman Catholic nuns from twenty-one different religious communities who served as nurses during the Civil War[2] (see fig. 1.1).

Historically, Catholic sister-nurses have had a mission to care for the sick, the injured, the aged, and the dying. In the competition for hospital

FIGURE 1.1 "THE SISTER," *Harper's Magazine* sketch of a Sister of the Holy Cross on board the *Red Rover*, May 9, 1863, 300. (Courtesy Sisters of the Holy Cross Archives, Saint Mary's, Notre Dame, IN)

services in the United States, they were around from the start. They adopted an economically based model that was established upon finding and servicing markets of consumers. One way of understanding their entrepreneurial roles, then, is that they went where Catholics and potential Catholics congregated and provided services for these specific groups.

Social and Medical Needs and the Hospital Marketplace

New medical markets developed in the nineteenth century as immigration brought diverse cultures and religions that crowded the East, Midwest, and West. "Push" factors in Europe such as famine and religious persecution and "pull" factors in the United States such as available jobs and land increased the number of immigrants and more than doubled the total number of Catholics by 1860. Between 1820 and 1840, over 260,000 Irish came to the United States. Fueled by the Great Famine that struck Ireland in 1846 to 1851, which resulted in the deaths of nearly two million people, over one million Irish left their country. Germans were the other Catholic immigrant group that settled in the United States before 1860, numbering approximately 1.5 million people. Even larger increases in immigration occurred after 1890 when other groups emigrated from southern and eastern Europe.[3] Medical markets also increased in response to the need for services by people congregating in urban, mining, and railroad centers who were detached from traditional family-based medical care. These problems intensified in the Midwest, Texas, and Utah as railway and mining centers increasingly attracted single, primarily immigrant, men who had nowhere to turn when they became ill except to a hospital.[4]

Catholic leaders worried over losing immigrants to rival social and religious enticements. Urbanization and industrialization had generated labor unrest and a breakdown of traditional sources of moral authority, especially the authority of the family and the Catholic Church. The diverse cultures and religions of the Midwest and Trans-Mississippi West challenged the church's authority as well. Leaders sensed that significant Catholic populations existed with inadequate spiritual institutions. To tap this growing group, the church created separate hospitals, orphanages, and schools and defined them along religious lines.[5] Nuns staffed these facilities in which they could preserve the Catholic identity. They focused much of their attention on social welfare for their own; that is, for working-class immigrants. As a result, nuns had a large role to play in the shift of medical practice from homes to hospitals that occurred in the late nineteenth century.

As sisters expanded their health care in the wake of immigration, most saw themselves as missionaries in a country dominated by Protestantism. To carry out their work and serve more people, they had to build their communities and institutions. As a result, the Sisters of St. Joseph, Sisters of the Holy Cross, and Sisters of Charity of the Incarnate Word, along with scores of others, fashioned new religious lives for themselves and developed the means by which they could carry out entrepreneurial activities in the public domain of the hospital. To understand their hospital roles, an exploration of the historical development of Catholic health care is helpful.

EARLY CHRISTIAN NURSING

A nursing tradition developed during the early years of Christianity when the benevolent outreach of the church included not only caring for the sick but also feeding the hungry, caring for widows and children, clothing the poor, and offering hospitality to strangers. The religious ethos of charity continued with the rapid outgrowth of monastic orders in the fifth and sixth centuries and extended into the Middle Ages. Monasteries added hospital wards, where to "care" meant to give comfort and spiritual sustenance. This provided a rationale for nursing the sick to become a function of community life for both male and female religious orders. The fact that nuns were nursing in hospitals did not mean, however, that they became nuns specifically to nurse and do other good works. Engaging in ministry was irrelevant to their primary goal of personal sanctification through asceticism or prayer. Thus, whatever work they performed was done not as a ministry but rather as ascetic training for the soul's perfection.[6]

A real innovation began in the seventeenth century and continued into the late nineteenth and early twentieth centuries when male and female "apostolic" or "active" orders developed with ministerial works as essential missions.[7] At that time, many women across Europe, both Catholic and Protestant, responded to their churches' calls for evangelical conversions and revival.[8] In particular, the Catholic Counter-Reformation in France witnessed a rapid expansion of new communities of women religious. An important development for nursing was the foundation of the Daughters of Charity by Vincent de Paul and Louise de Marillac in 1633. This "active" community of unmarried women and widows lived together and dedicated themselves to charitable works, including serving the sick poor.[9] Many other women followed the Vincentian framework, which joined humility, obedience, and simplicity to good works, and they practiced nursing as an imitation of Christ's charitable qualities.

Catholic Sisters in the United States

In the United States, nuns framed their hospital roles after Vincent de Paul's model. They had extensive experience caring for people outside the home environment. In the mid-nineteenth century, some "natural-born" or "professed" nurses cared for nonfamily members to provide an income for themselves, but most women in the United States were unaccustomed to caring for strangers. They provided nursing care in the home as part of their domestic duties and mainly tended family members or friends.[10] By contrast, when women joined a Catholic religious community, they intentionally accepted the inherent caretaker role for persons beyond their own circle of family and friends. During epidemics, when others fled cities, nuns remained to care for the sick and dying. While no formal training programs existed, sisters learned by experience in their hospitals and by visiting the sick at home.[11]

Sisters' hospitals evolved from a general institution for the indigent, which provided multifaceted services for the sick poor, widows, the aged, and children. Catholic hospitals also grew out of other more clearly medical contexts: epidemics, wars, railroad and mining injuries, and the need for hospitals for sick sailors.

The degree to which sisters were able to establish entrepreneurial programs of their choosing depended on their using a variety of strategies. By the 1850s, the American Catholic Church had moved away from lay trusteeism and congregationalism and had accepted the hierarchical authority centralized in the papacy. This model emphasized order, control, subordination, and disciplined uniformity.[12] In the nineteenth century, when nuns' communities were small, they sought legitimacy and support from local ecclesiastical authorities. As congregations grew, however, and circumstances demanded more extensive services, sisters resisted the limitations placed on them by the church hierarchy. Some orders remained under diocesan control, and the diocese rather than the religious congregation owned the hospitals. Others centralized their communities across diocesan lines, with a central motherhouse and female superior who would have authority over all the other houses. Eventually, provinces would be formed in areas where there were large numbers of sisters and institutions, and they remained tied to the motherhouse through a system of general government.

Sisters were careful to record their distinct governmental roles in their constitutions, to which they could appeal when necessary. Constitutions articulated sisters' beliefs about their ministerial priorities, rights, responsibilities, government structures, and relationships with ecclesiastical superiors. As nuns wrote and rewrote constitutions, they were not simply adopting standard forms of behavior. These documents, in fact, were extremely important in creating an area of specialty for the community to do certain work and maintain its independence. So valuable was nuns' independence that they spent a great deal of time refining constitutions to support their area of service.[13] While these revisions may appear muted because they took place within the framework of service, minor changes reflected major assertions of independence.

Women's congregations turned the increased church centralization to their advantage. By 1915, each of the three congregations in this book had established itself as a papal community. As such, they were directly responsible to the pope rather than the local bishop, and this checked bishops' interference with their work.[14] It would prove to be a key factor in sisters' hospitals, which they rather than the diocese owned.

Catholic Hospitals, 1823–1870

In the United States, Catholic sisters linked charity and market activities for charitable reasons. This strategy had long been successful for them in Europe, where they had contracted with government and medical authorities to run hospitals in which they could combine evangelism with nursing skill. In 1823, nuns first began staffing hospitals in the continental United States at the Baltimore Infirmary, where they charged a small fee for admission. Here, university officials asked the Sisters of Charity from Emmitsburg, Maryland (later known as the Daughters of Charity), founded by Elizabeth Seton, to staff the infirmary. Between 1828 and 1860, this congregation established eighteen hospitals in ten states and the District of Columbia, more than half the Catholic hospitals founded before 1860. They cared for medical and surgical cases and patients with mental disorders, and they were particularly active during epidemics.[15]

The epidemic-stricken cities of the mid-nineteenth century needed hospitals immediately. Another religious congregation that became permanently involved in nursing at this time was the Sisters of Charity of Nazareth. After the cholera epidemic of 1832, they began caring for the sick in Louisville, Kentucky, under the direction of Mother Catherine Spalding. In 1842, they started a hospital in Nashville, Tennessee. During the cholera and yellow fever epidemics between 1830 and 1840, the Sisters of Charity of Our Lady of Mercy worked in a hospital in Charleston, South Carolina. Although racial discrimination limited African Americans' institutional development, two communities of African American women—the Oblate Sisters of Providence, founded in Baltimore in 1828, and the Sisters of the Holy Family, founded in New Orleans in 1842—also cared for the sick during epidemics. The Oblate Sisters nursed over two hundred patients in the Baltimore Almshouse during the 1832 cholera scourge. In New Orleans in the 1850s, the Sisters of the Holy Family cared for victims of cholera and yellow fever and also established a ministry to the aged.[16]

As the unprecedented immigration of the 1840s and 1850s enlarged the medical market, social and religious roles for Catholic sisters expanded. The daily arrival of immigrants, the church's fear of Protestant proselytizing, and the social problems brought on by urban growth all provided opportunities for nuns to establish hospitals in the United States. While Protestant growth occurred particularly in the southern regions of the country, Catholic enclaves of European immigrants predominated in eastern cities such as New York, Boston, and Philadelphia, and midwestern cities such as St. Paul, St. Louis, and Chicago.

The Catholic Church was in the minority in Texas and Utah, but these areas attracted many immigrant miners and railroad workers from Catholic countries who were potential American Catholics.[17]

In the mid-nineteenth century, anti-Catholic nativist sentiments occurred in response to the growing Catholic population and influenced Catholic institutions. Protestant hostility arose from anxieties over Catholics' obedience to the pope and priest, which Protestants thought was incompatible with republican citizenship and religious freedom. Catholic leaders counterattacked nativism by attempting to demonstrate the church's compatibility with American democracy. Because of the prevailing anti-Catholicism, Catholics formed strong attachments to their own institutions.[18]

It is difficult to determine the exact number of hospitals that various women's religious groups established because of the lack of record-keeping and the humility of the nuns who did not wish to call attention to themselves. Nevertheless, some data do exist. From 1840 to 1870, nuns from thirty-four different congregations either established or took charge of more than seventy acute hospitals in the United States.[19] Many came from Europe, including the French Congregation of the Sisters of St. Joseph, who arrived in the United States in 1836. From 1849 to 1859, they staffed St. Joseph's Hospital in Philadelphia, largely to care for Irish immigrants. They also opened a hospital in Wheeling, Virginia (now West Virginia) in 1853 and St. Joseph's Hospital in St. Paul, Minnesota, in 1853.[20] Another important community was the Sisters of Charity of St. Augustine, who came from France to begin St. Joseph's Hospital in Cleveland in 1852 (later reestablished as St. Vincent's Charity Hospital).

Irish women were particularly active. A prominent community that augmented nursing in the United States after 1840 was the Sisters of Mercy, founded by Catherine McAuley in Dublin in 1831. The sisters arrived in the United States in 1843 with a history of caring for the sick poor in homes and in hospitals. The need for hospitals in the Midwest evolved much as it had for eastern cities as disease and injury followed the many immigrant laborers. In the 1840s, they established a hospital in Pittsburgh. Then in 1846, after bouncing in stagecoaches across Pennsylvania, Ohio, and Michigan, they arrived in Chicago, where they incorporated Mercy Hospital in 1852.[21] The Sisters of Mercy also went to Vicksburg, Mississippi, where they nursed victims of war and epidemics.[22] Another group of Irish Sisters of Mercy under the direction of Mother Baptist Russell arrived in San Francisco in 1854 and founded St. Mary's Hospital after a cholera epidemic had ravaged the city.[23]

Wars provided ideal proving grounds for sisters because their nursing during these conflicts helped improve negative perceptions of Catholics. Nuns' nursing service during the Civil War brought just such an opportunity. As a result, the public's perceptions of sisters and the Catholic Church itself improved dramatically.[24] Thereafter, congregations such as the Sisters of Providence of Saint Mary-of-the-Woods, Indiana; the Sisters of the Holy Cross; and the Sisters of Charity of the Incarnate Word became involved in health care.

Catholic women's congregations were particularly active in following the immigrant into new industrial, railroad, and mining centers in the Trans-Mississippi West. The Sisters of Charity of Nazareth became the nucleus of the Sisters of Charity of Leavenworth, Kansas, who established hospitals in Leavenworth; Helena, Montana; Denver, Colorado; and Butte and Anaconda, Montana; to care for miners, loggers, and railroad workers. The Sisters of Mercy opened pioneer institutions in Iowa and Nebraska, and the Presentation Sisters were active in South Dakota. Hospital care in New Mexico can be traced back to another branch of the Sisters of Charity, who established St. Vincent's Hospital in Santa Fe in 1865. In the Pacific Northwest, the French-Canadian Sisters of Providence were particularly active in hospital development. Led by Mother Joseph Pariseau, they came from Montreal in 1856 to open a hospital in Vancouver, Washington. In 1873, they established St. Patrick's Hospital in Missoula, Montana. By the end of the nineteenth century, they had established eleven hospitals.[25]

Sisters from Germany opened health-care institutions in areas with especially large numbers of German immigrants. The Sisters of the Poor of St. Francis immigrated to the United States in 1850 and established hospitals in Ohio, Kentucky, New Jersey, New York, Kansas, and Illinois. Another Franciscan congregation, the Sisters of the Third Order of St. Francis, established their first hospital in Philadelphia in 1860. A branch of this order, which became an independent community and called themselves the Sisters of the Third Franciscan Order, Minor Conventuals, cared for victims of leprosy in the Hawaiian Islands, a ministry that eventually included the facility at Molokai.[26]

Catholic Hospitals, 1870–1920

From 1870 to 1920, 189 different congregations established 275 Catholic acute-care hospitals.[27] By 1870, Boston had received large numbers of Irish immigrants, and about 20 percent were women whose mortality from childbed fever was especially high. In 1872, five Irish immigrant nuns from the Third Order of St. Francis established St. Elizabeth's Hospital for Women in Boston. The facility soon expanded to become all-inclusive, requiring a change in the hospital charter so that "its benefits should not be limited to female." Still, the hospital's commitment to women remained strong as it continued to care for women too poor and desperate to give birth at home.[28]

Because of religious persecution in Germany under Bismarck, additional German women's communities sought refuge in the United States and opened hospitals across the Midwest. In 1869, the Poor Handmaids of Jesus Christ established their first hospital in Fort Wayne, Indiana, followed by one in Chicago and another in Mishawaka, Indiana.[29] The Sisters of the Third Order of St. Francis expanded their work in Illinois, which included the founding of St. John's Hospital in Springfield in 1875. That same year, the Poor Sisters of St. Francis Seraph of the Perpetual Adoration opened St. Elizabeth's Hospital in Lafayette, Indiana, one of twenty health-care institutions they established across the Midwest in the late nineteenth and early twentieth centuries. Many of these hospitals were founded to strengthen group cohesion for German immigrants, particularly in the areas of language and devotional life.

Other hospitals followed similar paths. Between 1866 and 1894, the first community of nursing brothers in the United States, the Alexian Brothers, opened hospitals in Chicago; St. Louis; Elizabeth, New Jersey; and Oshkosh, Wisconsin. The Daughters of Charity continued their hospital expansion, opening St. Vincent's Hospital in Indianapolis in 1881 and many others across the United States. The Sisters of the Sorrowful Mother came from Rome in 1889 and opened ten hospitals in the Midwest and Southwest.[30] Beginning in 1891, Mother Frances Cabrini and the Missionary Sisters of the Sacred Heart established hospitals in New York, Chicago, and Seattle to care for Italian Americans. Also in 1891 Katherine Drexel, an heiress from Philadelphia, founded the Sisters of the Blessed Sacrament for Indians and Colored People, and this community staffed nine different hospitals. In association with the well-known Mayo Clinic, the Sisters of St. Francis of Our Lady of Lourdes opened St. Mary's Hospital in Rochester, Minnesota, in 1889.[31]

Sisters nursed in 1898 during the Spanish-American War, and eventually 282 nuns either volunteered their services or were asked to serve by government and military officials. Twelve Sisters of the Holy Cross and eleven Sisters of St. Joseph of Carondelet went to the Division Hospital at Camp Hamilton, Lexington, Kentucky; and then to different camps in Georgia, with the Sisters of St. Joseph going on to nurse in Cuba. At Camp Hamilton, Holy Cross Sister Lydia Clifford, a Civil War nurse

FIGURE 1.2 Catholic sister-nurses in the Spanish-American War. The Sisters of Charity are in the back row, Sisters of St. Joseph in the middle, and Sisters of the Holy Cross in front. (Courtesy Sisters of the Holy Cross Archives, Saint Mary's, Notre Dame, IN)

who had experience in other hospitals, was "Chief Nurse." Under her, fifty Sisters of Charity from Emmitsburg, Maryland, the eleven Sisters of St. Joseph, (fig. 1.2), and over fifty lay nurses shared nursing responsibilities with the Sisters of the Holy Cross.[32] Sisters also established specialty hospitals in the form of mental and tuberculosis institutions. By 1925, there were 581 Catholic acute and specialty hospitals in the United States, mainly under the auspices of nuns.[33]

This does not suggest that Catholic sisters were the only group of women motivated by religion to establish health-care institutions. Lutheran and Episcopalian deaconesses opened hospitals beginning in the mid-nineteenth century, and Mormon women established institutions in Utah in the early twentieth century.[34] Every denomination viewed health care as part of its mission. While many women's religious communities were involved in hospitals, the three Catholic congregations in this book were chosen to illustrate the theme of nuns' entrepreneurship in the Midwest, Texas, and Utah. Each group was active in the hospital field, and each possessed a distinct ministerial focus that gave members a special direction for their lives.

Foundations of the Three Communities

Sisters of St. Joseph of Carondelet

The Jesuit priest Jean Pierre Medaille founded the Congregation of the Sisters of St. Joseph in Le Puy, France, sometime between 1646 and 1651. The sisters aimed to serve the community, and, in spite of ecclesiastical law, did not observe canonical cloister. Their constitution stated that they were to carry out "all the spiritual and corporal works of mercy of which woman is capable." The sisters typically were daughters of farmers and laborers, and they performed a variety of services to their neighbors, including education of girls, service in hospitals, direction of orphans' homes, upkeep of dispensaries, and visitation of the sick poor. The flexibility they enjoyed by not being restricted to any specific work allowed them to respond to needs and situations as they arose.[35]

By 1789, the Catholic hierarchy held a privileged position in France, and it had the support of the aristocracy. However, the French Revolution shattered the church's dominant position, and religious congregations of men and women experienced tremendous upheaval. Hundred of priests and even some sisters were executed. In the aftermath, older nuns and new recruits reorganized the Sisters of St. Joseph community in 1807 under the direction of Mother St. Jean Fontbonne. She, too, had been imprisoned during the revolution but was spared from execution when Robespierre fell from power.[36]

As the Catholic Church revived in the post-Napoleonic era, the sisters expanded their works and prepared for missionary endeavors. In 1836, a wealthy French benefactor was aware of the sisters' flexible rule that supported their "readiness for anything," and when Bishop Joseph Rosati sought nuns for his newly established diocese in St. Louis, she convinced him to ask the Sisters of St. Joseph. Mother St. Jean agreed and sent six nuns in March of that year. They eventually established their motherhouse in Carondelet, just south of St. Louis. Between 1847 and 1857, they moved into other cities, including St. Paul, Toronto, Wheeling, Buffalo, Hamilton, Brooklyn, and Albany. In the following years, they expanded into regional provinces or organized within different dioceses.[37] As they established schools and orphanages, they obtained experience in business methods, which they could draw upon when they founded hospitals.

The sisters reacted spontaneously to needs as they arose. In the early years, they cared for cholera victims in St. Louis, Philadelphia, and St. Paul. They nursed in the Civil War and again in the Spanish-American War. After opening St. Joseph's Hospital in 1853 in St. Paul, the sisters took over St. Mary's Hospital in Minneapolis in 1887. Other health-care institutions included those in Kansas City (1874); Georgetown, Colorado (1880); Prescott and Tucson, Arizona (1878, 1880); the Minominee Indian Reservation in Keshena, Wisconsin (1886); Hancock, Michigan (1899); Fargo, North Dakota (1900); Grand Forks, North Dakota (1907); and Amsterdam and Troy, New York (1903, 1908).[38]

For their entrepreneurial activities to be successful, congregations needed ecclesiastical support. The sisters' coming to St. Paul resulted from networking between themselves and the area's local bishops, who were aware of the nuns' work in St. Louis. No doubt, their French connections made them attractive as well. Bishop Joseph Cretin of St. Paul was trying to establish a school for the many immigrants from French Canada, as well as local Native Americans and other European immigrants. After Mother Celestine Pommerel agreed to Cretin's request for sisters, particularly because his invitation gave them the opportunity they wanted to teach Native Americans, the French-born Mother St. John Fournier agreed to accompany, as their superior, three other Sisters of St. Joseph.[39] In St. Paul, however, bishops soon monopolized their work to serve European Catholics.

One of the earliest postulants was Sister Seraphine Ireland. Born Ellen Ireland to Irish immigrant parents, she entered the novitiate of the Sisters of St. Joseph in St. Paul in 1858. In 1882, she became provincial superior and led the group for the next thirty-nine years. Her patronage connections included her own family: throughout her tenure, her community had the support of her brother, Archbishop John Ireland of St. Paul. By 1900, the sisters listed 428 members in the St. Paul area. In addition to their hospitals, they staffed twenty-three other institutions that included schools, orphanages, and homes for dependent women. In 1905, they opened the College of St. Catherine.[40]

Sisters of the Holy Cross

Unlike the Sisters of St. Joseph, who brought a health-care tradition with them to the United States, the Congregation of the Sisters of the Holy Cross was not founded initially for nursing but rather as domestic helpers to priests and brothers at Notre Dame de Sainte Croix. Father Basil Anthony Moreau established the women's community in 1841 in Le Mans, France. Moreau's male order had an evangelical focus, and in 1841, the first band of Holy Cross men, including Father Edward Sorin, arrived in northern Indiana. The population of Native Americans in the area and eventually German and Irish immigrants, many who were nominal or

FIGURE 1.3 Mother Angela Gillespie, CSC. (Courtesy Sisters of the Holy Cross Archives, Saint Mary's, Notre Dame, IN)

potential Catholics, made northern Indiana prime missionary territory. In 1842, Sorin established what became the University of Notre Dame, and he requested sisters to help with domestic chores there. His letter to Father Moreau described his reasons for wanting sisters: "Once the sisters arrive—and their presence is ardently desired—they must be prepared not merely to look after the laundry and the infirmary, but also to conduct a school, perhaps even a boarding school."[41] The nuns arrived in 1843, and while they initially did housekeeping tasks for the priests and brothers, Father Sorin had opened up the possibility of a school. Soon, the sisters moved beyond domestic tasks to teaching and visiting the sick. In 1844, they established Saint Mary's Academy, which eventually became Saint Mary's College.

Father Sorin's influence on the sisters was profound, providing the classic example of the importance of ecclesiastical leaders to a religious order's interests and belief systems. He frequently used the language of assurance to convince the sisters of their importance. The Rules of 1871 were the first to contain the Preface which he wrote and which still exists in the 1982 constitution. The sisters were to accomplish their aims with a "spirit of faith" that would be a shield against all of life's tribulations, and their expectation of eternal reward should sustain and strengthen them.[42] Sorin's influence also affected the leadership of the community. From a prosperous family in France, he expected the sisters' leaders to have a similar cultural and educational background. Mother Angela Gillespie (fig. 1.3) met these qualifications.[43]

Mother Angela was born in Pennsylvania to second-generation Irish parents, and her relatives included statesmen and senators. Not only did she have political connections but also education, teaching, and business experience. These qualities gave her opportunities to wield significant influence. In 1853, she joined the Congregation of the Sisters of the Holy Cross and became the first American Directress of Saint Mary's Academy. She guided the sisters for more than thirty years.[44]

"Keeping with the needs of the times," from Father Moreau's 1841 circular letter, became the core of the sisters' mission.[45] They added practices according to how well they served the overriding purposes of their congregation. For example, during the Civil War, Mother Angela led nearly eighty nuns as nurses on battlefields, in hospitals, and on hospital ships, primarily in the western theater of war. They also nursed on the Union Navy hospital ship *Red Rover* as it carried wounded men to army hospitals in the North.[46] After the war, the sisters expanded their mission into hospital work. They established St. Mary's Infirmary in Cairo, Illinois (1867); Holy Cross Hospital in Salt Lake City, Utah (1875); St. Joseph's Hospital in South Bend, Indiana (1882); and other hospitals in Utah, Idaho, Dakota Territory, and Ohio, although teaching remained their primary work. They opened schools across the Midwest and Trans-Mississippi West and in Pennsylvania and Maryland. Membership grew from four in 1841 to 1,048 in 1915.[47]

Sisters of Charity of the Incarnate Word

The Congregation of the Sisters of Charity of the Incarnate Word was founded specifically to meet health-care needs in Texas. It grew from a French cloistered religious order, the Order of the Incarnate Word and Blessed Sacrament, founded in Lyons in 1627 through the work of Jeanne Chezard de Matel. For Mother de Matel, devotion to the incarnated Christ became the symbol for her order's way of life. Thus, the core of the mission was not solely Jesus' deity but particularly his humanity, which brought him into the full human community.[48] The Incarnate Word Sisters came to Texas in 1866 at the request of Bishop Claude Dubuis to open a hospital for victims of cholera and yellow fever. Since they dedicated themselves to nursing, the sisters inserted the word "charity" in their name and became the Sisters of Charity of the Incarnate Word.

In 1867, the nuns opened the first Catholic hospital in Texas, St. Mary's Infirmary, in Galveston. More French sisters came, and in 1869, Sisters Madeleine Chollet, Pierre Cinquin, and Agnes Buisson established Santa Rosa Infirmary in San Antonio, with Sister Madeleine becoming superior. A new constitution authorized expansion of the congregation's purposes and works in 1885. Besides seeking personal sanctification of members, sisters were to care for the "sick, the insane, the poor, the aged," and administer schools and asylums.[49] After working with smallpox victims, the sisters added the following to their 1885 constitution:

> In epidemics and contagious diseases the sisters must rise to the height of their sublime vocation, devoting themselves, at the peril of their lives, to the sick, who need their services, without regard to creed or color, and their most anxious care shall ever be for the poorest and most abandoned.[50]

This statement supports the idea that the mission of the community was charity to the poor, but it also provides insight into other aspects of the nuns' work. By caring for victims of epidemics, sisters had access to a population with a high mortality rate. Sister-nurses could bring not only physical comfort but also spiritual consolation. Furthermore, nursing was to be a sacrificial act in which nuns must be prepared to die to further their Christian message.

The Incarnate Word Sisters opened homes for the aged and mentally ill, rehabilitation facilities, and general hospitals in Boerne (1896), Amarillo (1901), Corpus Christi (1905), San Angelo (1910), and Paris (1911), Texas. They staffed already existing hospitals in Forth Worth (1885) and then in Marshall (1995). By 1890, they directed seven additional railroad hospitals in Tyler and Palestine, Texas; Las Vegas, New Mexico; Fort Madison, Iowa; and St. Louis, Sedalia, and Kansas City, Missouri. They began operation of Incarnate Word Hospital in St. Louis in 1902. In the process, they learned ways to procure land, buildings, materials, funding, and a growing clientele. In 1900, they established an academy for girls and young women in San Antonio that was the foundation for the College and Academy of the Incarnate Word. By 1919, the congregation had grown to 663 members. In addition to numerous schools and orphanages, they had twelve hospitals and two homes for the aged.[51]

Two women, in particular, were influential in the community's foundation. Although the sisters recognize Bishop Dubuis as their founder,

FIGURE 1.4 Mother St. Pierre Cinquin, CCVI. (Courtesy Archives, Motherhouse of the Incarnate Word, San Antonio, TX)

they also acknowledge Mothers St. Madeleine Chollet, the first superior, and St. Pierre Cinquin (fig. 1.4). Born to a wealthy family in France, Mother St. Pierre received her education from the Ursuline nuns. After entering the Incarnate Word convent in France and then immigrating to the United States, she became the second superior of the San Antonio community. Her entrepreneurial impulse to build her congregation was seen in its significant growth in personnel, institutions, and clients.[52]

Through their establishment of many institutions, nuns in all three congregations learned not only teaching and nursing skills but administrative ones as well, which they could apply as they managed large hospitals. By 1910, many of their health-care facilities held from one hundred to two hundred beds and typically admitted 1,000 to 2,000 patients per year. These hospitals were smaller than the large public facilities in the East, but according to a 1910 national study, sisters' hospitals were some of the larger ones in the country.[53]

Issues Regarding Work

Many factors influenced whether or not sisters' nursing and entrepreneurial activities in hospitals would be successful. First and foremost, there had to be a market for their services, a topic to be considered in the following chapters. The Sisters of the Holy Cross and Sisters of St. Joseph had to close miners' hospitals in Utah, South Dakota, Colorado, and Arizona when the mines failed and the nuns could no longer financially maintain the hospitals. For the same reason, they closed railroad hospitals when the railroad companies left an area.

Second, congregations needed significant numbers of recruits to staff the institutions. Preexisting networks of women from similar ethnic and socioeconomic backgrounds and those who were available for participation provided the focus for major recruiting drives for potential nuns. Ireland particularly was a fertile field for gleaning recruits.[54] Irish girls found communities in the United States especially attractive because many did not demand large dowries. Instead, they required education, which the Irish had. The Irish church also was the only European one offering English-speaking women. As early as 1845, the imbalance in favor of the Irish began for the Sisters of the Holy Cross. That year, eight women, all but one of Irish birth, received the habit.[55] During the Civil War, three-fourths of the nearly eighty Holy Cross sisters who nursed in the conflict were born in Ireland.[56]

An intense spirit of competition occurred among women's communities in obtaining Irish recruits. In the 1870s, Mother Angela Gillespie of the Sisters of the Holy Cross made several recruiting trips to Europe. She began in Dublin and spoke at places where large numbers of Catholic girls congregated, including sodalities, or parish devotional societies. From there she went to convents and schools across Ireland, including Kildare, Kilkenny, Limerick, Waterford, and Cork.[57] One Kilkenny priest remembered her visit: "She succeeded in getting *twenty-five* young ladies for her order in the United States, and they all persevered. She now desires twenty-five more and has come over to search for them."[58] On their part, Irish recruits desired opportunities to teach, nurse, and administer hospitals alongside the many Irish women already in American congregations. In 1873, of the ninety-three women who entered the Holy Cross congregation, sixty-one were Irish-born.[59] In 1898, fifty-seven aspirants left Ireland to join the Sisters of St. Joseph of Carondelet in St. Louis.[60]

Other historians have assessed the kinds of Irish families whose daughters were so readily drawn to convents in the late nineteenth and early twentieth centuries. Many of these families were headed by factory workers, shopkeepers, or cattle and dairy farmers. While some recruits

Table 1.1 Ethnic Background of the Sisters of Charity of the Incarnate Word

Year	Ireland	Germany	United States	France	Mexico	Canada	Other
1872–1900	45%	21%	16%	8%	4%	3%	3%
1901–1920	47%	21%	14%	2%	14%	1%	1%

Source: Archives, Motherhouse of the Incarnate Word, San Antonio, TX.

came from impoverished families in the south and west of Ireland, it appears that others came from both rural and urban middle-class or lower-middle-class families.[61]

Since the Incarnate Word Sisters settled in Protestant Texas, they had few Catholic candidates initially from which to recruit. Out of necessity, this congregation was particularly aggressive in recruiting women from Ireland. They obtained many from Irish sodalities such as Dublin's Children of Mary at Our Lady's Hospice, Harold's Cross. In 1900, Mother Mary John O'Shaughnessy, a former Child of Mary herself, brought back forty women to San Antonio from various locales in Ireland. Four years later, another Incarnate Word sister left Dublin with thirty-eight more.[62] After the turn of the century, the sisters continued recruiting in Europe, particularly Ireland and Germany (table 1.1). From 1872 to 1920, Irish women made up nearly half the congregation. The others came from Germany, the United States, Mexico, France, and Canada.[63]

Elements of Irish culture influenced the sisters' hospital foundations. Irish women were accustomed to a tremendous amount of physical labor. In Ireland, women often did the most strenuous jobs at home or on the family farm,[64] and they adapted well to the hardships of nursing in American hospitals. Furthermore, women from cattle-farming families in Ireland were used to hearing talk of buying, selling, and deal making. When, as superiors of hospitals, these women negotiated prices for the "best deal," they faced conditions they likely had experienced at home around the family table.[65] Hasia Diner has described Irish immigrant women in America as survivors. After the famine, they "saw themselves not as passive pawns in life but as active, enterprising creatures who could take their destiny in their own hands." Their optimism and their strong sense of self, their emphasis on economic priorities, combined with a rigorous Irish Catholicism that emphasized discipline, obedience, and devotion, facilitated their accomplishments in the hospital marketplace.[66]

This is not to say that French or German nuns did not have economic achievements, because they did. Nor is this to say that hard work and faith alone enabled sisters' successes. Nuns from Ireland, Germany, and other northern European countries accrued economic and social advantages from their acceptance as "whites." They worked in a society in which skin color determined social standing. Indeed, whiteness proved a valuable asset for doing well in the United States, an advantage the African American religious communities that had to function in a segregated society did not have.[67] Other Old World connections were important, as well. The Incarnate Word Sisters relied on the Lyons nuns to help in recruiting French women to the Texas community, especially in the early years. And there was a great reliance on social networks of family members, friends, and neighbors. Many women had birth sisters, aunts, or other relatives in a convent. Holy Cross Sister de Sales O'Neill, from County Cork, Ireland, had seven members of her immediate family in religious communities.[68]

European elements merged with a third factor influencing sisters' success: their willingness to adapt to changing circumstances. As nuns came to understand the American environment and the needs of their hospitals, they saw that adaptations had to be made if they were to survive financially and be successful in meeting their religious and entrepreneurial goals. Timing was important: they had to change as market forces changed. European women entering communities in the United States were especially influenced by the American sense of "fair play" and independence, which caused conflict when French motherhouses attempted to interfere with American groups. Furthermore, because of time and distance, communication problems developed between nuns in the United States and their French administrations.[69] By 1925, the Sisters of St. Joseph, Sisters of the Holy Cross, and Sisters of Charity of the Incarnate Word had become independent of their French motherhouses.

As they positioned themselves for growth, the congregations rapidly took on an American identity.[70] Americanization can be seen as a competitive response as institutions in the United States continued to grow. Indicating the imperatives of language, sisters began taking English lessons shortly after their arrival in the United States, and leaders had constitutions printed in English. The English language also was a recruitment strategy. Religious communities had to have American women to survive in the United States, and encouraging the use of English made congregations more attractive to American recruits.[71] Congregations deliberately sought American-born members soon after their arrival. Another significant element in the Americanization process was sisters' work as nurses during the Civil War and Spanish-American War.

Through their wartime experiences, sisters developed a deeper sense of identity as Americans, and they expanded their horizons. Because respectability was always a concern, nuns were anxious to show their patriotism, and their participation as wartime nurses not only affirmed their own loyalties but also symbolized those of the Catholic Church itself.

A fourth factor that influenced sisters' ventures was their support systems. Hospital successes typically reflected available funds, and nuns had to appeal to legitimate networks of patronage to gain the financial support they needed. The early enterprises of the Sisters of St. Joseph materialized primarily through their patronage relationship with the French countess who helped support them financially. Other superiors worked directly with prominent local citizens, businessmen and women, railroad companies, and mine owners to obtain support for their activities. Teaching young women from middle- and upper-middle-class families was a standard means through which nuns could cultivate relationships with wealthy parents. Despite the "token" support of the Catholic Church for black women's religious communities, Katherine Drexel was able to use the millions of dollars left to her by her father, a partner of the banker J. P. Morgan, to help African Americans.[72] Priests and bishops sometimes served as intermediaries for nuns. Archbishop John Ireland of St. Paul was known to have favored his sister's community, the Sisters of St. Joseph, over other women's congregations in his diocese, and he often maneuvered to give them advantages over certain territorial operations.[73]

Autonomy over their work was a fifth factor that influenced sisters' hospitals. Ordinarily, sister-superiors made nuns' work assignments and the final decisions regarding which new activities the congregations would undertake. Communities refused requests for their services when they did not have the available personnel, and superiors exercised this authority frequently. Often there were far more requests for services than nuns could accept. For several years, the Incarnate Word superior turned down an opportunity to open a hospital in West Texas because there were not enough sisters to nurse in another institution. They also left a facility after conflicts over a physician's financial management and his demand for lay nurses.[74]

Tensions persisted over the tasks that nuns should perform and who should be responsible for organizing them. In choosing opportunities for work, sisters cited the identity of the order and its mission. The Sisters of the Holy Cross, while professing obedience to superiors, were not eager to accept new housekeeping assignments. By 1870, their constitution clearly spelled out their work as teaching, nursing, and administering orphanages rather than housekeeping tasks that Father Moreau initially had stipulated. Thus, one way nuns could maintain independence was to cite their specialty as a defense. In this way, obedience could work in conjunction with autonomy.

Women's religious communities also called on their histories in defining their missions, and this influenced their decisions to take on new works. The Civil War experiences of the Sisters of the Holy Cross gave nursing a prominence in the congregation's identity that translated into more medically centered roles for them. Their prompt response for nurses during the Civil War influenced their decision to nurse in another national conflict, the Spanish-American War. Although the flexibility of the Sisters of St. Joseph enabled them to take advantage of a variety of opportunities, it also had its disadvantages. Sisters often became a cheap labor source for church committees and bishops, especially after the 1884 Third Plenary Council in Baltimore directed the establishment of parochial schools. Some bishops considered nuns as their own agents to summon when needed.[75]

Thus, sisters were subject to church authorities and were not expected to act alone. All major decisions by religious communities had to have the approval of the bishop or his representative. While sisters often wrote that a priest had invited them into an area, sometimes this merely meant permission granted for endeavors that superiors had already started. Often they "shopped around" for the best opportunities for their congregations to carry out their hospital work. In 1889, Mother St. Pierre Cinquin made all the arrangements to purchase Fort Worth's railroad hospital and then wrote the bishop "for his blessing." She had already obtained his permission to purchase land for building purposes, so she was reasonably sure that he would approve her actions. In the early twentieth century, another Incarnate Word superior was anxious to open a hospital in St. Louis, Missouri, where the sisters had recently established a novitiate. She corresponded with several medical leaders before accepting an offer.[76] The bishop's permission was merely a formality.

Sisters' initial agreements with hospital authorities were crucial to their entrepreneurship, and they tried to prevent as many problems as possible. These agreements reflect an acute sense of business. Before agreeing to a new venture, nuns inquired about access to the sacraments, adequate housing, and spiritual directors. Invariably, they insisted on full control of hospital operations. That the sisters could make such demands is not surprising. Nuns' successful organization and management of other institutions enhanced their bargaining power. Sometimes physicians asked for specific women's communities because they knew the sisters could financially support a hospital. Because of nuns' previous successes in hospital work, doctors trusted them with new financial ventures and often agreed to sisters' demands for control.

By the early twentieth century, Catholic sisters were active participants in the hospital marketplace in the United States. It was nuns, in particular, who went to new towns and frontier areas and became major players early in the hospital movement. They brought a tradition of nursing and hospital work that had been influenced by European sisters who had cared for the sick for centuries. As nuns took on American identities, they readied themselves to assert claims over nursing and hospital administration. They were not always able to realize their goals, however, without some form of compromise. This will be described in the next chapter.

2

"All the Advantages of a Religious Life":

RELIGION, GENDER, AND NEW PUBLIC ROLES

> Consider with me and see where have been gathered together more providentially to be benefited with all the advantages of a religious life a larger number of poor, unqualified, ordinary, and working class girls as all of us are.[1]
>
> Mother St. Pierre Cinquin, CCVI
> December 18, 1889

These words that Mother St. Pierre wrote to the Sisters of Charity of the Incarnate Word, most of whom had entered religious life without material resources, reveal that a religious vocation could bring certain advantages to women. Prevailing social trends limited some women's prospects, but by joining a religious congregation, Catholic women could create a space for themselves to nurse, teach, administer hospitals, and manage finances. In the convent, sisters obtained opportunities for job training and preparation for the marketplace, underscoring economic goals for them. Furthermore, although the clerical hierarchy of the Catholic Church excluded women, sisters developed alternative spiritualities that allowed them to stand apart from both the church hierarchy and other women.[2] This held considerable attraction for women who had few alternatives in the outside world.

In the context of church and societal ideas about gender and religion, Catholic sisters took on new aspects of entrepreneurship. However, they took vows that committed them to anonymity. While aspects of convent life arguably helped them, nuns did not oppose the Catholic Church's sex hierarchy, nor did they question their position in that structure. Furthermore, although sisters had identities that were distinct from other women, the Catholic Church did not formally invest them with power as it did priests. Sacramental laws gave priests certain functions that distinguished them from others, but the degree to which nuns acquired sacramental power was through identity formation. The construction and maintenance of personal and collective religious identities provided the basis for them to shape their lives and work. It was central in understanding women's willingness to invest their time and energy in their work and, hence, was important for a religious order's growth.[3] The religious congregation was the institution that gave meaning to a collective identity for women.

For sisters, the justification for religious life was to achieve spiritual perfection for themselves and others. These women followed a personal calling and believed they were doing God's will. Upon entrance into the novitiate, a Sister of the Holy Cross had to answer a questionnaire. Reasons for entering typically were "to save my soul" and "I loved its end [sanctification]."[4] Rather than focusing on a life of prayer and contemplation, however, the sisters gave priority to their work.

In Europe and the United States, beliefs about gender limited women's choices and influenced their work, marriage patterns, and opportunities. Barbara Welter has provided a comprehensive description of how ministers and other moralists constructed an "ideology of true womanhood" for white middle-class women in the nineteenth century. Women were to be submissive and pious and to practice domesticity to perfection.[5] While this cult was normative in many contexts, it was not observed in terms of actual behavior. Indeed, many women deviated markedly from this ideology, having neither the need nor the opportunity to stay at home.[6]

Roman Catholic writers promulgated a domestic ideology similar to that of middle-class white women. In his 1879 classic book on Catholic domesticity, *The Mirror of True Womanhood*, Bernard O'Reilly proclaimed the "true Catholic woman" to be pious, self-abnegating, and domestic. He particularly associated women with nursing.[7] While liberal Catholic writers argued for wider options, others upheld traditional Christian beliefs that God's appointed domain for women was the home.[8] Underpinning this tradition was the image of Mary, the mother of Jesus, embodied in the dogma of the Immaculate Conception. Both the ideology of "true womanhood" and the dogma of the Immaculate Conception idealized women as social guardians and purifiers and stressed their roles as caretakers.[9] In sermons and publications, ecclesiastical leaders and Catholic periodicals such as the *Ave Maria* and the *Catholic World* circulated this teaching.[10] Furthermore, by the late nineteenth century, fallacious scientific theories about feminine psychology and intelligence had developed to explain differences between men and women, yet their most significant social impact was to "justify" the role of women as subordinate caretakers.[11] For Catholic women who did not wish to be wives and mothers, however, the convent was an available option.

BENEFITS OF A RELIGIOUS VOCATION

A convent could offer women opportunities for personal fulfillment that they might not otherwise have. While most European orders required large dowries, overseas "mission" orders such as those in the United States did not. Many Irish Catholic women viewed the decision to become a nun in the United States as choosing the "better part," an alternative to a life of hard work or poverty in Ireland.[12] In postfamine rural Ireland, changes in inheritance patterns produced a surplus of sons and daughters, and women had few social or economic benefits. Demographic trends revealed infrequent marriages, high celibacy rates, gender segregation, and a massive female exodus as the country held fewer and fewer opportunities for women. Many women preferred to enter a convent rather than experience the perils of childbearing or tedious and backbreaking work on the family farm. As increasing numbers of young Irish women joined religious congregations and took vows of poverty, chastity, and obedience, they voluntarily experienced conditions that, in all likelihood, they would have faced as nonreligious women. With few marriage prospects and a future of dependence on family and relatives, hundreds of thousands of women fled their homes and joined convents in Ireland or elsewhere. By the late nineteenth and early twentieth centuries, Irish women dominated migration. This pattern was unique among European migrants.[13]

For other women, a convent could give occupational and educational options their families could not provide. For example, membership in a religious community could offer opportunities to rise to positions of influence.[14] Capable young women could aspire to become principals of schools, superiors of congregations, or administrators of hospitals. Not only did Irish women predominate within the Holy Cross congregation, they also held the leadership positions. Sisters Perpetua Wilson and

FIGURE 2.1 Sister Lydia Clifford, CSC. (Courtesy Sisters of the Holy Cross Archives, Saint Mary's, Notre Dame, IN)

Annunciata McSheffery emigrated from Ireland as children and eventually became superiors of the Sisters of the Holy Cross.[15] Another Irish immigrant, Sister Lydia Clifford (fig. 2.1), did housekeeping and other domestic work before she received training as a nurse. In addition to being "Chief Nurse" at Camp Hamilton during the Spanish-American War, she directed three different Holy Cross hospitals.[16]

Generalizations, however, cannot easily be made, since many women in convents did not rise in status. By 1910, the Sisters of St. Joseph, Sisters of the Holy Cross, and Sisters of Charity of the Incarnate Word had eliminated official internal class distinctions, such as lay sisters (who did domestic work in the convent) and those in the choir ranks (sisters who carried on teaching and administration tasks). Indeed, the Incarnate Word Sisters never distinguished among ranks. But the efficient running of a hospital relied not only on nurses and administrators but also on cooks and cleaners. Sister Aubin Shea did laundry and housework for seventeen years at Holy Cross Hospital before she had the opportunity to nurse the sick, a position she held for nine more years. That the convent could provide opportunities for entrepreneurship for some sisters is evident when one examines their work histories in more detail (table 2.1).

Table 2.1 Selected Work Histories

Name, Place of Birth, Year of Entry in Congregation	Dates, Places of Service
Madeleine Chollet, CCVI, France, 1867	1869–72: Administrator and Superior, Santa Rosa Infirmary ? Years: In charge of St. Joseph's Orphanage 1892–94: Assistant Superior General of Congregation 1894–1900: Superior General and Administrator, Santa Rosa
Robert O'Dea, CCVI, Ireland, 1896	1903: Organized School of Nursing, Santa Rosa Infirmary, San Antonio Superintendent of Nurses, Santa Rosa 1910–14: Superintendent, St. John's Hospital, San Angelo, TX 1915–18: Superintendent, St. Joseph's Infirmary, Paris, TX 1919–25: Administrator, Santa Rosa 1926–28: Administrator, St. Joseph's Infirmary, Fort Worth 1928–39: Administrator, Santa Rosa
Esperance Finn, CSJ, New York, 1884	20 years: Music Teacher, St. Agatha's Conservatory, St. Paul; and Director of two boarding schools, Hastings and Fulda, MN 1906–18: Administrator, St. Mary's Hospital, Minneapolis
Jane Frances Bouchet, CSJ, France, 1861	1872–74: Mistress of Novices and Asst. Provincial, St. Paul 1874–76: Trustee, Board of Directors, St. Joseph's Academy 1876–79: Superior and Administrator, St. Joseph's, St. Paul 1879–82: Provincial Superior, St. Paul Province 1882–88: Superior, teacher, various schools 1888–90: Administrator, St. John's Hospital, Winona, MN 1890–1906: Administrator, St. Mary's Hospital, Minneapolis 1906–18: Superior, St. Joseph's Convent and School, Marshall, MN 1918–21: Superior, Our Lady of Lourdes, Minneapolis

Table 2.1 continued

Name, Place of Birth, Year of Entry in Congregation	Dates, Places of Service
Augusta Anderson, CSC, Virginia, 1854	1856–61: Teacher and director of various schools 1861–65: Military Service, Civil War, Cairo and Memphis 1865–67: Administrator, Overton Hospital, Memphis 1867–70: Administrator, St. Mary's Infirmary, Cairo 1870–78: General Sect., Saint Mary's; founder St. Mary's Academy and Holy Cross Hospital, Salt Lake City 1878–82: Director of various academies 1882–95: Superior General of Congregation 1895–1903: Superior of academy, Washington, DC
Lydia Clifford, CSC, Ireland, 1859	1862–74: Teacher, clothes keeper, care of orphans 1863–65: Military Service, Civil War, Mound City, IL 1874–86: Director of various academies 1886–90: Administrator, Mt. Carmel Hosp., Columbus, OH 1892–96: Director of various academies 1896–98: Administrator, Our Savior Hospital, Jacksonville, IL 1898: Military Service, Spanish-American War, Chief Nurse, Camp Hamilton, Lexington, KY 1898–1901: Administrator, St. John's Hospital, Anderson, IN

Nuns, however, were not completely unique among women administering organizations and money. Lori Ginzburg notes the ubiquity of upper-class Protestant women administering large finances as well.[17]

In addition to social advantages, a convent could offer women political advantages. Some have linked the growth in religious vocations in postfamine Ireland to a rising Irish nationalism. The evangelical age of the nineteenth century saw a polarization and conflict between Catholics and Protestants that cemented each group's separate identity.[18] Furthermore, the Irish had been gradually losing their identity and language for nearly a hundred years before the famine. "Education, business, politics, and communication were all increasingly geared away from Gaelic to English as the Irish were being effectively Anglicized," Emmet Larkin writes. After the famine, the Catholic Church became a growing influence and authority. An Irish spirituality evolved that emphasized the authority of priests, the Mass and sacraments, a strong Eucharistic piety, and veneration of the Blessed Virgin and the saints. This devotional revolution offered a new cultural heritage with which Irish people could identify.[19] Afterward, the terms *Irish* and *Catholic* became interchangeable. These social, demographic, and religious factors combined to promote the adoption of Roman Catholicism as an essential part of Irish nationality.

Entering a religious order also could be a means of obtaining spiritual power for women. Despite subordination to men in the Catholic Church, nuns could balance the increasing power of the clergy through an alternative source of spiritual equality.[20] This brought them increased respect and status within their church and can partly explain the growth of women's religious communities. The belief that some men and women could achieve greater spiritual perfection than others by joining a religious community was a significant factor for them. A priest told the Sisters of the Holy Cross in 1896: "A few men and women are called by God . . . to rise to a higher sphere than that which reason can reach or Faith can indicate. We give them the name of religious persons." He continued, stating the Catholic Church, and the Catholic community from which they came, treated them as "a privileged class entitled to special favors . . . a pearl of inestimable worth and value."[21] Indeed, differential expectations about salvation were instrumental in recruitment of women for religious congregations.

Sisters' constitutions, prescriptions of religious superiors and founders, sermons, and manuals reflected Catholic teachings and influenced nuns' self-perceptions, their conceptions of nursing, and their worldviews. While these sources may reveal attitudes rather than actual practices, examination reveals a composite picture of what was expected of nuns. They were supposed to model the quintessence of feminine traits: to humble themselves, even to nothingness; and to be silent, submissive, self-sacrificing, serious-minded, reserved, docile, and obedient. A woman professing a religious vocation was to practice the virtues of self-abnegation, charity, modesty, and meekness. Bishops and priests publicly praised women religious but had their own views of the ideal nun. One bishop wrote, "The sister hides her name and work from the rough, loud world. . . . They never preach. . . . They belong to the great empire of silence."[22] Sisters' constitutions reflected similar views, exhorting nuns to remain "hidden." It must be acknowledged here, however, that monastic orders of men as well as women were founded on obedience and submission of the will. Utter obedience to the superior was essential to the development of a religious identity.

The Catholic Church elevated virginity as the holiest path women could take.[23] Through virginity, a woman could achieve fuller union with Christ. Founders of women's active communities in the seventeenth century upheld its ideal, as did nineteenth-century Catholics. In 1897, Father William Stang instructed priests to respect "the *consecrated virgins* of the Church. The priest who looks upon them merely as troublesome women ... has lost sight of the supernatural in them" (italics in original).[24]

On the other hand, underlying the virginity ideal was a theology that did not favor women.[25] For example, a priest counseled the Sisters of the Holy Cross that man should have dominion over woman. According to his view, woman was the first to sin and therefore should be the first to suffer, and she should expect a frightening punishment.[26] Particularly influential were Pauline interpretations of scripture and writings of church leaders such as Augustine, who assumed biological differences between women and men and beliefs in the supremacy of man. Furthermore, historians have argued that sexual morality was more central for women than men. Clerical apprehensions sometimes occurred over women's competing influences in the church, and writings degenerated into obsessive concerns for the nuns' purity. Male contact became a threat to that purity. Thus, constitutions and sermons frequently warned sisters of sexual temptations.[27]

Nuns did not verbally dispute Catholic theology. However, they defined their womanhood differently and created new identities that challenged prescribed gender roles. The vow of chastity became the chief defining behavior for women religious. Persisting through key growth periods during the Middle Ages, in seventeenth-century France, and in nineteenth-century Ireland and the United States, Catholics viewed chastity as superior to marriage and as the primary source of spiritual power for women.[28] In the late nineteenth century, a priest superior told the Sisters of the Holy Cross that sexual abstinence marked persons as being exceptionally close to the Spirit of God. Through chastity, their hearts were "more closely united to [Jesus'] Sacred Heart."[29] Indeed, one of the many attractions to a religious life for women was the opportunity to create positive new identities grounded in chastity that transcended the gender system.[30]

Sisters' celibate lives were the most significant departures from other women's gender roles. This mandated a "separate space" for nuns, and it was in this space that they created and ran their own institutions.[31] Within this space, sisters' gender roles sometimes overlapped with secular women and men. Nuns' vows, for example, bound them to exemplify womanly virtues. They tried to imitate Mary's humility, patience, modesty, and self-effacement. They spoke of their lives using female images, seeing themselves as "brides" of Christ. To indicate respect, they referred to each other as "sister" and to their leaders as "mother." Furthermore, their nursing fit in well with the developing role of woman as caretaker in the nineteenth century. On the other hand, to convey the message that they wished to relate to others on a deeper, more spiritual level, nuns consistently underscored their "asexual" identities, not merely by their vow of chastity but also through their religious dress, which concealed their physical bodies. They de-emphasized gender differences by taking on jobs such as hospital administration that men traditionally held. Some sisters took the names of male saints. They referred to the superior of the congregation as "Superior General," invoking the male military title. In these ways, they transcended the usual female stereotypes, and this had the potential of minimizing gender limitations.[32]

At the same time, sisters insisted on their own social and sexual legitimacy and derived strength and support from their conceptions of their womanhood. They conflated their gender and religious roles into a single identity. As vowed, celibate women, they belonged to a sacred order and lived both in and beyond the secular world.[33] In the words of one sister, Christ "refreshed their weary souls with a grace and a freedom that the worldly-wise [could] never know."[34]

While separation from the world defined their religious lives, sisters' vows gave them a public dimension. They were able to work in the community devoid of sexual connotations, and they could care for strangers in ways other women could not. Nuns' vows allowed them to walk through city streets unescorted when respectable women of almost any class could not. Sisters' elided sexuality protected them from scandal, and medical and military authorities showed them special respect. During the Spanish-American War, for example, Sister Liguori McNamara of the Sisters of St. Joseph wrote that two of the majors wanted nuns in every ward. Their "presence is a check to the trained nurses and doctors, as there [is] much of that kind of work going on here, particularly at night." Sisters' presence could "stop any scandal that takes place between the trained nurses and attendants."[35] Thus, sisters' gender and religious identities allowed nuns more space in the public domain of the hospital.

To Catholic sisters, then, a religious vocation clearly meant more than a forced submissiveness to an uncomfortable position in church and society. Some nuns on the receiving end of teachings often were self-critical of their failure to gain perfection and the spiritual purity that teachings and constitutions espoused. For most sisters, however, an internalized notion of themselves as weak or evil was not their dominant conception of themselves. To them, God called most people to live in the world but reserved only a small number of privileged men and women for religious life, and this enhanced their self-images. Thus, Mother St. Pierre Cinquin could say to her sisters, "You have given yourself to the most legitimate, most holy and most glorious course."[36] This positive self-identity along with the added respect it brought partly explain why so many women joined religious orders in the nineteenth century. This would prove particularly advantageous as they established and administered hospitals.

FORMATION OF A RELIGIOUS IDENTITY

The Catholic Church was the center for the development of a religious identity and consciousness for nuns. The process of identity formation involved spending one or two years in a novitiate during which sisters had intense initiations into traditions of active service. Novices absorbed community ideals as other nuns educated them into their new identities. They developed a religious identity that focused on an intense piety, charity, obedience, mental toughness, hard work, and fortitude. The bonding process included rigorous discipline, foregoing of physical comfort, and yielding one's individuality to group needs. Women were taught to believe that God called them to a work of service. This empowered superiors to say no to a bishop regarding what works to do, or to a doctor who wanted them to go against their constitutions. A strong religious formation could provide the spiritual, social, and emotional support necessary for women to persevere in tense situations that their work often brought.[37]

To develop a common purpose and group identity, each order had its own narrative of the foundress, the saintly bishop, and stories of the community's history. For example, the Holy Cross Sisters' experiences in the Civil War gave nursing a prominence in the congregation's identity. In fact, one congregational historian has noted that the Civil War experience became so all pervading for the sisters that, "in the consciousness of the Congregation, it has remained THE great response to emergency need made by the Sisters of the Holy Cross." No other activity has ever involved so many members. Until the congregation divided into provinces in 1931, the sisters from all over the country gathered at Saint Mary's in the summer to sing the Civil War song "Tenting Tonight" before going to their individual places of work.[38] Thus, memory of sisters' wartime nursing worked to keep a common mission alive in both old and new members. (See fig. 2.2.)

FIGURE 2.2 Civil War nurse Sister Paula Casey (Holy Cross), in wheelchair, surrounded by, left to right: Sister Servatius (St. Francis); Sister Patricia (St. Joseph); Sister Miriam (Mercy); Ellen Ryan Jolly (national chairperson of the Civil War nuns' monument committee of the Ladies Ancient Order of Hibernians); Sister Fidelis (Ursuline); Sister Electa (Charity); and Sister Manica (Providence), July 1922. (Courtesy Sisters of the Holy Cross Archives, Saint Mary's, Notre Dame, IN)

While an action-oriented spirituality guided the sisters in America, European ideas also informed their attitudes and practices. They performed daily, weekly, and monthly spiritual exercises and devoted several days every year to a retreat. Commitment mechanisms also involved self-abnegation and mortification activities. Women carried out rather debasing ritual practices of accusing themselves of faults. These de-individualizing mortification practices, while often humiliating, could be potent commitment mechanisms. They decreased one's sense of a separate ego and required appropriate behavior based on group membership.[39]

Congregational documents instructed that through the mother superior, God manifested his will. To build a sense of community, superiors wrote annual newsletters to all sisters in each establishment, including not only news items but also exhortations to self-dedication and ways to enhance spiritual development. These letters, along with constitutions, sermons, and manuals, employed the rhetoric of group unification. This language is one of reaffirmation and reassurance, and it explains to people who they are, why they are important, and what their mission is. In 1879, Father Sorin wrote the Sisters of the Holy Cross that they could look "to a richer inheritance" in the future. If they followed religious prescriptives, they would secure "the real ends of their creation. . . . a throne, a sceptre, and a crown, an endless bliss, an imperishable glory."[40] Mother St. Pierre Cinquin conveyed her enthusiasm for religious life to her Incarnate Word Sisters through frequent letters that proclaimed how "grand and noble" a religious vocation was.[41]

This sense of élan extended to instructions about self-sacrifice and suffering. By the late nineteenth century, a complex Catholic theology of pain and suffering had evolved that asserted that personal pain involved a sharing in Christ's pain and therefore could be redemptive.[42] Mother St. Pierre wrote, "Suffering is the predecessor of our Good Master. He blesses only those who suffer," and sisters were to be joyful in the struggle. Suffering was God's gift and a way of following Christ, who had suffered and died on the cross. Thus, sisters' suffering merged with Christ's own anguish and therefore could be sanctifying. To Mother St. Pierre, suffering could be a great teacher, making the sister "more fit for practical life."[43]

As charitable works became the basis for their spirituality, sisters began to elevate hard and servile work into a holy apostolate. Nuns were to see the recipient of their services as Christ himself. It was through envisioning Christ and being reminded that he also had endured sufferings that made the repugnance and drudgery of hospital tasks bearable. The nun's life also was to imitate Christ and exercise charity as he did, thereby making her work redemptive. Care of the sick thus had a heroic element that teaching and care of orphans lacked; nursing's unpleasant and often dirty work could act as an ascetic practice.[44] Internal documents often reaffirmed sisters in this work. The Incarnate Word Sisters' 1867 *Rule* stressed the need for unity, dedication, and adherence to community rules to sustain the nuns in overcoming the "natural repugnance" that accompanied care for the sick.[45]

Hospital work provided an additional challenge: it involved matters of life and death for both patients and nurses. Two Sisters of the Holy Cross died from illness when they nursed during the Civil War. Nuns who nursed in wartime and epidemics wore a badge of honor, both literally and figuratively. For example, the US Army gave bronze "Comrades to Nurses" medals to Civil War nurses, and Mother de Chantal Keating, a St. Joseph sister-nurse, proudly wore hers throughout her life.[46]

Although change was in the air by the early twentieth century, many of the concerns of the sister-nurses remained firmly rooted in the nineteenth century. An analysis of their suffering provides an example. Sisters' writings imply that their suffering reinforced boundaries between them and the outside world. It bestowed a unique strength and authority on them as well as a condition of sanctity. As an aspect of piety, it had more value if only a few people were victims. If all suffered equally, then it would lose its remarkable quality. Thus, nuns did not perceive their nursing commitment as costly but instead as beneficial. At the same time, through suffering, women could discharge their duties to the church as heroically as men. Most important, nuns' suffering could enhance their compassion and present them with opportunities of relieving the suffering of others.

Catholic sisters used their distinct gender and religious identities, formed in the religious congregation, to expand their public activities. As they competed in the hospital marketplace in the late nineteenth and early twentieth centuries, they emphasized their gender and religious roles to enhance the attractiveness of their hospitals over others. How they did this will be the focus of the next three chapters.

Part 2

Hospital Establishments in the Midwest, Texas, and Utah

3

Not the Traditional Institution:

CATHOLIC SISTERS IN THE HOSPITAL MARKETPLACE, 1853–1880

> Many a man who differed from the Roman Church widely in dogma, had nothing but admiring consent and approval for this self-abnegating and practical Christian work of the sisters at Santa Rosa Infirmary.[1]
>
> *San Antonio Weekly Express,* 1869

This newspaper quotation reflected the views of many non-Catholics of that era who, while suspicious of Catholicism itself, greatly admired the work and character of the sister-nurses. The statement serves as a starting point to examine the sisters' place among their constituents as they established hospitals in the Midwest, Texas, and Utah.

To explore this issue further, seven hospitals that developed before 1880 will be analyzed. Not all had the support of the local community that Santa Rosa Infirmary received. Four successful hospital ventures and three unsuccessful ones will be the focus of this chapter. The story is particularly worthy of attention because it shows the importance of an established market, physicians' support, and public and governmental backing in the determination of a hospital's success or failure.

The 1850s through the 1870s saw an expansion of hospitals resulting from a secular pious activism, traditional stewardship, and religious and ethnic responses to a growing immigrant population. Regional variations in hospital development reflected economic disparities. Particularly in the South and West, less private capital was available for private philanthropy, and this hindered the creation of voluntary hospitals.[2]

In some cities in the latter half of the nineteenth century, no hospitals existed to handle the burden of sickness. Sisters took advantage of this opportunity to care for the sick, and many of their institutions often were the earliest ones built.

When nuns established their facilities, they had to compete with multiple types of hospitals, each dedicated to caring for patients from certain social groups. Privately supported voluntary hospitals, products of Protestant patronage and stewardship for the poor, were managed by lay trustees and funded by public subscriptions, bequests, and philanthropic donations. Because of the status and influence those hospitals could give them, physicians treated patients without charge. Public or tax-supported municipal hospitals accepted charity patients, including the aged, orphaned, sick, or debilitated. For most of the nineteenth century, only the socially marginal, poor, or isolated received care in institutions. Inside the hospitals, patients had to recognize themselves as a dependent class. Hospital personnel sought to develop in the poor patients habits of proper behavior, speech, cleanliness, and Protestantism, all of which translated into a program of moral uplift. On the other hand, when middle- or upper-class persons fell ill, their family members nursed them at home.[3]

Catholic hospitals were not primarily started to provide wealthy benefactors a means of patronage. While some collaborative teaching ventures between sisters and medical schools existed, a Catholic hospital's main purpose was to heal and comfort the infirm, the sick, and the dying and to afford them the opportunity for repentance and spiritual solace. And in the wake of new threats, Catholic hospitals could not only manage unprecedented health problems of a growing population but also revitalize Catholicism itself.

FUNCTIONS OF CATHOLIC HOSPITALS

Other historians have analyzed the public/private ambiguities of hospitals that were dedicated to the public welfare while eventually depending on private-paying patients and governmental funding. These institutions developed exclusionary policies based not only on social class and race but also on diagnosis, as they prohibited admissions of those with chronic or contagious disease, mental disorders, alcoholism, and venereal disease.[4]

Catholic hospitals had some of these same elements as well. But because of their religious functions, nuns expanded the kinds of patients they admitted.

Although official notices stated otherwise, many of the sisters' general hospitals admitted patients with contagious diseases such as typhoid fever, diarrhea, syphilis, pneumonia, and tuberculosis.[5] Sisters also accepted persons experiencing delirium tremens. And nuns attended some individuals for as long as they lived. While this strategy certainly enlarged a hospital's financial base, it also allowed persons a comfortable place not only to die but also to live. This kind of service involved providing for basic needs and also for medical care. Furthermore, it was possible for a person to purchase a permanent place in the hospital. Thus, with Catholic hospitals, exclusionary claims were not so crucial, and functional boundaries appear to have been hazy.

What this means is that because of their religious functions, sisters' hospitals admitted different kinds of patients from the traditional voluntary hospital. Many of these patients were admitted without charge, but with the really destitute going to public almshouses, Catholic hospitals did not admit all poor patients. Furthermore, many of the indigent that Catholic institutions accepted had their care paid for by local or county governments. Charity admissions peaked in the 1870s and 1890s, possibly reflecting the financial crises throughout most of the country during those years. Catholic hospitals also functioned to assist with nursing, food, and other necessities during emergencies. For example, sisters opened their hospitals to military officials during wartime and to those who were victims of natural disasters. In economic depressions, unemployed workers turned to nuns' hospitals for food and shelter.[6]

Catholic hospitals appear to have been less concerned with moral reformation than Protestant hospitals described by other historians. Sisters' religious, ethnic, and class similarities to their patients likely were influential. Spiritual reformation, however, *was* a concern for nuns.[7] They provided religious instruction and encouraged devotional conformity among the Catholics who came as patients. If their patients could read, and the doctor permitted it, nuns passed out Catholic literature. They also helped patients reflect on their past behavior. The *Manual of Decrees* for the Sisters of St. Joseph, for example, prescribed that the sisters "instruct the patients in the truths of our holy religion, the necessity of living up to one's faith, and in the practice of the virtues of a truly Christian life." Thus, sisters' nursing could be a powerful means of spreading religious devotion into local and regional communities.[8]

Successful Hospital Ventures

St. Joseph's Hospital, St. Paul, Minnesota

The Sisters of St. Joseph of Carondelet began their path toward hospital development when they offered their school as a makeshift hospital for victims of a cholera epidemic that struck St. Paul in 1853.[9] The epidemic expedited work that Bishop Joseph Cretin had already begun on a new hospital, which opened in October 1854 on land donated by a benefactor. The three and a half-story structure had wards, private rooms, kitchen, and chapel. A newspaper reported in January 1855 that patients included those with "sufferings incident to poverty," sickness, and patients experiencing delirium tremens.[10] Even though separate mental hospitals became more numerous in the nineteenth century, St. Joseph's had mental patients in its wards. By 1876, however, the beginnings of change could be seen. Nuns renovated St. Joseph's when physicians suggested that they install a stove and pipe system that circulated fresh air and alleviated a persistent ventilation problem. They also converted an attic into an operating room, which relieved patients in the wards from having to witness "the sickening scenes."[11]

The hospital capacity at that time was fifty patients, with nine attending medical and surgical staff. While most surgeries would not be done inside hospitals until after 1900, the sisters realized early that surgery could bring in patients. In the 1870s, surgeons were adapting ether to in-home "kitchen surgery," since many physicians and patients feared the dangers of hospital infection. Yet, demand for surgery provided a means for hospitals to increase their earnings, and in 1871, the Sisters of St. Joseph advertised for surgeons in the *Northwestern Medical and Surgical Journal*. The nuns announced that they "disdained empiricism in any form" and selected the hospital staff "from the best of the city's regular physicians." Then, they asked physicians "to send [to St. Joseph's Hospital] those cases desiring operations . . . who . . . from their locality or peculiar surroundings can not be operated upon at home."

Significantly, the sisters promised that physicians "will be given the exclusive professional charge" of their patients while in the hospital, thus allowing private doctors to continue treating their clients.[12] This was an important strategy on the sisters' part. Hospital appointments had hitherto been concentrated among an elite group of medical men. Most practitioners were without hospital privileges, and professional fees and control over patients were contested issues. Doctors who referred patients to hospitals risked losing their patients and fees to hospital doctors who offered free treatment on the ward. Market factors likely drove the sisters' decisions. St. Luke's Episcopal Hospital and the City and County Hospital were in operation in St. Paul by the 1870s.[13] In such a competitive situation, which would increase over time, the sisters showed an understanding of future marketing trends. They established a policy that protected surgeons and enhanced their cooperation.

By the 1870s, St. Paul had a population of twenty-three thousand, with 43 percent being foreign-born. Of the latter, most had emigrated from the predominantly Catholic countries of Ireland and Germany, lending a ready market and support for the sisters' hospital. As the number of Catholics increased and St. Paul grew, so did the hospital. From 1876 to 1880, Mother Jane Frances Bouchet was superior, and in 1878 she directed the addition of a new wing.[14]

With the exception of some charity cases, the nuns charged patients for their hospital care: $9 per week for a private bed, and the weekly sum of $6 for a private ward bed, with medicine forming extra charges. Far from being necessary to the running of the hospital, some historians have suggested that patient charges served a symbolic function in attracting the "right kind" of people. They helped demarcate the new hospitals for the respectable from old charity hospitals where the poor congregated. To have to pay showed that one could pay and that the service was worth the money.[15] For Catholic patients, paying institutions could offer an enhanced dignity, and they could receive spiritual care from the nursing sisters.

Santa Rosa Infirmary, San Antonio, Texas

The same applied to other Catholic hospitals. After establishing a hospital in Galveston, Texas, only the second in the state,[16] the Sisters of Charity of the Incarnate Word took advantage of additional nursing opportunities in San Antonio after the Civil War when, in 1869, the city faced a disaster from the flooding of the San Antonio River. Outbreaks of typhus, typhoid fever, and dysentery erupted, and the city was unprepared for these medical emergencies.[17] San Antonio was an older city, originating in the early 1700s as a way station between the Rio Grande River and the East Texas missions. By 1870, Bexar County had a population of sixteen thousand, but no hospital services existed for the growing populace.[18] The hospital in San Antonio came from close collaboration between Bishop Claude Dubuis of Galveston and Mother Angelique Hiver, superior of the Order of the Incarnate Word and Blessed Sacrament in Lyons, France. Bishops often obtained sisters for their dioceses through family or boyhood connections. When Dubuis needed help in Texas, he went to his native Lyons to petition his friend, Mother Angelique, to help him find sisters. She sent Madeleine Chollet, Pierre Cinquin, and Agnes Buisson. Although Sister Pierre had very little nurse's training, if any, Sisters Madeleine and Agnes had trained under the nursing sisters in Galveston.[19] The nuns named the hospital after Rose of Lima, the first canonized saint of the Americas,[20] and located it in the west end of downtown at the corner of Cameron and Commerce streets.

At that time, the Incarnate Word Sisters had no regular income and relied on donations to establish the infirmary. They directed their advertisements to a variety of groups and also to physicians. When they announced the infirmary's opening in a newspaper on November 25, 1869, they targeted the city government in hopes of getting charity patients, and they also focused on doctors who would bring their patients to Santa Rosa:

> We hope to meet the wants of the patients entrusted to our care by providing for them healthy rooms, good food and attentive nursing; and for this reason we . . . solicit not only the assistance of the authorities with the welfare of the poor, but also the kind offices of the physicians of this place. . . . Every [physician] has a right to send in his patients, whether they be paying or charity patients.[21]

Thus, in 1869, when other hospitals were still restricting hospital privileges to a few elite doctors, the Incarnate Word Sisters established a policy from the outset that would allow a greater number of doctors access to the hospital. The paper also appealed for donations by using the language of charity: "In an affair of this kind, when the interests of a charitable association are identical with the public good, a generous liberality is compatible with the truest economy."[22] The *San Antonio Weekly Express*'s appeal to the public for hospital donations brought a positive response. In July, it reported that two gentlemen, John Twohig and Francisco Guilbeau, donated $1,000 each and several other benefactors gave $500 each. Twohig was a Catholic businessman who underwrote several of the sisters' projects, and Guilbeau was mayor of the city.[23] The founding superior, Mother St. Madeleine Chollet, was succeeded by Mother St. Pierre Cinquin as hospital administrator in 1872, and she led the congregation and hospital for the next nineteen years.[24]

Initially, the infirmary had only a few patients, and with a limited income the hospital approached bankruptcy. At its inception, the sisters charged patients $1 per day and an additional 50¢ for fire in the room. Frequently, however, they accepted patients for less. They entered into an agreement with the city to pay 50¢ for each pauper. When they took in farmers and ranchers from nearby towns, they often accepted meat, eggs, butter, and vegetables as payment for the hospital bill.[25] The sisters also relied on donations by Catholics from Ireland, Australia, Boston, and cities in Texas. These donors may have been relatives of the sisters or recipients of their services at one time or another.[26]

Debts continued to mount, however. Like other women's congregations, the Sisters of Charity of the Incarnate Word frequently prayed to St. Joseph for protection or for special favors. In the late nineteenth and early twentieth centuries, a distinct Catholic ethos was in place that particularly emphasized openness to the supernatural. A devotional worldview accustomed Catholics to petition saints as intercessors in everyday life.[27] Thus, Mother St. Pierre composed a prayer that specifically asked for money to help the nuns pay their debts. Showing the urgency of her situation, she prayed: "St. Joseph, we need 60 piastres to pay for that horse which Sister Mary of Jesus bought; 155 piastres to pay Mr. Grenett; 110 piastres to pay Mr. Woolfson; 60 piastres to pay Mr. Thalteyer." She reminded him that heaven's funds were "inexhaustible. Pay your debts, St. Joseph. We are asking for nothing superfluous but only for what is just and necessary."[28]

Gradually, as the nuns' reputation spread, and as hospitals throughout the country began to attract private patients, admissions at Santa Rosa increased. By 1875, the original hospital building proved inadequate, and the sisters occupied a building on West Houston Street (fig. 3.1), which became the permanent location. Twelve sisters and six novices staffed the facility, and the stone building could house fifty patients.[29]

St. Mary's Infirmary, Cairo, Illinois

The Sisters of the Holy Cross established St. Mary's Infirmary in Cairo, Illinois, in 1867. A view back begins with the Civil War, when the nuns staffed US military hospitals in Cairo and Mound City, Illinois. After the war, yellow fever constantly threatened these towns, and other diseases persisted, often brought by soldiers and camp followers. In 1867, Dr. Horace Wardman, who had worked with the sisters during the war, and two local priests requested that Mother Angela Gillespie begin a hospital. She assigned Sisters Augusta Anderson, who had headed Memphis's Overton Hospital during the Civil War, as superior and Matilda Hartnett as assistant. Postwar Cairo was not prospering financially, and its citizens could give little to support a new hospital. Although they were aware of the city's

FIGURE 3.1 Santa Rosa Infirmary on Houston Street, San Antonio, TX, 1875. (Courtesy, Archives, Motherhouse of the Incarnate Word, San Antonio, TX)

financial straits, the sisters began raising funds for a building. After obtaining $153, they rented a house on Eleventh Street in November 1867.[30]

In the 1860s, most people still associated hospitals with indigence and believed that their services were rudimentary. Hence, the sisters had difficulty attracting patients. In an effort to survive, they sought new client groups. Cairo's strategic location at the conjunction of the Mississippi and Ohio rivers made it an ideal site for a marine hospital. Mother Angela was aware of this, and in the fall of 1867, she went to Washington, DC, and contracted with the US Treasury Department for St. Mary's Infirmary to serve inland mariners. The marine clientele could increase sisters' access to patients as well as the hospital's income and visibility. Furthermore, as the frontier moved westward, demand for seamen's hospitals along the Mississippi and Ohio rivers rose. By 1870, the estimated number of men employed on riverboats was eight thousand with over seven thousand on canals. While the government created special marine hospitals for these patients, many were understaffed and poorly managed. Hence, in some cities, the government contracted with private hospitals to care for patients rather than build its own facility.[31] Undoubtedly, the government's subsidization of a privately owned hospital was more cost-effective than building and managing a public facility. Such was the case in Cairo.

In her negotiations, Mother Angela had to emphasize that her institution provided a service that was both attractive and beneficial. The contract read that the sisters would provide "good and suitable Board, Lodging, Nursing, Medicine and Medical Attendance," in return for government payments of $7 a week for each seaman, to be paid at the end of the month. In addition, the sisters assumed burial responsibilities for $6 per burial.[32] Mother Angela also contracted with the county whose officials needed a place for its invalids. The Holy Cross Sisters would "nurse, board and lodge" the sick and "furnish them medicine and medical attention at the rate of 92¢ a day," or $27.60 a month. As a further return for the sisters, a county judge agreed to pay the rent for a larger house, and the sisters moved the sick there on January 1, 1868.[33] In December 1869, however, newly elected judges renegotiated the contract with the sisters and lowered the county's payments to $16 per month for adult paupers and $14 per month for each child. The hospital benefited from these contracts: in 1883, St. Mary's received $7,371 for marine patients, $21.50 for county patients, $1,245 from the city, $500 from private patients, and $211 from the railroad. Without the government income in its early years, St. Mary's Infirmary likely would not have survived.[34]

The Holy Cross Sisters strengthened their connections with the local community and with physicians. Within two years of its opening, the original building proved inadequate, and in the spring of 1869, on land donated by a benefactor, Sister Augusta Anderson began directing the construction of a two-story frame building. By 1873, there were two attending physicians as well as Dr. Wardman, who served as resident medical officer. That year, the infirmary housed a daily average of twenty-one patients, with eight sisters in attendance. Income remained steady, with the nuns maintaining a surplus of $6,286.[35]

Holy Cross Hospital, Salt Lake City, Utah

After establishing St. Mary's Infirmary, the Sisters of the Holy Cross looked westward. Upon completion of the transcontinental railroad in Utah in 1869, the growing mining industry attracted many immigrant Catholics to the area. While Mormons made up the vast majority of Utah's population, Father Denis Kiely of Salt Lake City reported that individual mining camps often had a hundred or more Catholics.[36] In 1875, mine owner Marcus Daly, an Irishman, and other Utah miners appealed to Father Lawrence Scanlan of Salt Lake City for a hospital. Scanlan then petitioned Mother Angela Gillespie for teachers and nurses to open the first Catholic school and hospital in the territory.[37] Mother Augusta Anderson, who had started the Cairo hospital, received the assignment to work with Scanlan.

When she attempted to open Holy Cross Hospital, Mother Augusta wrote her superior in Indiana to "send those sisters on as soon as possible." She specifically wanted those who could speak different languages. "If they do not come I do not think I shall be able to do another thing for all our prospects will be blighted. I am in a state of great anxiety so pray, dear Father, help me out of it. We will lose more than you can ever imagine if you do not start the Hospital and give the languages."[38] This statement reflects the sense of urgency sisters felt to establish hospitals in the wake of a growing Catholic populace in the United States. During the next 120 years, the Sisters of the Holy Cross became firmly rooted in Utah, creating both educational and health-care institutions in Salt Lake City and the surrounding mining regions.

To achieve the goal of building a hospital, Mother Augusta engaged in a mix of religious and entrepreneurial activities. First, she and another sister spent the summer of 1875 negotiating for land and raising money in mining camps. In conjunction with other church efforts, the nuns visited towns and camps where Paulist priests had recently conducted Catholic missions, or revivals. In so doing, sisters collected not only money but also the personal interest and support of the miners. Then, they established contracts with local and regional mining companies to provide care for ill or injured workers. In a pioneer prepaid health insurance plan, nuns provided nursing care and hospitalization for a flat rate per month, taken from employees' wages. They asked for a subscription of $1 a month, payable in advance.[39]

On October 25, 1875, Holy Cross Hospital opened in a rented adobe building on Fifth East Street (fig. 3.2), under the direction of Sister Mary of the Holy Cross Welsh with Sister Bartholomew Darnell as assistant. After her arrival in Salt Lake City, Sister Mary of the Holy Cross wrote Father Sorin in Indiana, "I liked the appearance of the city better than I thought I would. The fresh water runs through the streets. It comes from the mountains [and] adds very much to the beauty of the place." The Mormon presence was obviously on her mind when she added, "I passed by Brigham's place last Saturday. . . . [A]s much as three blocks all round his place is enclosed with a big thick wall just like a fortification."[40] The nuns paid $50 a month for the adobe building that accommodated thirteen patients. Throughout the early years, miners' prepayments underwrote hospital expenses. During 1880, for example, Holy Cross admitted 107 patients, 71 percent of whom were miners.[41]

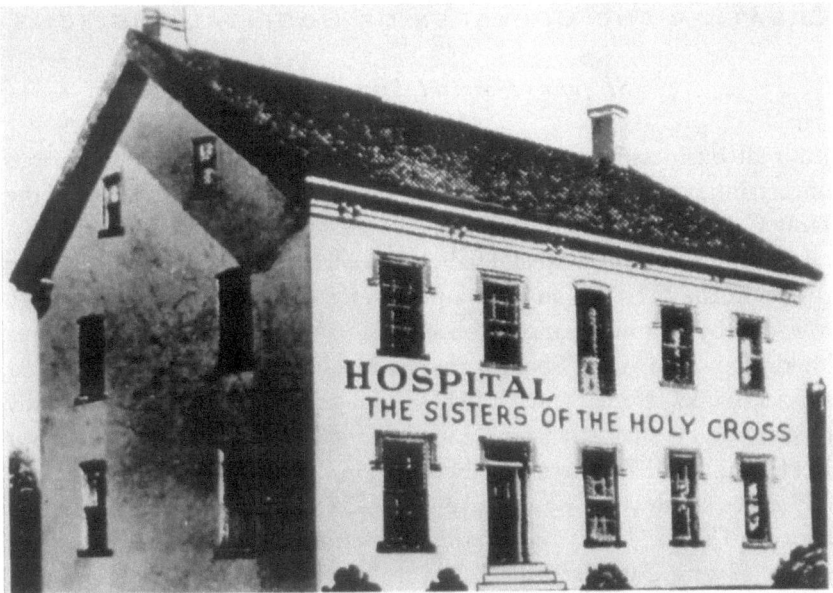

FIGURE 3.2 Holy Cross Hospital, Salt Lake City, UT, 1875. (Courtesy Sisters of the Holy Cross Archives, Saint Mary's, Notre Dame, IN)

The nuns admitted immigrants from several different countries, particularly Ireland, and many of the nursing sisters were as Irish as their patients. Of the 105 nuns at Holy Cross Hospital between 1875 and 1915, half were Irish-born. They had entered the Holy Cross congregation in the 1860s and 1870s and likely were part of the recruiting trips Mother Angela Gillespie made to Ireland. Many of those born in the United States and Canada were second-generation Irish.[42] To reinforce their cultural identity and that of their patients, occasionally the sisters brought in Irish entertainers. In 1884, a newspaper reported, "What a tonic, what a febrifuge a hearty laugh is! So must have thought the patients of the hospital of the Holy Cross last night, for they had a royal entertainment" by Morrissey's Hibernicon [Irish] Troupe.[43] On the other hand, when Father Denis Kiely wrote his archbishop in 1875 for sister-nurses and teachers, he emphasized that "there be one who can speak German, Spanish, Italian and French."[44] The sisters responded in kind: in the same sample mentioned above, five nuns were born in Canada, seven in Germany, and one in France.[45]

Creation and Collapse of Hospital Missions

St. John's Hospital, Silver Reef, Utah

Like all business ventures, Catholic hospitals were subject to various uncertainties and changing patterns in the marketplace. The Sisters of the Holy Cross administered and nursed in the short-lived St. John's Hospital for miners in Silver Reef, Utah, between 1879 and 1885. The mining rushes in the West began with a prospector making an initial discovery followed by communication to other miners who migrated to the area looking for a bonanza. Soon, corporate investors followed along with tar shacks, banks, stores, and churches. The communities were ethnically diverse, largely male, transient, and violent.[46] Such was the case in Silver Reef, Utah. In 1874, silver was discovered in the mountainous area located 375 miles southwest of Salt Lake City. The town peaked in population between 1878 and 1879, numbering approximately fifteen hundred, most of whom were Catholic miners.

Father Lawrence Scanlan of Salt Lake City built the Catholic hospital in 1879 with the understanding that miners would support it by being taxed individually $1 a month, and he offered it to the Sisters of the Holy Cross. Four nuns arrived after a treacherous four-and-a-half-day wagon trip in the summer of 1879. Sister Euphrosine Pepin described the trek in a letter to her superior. After experiencing an accident when the wagon overturned, they had to travel through a five-mile pass

> between the black ridge and an 300 ft.-deep ravine, through which the wagon had barely room to go; made Srs. Anacitus [Collins] and Beniti [Bryson] sick with fear. They insisted upon walking nearly the whole of it. The country after we left the R. R. is a barren, wild desert. It looks as though an earthquake had brought the bowels of the earth to its surface. . . . Not a blade of grass or a leaf of tree is to be seen.
>
> Nothing but miners' cabins surround us.[47]

One local resident recalled giant lizards, venomous rattlesnakes, fearsome tarantulas, the swift-moving centipede; many freighters, peddlers and wagons; saloon brawls and gunfights; Chinese inhabitants with their unusual merchandise and cooking; and hundreds of miners—Americans, Cornishmen, and Irishmen.[48]

After opening the hospital in a small building, the sisters averaged thirty to fifty patients over the next four years, with $1,700 to $3,000 collected in receipts annually. Fairs and donations brought in sufficient amounts to erect an addition to the building. Among the hospital inventory, the sisters listed bedsteads, linens, furniture, altar items, eating utensils, dishes, clocks, framed pictures, and spittoons. In this remote land, the nuns often experienced loneliness, and they wrote heartfelt, melancholy letters home. In March 1881, Sister Febronia Ward wrote Father Sorin, "The spirit of Faith you so strongly inculcate is the main support in this distant mission where even divine consolation seems withdrawn sometimes. . . . Regularity is the daily food of my soul. . . . Work is stopped in some of the mines since January—the Reef is slack."[49] By 1882, miners' wages had significantly decreased such that workers from all the mines except one went on strike. In 1885, the mines shut down altogether, and the sisters were forced to close St. John's.

St. Edward's Hospital, Deadwood, Dakota Territory

The Holy Cross Sisters also opened the first Catholic hospital in Dakota Territory. In January 1878, Father Bernard Mackin from Deadwood contacted the Sisters of the Holy Cross and asked them to establish a hospital there. Deadwood had become a booming mining town after the discovery of gold in 1874. By 1876 it had a population of nearly twenty-five thousand merchants, residents, and gold-seekers. Like other gold rush towns, it had its share of lawlessness, gunmen, gamblers, outlaws, and disreputable places of entertainment. Three miles away was Lead City, the site of the Homestake Mine, owned by a California company. Here, large corporate enterprises extracted gold by blasting from deep underground. Casualties resulting from disorderliness, blasting, and mining injuries, and occurrences of typhoid fever and diphtheria led to a growing demand for hospitals in both towns. It was this setting that the Holy Cross Sisters entered in 1878.

The local priest solicited the towns and camps for funds to erect a hospital and, with the help of some Protestants, started a subscription fund that amounted to $500. Five Sisters of the Holy Cross traveled by train from Indiana to some point in Dakota Territory, and the last two hundred miles by stagecoach in hot weather over rutted and dusty roads. After the uncomfortable trip, the sisters found the building in Deadwood unfinished, and they had to rent a house for $60 a month.[50] Without other funds, they wasted no time in seeking money. Sister Edward Murphy canvassed local businessmen but lamented to her superior, "Money is scarce and business dull at the present."[51]

The rhetoric of self-denial and mortification set nuns apart from others, and the secular press often used it to drum up community support for the sisters' work. On August 22, 1878, the Black Hills Daily Times noted,

Five Sisters of the Order of the Holy Cross chose to leave their home at St. Mary's, Indiana, and come to this place to devote their time to the care of the invalids at Deadwood and of those of the surrounding camps who wish to come under their care. Their first object is to build a hospital.... We are confident then that the generous inhabitants who wish to see Deadwood prosper and also to furnish an occasion to aid the suffering humanity, will, when called upon, give their assistance to this undertaking.[52]

On August 30, the newspaper announced a hospital benefit for the next day that was to include "the grand romantic and sensational drama of 'The Castle of Lausanne' and the highly amusing farce of 'The Irish Lion.'" It concluded, "In a community like this where so many strangers are sojourning away from their homes and friends, the necessity of such an institution [hospital] being established in our midst must be apparent to all."[53] The nuns eventually obtained enough cash to build a brick hospital, St. Edwards, on property purchased by the Indiana motherhouse. Over time, thirteen sisters, all but two Irish-born, staffed the facility.

At the same time, the owners of the Homestake Mine asked the nuns to open a hospital in Lead City. Three Irish immigrant nuns opened Miners' Hospital in December 1879 with $400 donated by the mining company and additional funds the sisters themselves collected. That month, Father John Toohey, a newly arrived Holy Cross priest, wrote his superior, "The sisters at Lead City have already entered their new hospital," aided by money from a "festival of three nights' duration by which they raised about $1,000 towards defraying the expenses of the building."[54]

The sisters cared for city and county patients as well as the miners. St. Edwards Hospital, in fact, usually held twenty-five county patients at a time, and money from the city clearly accounted for the majority of hospital receipts.[55] From the beginning, however, the sisters encountered difficulties in finances and personnel. One historian noted, "The type of patient made management without male nurses hazardous. The impossibility of securing maids and the high price of food, necessary for the sick, constituted another drawback."[56] In addition, the patients complained about the food. In October 1879, a fire in Deadwood left money scarce, and the county failed to pay its patients' bills at St. Edwards. In July 1880, the sisters lost their contract with the county, and the hospital had no patients. By then, the gold rush was over.

Further complications occurred as a result of a deteriorating relationship between the hospital directress, Sister Edward, and the local pastor. She wrote her superior, "Our pastor is making himself Superior not only of spiritual but temporal matters," over which he had no authority. "It is not good to have a Priest living in a house with Sisters who can not keep their place," she wrote. To make matters worse, she was losing the deference owed her as directress from her fellow sister-nurses. Most important, the nuns had failed to obtain written agreements from the physicians, who controlled the fund into which miners paid monthly sums entitling them to hospitalization. The doctors withdrew all the money in payment for their own services, leaving the sisters nothing to pay the hospitals' running expenses. Consequently, both hospitals closed in 1881.[57]

In May of that year, Bishop Martin Marty was still unclear about the sisters' position and wrote another local priest in Deadwood:

> I told Mother that I was sorry to see them go and lose partly the fruit of their labor, but that I had no hopes of others succeeding where they had failed. It will, of course, make a bad impression if that property which was bought for a hospital by the people is sold by the Sisters, but if they have the title one can not prevent it. I am very anxious to learn how things are now and how it came that the Sisters who seemed so zealous and devoted became so discouraged as to withdraw without giving you or me the opportunity of speaking and acting in their behalf. An appeal to the citizens made in the proper manner by one of us might have procured the means of perseverance and final success.[58]

That did not happen, and the sisters eventually sold the property to the Benedictine nuns. The Holy Cross Sisters were supposed to reinvest the $10,000 in a school in Sioux Falls, but the bishop failed to complete the arrangements, and the nuns believed they were justified in using the money for the congregation's other schools. In 1890, however, the balance due the sisters was $2,962.30. The Holy Cross Sisters dropped it since they eventually came to believe that it, in fact, did properly belong to the hospital.[59]

Providence Hospital, Terre Haute, Indiana

While the above hospitals were located in isolated mining regions and were subject to the changing fortunes of that business, another unsuccessful hospital venture occurred in a midwestern city. After the Civil War, the Sisters of Providence of Saint Mary-of-the-Woods, Indiana, a congregation that had been highly successful in education, were anxious to open a permanent hospital ministry. Founded in France in 1806 for the purpose of religious education of Catholic children, the sisters also cared for the sick poor in their homes. Six nuns came to Indiana in 1840 at the

Bishop of Vincennes' request to open schools in his diocese. Under the direction of Mother Theodore Guerin, the sisters founded Saint Mary's Institute for higher education for women and fourteen other establishments in Indiana. The French sisters took on an American identity shortly after their arrival, learning the English language and accepting women born in the United States into the congregation.[60] They established the motherhouse near Terre Haute, centrally located in the state.

The Sisters of Providence worked among a diverse Indiana population. French settlers from Canada and New Orleans comprised the early population, but by 1870, Catholics were in the minority.[61] Southerners from Kentucky, Virginia, and Maryland had migrated to the southern part of the state, while those from New England, Pennsylvania, and New York had moved to the north. Large immigration surges in the 1840s and 1850s brought German and Irish settlers. These immigration patterns significantly affected the Sisters of Providence congregation, since, thereafter, daughters of Irish immigrants entered in large numbers. The sisters also had to cope with prejudice as nativism against immigrant Catholics spread to the Midwest.[62]

The nuns' nursing opportunity came during the Civil War when Governor Oliver Morton requested their services in Indianapolis. Mother Mary Cecilia, superior general, wrote on May 15, 1861, "The wretched condition of the soldiers is such that the authorities are most anxious to see the Sisters come to take care of the sick. . . . This is an eventful occasion for the Community; to have a hospital has long been desired."[63] The sisters took over the nursing and general management of City Hospital, renamed the Military Hospital, under the direction of Sister Athanasius Fogarty. Born in Ireland, Sister Athanasius entered the community in 1855. She taught elementary school until she was assigned to manage the Military Hospital from June 1861 to August 1865, prompting physicians to credit the hospital's success to her ability rather than to theirs.[64] In 1861, the sisters also nursed sick soldiers in a temporary hospital in Vincennes, Indiana, where they cared for ill and injured soldiers after the battle of Fort Donelson. They turned down a request in Evansville because their authority as nursing supervisors would be divided with a male steward as hospital manager. To be under his surveillance was unacceptable.[65]

Through their wartime work, the sisters established a foothold in nursing work; and at their retreat in 1865 they elected to remain in the hospital field. In August of that year, Sisters Athanasius Fogarty and Mary Louise Maloney opened an infirmary in Indianapolis for sick veterans, St. John's Home for Invalids, at the request of Father August Bessonies. He had become increasingly aware of veterans' needs when he visited the sick in their homes. He did not have the resources at his disposal, however, leading the nuns themselves to purchase a house. They paid $3,000 down and borrowed $4,000 with interest, to be paid in one year. Ownership provided them the security to begin their work, and they hoped to support the hospital with fees of $8 a week collected from paying patients. At their own expense, they cared for the indigent sick. The *Indianapolis Sentinel* heralded the opening on October 10, 1865, and since the sisters had received only $300 in donations, specifically appealed for money until the hospital could support itself. By 1871, when other facilities were available in Indianapolis and the number of veterans had diminished, the nuns closed St. John's.

That same year, the sisters were in the planning stage for a hospital in Terre Haute. A colonel of the Indiana Volunteer Regiments had asked them to operate a temporary hospital in Terre Haute during the Civil War, but it did not come about because of prejudice against the nuns.[66] They encountered resistance again in the early 1870s during the short life of Providence Hospital.

In July 1869, at the request of Bishop Maurice de Saint-Palais, Mother Anastasie Brown purchased property in Indianapolis at the cost of $26,000 for a prospective hospital to replace the old St. John's Home for Invalids. At the same time, Chauncey Rose, a Protestant benefactor, offered $13,000 and a five-acre lot to entice the sisters to open a hospital in Terre Haute. The city had a population of over 33,500 people with no hospital to support them when ill. Those needing assistance who could not be tended at home went to the county's poor asylum. Believing that they could support two hospitals, Mother Anastasie took up Rose's offer.[67]

On September 12, 1869, Bishop de Saint-Palais and the sisters laid the cornerstone for Providence Hospital, located at Fifth Avenue and Thirteenth Street.[68] On August 25, 1870, the sisters agreed with Snapp and Haynes Contractors to have them construct the hospital at a cost of $22,331.28, payable in seven payments over the next year.[69] Contractors underestimated the expenses, however, and the entire cost of the structure, without furniture, ultimately amounted to more than $85,000. Citizens of Terre Haute contributed $4,290, and proceeds from a local fair and donations from friends of the sisters, $4,586. Chauncey Rose's gift, however, which eventually totaled $31,500, covered the bulk of the financing. Although he had hoped it would encompass the entire amount, it obviously fell short, and the sisters had to assume a debt of nearly $50,000 for the remaining expense. Still, the nuns wanted to make available the best modern and functional facility, and they expected it to be impressive.

Thus, they took on the debt. Shortage of funds interrupted the work several times, complicated by Mother Anastasie's discontinuance of sisters' begging tours, which had been used to solicit financial support. She did not believe the sisters had the ability for that kind of work. As a consequence, it took two years to complete the edifice.[70]

As the hospital neared completion in 1872, the sisters made plans for a dedication to be marked by a procession on the thirtieth of June, a Sunday. On June 26, the newspaper predicted the celebration to be "the most impressive solemnization ever witnessed in the city."[71] Opposition to the hospital was already beginning, however. During a recent smallpox epidemic, the sisters had volunteered their free services to the city pesthouse, but the mayor refused after he received an anonymous note threatening to burn the building down if the sisters entered. Although he suggested that perhaps the nuns' free services had upset the wage scale and alarmed the attendants employed in the hospital, the sisters wondered if more was involved. Then on June 29, an anonymous "Inquirer" attacked the idea of their holding the hospital procession on Sunday. Using the medium of the newspaper, he argued that the Catholic Church

> arranges for a procession to move at the very hour of the day when it is known that it will interfere most with the worship of the Protestant churches of the city. . . . In selecting the route of the procession, it arranges to pass the doors of at least four of the most prominent of the Protestant churches, at the time of service. Is this a studied insult, or is it the result of a carelessness hardly less culpable?

The sisters had advertised that the hospital would be nonsectarian, to which the writer responded, "Remembering the appeals made to Protestants and that the institution is built largely, if not chiefly, with Protestant money, if this is unsectarian [sic], is it quite courteous?"[72]

The procession went on the next day as scheduled, and it was an impressive one. Two trains of twenty cars brought a delegation from Indianapolis, and excursion trains also arrived from Vincennes and other nearby towns. Two wagons of sisters came from Saint Mary-of-the-Woods to receive the guests. The procession included eleven different Catholic organizations and societies totaling several hundred men. Demonstrating the high hopes of the sisters and church leaders, Dr. Theophilus Parvin, a Protestant and professor of obstetrics at Louisville Medical College, gave the dedication address, calling the hospital "the grandest of all" the things ever done in Terre Haute. Just as St. Paul's Cathedral in London was a memorial to its architect, Sir Christopher

Wren, so would Providence Hospital be a "noble monument" to Chauncey Rose and the Sisters of Providence. Responding to the "Inquirer" of the previous day, Parvin defended the propriety of holding the celebration on Sunday. Workers had no other day to spare for this purpose, and "their Master did not hesitate to heal and visit the sick on the Sabbath day." Following that example, Parvin endorsed the decision.[73]

On July 1, the *Terre Haute Weekly Express* described the new building: it was an imposing three-story brick structure designed for seventy-five patients, with every room having a fireplace. Verandas and porches provided patients with sunlight and fresh air. In addition, the building had two wash rooms on each floor, steam heat, underground cellars for provisions and coal storage, bakery, boiler room, kitchen, two refectories, china room, laundry with hot-air dryer, servants' sitting room, reception room, parlor, and office. Space for physicians included a consultation room, office, operating room, and pharmacy; and an oratory occupied the central front of the building. Two elevators linked the different floors.[74]

In its description of the hospital, the writer noted the donations of Rose and other citizens and then announced that the Catholic Church "has paid or assumed the remainder of its cost." By contrast, the "Inquirer" of June 29 had asserted that the hospital was built largely by Protestant money. Neither credited the sisters, who had, in fact, assumed the large debt. On July 6, to counter any false impressions that might injure the hospital's interests, the nuns responded in the newspaper themselves. They cited the expenses of the hospital as being between $85,000 and $90,000, with proceeds from fairs and donations totaling nearly $10,000, along with Rose's large endowment. Yet, the remaining $50,000 debt "has not been assumed by the Catholic Church, as some have supposed, but rests upon the Hospital, which is, in fact, under mortgage for a part of the amount. Bearing this in mind . . . the Hospital can, by no means, be exclusively for charity patients." The sisters then asked for more donations, "as our expenses are already so great, it will be impossible for us to make any considerable outlay." They appealed to men without families to provide for themselves in the hospital "as will best suit their personal interest," people in benevolent associations to have standing engagements with the hospital for their sick, priests and their congregations to contribute money to reserve beds when needed, and presidents of railroad companies to send their ill or injured employees.[75]

The hospital opened in September, with six nuns under the direction of Sister Gertrude Sherlock. Sister Athanasius Fogarty, who had ably administered the Military Hospital in Indianapolis and St. John's Home for Invalids, was scheduled to work at the new facility, but she sustained an injury when a window fell on her hand and she was never able to come. Patients did frequent the hospital at first. On September 28, 1872, the facility housed thirteen patients with several having already been discharged.[76] Over time, the "Register of Invalids" listed 170 patients: sixty-nine Irish, twenty-four German, and fifty born in the United States. Patients also came from England, Wales, Scotland, France, Canada, Prussia, Switzerland, Norway, and Sweden. The majority were working-class laborers.[77]

By 1873, the sisters' debts were mounting. In the hospital, they charged for various items. A sample bill included two weeks' board and nursing for $12.15, six prescription drugs ranging from 35¢ to 40¢ cents each, stimulants costing 10¢ to 15¢ each, and washing at 30¢, totaling $15.25. Another patient's bill totaled $13.70 for a two-week stay.[78] Even if all the patients had paid, it was hardly enough to cover the huge debt, because by then, the hospital had engulfed $125,000 over and above Chauncey Rose's gift. The sisters still had the property in Indianapolis where they had hoped to build a hospital, but the debt on that property, counting interest on the note, neared $50,000, as well. To their relief, but also to their sadness because they had desired a hospital ministry in Indianapolis, they were able to sell it to the Little Sisters of the Poor for the same price they had paid for it.[79]

Local opposition in Terre Haute did not end. In 1873, the Catholic Church's recent promulgation of papal infallibility fueled anti-Catholic sentiment among the general public. Additionally, the sisters did not have the support of local physicians, stemming from their choice of Dr. John Baty, a French physician whom they knew and trusted, as chief of the medical staff. Baty had been a surgeon in the French army and had graduated from Montpellier University. Although the sisters' own ties to the motherhouse in France had been inactive since the late 1840s, their French ethnic networks remained important to them. Baty took over in November 1872 when the tide of nativism was still high, and the nuns' decision was not popular with the local doctors who resented a "foreigner" as their chief. Aware of the negative feelings against him, Baty resigned in 1873, and Dr. Leon Willien succeeded him in the head position. Although Willien was born in Alsace-Lorraine and was a Catholic, he had been in the United States since childhood and had trained at St. Louis Medical College. His local ties also were deep—he had recently married a woman from Fort Wayne, Indiana.[80]

Additional opposition arose from the county commissioners. When patient numbers at Providence Hospital did not increase, the nuns offered to care for the city's poor at $4 per week, and in fact, did tend to some. But the county commissioners supported the county asylum rather than the Catholic hospital, and they spent large sums to renovate it. By December 1873, the poor asylum was ready to receive a hundred patients at a weekly rate of $1.25 for each patient. Alarmed over the possibility of losing these patients to Providence Hospital, the commissioners published the following in the *Terre Haute Express* on December 7, 1873:

> Whereas, The county has, at great expense, enlarged and refitted the county poor asylum, and made all the necessary arrangements for its existence and management ... and Whereas, The commissioners are often called upon by the Providence Hospital to pay large sums of money for taking care of sick persons in indigent circumstances; and Whereas, It is considered by this Board that under existing circumstances such allowances are but so much extra expense; therefore be it Ordered, That from this date no officer of this county, excepting the members of this Board, shall have authority to send any person or persons to Providence Hospital, to be taken care of at the expense of the county. . . .

The commissioners ordered that all county patients be removed to the asylum immediately.[81] This was the final blow to Providence Hospital.

Despite the sisters' attempts to interest different groups, their efforts failed to produce sufficient income, and they closed the facility in 1874. Dire financial straits led them to approach Bishop de Saint-Palais to persuade him to purchase the building for an orphanage. Although the sisters had invested $125,000 in the hospital alone, the bishop was only able to pay them $15,000 for the building and the land. By business standards, the purchase price could have been considered an insult, but the sisters were desperate, and after assuring themselves that the property would be put to proper Christian use, they acquiesced. The need for teachers and schools became so great that the nuns did not take up hospital work again.[82]

The Sisters of Providence of Saint Mary-of-the-Woods had many of the elements needed for success, including dedication, an early Americanization process, and a commitment to hard work. They certainly prayed that their work would succeed. And they marketed their project in the newspapers, directing their advertisements to a variety of associations. But the Protestant majority in Terre Haute coupled with nativist antagonism against immigrants contributed to problems. In 1870, the Germans and Irish were the largest immigrant groups in Terre Haute, and few French residents lived in the city.[83] Yet, the sisters chose to rely on a

French physician, an unpopular choice to local doctors who perceived him as "foreign."

Furthermore, while anti-Catholicism and ethnic tensions were real, the hospital's early demise also was due to market forces. A nationwide economic panic occurred in 1873, brought on by overexpansion of railroads and the Treasury Department's postwar withdrawal of greenbacks that contracted the money supply. It precipitated a financial crisis that lasted over the next several years and certainly contributed to Providence Hospital's woes. Also, one congregational historian has asserted that no preliminary canvas had been made to ascertain people's need for a hospital in Terre Haute. And the abandonment of the nuns' begging tours eliminated the sisters' main source of accessing this information.[84] Finally, at a time before the germ theory had taken hold in the United States, most of the ill received care at home, still fearing the social stigma of hospitals and their high mortality rates.

Unlike the other three congregations, the Sisters of Providence began their hospital with a large endowment. In hindsight, what surely seemed a gift from heaven in many ways turned out to be a curse. With the nuns having abandoned their begging and solicitation tours, it is likely that comparatively small numbers of citizens bought into the project. The people of Terre Haute had given only $4,290. Rather than being built by the pooled contributions of the common citizenry, the majority of the financing was primarily covered by a single wealthy donor. Hence, many never considered Providence Hospital as truly their own and felt little responsibility to help fill its beds.

Providence Hospital might have survived over time had the congregation itself not experienced a financial crisis in 1874. Mother Anastasie Brown, the superior general at the time, was a very optimistic, hopeful person, and she believed in the value of real estate as a good investment. Under her administration, the sisters had erected the hospital, schools, and convents that required enormous sums of money. At a time when additional money was unobtainable and creditors were demanding payments on existing loans, the congregation overextended itself and accumulated a large debt.[85] Along these lines, one has to wonder if the outcome of the sisters' efforts might have been different had they built a more modest building initially, which could be financed with Rose's $31,500 alone. They would not then have been saddled with a huge debt from the very beginning. When they erected such a large modern hospital in a primarily Protestant town, at a time when patients who could pay for their care stayed home, the formula for collapse had been made. The considerable debt taken on by the sisters, combined with the numerous empty hospital beds, resulted in a growing obligation they could not possibly cover.

As these examples have shown, the history of Catholic hospitals in the Midwest, Texas, and Utah during the 1850s, 1860s, and 1870s reveals a dependency on demographic, religious, economic, and ethnic factors. Catholic hospitals could provide a religious and ethnic identity not found in non-Catholic voluntary hospitals. Indeed, nuns' commitment to their ethnic heritage remained strong. Often this helped their institutions, since immigrants not only were prominent on hospital admissions lists, but they also served as an ethnic base for financial support. It proved difficult at other times, when sisters relied on networks that the public increasingly perceived as "foreign."

The Catholic institutions that were most successful had strengthened their connections with local and regional communities, church leaders, physicians, business leaders, governments, and other residents who expanded their investment in the hospital. By contrast, when hospitals lost physicians' support, county commissioners' income, and the general public's patronization, they had fewer chances for success. Most important, it is significant that the sisters whose hospitals succeeded during this time period started small with a manageable debt.

4

"An Institution for the Community and Not Narrowly Sectarian":

CATHOLIC HOSPITALS, 1880–1925

> The parade was one that did credit to the event that was being celebrated and it was watched with much interest by the throngs that lined its course. The societies that took part represented many different interests, showing an appreciation of the fact that St. Joseph's Hospital was to be an institution for the community and not narrowly sectarian to any degree.[1]
>
> *South Bend Times,* April 21, 1903

Under a rare warm sun in April 1903, Catholic officials placed the cornerstone for a new addition to St. Joseph's Hospital in South Bend, Indiana. It involved an impressive ceremony that started at St. Patrick's Church and included a parade of civic and religious societies, posts from the Grand Army of the Republic, and an imposing procession led by Bishop Herman J. Alderling. Thousands thronged the parade line. This auspicious ceremony reflected the broad base of support that sisters and the Catholic Church actively sought. The links nuns forged to make hospital building possible are important elements in the story of the medical marketplace after 1880.[2] Although hospital growth had clearly begun before 1880, changing social and economic conditions led to an aggressive expansion of hospitals in the last quarter of the nineteenth century and the first quarter of the twentieth. During this time, institutions became increasingly technological and market-based.³ Catholic sisters continued to carve out their own niche: in a 1910 government census, Catholic hospitals accounted for one-fifth of all the hospitals responding, and most were under nuns' direction.⁴ In recruiting patients, sisters had to negotiate in a society in which gender, race, class, religion, and ethnicity were important variables.

Entrepreneurship is a central characteristic of the actors in this chapter. Sisters took responsibility for building construction and the risks that accompanied large capital improvements, sought patients, and provided them with specific services. In addition, nuns gave doctors a site for certain forms of medical practice, providing them opportunities to practice private medicine without having to invest their own money.⁵

Sectarian rivalries within local and regional communities pressured sisters to improve their medical and nursing facilities so that they could remain competitive. In addition, the needs of local and regional communities for hospital treatment grew. Mainly, however, sisters believed their presence would create a beneficial environment for anyone facing a health crisis, and they especially wanted to provide quick spiritual care to any Catholic in need.

During this period, sisters had to compete not only with voluntary and public hospitals but also with institutions founded on different principles. Physicians had responded to competition by establishing proprietary hospitals, which operated to supplement the wealth and income of owners. By contrast, not-for-profit voluntary and religious hospitals took no share of hospital income to enhance owners' personal wealth. Physicians also had developed specialties such as ophthalmology and obstetrics and had opened their own institutions for this new kind of practice. All of these institutions experienced increased financial pressures and competition.

One of the defining characteristics of hospitals during this period was the way the power of science increasingly affected hospital decisions. By 1925, the American hospital had become an institution with recovery and cure the goals to be achieved by professional personnel and increasing medical technology. Like secular hospitals, Catholic hospitals functioned with the advantages of x-rays, laboratories, and aseptic surgery, making hospital operating rooms, with all their technical equipment and specialized personnel, the safest and most convenient places to perform surgery.⁶ Reflecting these transformations, the physical layouts of hospitals grew considerably. Expansions were consistent, although the sequence depended on when the sisters established the hospitals, what funds were available, and the degree of denominational competition in the area. In the details of the hospitals' programs of growth, one can obtain a view of the importance of local markets, religious and ethnic influences, and scientific imperatives.

As hospitals grew in number and complexity, members of the lower classes and the working poor, such as laborers, domestics, factory workers, and small craftsmen, entered them, as did larger numbers of the middle classes. Scientific medicine, surgery, the professionalization of medicine and nursing, and an emphasis on efficiency and order changed the character of hospitals. Growing deficits led administrators away from charity and toward the provision of services for acutely ill patients who could pay.

An Expanding Medical Market

While the Catholic hospital movement responded to economic realities, it also remained a spiritual movement to support the missions of the Catholic Church. In this way, Catholic hospitals departed from nonreligious hospitals. The Catholic Church's response to urban growth included hospital expansion, new churches, schools, and extra clerics. Hospitals, then, were only a part of the church's far-reaching plans to provide services. Paralleling these moves were vast increases in communicants. (See an ecclesiastical census, table 4.1.)

As medical problems increased in railway and mining centers, nuns moved into these regions. Mortality statistics for the mining and railroad industries show how dangerous those occupations were. High rates of homicides, gunshot wounds, and accidents occurred in mining camps. For example, in 1880, Utah had a 1:14 ratio of miners killed or injured to the number employed.[7] Mines were situated in isolated locations, and medical care was unavailable. Railroad workers faced similar hazards. Even though railroads were the principal agents of industrial development, they brought significant dangers from accidents. In 1888, the Interstate Commerce Commission (ICC) reported 2,070 railroad employees killed with 20,148 injured. Figures for 1911 showed 2,871 employees killed while on duty and a staggering 45,848 injured.[8]

To treat these injuries, most of the large western railroads adopted a hospital system in the late nineteenth century. This included a chief surgeon to act as director, consulting physicians and specialists at hospitals located at central points, and local surgeons to render first aid to the injured at emergency stations until removal to the general hospital.[9] Several of the companies contracted with Catholic sisters to provide hospitalization for sick and

Table 4.1 Hospitals, Churches, and Other Institutions in Selected Dioceses

Diocese	Estimated # Catholics	Catholic Hospitals / Charitable Facilities	Churches	Priests	Asylums	Academies/ Select Schools	Parish Schools
St. Paul, MN							
1885	...	3	195	153	7	10	69
1901	220,000	13	221	228	3	8	83
1910	260,000	9	248	305	3	7	85
Ft. Wayne, IN							
1885	...	3	122	109	2	7	60
1901	78,000	13	143	177	2	11	77
1910	99,196	15	153	206	2	13	86
San Ant., TX							
1885	...	1	50	47	1	3	25
1901	75,000	6	73	73	2	10	39
1910	85,000	8	73	89	2	19	36
Salt Lake City, UT							
1885	...	...	...	...	...	...	...
1901	8,000	2	20	22	1	2	3
1910	10,750	1	22	25	1	2	6

Sources: *Sadliers' Catholic Directory, Almanac, and Ordo* (New York: D. and J. Sadlier and Co., 1885); *Official Catholic Directory* (Milwaukee: M. H. Wiltzius and Co., 1901, 1910).

injured workers and their families. St. Joseph's Infirmary in Fort Worth, for example, began as a railroad hospital that the Sisters of Charity of the Incarnate Word staffed.

In the expanding medical market, hospital appointments became essential to the careers and priorities of ambitious physicians. In the nineteenth century, most physicians did not hold a hospital appointment; to have one was indeed a prize. Hospitals had few training positions, and social connections were particularly important in selecting candidates. Institutions functioned as a means for doctors to obtain opportunities for surgical practice, medical education, and clinical research. Doctors also sought hospital affiliation to acquire social prestige and to gain access to a population of experimental subjects. In general, however, by the late nineteenth century hospital appointments were becoming more widely distributed as sites for practice rather than prestige. Physicians consolidated their medical authority, and medical values increasingly shaped the modern hospital.[10] By that time, most physicians received a fee per service or case.

Four distinct groups of physicians emerged in late nineteenth-century hospitals: consultants who were older, distinguished doctors who had no customary duties; visiting or attending staff, consisting of active physicians who supervised treatment; resident or house staff composed of young doctors in training who handled treatment details; and dispensary staff who tended outpatients.[11] A parallel structure emerged in Catholic hospitals that essentially involved a two-tiered system. It appears that the nuns made a point of designating certain doctors as staff members, and they established medical boards that provided particular doctors with prestige. Over time, however, the hospitals moved toward granting open hospital privileges by allowing all qualified doctors in the area to admit patients, although it is unclear exactly when each hospital began that policy. The dual-tiered system that evolved consisted of distinguished physicians who had staff privileges and rank-and-file doctors who had hospital admitting privileges. This appears to be a pragmatic adaptation on the nuns' part to what the physicians wanted. Doctors, in turn, could trade off the attraction of having a hospital designation with the open staffing policies.

Expansion of Catholic Hospitals

St. Joseph's Hospital, St. Paul, Minnesota

In a letter to his father in 1891, a patient related having eye surgery at St. Joseph's Hospital, owned and managed by the Sisters of St. Joseph of Carondelet. He had seen his doctor in the office at ten o'clock in the morning and was directed to be at St. Joseph's at noon. Nothing is known about the exact nature of the disorder, except that the patient did not require chloroform anesthetic. After his arrival, the doctor accompanied the patient to the operating room, where he recalled having "some kind of medication injected in the eye lid." While lying on the table, he was aware of a sister-nurse beside him. He experienced some pain, stirred somewhat, and then the sister-nurse "took my hand for an instant in sympathy."[12] Indeed, when patients entered Catholic hospitals, they came with the

FIGURE 4.1 Sisters of St. Joseph of Carondelet at St. Joseph's Hospital, St. Paul, MN, 1897. *Front, left to right:* Sr. Cornelia O'Donnell, Sr. Elizabeth McGolrick, Sr. Blandina Geary, Sr. Irmina Dougherty, Sr. Emily, Sr. Melanie Kelly, Sr. Benigna Casey, Sr. Julitta Carroll, Sr. Beatrice Gleason. *Middle:* Sr. Isidore Troeger, Sr. Edith Hogan, Sr. Anatolia Ryan, Sr. Christina McNeill. *Back:* Sr. Aida Geary, Sr. Madeline Lyons, Sr. Florentia Downs, Sr. Loretta Vasey, Sr. Bernardine Maher, Sr. John Baptist McNamara. (Courtesy Archives of the Congregation of the Sisters of St. Joseph of Carondelet, St. Paul, MN)

expectation of receiving personal care by the religious sisters. Nuns' presence, influence, and authoritative control prevailed in all departments, including the operating room, x-ray, laboratory, kitchen, laundry, nursing, and pharmacy.

St. Paul's health-care services expanded in the decade between 1880 and 1890 when its population tripled. By 1890, more than 133,000 people lived in the city, with over one-third being foreign born and 39 percent Roman Catholic. Catholics outnumbered all other religious denominations combined, not only in the city but also in the state. Records from St. Joseph's from 1876 to 1883 show that over half of the total patients were born outside the United States, hailing from twenty-eight different countries but primarily Ireland, Canada, Scandinavia, and Germany.[13]

Mother Bernardine Maher (fig. 4.1) became superior of St. Joseph's in

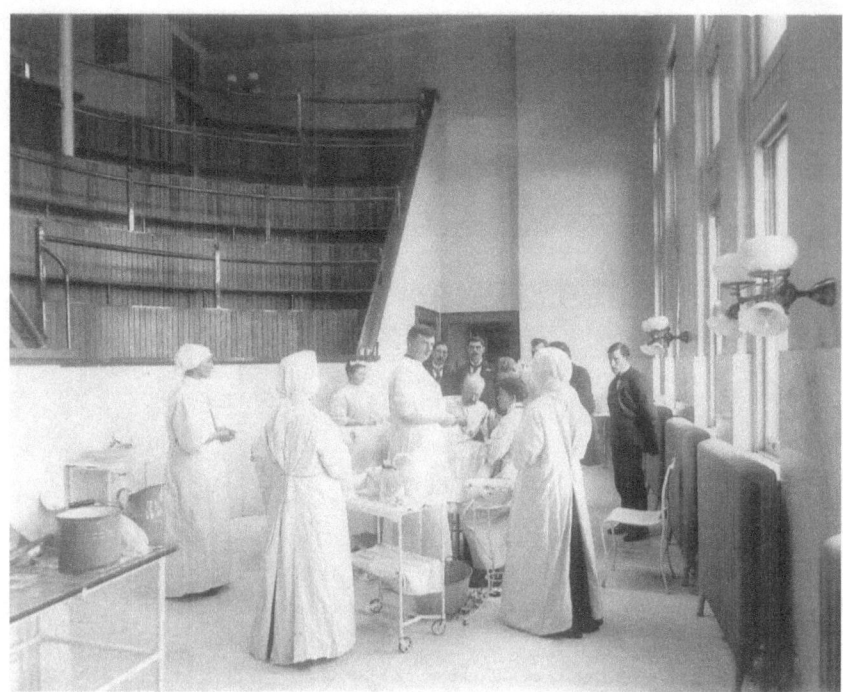

Figure 4.2 Operating Room, St. Joseph's Hospital, St. Paul, MN, approx. 1906. The photograph shows the surgeons without masks or gloves and nuns with white gowns covering their black habits. (Courtesy Archives of the Congregation of the Sisters of St. Joseph of Carondelet, St. Paul, MN)

1884, and she guided the hospital through its major development period over the next thirty-six years.[14] Under her direction, the sisters added an east wing to the hospital in 1885. In 1894, she and Dr. Harry J. O'Brien formed the St. Joseph's Hospital Training School for Nurses, one of the first in the region. Then in 1895, the sisters constructed a new main building at a cost of $75,000, bringing the total bed capacity to 150. The building contained offices, parlors, private rooms, and two operating rooms, one with a large amphitheater for medical instruction (fig. 4.2). The 1896–97 *Annual Report* described the operating room's "modern equipment, judicious management and scrupulous cleanliness," where more than fifteen hundred operations had been successfully performed since its opening. A widespread economic panic in 1896 increased the number of charity admissions to 28 percent of the hospital total for the year. Over time, however, St. Joseph's gained a reputation as more than a charity hospital. Table 4.2 shows that as early as 1900, charity cases comprised only 5 percent of admissions.[15]

Table 4.2 Personnel, St. Joseph's Hospital, St. Paul, MN

Year	# Marine Patients (%)	# Free Patients (%)	# Private Patients (%)	Male/Female	Total # Patients
1876	14 (19%)	12 (17%)	46 (64%)	50/22	72
1880	53 (15%)	18 (5%)	275 (80%)	272/74	346
1890	19 (3%)	3 (<1%)	655 (97%)	483/194	677
1900	9 (<1%)	68 (5%)	1,336 (95%)	761/652	1,413

Source: "Number of Patients Admitted Per Year, St. Joseph's Hospital, St. Paul, Minnesota, 1876–1901," 220. 2–1, box 1, folder 4, ACSJC-SP.

As the nineteenth century closed, St. Joseph's Hospital had grown in demand for its services. In 1902, Dr. Arthur Miller installed the first x-ray machine. That same year, Dr. James Ferguson, an intern at the hospital, converted a closet under the stairs into a laboratory; eventually it was moved to larger quarters to keep pace with the growing field. Annual admissions increased to more than 1,400 and in 1919 to 4,141, leading the sisters to start another building program. In 1921, they erected a new west wing, a six-story structure that included a chapel, additional patient rooms, and separate space for obstetric cases.[16]

As part of their development as paying institutions, Catholic hospitals accommodated orthodox medicine. This included adoption of antiseptic, and eventually aseptic, surgery. The sisters in St. Paul opened their facility to both Catholic and non-Catholic doctors. In its early days, St. Joseph's functioned with a small medical staff, and as in voluntary hospitals, the doctors tended the sick without pay. By 1880, nine medical and surgical staff attended patients, although it is unclear if other physicians had full hospital privileges yet. Dr. Justus O'Hage was a distinguished surgeon who had immigrated to the United States from Germany at a young age. After serving in the Union Army during the Civil War, he graduated from the University of Missouri in 1880. Following in the path of other late-nineteenth-century physicians who had the time and money, he did a short period of postgraduate work in Germany before setting up a practice in St. Paul in 1881.[17] As in other general hospitals, doctors in Catholic facilities could obtain clinical experience and opportunities to perform innovative operations. In 1886, O'Hage performed one of the earliest successful gallbladder operations in the United States.[18] By the 1890s, St. Joseph's had established specialty departments in orthopedics, eye and ear diseases, gynecology, medicine, and surgery. In 1912, the hospital had eight surgeons, thirteen internal medicine physicians, and thirty specialists. Accordingly, the proportion of surgical to medical conditions increased over time. By 1912, 80 percent of patient admissions were surgical cases.[19]

St. Mary's Hospital, Minneapolis, Minnesota

The Sisters of St. Joseph assumed authority over St. Mary's Hospital in Minneapolis in October 1887. Expanding their hospital mission to Minneapolis made economic sense, since sisters would be following the population. Between 1880 and 1890, the population of Minneapolis had quadrupled as Irish and German immigrants filled the city. Protestant numbers increased significantly, as well, with the migration of Scandinavian Lutherans.[20] Thus, ethnic and religious issues were important factors in the Minneapolis hospital market.[21] The Sisters of Mercy had first opened a twenty-bed hospital in Minneapolis in 1882 in what was known as the Murphy Mansion. With the bishop's permission, Mother Joseph Lynch journeyed east to raise money, a trip that proved successful, and the hospital flourished. By 1887, expansion was necessary, and Mother Joseph again collected money. This time, however, John Ireland was bishop of the St. Paul diocese. He apparently disapproved of her fund-raising methods and wanted more control over the sisters in his diocese, a classic example of problems women religious faced with ecclesiastical control. The conflict resulted in the Sisters of Mercy selling the hospital to Bishop Ireland for $30,000.[22] He, in turn, promptly asked his sister, Mother Seraphine Ireland, Provincial Superior of the Sisters of St. Joseph, to take over the hospital. She agreed to pay the bishop and assigned five nuns to open St. Mary's under the direction of Sister Ignatius Loyola Cox. None of the sisters were trained nurses at the time; rather, they learned from experience. It was not until 1900 that the sisters established a nurse's training school.[23]

From its beginning, St. Mary's provided physicians opportunities for professional practice and achievement. As in other hospitals, certain doctors had the designation of being associated with St. Mary's. On October 22, 1887, sixteen of the city's leading physicians and surgeons met with a local priest. They elected a board consisting of four physicians and four surgeons as attending staff members, with Dr. J. H. Dunn as president. Two others were specialists in eye and ear diseases. Six additional physicians and surgeons served as consultants and likely had fewer regular duties. One was mayor of Minneapolis, and another had practiced surgery in Minneapolis for twenty years before St. Mary's opened. Several of the

FIGURE 4.3 St. Mary's Hospital, Minneapolis, MN, constructed in 1890. (Courtesy Archives of the Congregation of the Sisters of St. Joseph of Carondelet, St. Paul, MN)

staff members were railroad doctors. Most served on more than one hospital staff, and only two were Catholic.[24]

The physicians and surgeons were prominent practitioners in the city, and several trained in Europe. Dunn, for example, had studied in Vienna and Heidelberg before he located in Minneapolis. Surgeon Frederick A. Dunsmoor helped organize the Minnesota Hospital College, which later became part of the University of Minnesota Medical School, and Doctors Dunsmoor and Dunn both served as professors of surgery. Another early surgeon was H. B. Sweetser, whose sons, grandsons, and nephews followed him as chief of staff at St. Mary's.[25] By naming a board of physicians, which the doctors likely wanted, the hospital retained a system of hospital appointments that other late-nineteenth-century hospitals had. While St. Mary's expanded hospital privileges somewhat by allowing a greater number of doctors to practice, it did not represent an opening of the hospital to all doctors at this time.

The Murphy Mansion was the site of St. Mary's from 1887 until 1890. As the only Catholic hospital in Minneapolis, St. Mary's beds were usually full. Like other early hospitals, the facility initially was poorly equipped and had no operating room. Surgeons performed operations in patients' rooms, hallways, or the sisters' dining room. A growing demand for beds centered around this specialty area, and in 1890 Mother Ignatius Cox, in consultation with physicians and architects, directed the construction of a new three-story brick building that cost the community $30,000 (fig. 4.3). It included two operating rooms, private rooms, elevators, steam heat, a new ventilation system, and male and female wards to accommodate a hundred patients. Nine sisters staffed the facility, and seventeen physicians and surgeons served on the medical staff. In its first three years, the hospital admitted nearly six hundred patients.[26]

An 1887 ledger reveals a list of sixty-three patients admitted during a four-month period, 73 percent of whom were foreign born. Nearly 30 percent of the foreign born were from Sweden, a predominately non-Catholic country. Others came from Ireland, Germany, Canada, Norway, Denmark, and Scotland. Sisters' ethnicity matched that of many of their patients. Three were born in Ireland, five in Minnesota or Wisconsin, two in Canada, and one in Germany.[27] Ethnic distinctions faded over time, however. Similarly, religious distinctions diminished: the 1920 *Annual Report* showed that only half of patients were Roman Catholic. The decline in ethnic and religious differences reflected the sisters' policy of accepting all patients regardless of religion or other distinctions. It also mirrored the decreasing number of foreign-born persons in the community.[28]

More building expansions occurred under Mother Jane Frances Bouchet, superior from 1890 to 1906, and Sister Esperance Finn, who led the hospital from 1906 to 1918. Both had experience in finance, management, and public relations before coming to St. Mary's. Mother Jane, in fact, had been one of the early administrators of St. Joseph's Hospital in St. Paul.[29] Under her direction, St. Mary's added a laboratory and a nurses' training school. Among the physicians joining the staff was Dr. Robert E. Farr, a pioneer in the use of local anesthesia. Sister Esperance worked closely with Dr. Richard J. Hill, chief surgeon for the Great Northern Railroad, whose patients sometimes filled an entire floor at St. Mary's. Under Sister Esperance's administration, a new six-story annex was completed in 1918. With a patient capacity of 225, it brought the hospital's total to 315 beds. At a cost of more than $500,000, it contained nine operating rooms, laboratories, x-ray and anesthesia facilities, electric elevators, and a paging system. And for the first time, it had separate facilities for a nursery and pediatrics.[30] Financial papers of Sister Esperance summarized some of her expenditures over her twelve-year tenure: payments for property, mortgages, elevator, x-ray equipment, new boiler, repair of the nurse's home, and erection of a new porch. She concluded, "Not a cent on either of these slips was borrowed. It was our own."[31]

After an eighteen-year tenure as administrator at a North Dakota hospital, Sister Madeleine Lyons came to St. Mary's as superior from 1918 to 1924. In 1920, 1,678 patients were admitted for the year. A sizeable number came for hysterectomies, appendectomies, and removal of tonsils and adenoids. The hospital medical staff grew to more than eighty physicians with nine interns, and both religious and lay nurses staffed the different units.[32]

Historians of medicine have documented how the changes in medical education requirements affected hospitals. Abraham Flexner's 1910 report to the Carnegie Foundation proposed more extensive laboratory and clinical experience for students. Medical schools thus had to affiliate with hospitals so that students could get access to patients and clinical experience.[33] Even before Flexner, both St. Joseph's and St. Mary's hospitals were teaching institutions, although they had not been organized with that expectation. St. Joseph's had students from the St. Paul School of Medical Instruction throughout the short life of that school (1871–1879), and from the St. Paul Medical School from 1885 until 1888. The University of Minnesota Medical School organized in 1883, and students from this institution interned at St. Joseph's and St. Mary's.[34] The hospitals were not well adapted for this purpose, however. Flexner visited the area in 1909 and noted, "[T]eaching opportunities were both limited in extent and precarious in character." The university was relying on hospitals that had not been "organized, equipped, or conducted" for education.[35] The state eventually appropriated funds to build a separate teaching hospital, but clinical teaching continued at both St. Mary's and St. Joseph's.

St. Mary's Infirmary, Cairo, Illinois

The situation at St. Mary's Infirmary in Cairo illustrates the varied roles of Catholic hospitals that continued into the twentieth century. Sometime in the 1890s, the Sisters of the Holy Cross admitted Marian B., a patient who suffered from "locomotive ataxia," a musculoskeletal condition that caused paralysis. The county paid the small sum of $10 for her care. For this amount, she received twenty years of medical treatment, which included massage therapy and therapeutic electrical treatment with a low-voltage electrical current. Most significantly, the patient received, for two decades, the personal nursing care of Sister Magdalen Kiernan.[36]

As the only hospital in Cairo for the public, St. Mary's Infirmary served paying patients while continuing to admit the chronically ill like Marian who could not pay their bills themselves. Continuing the policy of Mother Angela Gillespie before her, in 1887 Sister Adela Moran, the new superior, negotiated with the head surgeon of the St. Louis, Arkansas, and Texas Railroad to receive sick and wounded workers at $5 per week. A number of railroad companies ran their own internal insurance policies and obtained hospital funds through mandatory deductions from employees' wages. Like miners' prepayment plans, these fees guaranteed room, board, lodging, medicine, and medical attendance.[37] By 1890, four surgeons, including Dr. W. W. Stevenson, comprised the visiting or attending staff at St. Mary's. However, the sisters established a policy that patients could be tended by any physician they preferred, provided the doctor was in good standing in the profession.[38]

As the hospital increasingly relied on fees from private-paying patients, nuns began construction of facilities to compete for their patronage. While Sister Magdalen was caring for Marian, other building expansions occurred in 1890 and 1902. For the latter, the sisters spent $25,000 for a new operating room, kitchen, x-ray area, and additional private rooms. This raised the bed capacity to approximately a hundred.

Physicians helped in these expansion efforts. In 1901, Dr. Stevenson circulated a flyer that announced the construction of the new addition and specifically emphasized the increased space for private accommodations.[39] Dr. W. F. Grinstead paid for an additional operating room in 1907, which the sisters reserved for his use. To meet the growing demand for nurses, the nuns established a school of nursing in 1910, and they opened a laboratory in 1914. By 1925, the number of admissions reached 1,327, and only 10 percent were Catholic.[40] That same year, forty-two patients were victims of a tornado that had killed over seven hundred people. The survivors benefited from the newest addition to St. Mary's Infirmary, completed in 1922, which had cost more than $200,000. It included four operating rooms, x-ray room, heat and electrical therapy rooms, laboratory, kitchen, thirty-two private rooms, and an entire floor composed of maternity rooms, delivery room, and nursery with incubator equipment.[41]

Holy Cross Hospital, Salt Lake City, Utah

On February 9, 1884, a thirty-car freight train loaded with coal ore started eastward from Pleasant Valley Junction, Utah. A disastrous accident occurred shortly afterward that killed one worker and badly injured John T. Railroad workers took him to Holy Cross Hospital, most likely because of a contractual agreement with the sisters. There, doctors discovered that the lower part of his body was paralyzed. On February 10, physicians pronounced that he would never be able to walk again, and three days later he expired. The Order of Railway Conductors handled all the funeral arrangements.[42]

FIGURE 4.4 Holy Cross Hospital with chapel, Salt Lake City, UT, early 1900s. (Courtesy Utah State Historical Society, photo # 24101)

As the West transformed into a capitalistic and industrial economy, the Sisters of the Holy Cross committed increased effort and money to expand Holy Cross Hospital. John T. was attended to in a new facility on First South Street on land the sisters had purchased in 1883. The brick building was constructed in a Victorian style that was laid out in wards with a bed capacity of 125. By 1890, fifteen sisters staffed the institution and 914 patients received treatment. In 1895, reflecting a closing of some of the mines, the annual census decreased. By then, however, the local market for medical and nursing care was expanding in other directions. Salt Lake City had a population of eight thousand Catholics in 1895.[43] At that time, the sisters were competing with Protestants as well as Mormons for hospital physicians and paying patients. In 1872, leaders of the Episcopal Church had established St. Mark's Hospital to care for miners.[44] The organizers were leaders in Utah's business community and included bankers and mining company managers. Likely it was to compete with this facility that Catholic mining leaders approached Father Scanlan in 1875 for a Catholic hospital. Mormons were also active in the urban hospital market. In 1882, women of the Mormon Relief Society established Deseret Hospital, which became a center for training nurses and midwives and teaching health and hygiene to Mormon women. A dentist donated resources to help the Mormon Church build Latter-day Saints Hospital in 1905.[45] St. Mark's expanded in 1893, 1896, and again in 1903. This last addition gave the hospital the same bed capacity as Holy Cross Hospital until the following year when the sisters' new expansion increased Holy Cross's beds.

Holy Cross was the only Catholic hospital in the area, and as the city grew, the need for more space arose. In 1901, Sisters Lidwina Butler and Cordelia Gahagan started a school of nursing. Encouraged by physicians in 1904, Sister Lidwina, as hospital administrator, presided over the construction of a new west wing and an enlarged operating room that cost over $122,000. While the first building had consisted of wards for miners and railroad patients, the new wing had more private rooms and brought the total bed capacity to 155. Hidden behind the façade of the hospital was a new chapel, located at midpoint in the hospital complex (fig. 4.4).

Table 4.3 shows the expanding number of private paying patients at Holy Cross compared to contract and charity patients. In 1914 and again in 1919, the sisters provided additional operating rooms, an updated x-ray department, laboratories, a pediatric department, and a maternity unit. These facilities enhanced the hospital's attractiveness to private patients: by 1925, 3,381 patients were admitted to the two hundred-bed facility.[46]

A key characteristic of the mining and railroad labor forces was their ethnic and racial diversity, and after the turn of the century, Holy Cross Hospital continued to admit a heterogeneous group of patients. From 1908 to 1915, they came from twenty-seven countries and every state in the United States. Most of the foreign-born miners and laborers came from Ireland, England, Canada, France, Germany, Scandinavia, Italy, and Greece. Countries such as Ireland, Italy, France, and Germany were heavily Catholic, but others such as England and Scandinavia were not. Sisters' ledgers indicate that they also cared for Mormons but few Asians, suggesting either that Chinese miners did not appear in large numbers in Utah as they did in California and other western states, that they did not utilize Western medicine, or that hospitals excluded them. Nearly three-fourths of the hospital population, however, was native born. Ethnic distinctions may have had some bearing on the performance of surgery. Between 1908 and 1915, the majority of all surgeries involved those born in either the United States or northern Europe. Most of the foreign born classified as medical cases came from Italy and Greece.[47]

Table 4.3 Personnel, Holy Cross Hospital, Salt Lake City, UT

Year	# Free Patients (%)	# Mining Patients (%)	# Private Paying Patients (%)	Total Patients/Year
1880	15 (14%)	77 (71%)	15 (14%)	107
1905	32 (3%)	106 (8%)	1,105 (89%)	1,243

Source: Holy Cross Hospital Record Book.

Until 1896, the original medical and surgical staff of Holy Cross Hospital consisted of five members, and most were not Catholic. One distinguished physician was Dr. F. A. Meacham, who had studied bacteriology at Johns Hopkins University and was instrumental in teaching surgical antisepsis in the intermountain region. In the late nineteenth and early twentieth centuries, as hospital appointments became more widely distributed, administrators began reorganizing their medical staffs. St. Mark's had enlarged its staff in 1895 and extended privileges to all reputable physicians in the city. Sister Lidwina Butler soon followed suit. In 1896, she reorganized the Holy Cross staff to include six members, primarily the physicians who brought the greatest number of patients. She also granted physician privileges to doctors not on staff, leading to the two-tiered structure developed in other Catholic hospitals. Dr. Allen Fowler became medical director and, although he did not become a Catholic until shortly before his death, he was very influential during his twenty-seven years at Holy Cross Hospital. The sisters also admitted Dr. Emerson F. Root, a graduate of Western Reserve Medical School, to the staff along with other doctors who had studied in the United States and Europe. By 1907, the hospital had eight staff physicians, but according to one hospital history, seventy doctors treated patients between 1896 and 1904.

The Medical Department of the University of Utah organized in 1905. Through this program, the Sisters of the Holy Cross established an intern service.[48] Abraham Flexner labeled the Medical Department a "half school," however, after his visit in 1909 because the program offered only the first two years of a full medical course. Medical students had to transfer to four-year schools in the East or Midwest to complete their training.[49]

In the 1870s and 1880s, medical cases such as lead poisoning, gastritis, and fevers made up most of the admissions, but by the end of the century, reflecting national trends, surgical services had expanded. By 1915, surgeries accounted for 69 percent of total admissions.[50] One of the most frequently reported surgeries was appendectomy. While inflammation of the appendix had been recognized since the eighteenth century, the first definitive description and treatment came in 1886 by Boston physician Reginald Fitz.[51] Within five years of Fitz's publication, appendicitis appeared in Holy Cross Hospital records and soon became the principal disease treated surgically. Diseases of the ear, nose, throat, and genitourinary organs, which were typically managed by surgical specialists, also increased. In 1896, Holy Cross Hospital appointed Dr. Harry Niles to the surgical staff. He particularly excelled in abdominal surgery, many of which were excessive procedures on the ovaries and uterus.[52]

St. Joseph's Hospital, South Bend, Indiana

South Bend, Indiana, the site of the congregation's motherhouse, was without a hospital until August 1882, when the Sisters of the Holy Cross opened St. Joseph's at the corner of Cedar Street and Notre Dame Avenue. In the 1850s and 1860s, several manufacturing companies had transformed the city into an industrial center, and thereafter the population nearly doubled every decade. By 1880, 13,280 people populated the city, one-third of which were foreign born. Many were immigrants from Ireland, Germany, and Poland, largely Catholic countries. In 1890, although fewer than the total number of Protestants, Catholics comprised the largest single denomination in St. Joseph County.[53] Their lack of a hospital provided an opportunity for a sister-run hospital similar to those in Cairo and Salt Lake City.

Sister Edward Murphy and two other sisters opened St. Joseph's Hospital on October 20, 1882, with sufficient space to care for thirty to forty patients. Sister Edward came to the hospital with considerable experience. She had nursed in the Civil War and had been director of St. Mary's Infirmary, Cairo, and the sisters' hospital for miners in South Dakota.[54] Although the press had offered enthusiastic support for the hospital, the public did not contribute money. To generate a hospital fund, Sister Edward canvassed local merchants. The hospital still did not attract many patients, and the situation became more complicated when some townspeople started planning a Protestant hospital across the river in direct opposition to St. Joseph's. While this did not become a reality until 1894 when Methodist deaconesses established Epworth Hospital and Training School, St. Joseph's only slowly attracted patients.[55]

In 1895, the general council at the motherhouse authorized the third superior, Sister M. Sophia Rooney, to renovate the operating room and organize a medical staff. During the 1890s, the sisters admitted approximately 150 patients annually, but the daily average of resident patients was less than twenty. In the early 1890s, the township trustees sent indigents to St. Joseph's, but by 1897 they were using Epworth. "Epworth Hospital is a great injury to St. Joseph's," noted a sister in an archive entry. "The Township Trustee favors the Protestant Hospital, and as he largely controls the county patients, none are sent to St. Joseph's except the few Catholic patients who refuse to go to the Epworth."[56] In 1901, the annalist again noted the competition in hospital work in South Bend and St. Joseph's dependence on income from the county: "The Protestant denominations are nearly a unit in working for the Epworth Hospital and against St. Joseph's. To the County Physician, Dr. W. F. Mills and the Township Trustee Mr. James D. Reid we are under many obligations for a larger share of County patients."[57]

Surgical cases were increasing, however, and sisters occasionally had to turn patients away because of lack of space. In the early years of the new century, the nuns planned their first major addition. It opened in 1904 with a new operating room and additional private rooms. In 1907, the sisters established a nurse training school under the direction of Sister M. Holy Cross, the former superior at Holy Cross Hospital in Utah. Two years later, she assumed the role of hospital superior. The sisters cared for persons outside the hospital by opening a clinic for the poor in 1914, and clinic patients who needed hospitalization were admitted to the hospital.[58] A large debt had been incurred with the 1904 addition, which the nuns did not significantly reduce for many years. Thus, it was not until 1922 that they undertook any new construction. At that time, they added a west wing that increased the hospital's bed capacity to 142.[59]

As with the other hospitals, the medical staff consisted of prestigious local practitioners. Dr. J. B. Berteling had graduated from the University of Notre Dame, studied medicine in Cincinnati, and then became attending physician at Notre Dame. Dr. C. A. Daugherty attended Indiana Medical College, graduated from the medical department at Butler University, and then spent several months of study in Vienna and New York. He later became associated with Epworth Hospital and eventually served as its chief of staff.[60] In 1902 and 1903, other leading doctors, mostly Protestant, attended patients at St. Joseph's. By 1920, when a formal medical staff organized, seventy-three physicians were members.[61]

Conflicts developed in secular voluntary hospitals between trustees and physicians over staffing patterns, and similar tensions occurred between doctors and nuns at St. Joseph's. Protestant/Catholic issues no doubt added to the problem, and competition between the two South

Bend hospitals could be intense.⁶² From the beginning, St. Joseph's advertised that any patient could choose his or her physician,⁶³ and this staffing policy angered some local physicians who wanted to limit hospital privileges to a small elite. Unfortunately, there are no minutes of staff meetings, and what is known about the sisters' dealings with physicians is revealed only in the nuns' writings. In 1905, when the sisters refused to give a set number of physicians and surgeons exclusive rights to treat patients, the doctors staged a boycott against the hospital. An annalist justified the hospital's actions by noting that none of the practicing surgeons had been specially trained. "So little confidence did the people of South Bend have in the surgeons of the city, that most of those needing surgical operations and who could afford it went to Chicago."⁶⁴ The very doctors who wanted control of St. Joseph's patients were also on the staff of the rival Protestant institution. The sisters feared that "to have placed them in charge of our hospital, would have created for them a monopoly of the treatment of the sick of South Bend, and have cut the hospital off from securing better men who might present themselves."⁶⁵

During the boycott, many of the physicians sent their patients to Epworth Hospital. Consequently, the two hundred patient admissions at St. Joseph's were half what Epworth admitted in 1905. Always with an eye toward spiritual returns, however, the annalist noted that even though surgeries and admissions were down, "five baptisms and several remarkable conversions more than compensated for the labor and hardships of the year."⁶⁶

Since surgery was the largest work in the hospital, the boycott left the sisters in the position of having to recruit a new medical staff. They were relieved when Dr. Thomas Olney from Chicago established a practice in South Bend and became identified with St. Joseph's. He had been a surgeon in two large Chicago hospitals and an instructor in anatomy at Rush Medical College for ten years. Within a short time, he was performing the majority of the surgeries at St. Joseph's. The annalist wrote, "He was soon the target for shafts from the other doctors, who saw in him a menace to the patronage they controlled."⁶⁷ The doctors stepped up the fight by branding the sisters as untrained and incompetent. Indeed, the nuns did not establish a nurse's training school until two years later. What was especially appalling to the sisters was that the physician who led the boycott was a Catholic. Eventually, other physicians brought in more patients so that slowly the sisters recovered financially, and patient numbers came back up by 1907. After a third expansion, surgeries had increased from 30 percent of total admissions in 1897 to 54 percent in 1923.⁶⁸

This Indiana hospital experienced similar Protestant/Catholic tensions that had affected Providence Hospital in Terre Haute, Indiana, in the early 1870s. Although St. Joseph's still lay under the shadow of nativism, its establishment came after the critical period of anti-Catholic sentiment over papal infallibility in 1873. Most important, by the mid-1880s, more physicians had accepted Joseph Lister's views on antisepsis than they had in the 1870s.[69] The Holy Cross Sisters benefited from new applications of the germ theory and medical science, which resulted in fewer hospital infections and more patients entering hospitals, especially for surgery. Thus, for successful ventures, timing was crucial, and the Holy Cross Sisters were able to weather the storm.

Santa Rosa Infirmary, San Antonio, Texas

Showing the mix of charity and acute cases along with evangelical and skilled nursing in Catholic hospitals, an Incarnate Word Sister at Santa Rosa Infirmary recorded several patients admitted in January 1899. On the tenth, a woman with two children requested "to be allowed to warm the baby, a little girl six weeks old, and so thin and tiny that you could never imagine." The sisters admitted her and placed her and her children in a semiprivate room. On the eleventh, a patient died and Dr. Adolph Herff performed a postmortem examination. Before death, however, the patient allowed one of the sister-nurses to "repeat some aspirations and prayers with her." That same day, another patient had an operation for laceration of the womb. "Miss Rosa gave the chloroform, and Sister Remigius also assisted." On the twelfth day of the month, a patient came in with measles and was placed in an isolation room for contagious diseases. Early the next morning, another patient gave birth to a baby, and once again, Sister Remigius attended.[70]

In the 1880s, in an attempt to expand their clientele, the sisters initiated a plan to admit workers of the Southern Pacific and Aransas Pass railroads at reduced rates. In 1897, doctors and sisters treated a total of 1,655 patients for the year, 73 percent being railroad patients.[71] By 1899, three different building expansions had occurred at Santa Rosa—in 1884, which included the first operating room; in 1894; and again in 1896, when the nuns added a separate tuberculosis ward, kitchen, chapel, dining room, and additional operating room.

By 1900, Santa Rosa had become the primary medical facility in the area, and it attracted patients from New York, St. Louis, Chicago, and Mexico.[72] Sisters called on ethnic priests for their Polish, Mexican American, German, and Irish patients. They also cared for African Americans, Italians, Norwegians, and American-born groups, mostly non-Catholic, who had congregated in the city. With such a diverse population, the hospital needed nuns with language skills. Most of the Incarnate Word Sisters were born in Ireland, Switzerland, Germany, or France. To care for Mexican Americans, Mother St. Pierre frequently reminded the sisters that they had to learn Spanish.⁷³

By 1910, Santa Rosa was treating more patients than the other general hospital in town, City Hospital. The nuns opened a school of nursing in 1903, a laboratory in 1910, an x-ray department in 1912, and a free clinic in 1915. In 1919 and again in 1926 the sisters expanded the hospital. Under the direction of Mother Robert O'Dea, the 1926 addition cost $300,000.⁷⁴ While railroad patients dominated admissions in the 1880s and 1890s, by 1922 private-paying patients outnumbered all other cases at Santa Rosa. The annual report for that year revealed that 3,383 patients were admitted, with 10 percent "free" cases and 12 percent "part pay."⁷⁵

When Flexner visited the state medical schools in 1909, he noted that Texas was badly overcrowded with physicians who had studied in the state's inferior medical schools.⁷⁶ Nevertheless, it seems that some well-qualified physicians practiced at Santa Rosa. An especially close association developed over the years between the Incarnate Word Sisters, Dr. Ferdinand Herff, and members of his family who followed him as surgeons in the San Antonio area. An immigrant from Germany, Herff had trained at universities in Bonn and Berlin before taking his final two years at the University of Geissen. Closely associated with Herff was George Cupples, born in Scotland and trained at the University of Edinburgh and in Paris. For these men, hospital appointments were helpful in establishing practices in a new land, and Santa Rosa provided them that opportunity. Before the turn of the century, Dr. Aureliano Urrutia, who had fled Mexico's political situation, joined the staff; and his four sons followed him as staff members. Sisters sought other prosperous physicians as well, including Doctors William Wolf, a member of the American College of Surgeons; Amos Graves, a railroad surgeon; Julius Braunagel; A. S. McDaniel; and Adolph and John Herff.⁷⁷

Dr. Ferdinand Peter Herff compiled a three-generation memoir of his family's experiences as physicians at Santa Rosa. As a descendant of a Protestant German family, he noted that an "unlikely partnership" developed between the Catholics and the German population in San Antonio. Through health-care endeavors, "the [Catholic] Church and a descendant of its enemies [the Huguenots] embarked upon the same pursuits, dedicated to the same goals, upholding the same high standards."⁷⁸ Both physicians and nuns, then, shared pride and responsibility for the hospital's achievements.

St. Joseph's Infirmary, Fort Worth, Texas

After their success at establishing Santa Rosa, the Incarnate Word Sisters were approached by railroad directors, physicians, and church officials in 1885 to staff the Missouri Pacific Railroad Hospital in Fort Worth. This ranching, agricultural, and railroad center was a fertile breeding ground for the medical market. In 1880, Tarrant County had a population of 23,782 American-born and 889 foreign-born residents who came mainly from Germany, Ireland, and England.[79] In addition to injuries from railroad accidents, wounds from personal violence frequently occurred. The prospect of serving this growing population was not lost on Mother St. Pierre Cinquin, but she was reluctant to accept the offer, mainly because the hospital would not be under the sisters' direction. Rather, secular authorities associated with the Missouri Pacific Railroad ran the hospital. Furthermore, her training in the cloistered Lyons convent convinced her that contact with secular officials would present many temptations for the sisters' religious vocations. The nuns would receive salaries, however, which would help alleviate the debt incurred in Santa Rosa's 1884 expansion. In the end, Mother St. Pierre's desire to have the opportunity to influence the many immigrants the railroad employed overcame her resistance, and she accepted the offer.[80]

Even though the physicians were not Catholic, they wanted the sisters as nurses and granted them religious freedom. In March, Mother St. Pierre assigned eleven sisters to staff the facility under the direction of Sister Mary of the Assumption. Although the hospital market offered sisters opportunities to care for body and soul, it also brought risks. Fire destroyed the original building, and the sisters moved the patients to an already existing hospital in Marshall, and began working there. Eventually, a new hospital was built in Fort Worth, and the sisters resumed their work at the Missouri Pacific. At that time, officials of the Missouri Pacific Railroad moved out of Fort Worth to expand into the Midwest and wanted to sell their hospital. Mother St. Pierre saw this as a good investment and acted. She began negotiations to purchase it with Dr. R. C. Volker, who first suggested $30,000 to $35,000 as an appropriate price. Knowing that the doctors were anxious to sell, she would not agree. She wrote to Dr. W. B. Outten, the chief surgeon, and dictated her own terms: up to $15,000 down plus $10,000 in installments of $1,000 per month. Outten accepted the offer.[81] In May 1889, Bishop John Neraz dedicated the facility under a new name as St. Joseph's Infirmary.

In an effort to gain private patients, and thus stimulate business for themselves and the hospital, two railroad doctors issued a circular describing the hospital as "spacious and artistically laid out." It was situated on a hill "facing south, thereby insuring the full benefit of our prevailing breezes." It housed an operating room, a pharmacy, private rooms, and wards for a hundred patients.[82] The nuns also arranged with the Fort Worth and Denver; Texas and Pacific; Santa Fe; and Missouri, Kansas, and Texas Railroad Companies to receive their patients, typically at a daily rate of 90¢ per person, to cover nursing, board, and lodging. As in other facilities, workers contributed a sum for support, which guaranteed them care. Fort Worth had no city or county hospital at the time, and the mayor requested that the nuns receive the city's poor at reduced rates. From the beginning the hospital accepted patients of all ages and races. In 1890, they included city charity cases, firemen, policemen, and private patients, but railroad patients comprised the majority.[83]

As at Santa Rosa, the sisters granted hospital privileges to all qualified physicians in the area. After the congregation bought the hospital, Mother St. Pierre negotiated with Dr. Francis Farrar to become resident physician.[84] Doctors W. A. Adams and F. D. Thompson, who had worked with the Missouri Pacific hospital, continued their practice at St. Joseph's. Adams received his medical degree from the University of Georgia Medical Department in 1876 and Thompson from Louisville Medical College in 1875. Others joined the staff, including Bacon Saunders, another graduate of Louisville, who became a well-known railroad surgeon in Texas. He also served as professor of surgery at the Medical Department of Texas Christian University and was chief surgeon at St. Joseph's.[85]

St. Joseph's Infirmary slowly but steadily grew. Expansions in operating room facilities, chapel, and emergency services occurred in 1897 and again in 1905 (fig. 4.5). At the urging of physicians, the sisters added more private rooms in the 1905 expansion. They opened a school of nursing in 1906, the first in the city.

While Medical College Hospital, a private corporation, was established in 1906 and the first city hospital opened around 1907, St. Joseph's remained a primary medical facility for the public. During the outbreak of the Spanish influenza after World War I, the hospital accommodated sick soldiers from nearby Camp Bowie. The increase in patients convinced the sisters of the need for another building, but appeals to the congregation's general administration for funds were denied. One historian of the congregation noted that "the works in San Antonio ... always seemed to take precedence," particularly the new college the sisters were establishing at that time. It was not until 1927 that the nuns in Fort Worth obtained approval to construct a five-story building at a cost of $500,000.

FIGURE 4.5. St. Joseph's Infirmary, Fort Worth, TX, 1904. (Courtesy Archives, Motherhouse of the Incarnate Word, San Antonio, TX)

Designed in a Jacobean classic style, it had surgical suites, electric elevators, sun porches on each floor, and two hundred additional beds. It appears that surgery was not commonplace in the late nineteenth century in the Incarnate Word hospitals. Of the surgeries performed, most were amputations from accidents or lacerated wombs from childbirth complications, since sisters mainly cared for railroad patients and their wives. By 1925, however, the majority of patients admitted were for surgery.[86]

DEMOGRAPHICS IN CATHOLIC HOSPITALS

Demographic patterns reveal that a main distinction between these hospitals and others in the East was the diversity of the population in terms of ethnicity and religion. Sisters' ecumenism of treating people regardless of creed made them acceptable to a variety of cultural groups. Indeed, clientele sometimes included more non-Catholics than any other group.

Similar findings are seen in the sex, age, and occupational distributions of the patients. In the early years, most hospital admissions were of young adult males, but by 1910, reflecting national trends, all the hospitals admitted more female patients and patients of various ages than previously.[87] In the 1880s and 1890s, railroad and mining patients dominated admissions, but by 1925, the largest patient groups were society's newest consumers, the working families.

The importance of ethnicity in sisters' decisions to work with railroad workers and miners cannot be overlooked. The Irish immigration to the United States that had begun in the first half of the nineteenth century continued for eighty years. By the 1870s, the earlier-arriving Irish were in place to provide some form of cultural continuity for the newcomers who filled the mining and railroad centers in the West. For example, many Irish miners worked for Irish owners and superintendents such as Marcus Daly. He was superintendent of two local mines in Utah in the 1870s and was known for his support of the Irish and their causes.[88] In Fort Worth, the presence of large numbers of Irish railroad workers particularly influenced Mother St. Pierre Cinquin's decision to staff the railroad facility there. She knew that, as sister-nurses tended physical needs, they also could ensure that patients received the sacraments and Catholic teachings about the spiritual meaning of sickness. She wrote, "We had firmly resolved not to take any more establishments for a time, but with this opportunity of doing so much good we could not refuse."[89]

At the same time, one of the challenges facing hospitals was how to respond to a segregated society. The Catholic Church failed to speak out against slavery or the segregation that followed emancipation, and many priests and bishops aligned with the white social order.[90] White private patients often avoided hospitals in which they might have to share a room or floor with black patients, and sisters had to reconcile these issues with notions of charity. Segregation was strongly entrenched, particularly in the South. Furthermore, as the number of European Catholic immigrants grew after the Civil War, ministry to them became the Catholic hierarchy's top priority. Consequently, fewer resources were available for other groups such as African Americans, Native Americans, and Mexican Americans. From the beginning, hospitals of the Sisters of St. Joseph, Sisters of the Holy Cross, and Sisters of Charity of the Incarnate Word admitted black patients, although in separate wards or annexes that often were inferior to other facilities.

In Cairo, African Americans comprised nearly half the population of the county, and they had no other hospital to enter except St. Mary's. Sisters also allowed African American and Mexican American physicians to attend patients in their hospitals.[91] It appears that class status played a role as well. While some Mexican Americans stayed in a separate ward at Santa Rosa, others from Mexico paid for private rooms and care from Mexican-born physicians. In the late nineteenth and early twentieth centuries, for example, Dr. Aureliano Urrutia performed surgery at Santa Rosa on many patients from Mexico's upper-class families.[92]

These hospitals arose as Jim Crow laws in the South were institutionalized and racial tensions in the North increased. The relationship between the Sisters of the Holy Cross and the city of Cairo was mixed, ranging from supportive to critical. Besides the economic poverty of the city, racial prejudice was harsh. Segregation ruled for almost a century and did not change until the 1960s. Throughout that time, sisters battled doctors and city leaders as nuns admitted blacks and hired black workers.[93] In other hospitals, authorities might have problems finding staff for African American wards. There is no recorded incident, however, where individual sisters objected to their nursing assignments with African Americans. Nuns vowed obedience to the superior, and in light of this it is unlikely that any opposition arose.

Nuns' segregation of African Americans was an accommodation to community standards. Since the middle of the nineteenth century, immigrants in Catholic America held a deeply ingrained racial system that distinguished between "black" and "white." Some historians have argued that Euro-Americans separated themselves from the "colored" side of the American racial divide by claiming a shared identity based on skin color.[94] There is no evidence that, in their hospitals, sisters dealt with this issue in these ways. More important for this study is Margaret Susan Thompson's assertion that late nineteenth- and early-twentieth-century nuns most likely did not perceive the racial issue in their hospitals as a dilemma. Sisters lived and worked for eternity, and salvation through baptism was the foremost objective of their missionary work. Through baptism, all were equal before God, and earthly inequality mattered less than the soul's destiny.[95] In 1872, religious prescriptions for the Sisters of Charity of the Incarnate Word directed them to alleviate all the sick, "which are their brothers in Christ." Then in 1906, they expanded these rules to include caring for "all without distinction of disease, age, character, fortune, color or even religion, making themselves all to all, to gain all to Christ."[96] Indeed, nuns held to the assurance that all would be of equal status in the context of eternity.

Hospital Patterns

Using government and hospital surveys, table 4.4 offers some comparisons among the Catholic hospitals regarding growth in patients and personnel. The midwestern cities of St. Paul and Minneapolis, with their sizeable Catholic populations, admitted the most patients. Santa Rosa's increased patient population likely reflected the fact that it was the only private, general hospital in San Antonio in the early part of the twentieth century. It also was a well-established hospital, having been around longer than any other in the city. Large cities were havens for aspiring physicians and specialists because of the better chance of making a name for themselves and being successful in private practice. Thus, hospitals in St. Paul, San Antonio, and Fort Worth had the most physicians. Growth in nursing personnel reflected the development of the sisters' nurse training schools, with their significant numbers of nursing students. The hospitals did not report the average length of stay, but according to data in a 1904 governmental census, the average number of days in ecclesiastical hospitals was twenty-eight. This was comparable to nineteen days in private secular hospitals and thirty-one days in government-supported hospitals.[97]

As the market expanded after 1900, some hospital leaders were already complaining that there were too many small hospitals in the United States. In 1911 one wrote, "If many hospitals in each city could pool their interests, the result would be greater efficiency and greater economy—and yet nothing is more unlikely than that independent, privately controlled hospitals will pool interests."[98] He primarily criticized inadequately financed institutions, many of which had fewer than fifty beds. This would not have included the seven Catholic hospitals represented in this book. Nevertheless, integration of services did not occur. Hospital systems in the late nineteenth and early twentieth centuries had no set design, and they developed without any long-term vision of adequate services. In a cross-national study of hospitals, William A. Glaser found that in countries such as the United States, where greater denominational competition existed, religious groups maintained hospitals to fortify their influence. In many cities, Catholic, Protestant, ethnic, and public hospitals existed "where a neutral national planner might have established only one large hospital."[99]

Hospital numbers, however, do not tell the whole story. In smaller towns like Cairo, Illinois, the Catholic hospital was the only one in town. While patient admissions at St. Mary's Infirmary were fewer than in other hospitals, there was widespread use by people of all faiths and by those with none at all. The same was true in the early years in Utah. The

Table 4.4 Hospital Census Data

Hospital	1904 Patients	Doctors	Nurses	1910 Patients	Doctors	Nurses
St. Mary's, Minneapolis	1,164	18	24	1,490	nd	40
St. Joseph's, St. Paul	2,010	5	50	2,843	33	86
St. Mary's, Cairo	478	nd	7	560	nd	14
Holy Cross Hospital, Salt Lake City	1,332	8	20	1,150	8	36
St. Joseph's, South Bend	90	24	8	392	nd	16
Santa Rosa, San Antonio	1,149	Nd	25	2,000	22	56
St. Joseph's, Fort Worth	848	13	25	1,491	66	64

Source: Department of Commerce, Bureau of the Census, *Benevolent Institutions, 1904* (Washington, DC: Government Printing Office, 1905); *Benevolent Institutions, 1910* (Washington, DC: Government Printing Office, 1913).

fluid environment and the lack of long-standing religious prejudice in burgeoning western towns created a situation of interdenominational cooperation. Nuns at Holy Cross Hospital hired Mormon doctors as well as Catholics and Protestants, and they cared for migrating Jews, Greek Orthodox, and members of other faiths. Indeed, Mormon children often followed the Sisters of the Holy Cross whenever they walked the streets of Salt Lake City.[100] A focus of the next chapter will be how Catholic hospitals, which rarely had large endowments, obtained financial income that they could depend upon for growth in an expanding hospital marketplace.

5

"Debts Are Our Only Wealth":

FINANCING AND MARKETING CATHOLIC HOSPITALS

> Debts are our only wealth.... We do the best possible to receive paying patients in order to live ourselves and care for [the poor]. ... If we did not have a paying infirmary, we would have to steal in order to live ... the poverty is so great.[1]
>
> Mother St. Pierre Cinquin, CCVI
> December 15, 1885

As limited income led to mounting debts at Santa Rosa Infirmary, Mother St. Pierre anticipated the difficulties of keeping it functioning without having adequate resources to do so. This brief account to her French superior encapsules the anguish Catholic sisters experienced as they struggled to remain true to their missions of serving the needs of the poor while simultaneously managing the realities of business economics. Mother St. Pierre's words had an apologetic tone as she explained why a charity-based infirmary still had to serve paying patients. Virtually all sister-administrators of hospitals ultimately would have to face and resolve this clash of spiritual motives and business realities. Some, no doubt, faced their tasks with hesitancy and trepidation. Many others, however, did so with enthusiasm and creativity. Sisters raised funds by bringing in patients, and their marketing became crucial to their success. Although fund-raising and marketing were traditionally viewed as male activities, the sisters found ways to carry them out while underscoring the strengths of their religious and gender identities.

Personnel allocations typically reflected available funds, and nuns had to appeal to legitimate networks of patronage to gain the financial support they needed. Ecclesiastical and lay supporters often served as intermediaries between the congregation and general public. The early enterprises of the Sisters of St. Joseph materialized primarily through their patronage relationship with the French countess who helped support them financially. In the United States, Mother Angela Gillespie sought specific networks of power with doctors and US government officials during the Civil War and afterward when the Sisters of the Holy Cross opened their first hospitals. Other superiors worked directly with prominent local citizens, tradesmen, contractors, railroad executives, and mine owners to obtain support for their activities. Teaching young women from middle- and upper-middle-class families provided nuns the opportunity to cultivate relationships with wealthy parents who could help support their enterprises. Through these contacts, sisters obtained the regular services of lawyers and bankers. Priests and bishops sometimes served as intermediaries for nuns. Some clergy, like Archbishop John Ireland of St. Paul, were either related to the sisters or were family friends.

As communities expanded their membership, their financial dealings became more complicated, and they had to clearly delineate in their constitutions who had ultimate authority over finances. Nuns also changed their constitutions to allot greater authority to the mother superior.[2] These modifications were crucial to sisters' control over their organizations. As they acquired properties such as hospitals and schools, they did so in the convent's name. Thus, sisters did not violate their individual vows of poverty because they did not obtain property in their own names. Rather, it belonged to the religious community as a whole.

As Catholic hospitals underwent demographic, architectural, and technological change, nuns had to obtain new sources of capital. Unlike European women's religious orders that often had wealthy members, most sisters in the United States were not from the upper classes and did not have large dowries to finance their institutions. Furthermore, late-nineteenth-century Catholic hospitals typically did not have endowments, nor were many the recipients of large donations from the wealthy, the traditional supporters of other nineteenth-century voluntary hospitals. Only one feasible avenue for income was available to the sisters, and that was to generate their own capital. In effect, poverty and a dearth of donors led Catholic nursing congregations to embrace capitalism and entrepreneurship. Marketing replaced donations as the primary funding strategy.[3]

Financing Catholic Hospitals

In the early years, nuns made collection tours to raise money in towns, forts, and mining camps where Catholics typically could be found. Collections partially paid for the first building of Holy Cross Hospital, Salt Lake City, in 1875. Utah's Father Lawrence Scanlan affirmed the sisters' abilities as he described their collection for the hospital: Nuns were "*good collectors*. . . . The Sisters can collect 5 dollars to a priest's one"[4] (original emphasis). And as demonstrated in chapter 3, "begging" (or solicitation) tours could also gain the local people's personal interest and support for a hospital.

These measures were not always successful, however, and all three women's congregations courted government help through municipal or county subsidies for the indigent.[5] As early as the 1850s in St. Paul, the Sisters of St. Joseph cared for patients whose expenses the city and county paid.[6] In Cairo in 1867, Mother Angela Gillespie contracted with the county whose officials needed a place for its invalids. And it was the loss of county subsidies that contributed to the demise of Providence Hospital in Terre Haute in 1874.[7]

Another strategy to underwrite hospital expenses was the beneficial society. In Salt Lake City in 1886, the Sisters of the Holy Cross agreed with a Mutual Hospital Aid Association to provide room, board, medical attendance, nursing, and "all necessary surgical instruments and medicines" to participants, with the association compensating the sisters one dollar a day for a ward and $1.25 for a private room. All of the patients who applied to the association would go to Holy Cross Hospital.[8] In many of the hospitals, however, sisters maintained wards that they reserved specifically for charity patients who were unable to pay for their care. In later years, the sisters at St. Joseph's Infirmary, Fort Worth, allotted over a fourth of the operating budget to free and discount patients.[9] And nuns tried to obtain funds specifically for the needy. In the 1890s sisters at St. Mary's, Minneapolis, generated funds to care for the poor by issuing "Sisters' Tickets." By donating $100, a patron could send any needy person to the hospital for care and treatment.[10]

While hospital rooms remained available to full charity patients who could not pay, sisters' advertisements aimed largely at a paying population. Inside the hospital, social class stratifications were evident. Like voluntary hospitals, Catholic hospitals typically offered three classes of accommodations, including ward beds and private beds. The ward beds were further divided into public and private. Poorer persons usually stayed in the public wards and received care from city or county doctors. Ads claimed

FIGURE 5.1 Private room, Holy Cross Hospital, Salt Lake City, UT, 1908. (Courtesy Utah Historical Society, photo # 28541)

that private patients could have their own doctors, a special prerogative for those who could pay for their care; and stay in rooms that offered a stove, water closet, and hotel-like furnishings (fig. 5.1).

Other hospitals had similar policies. In Minneapolis and St. Paul, a private room went for $10 to $20 a week.[11] In San Antonio, the Incarnate Word Sisters charged the county 50¢ per day for indigent patients in the ward, while those in private rooms typically paid a weekly rate of $7 to $10.[12] Hospital stays were not cheap, and these costs would have been a significant burden on many families.[13] Whether or not poor patients actually received a different quality of service from that of private-paying patients is unknown. Sisters apparently were sensitive to this possibility, however, and their publications claimed that there was no difference in care. A pamphlet for St. Mary's Infirmary, Cairo, for example, advertised that charity patients had access to hospital services "in exactly the same measure as would be given to the richest and best paying patient."[14]

Typically, the superior of the hospital determined rates. Sometimes, she charged patients different amounts for similar services, based on ability to pay. Superiors worked directly with the patients and might bargain for their work in return for room, board, nursing care, and medicines.[15] As hospital costs rose, superiors increased rates. In 1908, after surveying Catholic and non-Catholic hospitals in Chicago, Denver, and Rochester, Minnesota, Sister Lidwina Butler raised room rates for Holy Cross Hospital in Salt Lake City. In 1916, the new superior increased them again "owing to the cost of all commodities," with wards costing $12 for a week's stay and the cheapest private room $20 a week.[16]

Payment of fees was never certain, however. Santa Rosa records reveal that patients often left the hospital promising to pay later and then failed to do so.[17] Sisters did not hesitate to write former patients for money past due, even if they were priests.[18] Likewise, the government did not always follow through on its payments. Although the Incarnate Word Sisters nursed San Antonio's indigent in the public hospital from 1885 to 1892, the city did not pay them until the sisters took the matter to the City Council in 1896. Similarly, the city of Fort Worth delayed paying the sisters in 1890 and again in 1892, and the superior had to go to town to collect the money.[19]

Part of nuns' marketing strategies involved actively seeking groups of new clients who were ready sources of revenue. Sisters turned to the businesses and corporations that had the capital resources—railroad and mining businesses whose production and profits depended heavily on the good health of the working-class laborers. Sometimes the nuns sought out the industrial companies first. In the case of Holy Cross Hospital, however, it appears that mine owners took the first step and approached the bishop for a Catholic hospital.

In the prepayment plans with mining companies, sisters did not set hospital rates by themselves but instead negotiated with owners or more typically with the company doctors. While some owners set up claims departments and relief associations to cover medical expenses and support disabled workers, many did not negotiate hospital rates on behalf of workers themselves as a union would.[20] Indeed, from the companies' views, owners were not really trying to get the lowest hospital rates, because deductions from workers' wages rather than the companies themselves bore the cost. Owners could always raise deductions if costs began to soar. Thus, it was not a market that necessarily gave workers the best price for hospital care, because the company acted as the middleman.[21] The sisters themselves, however, were not in the actuarial business. Rather, the company determined the insurance premiums, deducted funds from the employees' wages, and directly paid the hospital for care. Nevertheless, the rates nuns charged were comparable to or less than what they charged their other patients. In some Catholic hospitals, miners could choose their own doctors, but in others, they could not.

Sisters' hospitals were not simply an auxiliary to late-nineteenth-century capitalism. Nuns and industrial owners each had something the other needed. Both parties strove for the same outcome of lower mortality and injury rates. Mining and railroad industries, to which the nuns concentrated much of their marketing efforts, were dangerous working environments, and lawyers of that era were increasingly targeting companies for litigious actions. Owners considered it prudent business practice to provide medical benefits to workers, thus reducing the risks that ruinous lawsuits would bring.[22] On their part, the sisters viewed the medical outcomes as a reflection of their mission to serve the poor and needy workers. They wanted to care for their own and tried to make them well. No doubt, the fact that the workers and miners were potential Catholics affected sisters' decisions.

Furthermore, a large number of the laborers were Irish immigrants, drawn from the same cultural group as many of the sisters themselves. Catholic hospitals could offer care to immigrants who otherwise had no access to medical and nursing services. Mother St. Pierre wrote of Irish railroad patients in Fort Worth: "If they do not go to this hospital they are obliged to pay their own expenses elsewhere—which most of them would not be able to do because all of them belong to the working class and have no resource other than their work."[23]

And yet, sisters' hospitals should be understood not only in terms of service or cultural continuity but also in terms of entrepreneurship. A close inspection of nuns' writings makes it clear that caring for miners and railroad workers was an expedient means of financing hospitals, particularly during startup periods when financial stability was precarious. Miners' and railroad workers' prepayment plans helped significantly to underwrite hospital costs. At Holy Cross Hospital in Salt Lake City, the mandatory deductions from miners' wages initially financed the facility and kept it financially viable through the 1890s, accounting for 40 to 60 percent of receipts. This income was especially needed since, throughout the late nineteenth and early twentieth centuries, donations never accounted for more than 9 percent of total receipts.[24]

Sisters' hospitals' successes may have led some people to perceive them as being too financially independent to need philanthropists. Even the rare hospital that did have an endowment, such as Providence Hospital in Terre Haute, was not guaranteed success. Still, nuns always sought benefactors, and religious and ethnic networks were particularly important. Immigrant laywomen and men, miners, railroad workers, and other laborers gave their hard-earned money. After the turn of the century, members of the rising middle class or wealthy Catholic laity, largely Irish or German, donated to the hospital cause. In Salt Lake City, nuns borrowed money from the Hibernia Bank, and many donations and credit extensions came from local Irish and German merchants.[25]

There were other benefactors. The wealthy Clem Studebaker donated a carriage and harness to St. Joseph's Hospital, South Bend, in 1904, and his wife gave land.[26] These donations added to the sisters' assets, and gifts of land could be liquidated if necessary. For example, the Incarnate Word Sisters in Fort Worth received land from a railroad patient in 1890, which they promptly sold for $1,000.[27] The Sisters of the Holy Cross took advantage of their location in mining regions when they were given a claim to a mine in Deadwood, South Dakota. They considered selling it at the same time they sold the hospital.[28] It would be several more years, however, before most Catholic hospitals would receive the large bequests of wealthy patrons on the scale of the $60,000 the Studebaker family gave to the Protestant Epworth Hospital in South Bend in 1900.[29] Business self-interests played a role in some of these charitable activities, since the maintenance of a healthy workforce in industrial cities such as South Bend required that workers have access to medical care.[30] But a Catholic hospital was also a place to which people could give gifts in exchange for sisters' prayers, and nuns did not forget their benefactors. Sometimes they acknowledged them publicly, but more often they prayed for them, particularly on special holy days and on other such occasions. And Catholics depended on sisters' prayers.[31]

Catholic hospitals also owed much to the financial backing of laywomen. Local and regional community fund-raising projects were launched during periods of hospital establishment and expansions, and laywomen often headed these events. Fairs typified fund-raising events in the early years. After the turn of the century, other types of fund-raisers supplanted fairs, reflecting the presence of a Catholic middle class. Women's auxiliaries became prominent, and they held galas such as opera concerts, sewing projects, raffles, and bake sales.[32] In the smaller community of Cairo, Illinois, the people especially took pride in their hospital. In a show of widespread community involvement, Protestant and Catholic women held a bazaar and concert in 1902; and in 1912, Jewish, Catholic, and Protestant women held a "lawn fete" to raise money for St. Mary's Infirmary.[33] Sisters listed creditors in their records, and these included Irish women such as Ellen Fitzpatrick, Rose Conway, Mary Davis, and Bridget Gaven. In many parishes, Irish women were the most significant contributors to the church, and it appears their generosity extended to hospitals as well.[34]

While competition remained keen between St. Joseph's and Epworth Hospitals in South Bend, the city inaugurated a novel plan to raise funds for both facilities in 1904. The two divided the proceeds equally from what became an annual community-wide event called "Tag Day" to help cover expenses for the coming year. With local community patrons, then, the two hospitals cooperated to collect money for both institutions. The Sisters of the Holy Cross obtained from $800 to $1,400 yearly from these events.[35]

Early in the twentieth century, in a conscious effort to keep up with growing competition, some women's congregations borrowed a specific strategy from voluntary hospitals' fund-raising methods. A ploy often used by trustees was to solicit endowments for free beds, and they assured prospective donors that they could choose the bed's occupant. In the early twentieth century at St. Joseph's Hospital, St. Paul, a donation of $10,000 endowed a room in perpetuity, $5,000 a bed in perpetuity, and $300 a bed for one year. The sisters also solicited bequests. In 1915, nuns at St. Mary's, Minneapolis, received over $4,000 in donations and bequests, although it accounted for only 5 percent of the total hospital income.[36]

Sometimes sisters relied on priests' patronage. In 1882, when few patients came to St. Joseph's Hospital in South Bend, the priests at Notre Dame helped the Sisters of the Holy Cross by sending paying patients. Some priests secured loans for the sisters or lent them money themselves.[37] Archbishop John Ireland took great interest in the work of his sister, Mother Seraphine. After paying the Sisters of Mercy $30,000 for St. Mary's Hospital in Minneapolis, he lent the Sisters of St. Joseph money to buy the hospital, but only if they agreed to pay him interest. A note of March 9, 1894, tallied the sisters' debt to the archbishop: the original cost of St. Mary's property, $30,737.83; interest and expenses incurred in improvements, $33,978.64; and $31,810 for the 1890 addition to the hospital. When Mother Jane Frances Bouchet became superior of St. Mary's in 1890, she inherited the congregation's debt. Although a formidable one to retire, the sisters succeeded in paying it back with money from hospital receipts, collections, and fund-raising fairs.[38]

When the Sisters of the Holy Cross opened St. Joseph's Hospital, South Bend, in 1882, they purchased the building from the Holy Cross priests at the University of Notre Dame for $15,000. The nuns obtained five notes from Notre Dame for $3,000 each, payable over seven years at 4 percent interest. One might expect this offer to have been insulting to the sisters, considering the many years of unpaid domestic labor they had given Notre Dame in the past. But the interest rate was low compared to Indiana's average 1882 interest rate for real estate mortgages, and no records suggest that the sisters were offended. In fact, in 1892 the priests forgave the unpaid balance as a recompense for the sisters' labor over the past twenty years. After receiving a Quit Claim Deed from the diocesan bishop, who held the land as church property, the sisters became full owners.[39]

Central to the nuns' entrepreneurship was their financial independence from the local diocese. Except in the case of Archbishop Ireland, neither dioceses nor parishes provided the sisters any regular financial assistance. Bishop Claude Dubuis, who had first brought the Incarnate Word Sisters to San Antonio in 1869, expected the women to shoulder all their hospitals' debts. In 1885, Mother St. Pierre remarked that he "left *us* only with debts . . . without revenue, without resources, having confidence only in the providence of the Incarnate Word"[40] (original emphasis). Ironically, what appeared to be a financial disadvantage turned into a practical advantage for the sisters. They did not depend on the church hierarchy for financing and instead had to find their own sources of funding. This allowed them to exercise administrative control over their hospitals without interference from local bishops.

Sisters also incorporated their hospitals with the state, which gave them legal ownership and control of their own property and freed them from financial dependence on the diocese. Nuns' strategies to incorporate, however, raise more questions regarding the tension between a charity and a business. Through incorporation, sisters essentially organized their charity work using a business model. The nuns themselves served as officers, board members, and corporate members, and all property belonged to the respective corporations. Articles of Incorporation gave officers the right to raise and borrow money; accept bequests; avoid taxes; make contracts; sue and be sued; and own, buy, and sell real estate. Furthermore, as members of their own boards, nuns could establish contracts without relying on a male cleric's signature.[41]

The sisters incorporated at various stages of their hospital development. The Congregation of the Sisters of Charity of the Incarnate Word filed for Articles of Incorporation on January 23, 1881, for Santa Rosa Infirmary, although St. Joseph's Infirmary in Fort Worth did not incorporate until 1917.[42] In 1894, the Sisters of St. Joseph of Carondelet formed St. Mary's Hospital Corporation. It was at that point that Archbishop Ireland transferred the title, which he had kept in his name, to the sisters. St. Joseph's Hospital, St. Paul, incorporated the following year. It had begun as a diocesan institution founded on land donated to the diocese, but when the hospital incorporated in 1895, the hospital and land passed into the sisters' hands. The diocese did not want the burden of a $60,000 debt on the new hospital, and it gladly transferred the whole matter to the nuns' corporation.[43] Mother Seraphine Ireland was the first president of both St. Joseph's and St. Mary's corporations. Records of boards of directors' meetings indicate that sisters met to act upon propositions to borrow money, elect board members and officers, and approve bylaws.[44] In 1903, the Sisters of the Holy Cross created the Holy Cross Hospital Association.[45] A problem had arisen after Father Sorin's death as to who would hold the title of Holy Cross Hospital in Salt Lake City. The title had been vested in him, and the sisters needed "proper proof of succession in trust" in order to take out any mortgages. According to the new articles, all hospital property came under the sisters' corporation.[46]

Incorporation gave sisters' organizations significant advantages. It enhanced women's administrative efficiency in financial management.[47] While the religious orders as corporate bodies were entrepreneurs, so were the individuals who ran them. Mothers Angela Gillespie, Seraphine Ireland, and St. Pierre Cinquin particularly were successful in building their congregations' services. They courted the influence of government leaders, church authorities, corporate owners, and lawyers to help in their endeavors. This accorded their religious communities unusual influence and significance.

Sisters allocated resources to their hospitals by using several strategies. To help with startup projects, the motherhouses had assets from a variety of sources. Nuns in each of the three congregations taught in private schools, and tuition fees frequently showed up on sisters' hospital ledgers. When they taught in public or parish schools, sisters received salaries. To help make ends meet, nuns also practiced strict economy in their personal expenses; indeed, their vow of poverty compelled them to do so. They often had vegetable gardens behind their hospitals, raised chickens, and owned cows.[48] Furthermore, they cooked and cleaned for themselves, and the free labor they furnished as nurses, cooks, housekeepers, and laundresses undoubtedly was beneficial.

After the congregations formed centralized governments, general councils and superiors decided to use congregational assets in particular ways. Since they lived communally, sisters held their funds in common with all salaries paid to the superior general. After deducting community expenses, the superior and her council exercised discretion over the remaining funds. For example, on September 11, 1875, the general council of the Sisters of the Holy Cross granted $6,000 to Mother Augusta Anderson to open Holy Cross Hospital.[49] A week earlier, Mother Augusta had asked her priest director, Father Sorin, to borrow the money and charge it to her. In reply, however, Sorin directed her to obtain the money from Saint Mary's, the sisters' motherhouse in South Bend.[50] Likely, he knew the motherhouse either had the money or could get it. And since interest rates in Salt Lake City were much higher compared to Indiana, the sisters recognized the wisdom of obtaining the money from the motherhouse rather than borrowing it in Salt Lake City.

Five years later, on December 28, 1880, the general council debated whether or not to take responsibility for a hospital in South Bend. The congregation was heavily in debt for money it had advanced to other establishments, and it had been unable to erect convent buildings and a chapel at Saint Mary's that the community needed. The council considered the convent and chapel to be "so absolutely necessary to maintain and to develop the Religious Spirit at the Mother house" that the members voted to "appropriate all funds they may realize for the next few years to the erection of the aforesaid buildings."[51] For that reason, they did not begin a hospital, which would have incurred an even larger debt. A year later, however, when the mines closed in South Dakota and the sisters sold their hospital, they used the money for other projects. They not only shared monetary assets from one institution to another but also personnel. It was from the South Dakota hospital that Sister Edward Murphy came to St. Joseph's in South Bend in 1882. The fact that the nuns had an experienced person to administer the institution undoubtedly affected the general council's decision to open the hospital.[52]

The sisters undertook aggressive financial strategies at the congregational level. Availability of modern facilities was crucial to the success of hospitals, and sisters spent tremendous amounts of money not only to erect them but also to expand and update their facilities. In 1897, Mother St. Madeleine Chollet asked local physicians to help her obtain a loan for a new addition to St. Joseph's Infirmary, Fort Worth, but they did not come forth with help. Relying instead on the patronage of a benefactor in Europe, she wrote to Gabriel Wiegman in Holland and secured a $10,000 loan.[53] The Incarnate Word Sisters had contacts in Germany and Holland, having recruited sisters from these areas in previous years. Whether Wiegman was a friend or relative of one of the nuns is not clear; at any rate, he lent the money at 5 percent interest, a rate considerably lower than the average rate in Texas. Records do not indicate if he required collateral.[54]

Before incorporation, general councils gave individual hospital superiors permission to borrow money to expand facilities.[55] After corporations formed, loans were made to the organization and signed by the president and board of directors, who were sisters. When applying for loans, sisters did not have stocks and bonds to serve as collateral; rather, the main securities for their bank loans were their hospitals, which they mortgaged.

Table 5.1 Financial Statistics, St. Joseph Hospital, South Bend, IN

Date	# Patients/year (average/day)	Receipts ($)	Expenses ($)	House Owes ($)
1891–92	106	3,123	2,525	2,161
1894–95	123 (11)	5,258	4,279	19,356
1899–1900	142 (14)	3,393	3,222	20,437
1904–05	200 (25)	11,300	41,064*	106,167
1909–10	361 (23)	15,163	14,822	117,316
1914–15	518 (25)	18,730	16,899	111,600
1919–20	1,185 (35)	52,823	41,470	54,900
1924–25	1,661 (55)	146,892	122,724**	308,480

Source: *Archive Book, St. Joseph's Hospital, South Bend, IN.*
* Building expansion, 1904
** Building expansion, 1922.

After the Sisters of the Holy Cross incorporated in 1903, they began major construction projects at both Holy Cross and St. Joseph's Hospitals, with combined costs totaling more than $220,000 in a three-year period. In 1903, to erect the new addition to Holy Cross, they mortgaged the hospital property, borrowed money, and sought donations.[56] These funds, along with congregational savings and hospital assets, paid the construction expense of over $126,000. Clearly, the hospital itself and the sisters' motherhouse had assets to assure relatively rapid payment of major debts. Hospital records indicate that the sisters paid all loans by 1907 and then expanded the hospital again in 1914 and 1919.[57]

At St. Joseph's Hospital, South Bend, the Holy Cross Sisters began planning a major expansion project in 1903. The motherhouse lent them nearly $14,000 to begin construction, with the expectation that the hospital nuns would repay the loan. In addition, the sisters obtained over $11,000 in private loans from individuals at interest rates that were only 1 to 2 percent. The sisters then mortgaged the hospital for $30,000, which had to be repaid in cash the following year.[58] This prompted the corporation to obtain a ten-year loan of $50,000 from the Massachusetts Mutual Life Insurance Company, and to secure this loan the sisters mortgaged the property again. Table 5.1 shows that their total debt for 1905 was $106,167. It was 1919 before the debt was significantly reduced.[59] Not to be deterred, the sisters embarked on another building campaign in 1922, increasing the debt yet again.

Expansion of St. Joseph's clearly was a priority for the sisters, given the competition with the local Protestant hospital. Although the nuns kept up with modern scientific discoveries and wanted to make the best facilities available to their patients, market factors also drove their actions. Epworth Hospital had recently renovated its operating room, aided by the $60,000 gift from the Studebaker estate.[60] A new hospital addition was especially important so that St. Joseph's could attract paying patients and physicians.

Table 5.1 shows that the number of patients and income increased after the sisters expanded the hospital. In 1900, St. Joseph's maintained a daily average census of only fourteen patients. Reeling from the 1905 physician boycott over hospital control, the sisters worked hard to get other doctors who would bring in paying patients, since St. Joseph's had no mining or railroad prepayments to supplement income. Over time, expanding the hospital paid off. By 1915, receipts had markedly increased, and patient admissions had risen to 518 annually. This growth persisted over time and was largely due to the opening of new wings with more private rooms and updated operating rooms, which attracted new surgeons and their patients.[61]

As these data indicate, hospitals were not immediate financial successes. After they became well established, however, hospital assets could be used to fund other institutions. Indeed, hospital work became a major source of income for the rest of the congregation.[62] Once the Incarnate Word Sisters were well established in San Antonio, the motherhouse regularly sent checks to meet the debt on hospital property in Fort Worth.[63] Surpluses from the hospitals themselves sometimes paid for new additions.

Comparisons of Catholic and Non-Catholic Hospitals

Accurate comparison of financial status among all seven hospitals is not possible due to scarce records and incompatible accounting methods; nevertheless, extant sources allow some generalizations to be made. In the years before government and insurance regulations made accounting rules more complex, sisters kept records of cash receipts and expenditures, which they compared each year to see if serious deficits occurred over time. Congregation superiors making their annual visits scrutinized financial records. Cash was the most liquid asset of the hospital enterprises, and available records show that the nuns kept positive cash balances. Hospitals needed them to maintain their credit rating with

Table 5.2 Income Comparisons to Other Hospitals in Regions, 1904*

Hospital	Dividends, Rents, Invested Property (%)	Subscriptions, Bequests, and Donations (%)	Legacies (%)	Patient Payments (%)	Misc. (%)	Total $
St. Mary's, Minneapolis (100 beds)	Rent: 77 Items sold: 88 Total: 165 (0.6%)	870 (3%)	... ...	28,017 (96%)	... ...	29,052
Presbyterian, Chicago (250 beds)	34,100 (21%)	24,955 (16%)	10,965 (7%)	87,644 (55%)	1,807 (1%)	159,471
Holy Cross, Salt Lake City (150 beds)	Items sold: 4,350 (9%) 97 (0.2%)		... ...	45,108 (91%)	87 (0.2%)	49,642
St. Luke, San Francisco (111 beds)	29,769 (33%)	135 (0.2%)	452 (0.5%)	58,982 (66%)	...	89,338

Source: Holy Cross Hospital Annual Account, 1904-05; Sir Henry Burdett, *Burdett's Hospitals and Charities* (London: Scientific Press, Ltd., 1906).
* St. Mary's Hospital Financial Report (for the year 1906).

financial institutions.[64] Another asset that could be liquidated quickly was merchandise. Sisters carefully recorded sales of items such as buildings, horses, and wagons. They also noted money due the hospitals from patients, although these were sometimes uncollected outstanding accounts and could not be liquidated as quickly. Nuns' hospitals usually operated in the red only when they had major construction projects. While their ledgers seldom showed current-year deficits, their payments to creditors during building years could be quite large. Clearly, these sisters were not afraid to take risks. In 1910, the sisters in Utah reported the value of Holy Cross Hospital as $350,000, but they had notes due that amounted to $117,316.[65]

Tables 5.2 and 5.3 compare early-twentieth-century income and expenditures of two Catholic hospitals with two non-Catholic hospitals from the same western and midwestern regions. A glance at table 5.2 confirms just how dramatically different were the income sources of Catholic and Protestant institutions, especially in the area of dividends, rents, and investments in property. These items accounted for nearly one-fourth of the total receipts at Presbyterian in Chicago and one-third at St. Luke's, San Francisco. The Catholic hospitals, however, obtained less than 1 percent of receipts from these sources.[66] Subscriptions and bequests at Presbyterian were particularly high, but interestingly the Catholic hospitals drew in more money from subscriptions and bequests than St. Luke's in San Francisco. The Catholic hospitals recorded no legacies, although this changed in later years. For example, in 1914 the sisters at St. Joseph's, South Bend, received enough legacies and donations to pay off the Massachusetts Mutual Life Insurance loan which expired that year.[67]

In summary, income from donations, investments, and legacies accounted for 44 percent of receipts at Presbyterian, Chicago, and almost 34 percent at St. Luke's, San Francisco, compared to only 3 percent at St. Mary's, Minneapolis, and 9 percent at Holy Cross, Salt Lake City. It was income from private patients that brought in the greatest income for the Catholic hospitals. Different results are found, however, in a comparison of Holy Cross Hospital with its rival Protestant facility in Salt Lake City, St. Mark's. In 1910, receipts from the care of patients there brought in 92 percent of the total income.[68]

In recording expenditures, hospitals used separate categories for personnel, food, fuel, medical supplies, printing, wages, and so on. Medical care was not included since hospital rates did not include physicians' fees. Table 5.3 shows that in the early twentieth century, most of the sisters' hospital budgets went for food and other provisions. The greatest difference between the Catholic and non-Catholic hospitals was in salary and wages. These were never large budget items in the early-twentieth-century Catholic hospitals because nuns provided most of the labor. However, they resided in the hospital, and their living expenses were considered part of the overall hospital costs.[69] Nevertheless, their unpaid labor supplemented limited donations and endowments. By contrast, more staff in non-Catholic institutions lived outside the hospital, and wages became the largest single category of expenses in those facilities. The fact that nuns constituted inexpensive labor gave Catholic hospitals a distinct advantage over their competitors and helped them to survive in the hospital market.

Table 5.3 Expenditure Comparisons to Other Hospitals in Regions, 1904*

Hospital	Provisions (%)	Fuel (%)	Furniture/ Bedding (%)	Drugs/ Surgical Supplies (%)	Salary & Wages (%)	Repairs (%)	Printing etc. (%)	Misc. (%)	Total $
St. Mary's, Minneapolis (100 beds)	10,231 (36%)	1,342 (4%)	848 (3%)	1,643 (6%)	3,418 (12%)	1,110 (4%)	101 (0.3%)	9,834 (35%)	28,540
Presbyterian, Chicago (250 beds)	31,777 (23%)	14,581 (10%)	2,724 (2%)	15,628 (11%)	50,950 (36%)	4,987 (4%)	1,303 (1%)	17,822 (13%)	139,937
Holy Cross, Salt Lake City (150 beds)	7,293 (29%)	1,476 (5%)	864 (3%)	1,992 (8%)	2,182 (9%)	1,797 (7%)	297 (1%)	9,618 (38%)	25,519
St. Luke, San Francisco (111 beds)	16,159 (19%)	4,770 (5%)	...	5,660** (6%)	20,717 (24%)	2,802 (3%)	500 (1%)	37,038 (42%)	87,546

Source: Holy Cross Hospital Annual Account, 1904–05, CSC; Sir Henry Burdett, *Burdett's Hospitals and Charities* (London: Scientific Press, Ltd., 1906).
*St. Mary's Hospital Financial Report (for the year 1906).
** Figures for 1903.

Marketing Strategies

Since sisters raised funds by bringing in patients, their marketing strategies were central to their success, and they used a variety of strategies to expand their clientele. First, they had to encourage those who needed their hospitals to use them, because many people still received care at home by private family doctors. Advertisements also emphasized the institutions as the providers of worldly services. Reports spoke of comfortable, convenient, homelike environments. As late as 1908, the annual report for St. Joseph's Hospital in St. Paul emphasized the "bright, airy and pleasing appearance" of each ward and private room. Second-floor private rooms could accommodate patrons "who desire the convenience together with the comfort of a beautiful home."[70] Sisters wanted to remove any impediments to hospital use, particularly lingering images of hospitals as places of death. Hence, their advertisements focused on their low mortality rates, such as the 2 percent that St. Joseph's, St. Paul, reported in 1905.[71] Sisters also frequently used newspapers, which could not only stir up community interest in their projects but also help financially. And they gave the media important news items such as fund-raising events and completions of new buildings.

The opening of new hospitals also received special attention. In 1875, the Sisters of the Holy Cross announced the opening of Holy Cross Hospital by emphasizing that it would be "under the immediate supervision of the Sisters themselves, and will be attended by a corps of the best Physicians of the City."[72] Advertisements often targeted specific consumers. St. Mary's Hospital in Minneapolis designed an advertisement card in 1890 (fig. 5.2) to appeal to private patients, holders of national benefit association certificates, and union hospital companies whereby workers would be eligible for certain services.[73] Notably, the words "Sisters of St. Joseph," as hospital owners, held prominence in the ad. In each of these announcements, sisters' gender and religious identities stood out as the nuns emphasized that they would be in charge of the hospital and nursing care. In terms of the culture and work environment, it was very much their hospital.

While working in the public domain of the hospital, sisters' vows of poverty, chastity, and obedience helped to project the image that they were untarnished by self-interest in their work. In Mother St. Pierre Cinquin's negotiations with the chief surgeon for the Fort Worth hospital, she wrote, "Remember, dear doctor, you have not to deal with business and speculative purchasers, but I dare say with honest and upright dealers."[74] During the Civil War, Frederick Law Olmsted of the US Sanitary Com-

> **St. Mary's Hospital,**
> MINNEAPOLIS, MINN.
> IN CHARGE OF THE
> **Sisters of St. Joseph.**
>
> MEDICAL AND SURGICAL STAFF.
> J. H. DUNN, M. D., President.   W. A. JONES, M. D., Secretary.
> ATTENDING PHYSICIANS   ATTENDING SURGEONS.
> J. W. BELL, M. D.   W. A. HALL, M. D.
> H. B. SWEETSER, M. D.   J. H. DUNN, M. D.
> C. A. McCOLLOM, M. D.   F. A. DUNSMOOR, M. D.
> J. P. BARBER, M. D.   FRANK BURTON, M. D.
> CONSULTING PHYSICIANS AND SURGEONS.
> A. C. FAIRBAIRN, M. D.   A. H SALISBURY, M. D.
> W. A. JONES, M. D.   J. W. MURRAY, M. D.
> H. H. KIMBALL, M. D.   A. A. AMES, M. D.
> EYE AND EAR SURGEONS.
> C. J. SPRATT, M. D.   FRANK ALLPORT, M. D.
>
> St. Mary's Hospital is delightfully located on the bank of the Mississippi River at 2416 Sixth Street South, adjoining Riverside Park. It was opened for the reception of patients October 1, 1887, since which time nearly 600 patients have been cared for. It has spacious wards and neatly furnished rooms for private patients. Its capacity has been trebled by the erection of additional buildings constructed upon the latest improved sanitary plans.
>
> Its Medical and Surgical Staff is composed of some of the ablest talent of the Northwest.
>
> The unparalleled success which this Hospital has achieved during the past two years is a sufficient guaranty of its popularity and good management.
>
> Holders of National Benefit or Union Hospital Companies' Certificates Admitted.
>
> Terms on application at the Hospital, or address
>
> **SISTER SUPERIOR,**
> St. Mary's Hospital,   MINNEAPOLIS, MINN.
> To reach the Hospital take Riverside Ave Cars to 24th Ave S.

FIGURE 5.2 Advertisement, St. Mary's Hospital, Minneapolis, MN, 1890. (Courtesy Archives of the Congregation of the Sisters of St. Joseph of Carondelet, St. Paul, MN)

mission favored religious sisterhoods, "whom the odour of sanctity might be hoped to preserve from scandal." They were unlike other female nurses who had to be "constantly watched for evidences of favor to individuals and for grounds of scandalous suspicion...."[75] In the same manner, mine owners may have preferred the sexual discipline of Catholic hospitals for their male employees. The rapid changes brought about by mining and railroad expansion had resulted in social turmoil, amoral behaviors, and violence among the workers. Catholic hospitals, owned and managed by religious women, offered a setting where undisciplined behaviors and sexual bantering were at a minimum. This allowed the hospital environment to project a calm and safe aura for patients and hospital staff alike. And patients cognizant of the sisters' self-sacrificial spirituality and distinctive gender identities could find it comforting to place their care into sister-nurses' hands.[76] Thus, not only did nuns' advertisements focus on specific consumers but also on the providers of care—the sisters themselves.

Although it was clear that these were Catholic institutions, they had policies that accepted non-Catholic patients. This was important for successful participation in the medical market. To counter any charges that sisters proselytized, a brochure of St. Mary's Infirmary in Cairo, Illinois, announced, "The religious convictions of patients are not interfered with in any way, nor is preference given to patients of any special nationality or religion."[77] Still, sisters marketed their spirituality in subtle ways, even to non-Catholics. Another Cairo brochure claimed that although sisters did not introduce their religion to patients, they tried to make their lives "an example of purity and Christian duty, in the service of our Master; and to aid and comfort unfortunate and afflicted humanity." This circular was designed to obtain money to defray construction costs to the Cairo hospital. By presenting themselves as motivated by self-denial and self-abnegation, nuns were less likely to be seen as profit-seekers for themselves alone.

And although they directed the ad to the middle and upper classes, they also emphasized that the poor could "find succor here without price."[78] The *Irish Standard*, a Catholic newspaper in Minneapolis, was bolder in its marketing tactic. It directly appealed for money to complete a new addition to St. Mary's by highlighting the exalted spiritual status of nuns: "[W]e hope that all Catholics in the city will see that their names are enrolled among the names of subscribers to this worthy institution. Here is where every Catholic can go when sick and receive the attention of trained nurses and holy women."[79]

Marketing Hospitals as "Sacred Space"

One of the most important reasons sisters raised funds and marketed their hospitals was to provide an institution that included both separate "sacred" space and integrated "holy" activities within the medical space of

FIGURE 5.3 Entrance to Holy Cross Hospital, 1908. (Courtesy Utah State Historical Society, photo # 28542)

the hospital. Catholic architecture itself could mediate religious meanings. Light entering through the windows, the presence of statues, pictures of saints, fonts of holy water, and crucifixes in patients' rooms and hospital corridors all could give one the impression that the building was sacred.[80] (See fig. 5.3.) Reflecting Catholic interests in medieval architecture, Holy Cross Hospital in Salt Lake City was constructed in a Gothic style with steeply pitched gabled roofs and stained-glass windows.

As they modernized their hospitals to accommodate technical advances, sisters also built new hospital chapels. Because sacraments were important, chapels were essential for any Catholic institution that sheltered the sick and dying. Nurses and patients gathered there to offer prayer and find solace. In 1883, a newspaper article described Holy Cross Hospital's chapel as "a perfect gem of its kind."[81] A later brochure described it as a "European Basilica" and a "holy place."[82] Figure 5.5 shows its large stained glass windows, three altars, paintings, and statues. Many chapels were quite large and could seat up to two hundred people.

FIGURE 5.4 Interior, Holy Cross Hospital chapel, early 1920s. (Courtesy Utah State Historical Society, photo # 22852)

Sisters dealt with tensions between medical and sacred space by locating their chapels away from operating rooms and other areas that required more rigorous attention to germ-free environments. Even in sterile operating rooms, however, a patient might find a crucifix on the wall.

Chapels were close to patients' rooms or wards so that those who could not attend personally could have their beds moved into nearby hallways and attend Mass. At St. Mary's, Minneapolis, the chapel's altar could be visible from the hallway on the third-floor south wing. A Catholic bulletin stated, "Secular hospitals and sanatoria may embody in their structure and equipment, even as does St. Mary's, the latest and best ideas of the scientific builder," but only Catholic hospitals had chapels "wherein abides the Author of life and the Hope of those who die.... The spirit that inspired a wise solicitude for soul and mind as well as body in the fifteenth century hospitals, lives still in St. Mary's of the twentieth century."[83]

Nuns also dedicated their hospitals to patron saints so that even the names reflected a religious identity. When the Incarnate Word Sisters purchased the Missouri Pacific Railroad Hospital in Fort Worth, they immediately changed the name to St. Joseph's, the patron of the Catholic Church.[84] They also renovated the building to reflect their Catholicism. A priest blessed each room in the hospital, stables, and outdoor buildings and nailed holy medals to infirmary doors. The motherhouse in San Antonio sent crucifixes, fonts, saints' statues, and water that a priest had blessed. Four stained-glass panels in the chapel windows incorporated several symbols of Christ. Together they conveyed the message that Christ delivered the faithful from sin and death.[85]

Measures of Success

Nuns measured their successes by keeping several sets of statistics: balanced account books, medical and surgical cures, numbers of private and charity patients, and numbers of baptisms. Indeed, financial profitability did not supplant sisters' overriding religious mission. Regardless of whether a patient could pay or not, nuns' work could be "profitable" if they had opportunities to minister to patients' spiritual needs.

Comprehensive financial statements from two hospitals reveal that growth occurred in admissions, money received and expended, and hospital personnel. By including the previous year's surplus with revenues for the current year, financial accounts showed a positive balance that would be available to cover hospital costs for the following year.[86] Table 5.4 shows that, while receipts at Holy Cross Hospital and St. Mary's, Minneapolis, increased between 1905 and 1915, expenses nearly doubled as nuns constructed new buildings, updated their equipment, introduced steam heat, installed telephones, and piped in water.[87]

By 1925, a greater percentage of hospital budgets went to medical and surgical costs. As surgery increased, nuns met the associated rise in costs by charging separately for surgical supplies and operating room, delivery room, and x-ray use, which could comprise as much as 15 percent of all receipts.[88] As in other hospitals, nuns also derived income from special nursing cases, although the system was controversial everywhere since it often involved using student nurse labor. Income from "special nurses" began showing on the 1909 financial statement for St. Mary's Hospital, Minneapolis. By 1915, it accounted for 18 percent of total receipts, although thereafter the percentage diminished over time.[89]

While income from paying patients had always been a condition in Catholic hospitals, by 1900 the proportion of paying patients in hospitals had increased all over the country.[90] The reliance on private, paying

Table 5.4 Annual Accounts, Holy Cross Hospital, Salt Lake City, and St. Mary's Hospital, Minneapolis

	Holy Cross Hospital			St. Mary's Hospital		
	1904	1910	1915	1906	1910	1915
Receipts	$47,172	$54,054	$106,051	$30,186	$52,463	$78,313
Expenses	$40,452	$47,461	$76,787	$28,540	$51,901	$59,191
Balance	$6,720	$6,603	$29,264	$1,646	$562	$19,122

Sources: "Financial Reports, St. Mary's Hospital"; *Quarterly Accounts, Hospital of Holy Cross.*

patients was necessary to meet escalating day-to-day hospital budgets. Whether in small towns or larger cities, other hospitals experienced similar developments.

Nuns' hospitals were part of an enlarged model of social institutions that reflected a Catholic ethos of service. They justified their actions by their religious responsibilities. Hence, they resisted treating hospital care purely as a commodity.[91] As early as 1871, the Sisters of St. Joseph in St. Paul advertised that even though they wanted to make their hospital work a charity, financially "they were utterly unable to do so." Nevertheless, "doing what few would have the courage or self-denial to undertake, the Sisters give their whole time and attention to the sick, and charge only so much for board and medicine as will absolutely cover the cost."[92]

By the first decades of the twentieth century, when commercialization of hospital services had grown, nuns and church leaders felt obligated to defend their charitable images by reminding the public of their service roles. On the one hand, they insisted on the right to sell their health care, but on the other, they defended their responsibility to provide a charitable service and avoid crass materialistic goals. After its formation in 1915, the Catholic Hospital Association became a platform to address this issue. Many of the papers at its national meetings and in its official journal, *Hospital Progress,* reflected this concern. In one paper, a physician noted that the Catholic hospital should always remain "solely a service" rather than becoming a business, although he had few suggestions as to how else to maintain financial viability.[93] Hospital supply companies advertising in *Hospital Progress* used the service rhetoric, as well. One company advertised its "pure nitrous oxide and oxygen gas" to superiors of America's Catholic hospitals by stating, " 'Service' is our middle name. Try it!"[94] For the sisters, service remained paramount. They continued to proclaim that their hospitals existed to provide Christ-like care to all patients, regardless of race, creed, religion, or financial status.

As nuns expanded their clientele after 1900, they assumed larger debts to finance their growing institutions. By this time, an array of backers supported their hospitals: individuals, parishes, business groups, and local governments. It was income from private patients, however, that primarily sustained the institutions and defrayed the expenses of nonpaying patients. One cannot fully comprehend sisters' work, however, without some appreciation of their sacramental roles and their sense of calling. This religious mission drove their entrepreneurship. The next chapter will explore this issue more fully.

Part 3

Religion, Gender, and Autonomy in Catholic Hospitals

6

"Our Heels Are Praying Very Hard All Day":

NURSING IN CATHOLIC HOSPITALS

> The great grace he has received is to be attributed to the intercession of our Lady of Lourdes as the Sisters made novenas for him and we gave him some of the water to drink.[1]
> *Remark Book, Santa Rosa Infirmary*
> January 18, 1898

The Sisters of Charity of the Incarnate Word used this language to explain a miracle of a railroad worker's conversion at their hospital in San Antonio. Catholic teachings emphasized miracles, usually due to intercession of Jesus, Mary, and the saints, that often involved the use of holy water. Stories from the Bible frequently associated water with miraculous healing. To devoted Catholics, not only did holy water have protective and curative powers, it also had sacramental properties that would remind persons of their baptism. In the Catholic imagination, then, water could be a major source of spiritual restoration and protection.[2]

This account of holy water and its use in what was viewed as a miraculous conversion is just one of many examples of how the nuns wove their religious beliefs and practices into their nursing service. A conception of health care that understands it solely in terms of the prevention of suffering, illness, and death would see sister-nurses simply in an auxiliary role of fulfilling a duty of charity. However, the significance of their nursing was much broader because the meanings of suffering, illness, and death were much broader. To comprehend nuns' nursing and hospital establishment in the late nineteenth and early twentieth centuries, it is important to understand the ways in which disease, death, and healing simultaneously were issues of body and spirit. These formulations of meaning lay at the very heart of nuns' hospital establishment and nursing.

An emphasis on religious practice, however, sometimes contrasted sharply with the day-to-day reality of sister-nurses' work. During one particularly hectic week in 1889, the Incarnate Word Sisters at St. Joseph's Infirmary, Fort Worth, admitted nineteen patients, discharged six, transferred one to another room, and cared for twenty-four others, prompting the annalist to remark, "Our heels are praying very hard all day."[3] Thus, while spiritual concerns fueled their nursing, on their stressful hospital wards where they were exposed daily to life-threatening illnesses and emergencies, nuns' nursing dispelled the notion of them as passive praying creatures.

Meaning of Sickness in the Roman Catholic Tradition

Multiple explanations for sickness existed simultaneously for Catholic sisters, including both religious and medical, and there were equally complicated understandings of remedies. The point, here, is not to emphasize the conflicts and tensions between religious and medical missions, but rather to illustrate how Catholic sisters integrated them. Nursing the sick and dying placed nuns in situations that linked the worldly and the divine. It was a means by which sisters could participate in important and dramatic religious experiences, and this conferred on them a special mission.

In the American Catholic tradition of the nineteenth century, no clear distinction existed between the healing effects of secular medicine and the comforts of religion. Both religious and nonreligious explanations prevailed when one became ill. These included a concept of disease as a deviation from normal health, caused and potentially correctable by natural means, but also other perspectives that involved an emphasis on supernatural causes and healing by religious measures. For example, belief in the natural causation of disease associated medicine as part of the natural order. Often, however, natural causes were subsumed under ultimate supernatural causes that only divine intervention could ameliorate.[4]

At this time, recognition of the inevitability of pain and suffering was still part of the American Catholic ethos,[5] although certain tensions prevailed. Caring for the sick could ease suffering, and it was a characteristic demonstration of charity. Yet, suffering was also an invitation to share in Christ's redemptive sufferings. While this did not translate into a view of suffering as good in and of itself, it could advance the glorification of the sufferer and the self-sacrificing caretaker, in whom suffering could awaken compassion and present opportunities to relieve the sufferings of others.

Writings by nineteenth- and early-twentieth-century theologians as well as the nuns reveal the full range of interpretations of illness and suffering. The 1888 *Manual of Decrees and Customs* of the Sisters of St. Joseph of Carondelet recorded a statement on sickness as a guide for sister-nurses. Indicating God's hand in illness, it stated: "God's fatherly providence frequently visits negligent Christians with sickness, in order to lead them back to the fold from which they unfortunately strayed."[6] Similarly, in his 1908 sermon entitled "Sickness a Season of Divine Mercy," James Gibbons, the cardinal archbishop of Baltimore, justified sickness as somehow deserved:

> Seeing that we have not the courage to subject ourselves to voluntary deeds of penance, or even to observe those of the Church, God in His mercy visits us with a remedial penalty of His own selection. This consideration should prompt us to accept ailments and other corporal pains with patience and cheerful resignation.[7]

To Cardinal Gibbons, the best kind of penance was sickness and other afflictions, which God imposed. God might send sickness and suffering to punish an individual's sin or to strengthen one's character and deepen one's faith. How many sick, he asked, "would have exulted in their strength and have plunged like untamed colts into the precipice of vice, if they had not been restrained by the bit and curb of a spell of chastening malady[?]" Illness, in other words, could be an opportunity for spiritual growth. Gibbons described the biblical Job's sufferings as sent to try his faith rather than to punish his sins. God allowed Job to be afflicted with a "loathsome illness, that he might serve as an example to posterity." Indeed, "a sickness visitation is a season of grace, not only to the patients themselves, but to the other members of the family as well." He concluded: "Let these be your sentiments when you are ministering to the sick. The Lord will restore your cherished patient, if it is expedient for his salvation, or if the sickness is unto death he will give you interior grace to bear the cross." Thus, while God could cause illness, God surely could cure it or help one more easily endure it. Significantly, Gibbons emphasized a combination of regular medicine and faith when treating the sick: the physicians' and nurses' ministrations were important and were complementary to God's work. While the doctor's skill should be invoked, one should not overlook the aid of the "Divine Physician."[8]

Spiritual Agents of Care

It followed that Catholic sister-nurses viewed illness not only in biological terms but also within a spiritual framework. The message of priests was to endure suffering as a means of strengthening faith, whereas the sister-nurses placed greater emphasis on alleviating pain and comforting the sufferer. They supplemented their nursing care with prayer cards, icons, and other religious symbols designed to provide comfort and healing. At the same time, by caring, serving, and treating the poor, the sick, and the dying, sister-nurses were involved in important religious experiences. In their hospitals, nuns could do spiritually important work for their patients while obtaining sanctity and grace for themselves.

Because Catholic sisters were committed to the vowed life, part of their formation as nurses included the development of a role that had a strong religious identity. Before they established their own nurse training schools at the turn of the century, nuns received on-the-job instruction in the care of the sick from doctors and experienced nursing sisters. As they gained experience through practice, these women in turn taught nursing tasks to new members. Most communities had a period of training either during or after the novitiate when young sisters trained for their future work. Their convent training included not only nursing education but also instructions on prayer, Mass, and other religious practices.[9]

Several written documents provide insight into the training and nursing practice of Catholic sister-nurses. Constitutions articulated how the sick were to be treated, what daily schedule nurses should follow, how they should relate to physicians, how they were to prepare food and medicines, and most important, by what means the nuns should prepare a person for death. Sisters were to speak softly and to work gently, quietly, and unhurriedly. Most patients until the twentieth century were males, and nuns tried to obtain male nurses to help with them. As far as can be determined from the records, however, there were not enough to make it possible to enforce this rule. Thus, directives also emphasized the need for modesty.[10] Prescriptions also focused on caring and compassion as necessary attitudes for sister-nurses. The Incarnate Word Sisters were to "serve [patients] with a tireless zeal," and entertain for the sick, not only a compassion, kindness and devotedness, but likewise a great respect." The Sisters of the Holy Cross were to be mild, vigilant, patient yet firm, and compassionate for the suffering of others.[11]

For Catholic sisters, nursing itself was a religious discipline. This can be seen in one of the earliest Catholic texts for sister-nurses, a handwritten one from 1796. It is located in the archives of the Midwestern Province of the Daughters of Charity of St. Vincent De Paul and is composed of two parts. In the first section, an anonymous priest in France wrote a catechesis for the religious Hospitallers at the time of the French Revolution. Because priests could not exercise their clerical functions at that time, much of the religious instruction of the sick passed to the Sisters of Charity as nurses. This first section was recirculated in 1841 when Mother Xavier Clark, superior of Elizabeth Seton's Daughters of Charity in the United States from 1839 to 1845, wrote the second part, "Instructions for the Care of the Sick."[12] Nuns could carry the text in their pockets as a supplement to directions of doctors and experienced sister-nurses. At the beginning of her "Instructions," Mother Xavier set the book's spiritual focus: "Our charity must be extended to all; all are the redeemed souls of our Savior."[13]

Mother Xavier taught her nurses to exercise authority and good judgment. The experienced sisters must guide the others; indeed, "they must know everything." This included advising the less experienced nurses when they were not yet skilled enough to care for the sick. Furthermore, the sisters would teach the men who were caring for male patients. While the nuns' model emphasized self-abnegation, deference, and loyalty, the nurse also was to seek knowledge and ask questions. In addition, the sister-nurse was to be decisive. Mother Xavier gave specific instructions for admitting new patients and steps to take if the person required immediate attention, either physically or spiritually.[14]

Nuns were to be concerned with practical nursing care. Mother Xavier reminded her sisters that when they gave patients a drink of water to remember Jesus' thirst while on the cross. She also exhorted them to anticipate the patient's wants without waiting to be asked. They were not to ignore physical problems, indeed were to care for them first, because "the union between the soul and the body is so close that when the latter is suffering a great deal, the other, attentive to its wants, cannot think of anything else." She insisted, "But remember one thing—never begin to speak of religion before you have afforded them all the little relief and comforts you can to the poor body. By these you will find your way to the soul."[15]

Mother Xavier gave detailed instructions on how to give medicines. These included purchasing the best medicines, knowing the correct doses, looking at the label to avoid mistakes, keeping medicines covered to prevent evaporation, and learning the "weights, measures, and the signs" which the doctors used to write prescriptions. If they did not know the signs, or could not read the physician's writing, they should always ask one who knew more than they did. Sisters were to "pay great attention" to vessels in which they mixed or boiled ingredients and never "mix medicines in vessels that have had other remedies in them without first washing them well." Alluding to drug interactions, she taught, "The qualities of a medicine may be destroyed by another and . . . does not produce the desired effect," and might even lead to death of a patient. Furthermore, "Everything ought to be very clean," including the food. "Good and clean water should . . . be used in all the preparations, etc."[16]

Examination of sister-nurses' daily schedules also reveals the integration of religion and nursing in their practice. Nuns began and ended each day with prayer and meditation and had specific times for work, meals, and recreation. Their hospital work followed this same pattern. For example, the 1867 *Rule* for the Sisters of Charity of the Incarnate Word directed sisters to rise at four thirty in the morning and have prayer and spiritual recitations at five. At 5:45 AM, they visited the sick in the dorms, made beds, and distributed drinks, potions, and soup. They attended Mass at six thirty and then ate breakfast at seven thirty. At eight they accompanied physicians on rounds, at which time the head sister wrote their orders in a register. She then gave the register to the pharmacist for the preparation of medicines. At nine o'clock, the sisters served patients breakfast, then performed other religious exercises and ate their own lunch at eleven. They were to go to the chapel for prayers after lunch, have recreation until 1:00 PM, and then do "common tasks." More visits to the wards came in the afternoon, followed by overseeing patients' supper at five o'clock in the evening and eating their own at six. They visited patients again at 6:45 and retired after evening prayer and meditations at 8:25 PM.[17] These tasks changed after 1900, when sister-nurses spent more time with patients, but even then, their spiritual exercises and personal lives continued to mesh deeply with their nursing.

Sisters' nursing practices conveyed a distinct religious vision and were important in a religion such as Catholicism that emphasized ritual. For Catholics, the central rituals were the Mass and sacraments. Thus, nuns often accompanied patients to Mass in hospital chapels. They also incorporated various healing practices associated not only with regular medicine but also with devotions and rituals. These included devotions to the saints and the Virgin Mary who, Catholics believed, had power over disease. During the nineteenth century, the Catholic Church revived other exercises such as the rosary, forty hours devotion, benediction, and devotions to the Sacred Heart and the Immaculate Conception. These devotions were a form of personal piety that especially helped immigrant Catholics who were displaced from their homelands to preserve their faith. Associated with saints were novenas, or nine-day devotions to honor a saint or make a particular request. Relics were particularly popular with Catholics, and nuns used beads, scapulars, medals, prayer books, and holy pictures to heal or at least to lead a suffering person closer to God.[18]

Sister-nurses also promoted elaborate religious ceremonies in their hospitals. The Incarnate Word Sisters and their patients celebrated religious feasts, held forty hours of adoration in chapels, and processed in hallways and on hospital grounds.[19] Nuns faithfully recorded different feast days in their annals. On August 15, 1896, they held a procession through the hospital grounds of Santa Rosa in honor of the Blessed Virgin's Assumption into heaven.[20] Catholic sisters participated in all of these activities in their traditional dress. The hospital's Catholicism was unmistakable.

Prayers for the sick and dying had a long history in the Catholic Church, and references were particularly prominent in nuns' writings. Combined with the sacraments, Catholic belief held that prayer could lead to graces and favors from Jesus and Mary, cures for the sick, and intervention in the course of events. Lay Catholics requested sisters' prayers, believing they were more effective than those by laypeople. In 1897, when death seemed imminent, a patient requested his remaining salary to go to the Incarnate Word Sisters so they would pray for him after death, thereby, according to Catholic belief, releasing his soul from purgatory to rest in heaven.[21] A few months later, family members removed the remains of a woman from one cemetery to another in closer proximity to the Incarnate Word Sisters so they could pray for her.[22]

Given the emphasis the Catholic Church placed on charitable works for personal salvation, nursing became a prominent means by which nuns could satisfy their desires for evangelism. During the Civil War, Mother Angela Gillespie wrote the prominent Catholic Orestes Brownson from the Mound City, Illinois, hospital. She emphasized the important spiritual work that wartime nursing could bring for Catholic nuns. By the time she wrote her letter in 1862, the Sisters of the Holy Cross had baptized 154 dying soldiers in the Mound City hospital. "We have the happiness to think we are recruiting subjects for the Church Triumphant," she wrote. "Should the war continue much longer we may have a full Regiment!"[23]

In their evangelical work, sisters' rules and constitutions provided guidelines. The 1888 *Manual of Decrees* of the Sisters of St. Joseph stated that they were to attend to a patient's bodily wants while being "very solicitous for the welfare of his soul." They were to avoid actively seeking Protestant converts, though, and to respect their religious convictions.[24] Yet, sisters' very work was a powerful form of evangelization. They proselytized by the virtue of their deeds and accomplished conversions in this way. Upon going to Utah in 1875, Sister Augusta Anderson remarked that the best way to do any good with the Mormons was "to have little to say, and give them good example."[25]

The power of "good example" was a strategy sisters frequently used in their nursing and hospital work. Because of their association with immigrants, their distinctive dress, and their unfamiliar belief system, nuns employed various strategies to break down non-Catholics' fears. They based their position on political necessity. Securing capital and community acceptance was crucial to any hospital endeavor. Legitimation was important, since much of the support had to be obtained either in patient fees or donations. Thus, to allay nativist fears of proselytizing, nuns often relied on good deeds rather than sermons. Sometimes, however, proselytizing methods could be subtle. During the Spanish-American War, the Sisters of St. Joseph shared scapulars, crucifixes, medals, and beads with Catholic soldiers. As they did, they were conscious of non-Catholics in nearby beds who were listening to what they said. Thus, Sister Liguori McNamara could write that both Catholic and Protestant soldiers asked for medals.[26] Some non-Catholics requested to join the Catholic Church as they neared death.

Sacramental Power

Hospital work also allowed Catholic sister-nurses an opportunity to be centrally involved in important sacramental occasions that involved sickness and death. The Council of Trent in the sixteenth century set the directions of the Catholic approach to health care in the nineteenth century. To counter Martin Luther's doctrine of justification by faith alone, the bishops at Trent reaffirmed that both faith and charity through good works brought salvation.[27] Most important for sisters, bishops affirmed the sacramental principle and its corollary, mediation. According to the sacramental principle, signs manifested in rituals and symbols can mediate God's presence to humans. These visible channels of God's grace can be natural, such as the world itself as God's creation, and the more formal sacraments, all of which signify God's reality.[28]

Spanning three centuries, these strands of belief required accommodation to new circumstances. Still, any accommodations were viewed through the lens of the Catholic faith. A problem for sister-nurses was that only male priests could administer the formal sacraments. On the other hand, Trent had insisted upon a wider view of the sacramental principle by linking sacramentality with every aspect of a Christian's life.[29] Any ritual, object, person, or place could be "sacramental" if it represented something that was sacred, even mysterious. Thus, nursing took on new meaning for sisters. Sickness and dying could be sacramental experiences in which the body could be an important way for contact with the divine. Nuns' comforting, feeding, and sheltering the sick and dying, and their whispers of consoling prayers to the patient in pain or near death functioned as invitations to religious experiences and means for patients to meet God. God could also be encountered through created, finite things. Churches, temples, and even hospitals could be sacred places. Pictures, statues, religious garb, or food may be hallowed objects. Sacred persons could be priests, kings, gurus, and virgins. Indeed, there could be a sense of sacred importance and power in these places, persons, and things, because they pointed to something transcendent, "something beyond themselves."[30] Thus, Catholic hospitals were key centers of ritual, hope, and reconciliation and represented "sacramentally" the presence of Christ.[31] In this way, even though nuns' nursing tasks did not require ordination, they served as an independent means for women to acquire sacramental authority. Sister-nurses could strengthen the sick or dying person's soul and help him or her more easily bear illness and resist temptations. In the process, the nuns could be mediators to God.[32]

THE HOUR OF DEATH

The care of patients at the time of death was particularly significant for its sacramental potential. Notwithstanding prevailing attitudes that a good death was one that occurred at home, late-nineteenth-century Catholic writers asserted that a Catholic hospital was the best place for Catholics to die. Patients could receive not only physical care based on modern technology but also the sacraments that the church sanctioned, and nuns would be present to see that important deathbed rituals were carried out. Catholic theology held that grace, which the sacraments conferred, could save the soul of the dying. Thus, to die in a state of grace, it was absolutely necessary for a person to have opportunities to make a last confession and receive the sacraments. In his sermon on sickness, Cardinal Gibbons focused on the sacramental role of Catholic hospitals: "Rarely, indeed, do any patients die in these institutions without being chastened by repentance and fortified by the grace of the Sacraments, especially when their sickness is prolonged."[33]

Sister-nurses' notations confirm that they hoped to restore patients to physical health but also to help them with a "good death." As an example, the booklet written in 1796 instructed the Daughters of Charity to fulfill three duties with their patients regarding their souls: "to instruct them; to prep them gently and prudently towards their conversion; and lastly to help them to die well."[34] A history of the Sisters of Charity of the Incarnate Word recorded that their hospitals had a long record "of frequent restorations to health, and of beautiful and edifying deaths."[35]

While sisters were to follow the doctor's orders for medications and physical care, they also were to assist the sick and dying in their spiritual maladies by exhorting them to penance, resignation, and prayer. Mother Xavier Clark had joined the Daughters of Charity after her husband and son died; thus, she had early experience in the care of the dying. In her "Instructions to the Care of the Sick," she wrote that the sister-nurse must do all she could to help the dying patient "in this last dreadful moment" because "it is the time for the enemy of salvation to use all his power" to entrap and "tempt the soul he sees so near the gates of heaven." The drama of the sickroom scene and the sister-nurse's important role with the dying were such that she devoted an entire chapter to ministrations for the dying. Sister-nurses were to strive to bring their patients into a state of grace and prepare them to make a good confession. While nuns were to offer silent prayers for a deathbed conversion of Protestant patients, the nurses had detailed instructions and prayers for Catholics.[36]

Typical of many religious communities, the Incarnate Word Sisters' 1885 constitution emphasized that, in caring for the sick, sisters especially were to "induce those who are in danger to receive the last sacraments, and to prepare worthily for that great action." Similar instructions continued well into the twentieth century.[37] To nuns, death did not mean *losing* a patient. Indeed, they considered it a "great grace" that a person died after having been baptized. To lose a patient, to sisters, meant they could not reclaim the person's soul. In 1896, the Incarnate Word nuns wrote of a patient in their hospital: "We regretted to see him die a Free Mason, but could not do good for his soul."[38] It appears, then that some patients did not accept nuns' ministrations. Other patients may have reluctantly resigned themselves to them. In 1896, one sister-nurse wrote, "The poor man was brought back to the right path in a few days." By then, "He was well prepared to die."[39]

The supernatural drama of dying was such that nuns had to be acclimated to the event. When the Sisters of St. Joseph first took over a hospital in Philadelphia in 1849, Mother St. John Fournier described the fear the nuns experienced: "Our sisters were so afraid of the dying that I had to stay with them during the night.... Little by little these poor children got accustomed to working for the sick and dying."[40]

Because sister-nurses were at the bedside during critical moments, they were the first to notify priests to perform the sacraments of baptism, penance, and extreme unction. Baptism was particularly important in a hospital, since Catholics believed that if a person died without it, he or she could not be saved. When priests were unavailable, nuns baptized dying patients. Manuals on nursing and pastoral medicine gave explicit instructions on procedures to follow, including where to place the hands, what words to say, and how much water to pour.[41]

Preserving the body at death also was an important role for Catholic sister-nurses. Incarnate Word Sisters frequently held wakes in their parlor at Santa Rosa, and they kept a "dead house" behind the hospital where they held bodies of the deceased until relatives arrived.[42] Families often requested sisters to attend to burial services, and nuns made funeral arrangements and paid for expenses. A stark contrast can be seen here between hospitals where the body of a deceased working-class patient died with dignity and the public hospital where the body was conceived as a source of cadavers for dissection. Rather than experiencing the fear and apprehension accompanying expectations of dying in a public facility, lay Catholics could trust sisters to dispose of the corpse in a respectful way.[43]

Congregations often kept statistics of successes with baptisms and "good deaths," mainly for the community's motherhouse. Indeed, a major goal of their nineteenth- and early-twentieth-century hospital work was to save souls, either through baptism or reclaiming lost Catholics to the church.[44] In productivity terms, the number of baptisms was not large. Many lapsed Catholics did come back to the church's fold, however, and sisters took great pride in these spiritual successes. One annalist exulted, "How grateful we ought to be to God for the great grace of redeeming a soul out of the snares of the devil."[45] In later years, sisters at St. Mary's Infirmary, Cairo, were especially fruitful. In 1925, they recorded eighty-five deaths, sixty of whom were baptized, and fifteen who received the last sacraments.[46] By far the majority of patients at the hospital that year were not Catholic. Even if the nuns kept to their prescriptions against proselytizing, it appears that at times they ensured that practices distinct to Catholicism were carried out.

Sisters inherited a multivalent set of significances of Christian responses to death. Early Christians viewed death as a time of great joy as well as grief.[47] Death also brought an enormous sense of vulnerability, since it was a time when heaven seemed most accessible. As Philippe Aries points out in his magisterial survey, however, Christian responses to death varied with time and place. During the Reformation and Counter Reformation, both Protestant and Catholic martyrs went joyfully to their deaths and powerfully influenced others. On the other hand, French texts and artwork between the twelfth and fifteenth centuries reveal a representation of the torments of hell and a fear of what lay beyond death. For Europeans terrified by the plague, opportunities for confession and the benefits of the Eucharist gave increasing importance to the deathbed scene, where one's fate could be decided for the last time. Death was the moment when the individual could gain or lose all. One's existence for all eternity would be determined at that time, and hence, it was the decisive moment in a person's life.[48]

Nuns were working in a heritage where all these ideas were present. The sickbed became the "arena of a drama" in which the dying person's fate could be decided for the last time. Thus, deathbed conversions and preparation for eternity were immensely important.[49] Nineteenth-century sermons directed that death would bring "rest after the hardships of the day." At the same time, a sermon entitled "The Last Judgment" taught of a vengeful God that would separate the just from the unjust. It described that terrible moment: "Oh fearful moment, when wilt thou arrive? O unhappy moment! Perhaps in a few days from now we may observe the harbingers of this, for sinners, so terrible a day of judgment."[50] Thus, to nuns who firmly believed in life beyond the grave, death was a momentous and even risky time. Mediators of this critical event could be very powerful. Indeed, in their hospitals, nuns found a place to exercise power at a crucial moment. Through their role in deathbed conversions, nursing became a priceless opportunity for sisters to further God's kingdom.[51]

There is certainly a tension, even a paradox, about the sacramental role of hospitals that requires some comment. Hospitals were and still are, to a degree, places of death and, hence, places of spiritually important work for Catholic sisters. It should not be thought, however, that sisters intended their patients to die or that they failed to provide them the best care they could. However, given the kinds of conditions hospitals treated and the limited means of medical intervention available, until quite recently they were places of death, not intentionally but inevitably. Sisters' involvement with health-care institutions in the late nineteenth and early twentieth centuries must be understood in relation to hospitals as they were and not in light of what they have become, with much more powerful possibilities for medical intervention. Furthermore, while in the past, death was a highly public event that had major significance for the person, family, community, and caretakers, currently death typically takes place among strangers. It is accompanied by secular practices involving professional caretakers who extensively employ drugs and other treatments.[52] In the late nineteenth and early twentieth centuries, however, sister-nurses dealt with death in ways that are no longer the case in the twenty-first-century hospital.

In sum, nuns considered the welfare of patients not only in terms of the present but also with a view to eternity. In their view, because the body was only a temporary dwelling place of the soul and the soul was immortal, it must be saved. If physical death was the access to eternal life, so too the sickness that led to it. Pain and suffering had special meaning and purpose. Sometimes they were necessary, not only for the natural welfare of men or women but also for the supernatural welfare of their souls. Suffering could be a means of redemption. Whereas in health one might be indifferent to religious practices, when sick he or she might be more receptive to renew the faith. Through physical distress, one might find his or her way back to the church, and this renewal would affirm sisters' ministry.

OTHER NURSING PRACTICES

In addition to battling for souls, records make it clear that nuns' concerns for making their patients well were characteristic elements of their nursing. The *Manual of Decrees* for the Sisters of St. Joseph prescribed practical nursing tips: "She tries to be exact in carrying out the directions with regard to the remedies ordered, either by the physician or by Superiors, and does not, except by the doctor's advice, give any but ordinary remedies."[53] Likewise, the Sisters of Charity of the Incarnate Word were to heed physicians' orders for medicines, hygiene, "and everything connected with the purely bodily alleviation of the sick."[54] By the latter decades of the nineteenth century, sister-nurses were taking temperatures, pulses, and respirations; preparing and applying dressings; and using hot and cold body packs for fever cases. They administered laudanum (opium in its liquid form), ointments, and poultices for pain relief. Like secular nurses, sisters' nursing care involved comfort measures and assistance with feeding and personal hygiene. Nurses bathed patients, changed their linen, gave medications, and prepared and administered food for special diets. They kept the sickroom clean and well ventilated, protected the patient against contagious diseases, and prepared corpses. They also observed patients for signs and symptoms of disease and its complications, recorded these in the clinical record, and reported them to the physician.[55]

Nuns typically worked a seven-day week, including night shifts, and usually lived in the hospital itself. One physician who had worked with the Sisters of Charity of the Incarnate Word recalled: "The sisters worked fifteen hours a day and often slept just where they found a place. They worked too hard—too many died too young."[56] As more severely ill patients came to hospitals in the late nineteenth century, nuns had to deal with more time-consuming procedures, leaving them less time to perform religious exercises.

In hospitals for miners and railroad workers, patients with lead poisoning and typhoid fever were numerous. Lead poisoning reflected the poor working conditions in the mines, while typhoid fever showed the unsanitary conditions in mining and railroad camps.[57] These hospitals also became centers for the treatment of traumatic injuries, and sisters handled frequent emergencies. Besides sustaining injuries from personal violence, men fell from mining shafts, were crushed by boulders or large equipment, or injured from exploding gunpowder. Many had suffered burns, head injuries, and broken limbs and backs.[58] Accidents among ranchers also were frequent. Sisters ran their own ambulance services (fig. 6.1), and in later years, interns accompanied attendants so they could provide immediate emergency care.

Nuns' discipline helped them manage sudden influxes of large numbers of patients. In 1890, the Incarnate Word Sisters often received up to six new patients a day, including those with throat injuries, fractured backs, and knife wounds to the head. On October 18, 1895, the nuns at Santa Rosa Infirmary admitted a twenty-month-old child who had a pecan shell in his larynx. And during one week in 1897, sisters admitted a stabbing victim and four badly burned patients.[59]

Nuns' nursing was not without risk of physical violence. They frequently had to deal with patients who were victims of assault or who were going through withdrawal delirium from alcohol abuse. Late in the nineteenth century, neighbors of Holy Cross Hospital in Salt Lake City complained about the inability of the sisters to manage their patients, prompting the physicians to come to the nuns' aid in the newspapers. Sometimes sisters had to go after patients who had run away from the hospital. Occasionally, when patients were extremely violent or suicidal, nuns resorted to the use of protective beds or even straitjackets.[60] In the United States,

FIGURE 6.1 Horse-drawn ambulance, St. Joseph's Infirmary, Fort Worth, TX, undated. (Courtesy Archives, Motherhouse of the Incarnate Word, San Antonio, TX)

views at the end of the nineteenth century supported moderate use of restraints because it prevented accidents and injuries, and the "peculiar violence" of American insanity required it.[61] At times, sisters provided private nursing to those at risk of violence to themselves or others. In September 1889 at St. Joseph's, Fort Worth, a sister had an especially rough night when she admitted a man who threatened to kill both her and his wife. Driven by hallucinations or delusional fears, this patient received close observation throughout the week.[62]

Besides the routine daily care of patients, a typical week in the 1880s and 1890s saw nuns assisting with surgeries, tending to visitors, handling finances, negotiating hospital charges, and admitting and discharging patients. On January 16, 1892, a physician telephoned St. Joseph's Infirmary in Fort Worth at 5:00 PM. He wanted the sisters to have everything ready within the hour for an emergency operation for a skull fracture. After doctor, nurses, and equipment were in place, the annalist noted that "the patient never showed up." Yet, two weeks later, the sister-nurses did assist in an actual emergency that required an operation for a skull fracture. In one forty-eight-hour period in 1896, sister-nurses at Santa Rosa had to chase a delirious person who left the hospital with only a shirt on his back, tend to a patient with a high fever and convulsions, nurse a postoperative person with cancer, and provide emergency care for one who hemorrhaged.[63] Flexible constitutions certainly helped, since sisters' activities often broke with rules about caring for male patients. While male orderlies assisted the nuns with violent patients, records indicate that the turnover of male nurses was high.

Knowledge of signs and symptoms of complications was essential, and sisters learned to respond quickly to emergencies such as hemorrhage or suffocation. The following example shows how sister-nurses relied on a combination of regular medicine and faith. On June 10, 1889, a patient at St. Joseph's Infirmary in Fort Worth began hemorrhaging early one morning, prompting the Incarnate Word Sisters immediately to telephone the attending physicians. Unable to locate anyone, the nuns tried several remedies, but none stopped the bleeding. At last they reached one doctor who ordered interventions they had already tried. Eventually the bleeding stopped, but not before the nuns spent several anxious hours observing and praying for the patient.[64] As this example shows, the sister-nurses performed emergency measures first, called the physician, and then tried other remedies. Equally important, while they waited for the doctor, they prayed.

Criticisms of Nuns' Nursing

Although secular nursing leaders and physicians admired sisters for their devotion and the amount of time they spent in hospitals, some groups criticized them, for several reasons. According to some, nuns' "misplaced" religious behaviors and beliefs—such as the body as an occasion for sin, or suffering as a route to spiritual salvation—threatened proper care for patients. Florence Nightingale disparaged religious nursing orders that aimed "always, more or less, to prepare the sick for death," compared to the secular nurse, whose goal was "to restore them for life." Charging that the nuns neglected their patients' general conditions, she accused them of allowing a patient to "die of a bedsore, because the nurse may spread the dressing for it, but must not look at it." At night, they left the wards "in sole charge of subordinates."[65] Reflecting her concerns, she wrote her father, William Nightingale, that being "concerned with one's own salvation was like being concerned with one's own dinner."[66] One must be cautious about making simple generalizations, however, when discussing a group as heterogeneous as the nursing sisters. Nightingale's criticisms applied to particular European groups. She greatly admired the Irish Sisters of Charity, and her ally and friend during the Crimean War was a Sister of Mercy.[67]

Others disparaged outdated nursing practices and constitutions of Catholic women's nursing orders. In 1895, Thomas Dwight, a physician and Catholic convert, asserted that nuns were not doing the best nursing. Sisters' hospitals "may have been the best places for a Catholic to die in; [but] they were not the best for him to get well in."[68] These critics were correct that preparing patients for death was important to nuns. However, sisters also carried out medical orders, gave emergency care, and tried to make their patients well. Catholic sister-nurses did not see any contradiction in healing as spiritual and as somatic, and they performed measures for both.

As they interacted with European immigrants and American-born patients in hospitals, army camps, and homes, sisters were both caretakers and missionaries. Yet, conflict sometimes developed between nuns and their patients. As in secular hospitals, sisters served meals at certain times; had specific visiting hours and times to go to bed and to awaken; and routines for hygiene. They viewed discipline as necessary to enforce appropriate behavior, but to some patients the discipline appeared oppressive. Historians of the post-Foucault era have emphasized hospitals as sites of control.[69] Yet, this literature loses sight of the function of hospitals as institutions of care. Care and control could necessarily be bound together: to provide care was to take control of patients' well-being physically, psychologically, and spiritually when they could not care for themselves in their homes. Ultimately, then, control and care were not clearly distinct.

This could especially be evident when care was understood to include spiritual sustenance. Priests brought the sacraments to sick patients for religious succor, but nursing sisters cared for and consoled the sick and dying day after day. It is unknown how patients reacted to the dying experience, whether readily accepting death or bitterly resenting it. It is also unknown if nuns forced their patients to accept death. While the evangelical nature of their work may have offended some patients, it is possible that religion appealed to those who knew they were about to die and render an account of their lives. While it may have been an appeal based on fear, a return to the Catholic Church or conversion to the faith could also satisfy a need to find meaning to one's existence. For some, hearing Mass was important as a means to receive the Holy Eucharist. For others, religious practices and the care by nuns in Catholic hospitals could satisfy a need for encountering the sacred, participating in healing mysteries, or finding hope for eternal life.[70]

Catholic Nursing: Skillful and Evangelical

As they cared for the poor, nuns did not engage in public discussions about the causes of poverty. Their emphasis was on improving the individual.[71] They remained socially active in their local communities, although they were not gainfully employed as visiting nurses in city slums.[72] The Sisters of Charity of the Incarnate Word could visit the sick in their homes, if necessary, but their constitutions forbade them from earning money from this type of nursing. In 1890 in Fort Worth, a physician asked the sisters to accompany him to the home of a patient who needed emergency surgery. A nun gave chloroform while the physician operated.[73] The Sisters of St. Joseph could visit the sick and imprisoned as part of their broad service ministry. Nuns had been working with the poor in inner cities long before secular women reformers established settlement houses. During epidemics, sisters had gone into the streets, lanes, and alleys carrying food baskets and medicine that were necessary for health restoration. Since the middle of the nineteenth century, they had established orphanages, Sunday schools, free schools for the poor, hospitals, and homes for dependent girls and women accused of prostitution.[74]

In all these cases, through their nursing, prayers, and devotions, nuns tried to make certain that no one would be denied physical or spiritual care. As they administered laudanum for pain relief, they also said rosaries, made novenas, accompanied patients to Mass in their chapels, and maintained hospital shrines. Thus, they conveyed an alternative to official medicine and church doctrine. Sisters had confidence that healings would occur. Indeed, their practices contrasted sharply with the Catholic devotional ethos that emphasized enduring suffering and pain. Nuns' practices also were subtly resistant to the authority of male physicians and their narrowly focused medical goals.[75]

Sisters were extremely sensitive to criticism of their hospitals and their nursing, and they firmly believed they were providing a valuable and needed service in ways other women could not. In their hospitals, sister-nurses had enormous potential to blend spiritual and somatic healing. They used their authority to effect changes not only in physical health but also in attitudes and behaviors through provision of religious instruction and guidance. Nuns also had an opportunity to claim authority over the living and the dying. At the moment of death, when the carnal intersected with the spiritual, and the finite became the eternal, the sister-nurses' roles in this transition epitomized their religious purpose and identity.

The gendered emphasis on obedience and reverent devotion and the romantic construction of pain and suffering often contrasted sharply with the realities of everyday work. Just as important, physicians had confidence in the sisters' competence. When the Incarnate Word Sisters encountered a hemorrhaging patient, they did not hesitate to take the appropriate steps, which the doctor's orders later affirmed. When a physician called them quickly to prepare the operating room for emergency surgery, he knew he could trust them to do so. Furthermore, nuns were "in charge" of both secular and religious nurses. And in the eyes of the laity, sisters had the power to effect change through their prayers. Most important, nuns' very presence could be a sign to others of a dimension beyond the visible world of everyday experiences.

7

Power Sharing:

BUSINESS NEGOTIATIONS IN CATHOLIC HOSPITALS

> [These] devoted creatures in the Catholic Church [could be seen] leaning over the bed of the suffering, wiping away the sweat of death from the pale forehead of the dying man, soothing his declining moments... alleviating his sufferings in life... all these acts performed for no earthly reward, but through love of humanity....[1]
>
> Bishop Lawrence Scanlan
> October 12, 1876

As Bishop Scanlan described the Sisters of the Holy Cross after they opened Holy Cross Hospital in Salt Lake City, he reflected the clergy's typical perceptions of sister-nurses. Such idealized sentimentality was characteristic of the clerical need for the "cult of true womanhood."[2] However, Catholic sisters who stood at the threshold of establishing and operating hospitals in the growing competitive market of the late nineteenth century challenged prescribed gender roles. Much more was required of them than mere acquiescence to self-sacrificial feminine service.

One of the defining characteristics of the Catholic hospital in the late nineteenth and early twentieth centuries was the way religious, economic, and social boundaries altered the authority within Catholic hospitals run by women religious. Nuns maintained a unique hierarchy over their hospitals' administrative and nursing affairs, but at the same time they had to use certain diplomatic strategies when working with medical and episcopal authorities. They also had to deal with the romanticized images assigned to them that emphasized their feminine spirituality while obscuring their technical and professional skills.

This chapter will focus mainly on sister-administrators, or superiors. The average sister did not have the individual authority that the mother superior had because each gave up individual power to the congregation's good as a whole. In this chapter, power is treated in its material forms but also as a means of fashioning identities and behaviors. Nuns' actions reflect a complex relationship between power and manners. While superiors often negotiated through tensions by confrontation and resistance, at other times they openly embraced assigned roles of meekness and deferential service. This removed the visible trappings of power and influence and reduced their threat to the bastions of male power. Ironically, it also enabled sisters to move with skill and purpose in fulfilling their service missions.

Relations with Physicians

Although sister-administrators appointed the hospital's physicians and exercised inherent power within that role, nevertheless they had to remain cognizant of their identities as females and religious servants. They could not afford to openly challenge the prerequisite authority of the doctors. Indeed, nuns were very aware of their need for public association with physicians, whose social prestige was already accepted and on whom sisters relied for patients. In turn, the doctors, many of whom were Protestant, remained keenly aware of their indebtedness to the sisters for their employment within the Catholic hospitals. Thus, when conflicts arose, both sides were more likely to compromise than to engage in lengthy or contentious struggles.[3]

From the beginning, nuns deferred to physicians in medical matters. The first advertisement by the Sisters of Charity of the Incarnate Word for Santa Rosa Hospital in San Antonio promised physicians that they would "have the entire control over [patients] in the Hospital; and his prescriptions with regard to food, nursing, and medicines, will be strictly followed."[4] The 1867 constitution prescribed that, in working with the doctor, sister-nurses "will take care not to control his prescriptions or find fault with his manner of acting."[5] In their annual reports, nuns always credited physicians' roles in the hospital's success. A report from Santa

Rosa Infirmary was typical: "We could not have a hospital without our doctors. ALL HAIL TO OUR DEVOTED DOCTORS!"[6]

Sisters also generally respected physicians' professional freedom. One doctor recalled that, at Santa Rosa Infirmary, whether they were engaging in new surgical techniques or trying out suggestions by other surgeons, "our efforts never met discouragement or insurmountable opposition from the officials at Santa Rosa." Had the physicians encountered outright refusal or even words of caution at every turn, they believed their effectiveness as surgeons would have deteriorated. He described the ideal relationship between a physician and hospital as "one which not only allows freedom to innovate, but freedom not to do so, the option of rejecting change if its institution represents no improvement. To our lasting benefit and that of the community which we served, Santa Rosa offered this freedom."[7]

Yet, because Catholic hospitals were both medical and religious institutions, a tension developed between medical men and women religious who were the hospital administrators. Each group expected to have power, and conflict between the two groups inevitably flared from time to time. Gender and religion often were determining factors in these internal struggles. Although their nursing fit in well with the developing role of woman as domestic caretaker, in their hospitals sisters also took on administrative jobs that men traditionally held. In these positions nuns had unusual authority, a quality typically considered "masculine." On October 27, 1903, at Sister Lidwina Butler's expressed wish, members of the Holy Cross Hospital medical staff held their first formal meeting. While doctors wanted more control in making decisions that were in their own best interests, they were not always able to get it. Their records repeatedly document them merely "seconding" and "advising" the superior, in this case, Sister Lidwina. In one case, the physicians noted that "as things are now we could only express a wish, which doesn't amount to much in practical results." Nevertheless, the physicians devised a constitution that spelled out ideas for their own organization. They had to submit it to Sister Lidwina "in order to determine what and how much she would approve, that we might act in accordance with her desire."[8] The physicians reflected their circumscribed position, however, when they stated, "We might as well burn it."[9]

This relationship between sister-administrators and physicians was unusual. By 1910, American medicine had made large strides toward increasing its social power. In large teaching hospitals such as Johns Hopkins, physicians managed the hospital budgets and subsumed nursing school finances under their own control. In other hospitals, male boards of trustees handled detailed operations and judged which patients were worthy of admission. As charity hospitals transformed into medical institutions and financial problems increased, trustees sought men with backgrounds in business and in medicine for administrative roles.[10]

By contrast, nuns exerted a greater degree of authority as they developed and administered comprehensive medical institutions. They did not primarily rely on charitable contributions for funding, and donors and subscribers did not have a say in management. Furthermore, nuns could balance the increasing power of medicine through an alternative source of spiritual power. As "brides" of Christ and representatives of the Catholic Church, nuns had their own special status, and no layman could rival it.[11] Catholic tradition was the basis upon which sisters claimed legitimacy, and they had the support of the Catholic Church behind their endeavors.[12] One cross-national study of secular and religious medical settings recognized the special status that nuns had in Catholic hospitals. Sisters' supernatural frame of reference, based on their religious vocations and church affiliations, gave them a distinct charisma. Only the senior doctors' medical charisma could match the nuns' religious charisma. Thus, the only laymen whose authority the nuns recognized were the medical staff.[13]

Sisters modeled their hospital organization on the hierarchical structure of the Catholic Church. A superior led the hospital sisters, and she had control over the management and direction of the facility. While nuns yielded medical authority to physicians, their constitutions stated that sister-nurses were to obey the authority of the sister-administrator in everything "temporal" and were not to submit to anyone, doctor or others, who disregarded their rules.[14] Sisters served as hospital trustees, nursing supervisors, and heads of different floors and hospital departments. (See fig. 7.1.)

The superintendent of the nurse training school usually was a member of the religious community, as well. Sister-nurses also rarely worked under secular nurses. Nuns expected secular employees to obey the sisters and sometimes discharged them if they did not follow the nuns' directions. In the hospital, all reported directly to the superior.

Relations between doctors and nuns differed in another way. Physicians were not deeply involved in the establishment of Catholic hospitals, and nuns' status as owners could not be forgotten. The sisters' hospital corporations held overall authority and responsibility for policy formation and operation decisions. Through their board presence, the nuns formulated philosophies and missions and protected the hospitals' assets. The superior of each individual hospital exercised close control over equipment purchases, nursing assignments, applications for admission to the attending staff, and admission and billing procedures.

FIGURE 7.1 Nursing staff of Holy Cross Hospital, Salt Lake City, UT, approximately 1883. (Courtesy Utah Historical Society, photo # 19836)

With a different perspective, Bayard Holmes, a Chicago physician writing in a medical journal in 1906, illustrated the unusual relationship that members of a religious order had with doctors. Specifically, Catholic hospitals could give physicians opportunities to obtain patients for their practice. Holmes acknowledged that "the interest of the religious sect or solidarity by which the hospital is organized makes each member of that association or body far and near a crier and drummer for their hospital," and only incidentally for staff members. Yet many patients of the same religion were drawn there. Hence, "[t]o have a fervid religious sect, with a substantial, numerous and loyal hierarchy behind his hospital to sanctify it and fill it with devotees" was "worth more to a physician and surgeon than six columns a week" of blatant advertising in newspapers.[15]

Sister-administrators also had unusual relations with medical interns, who typically were subordinate to both the superior and the medical staff. The superior and Intern Committee made interns' schedules and assignments in the various departments. But because many of the senior medical staff visited hospitals only a few hours each week, specific rules for interns gave considerable authority to the superior as superintendent. Once interns arrived, they had to follow regulations similar to those for student nurses. In this way, sister-administrators and physicians hoped to impose order and control over interns' behavior. Rules at St. Joseph's Hospital, St. Paul, advised interns to maintain tidiness and order in their quarters and refrain from loud talking. They were expected to observe the "strictest decorum and the utmost courtesy to the nurses on duty."[16] Interns could smoke only in their quarters, could not play musical instruments or radios after 10:00 PM, and had to eat at specific times. Rules strictly forbade the use of alcohol, and interns found with it in their possession or who appeared at the hospital under its influence were subject to dismissal upon the superintendent's complaint to the medical board. Interns could not professionally treat hospital employees unless requested to do so by the hospital authorities, including the superior or her representative. At St. Mary's, Minneapolis, interns could not remain outside the hospital after 11:00 PM without the superior's consent, and they had to accept her surveillance of their rooms.[17]

The superior and physicians at St. Mary's held that interns needed careful supervision in their relationships with patients as well. Reflecting the view of patients as recipients of Christian charity, rules directed interns to remember "that those placed professionally under their care are sick and helpless and thus especially objects of compassion. They are, in voice and manner to treat them as they would wish to be treated themselves, were the positions reversed."[18] Interns were to report any insubordination or violation of rules promptly to the superior and communicate with her about all matters affecting the welfare of the hospital and its patients. Understandably, interns had ambivalent relationships with superiors. While they held them in awe, they also feared them. One would hide in an elevator when a superior came on the floor.[19] The daily routines, discipline, decorum, and maintenance of order reflected the sisters' own convent training and indicated how important order and personal behavior were to the hospital environment. They also showed the respect that sisters expected, both for patients and for themselves.

Hospital Control

Nuns reserved the right to make executive decisions. At administrative meetings, sister-administrators and board members discussed business transactions, weekly expenses and receipts, and the hiring and firing of personnel.[20] With doctors' potential for power growing due to their increased numbers, however, conflicts sometimes occurred between them and the nuns over hospital policies and staff. As owners and administrators, nuns held a measure of control over staff appointments. In the early twentieth century at Holy Cross Hospital, the superior first received the applications, after which physicians reviewed the applicants' qualifications. Doctors then made recommendations to the superior, who had the final authority to accept or reject their decision.[21] Both groups usually agreed, but the superior did not always approve the doctors' choices. She controlled not only the hiring but also the firing of physicians. In 1909, the members of the Holy Cross Hospital medical staff were displeased over a pictorial history of the hospital that a physician had issued. Apparently he failed to mention the doctors. They requested that Sister Lidwina ask him to resign, which she refused to do.[22]

Conflict also occurred over hospital privileges and open staffing policies. The Catholic hospitals did not restrict physician privileges to an elite group. Rather, by the turn of the century, most allowed "open-staffing" patterns that involved unrestricted use of the facility by any qualified doctor. On their part, nuns were pragmatic about allowing qualified physicians to practice. Sisters' religious missions impelled them to grow in terms of numbers of patients served. Furthermore, they always felt the need to increase income. One way of meeting both imperatives was to increase the number of physicians whose patients could help fill hospital beds.

An editor of a national magazine noted that the move toward open staffing indicated in "which direction the current is moving. . . . Experience has proved conclusively that 'the open door' to the hospital is a benefit, not only to the rank and file of doctors, but to the hospital. It pays in dollars and cents." In 1909, a hospital administration guide stated, "If the staff had large and profitable practices, then a sufficient amount of money can easily be realized to defray the entire running expenses of the institution, supplying the care not only for the private patients, but also for the charity inmates."[23] Likely, this compelling argument tapped sisters' entrepreneurial interests and influenced their decisions to open up the staff.

At the same time, hospitals were becoming essential to a doctor's successful practice. Not only did hospitals provide access to patients but also to the x-ray, laboratory, and surgical equipment necessary for diagnosis and treatment. For various reasons, many doctors preferred closed staffing policies that restricted the institution to certain physicians. Those in closed facilities could treat greater numbers of patients than their colleagues and competitors in other hospitals. Often this meant excluding African American, foreign-born, Catholic, and Jewish doctors.[24] In 1903 and again in 1904, doctors at Holy Cross Hospital criticized the open-staffing method, arguing that it led to disorganization, inefficiency, deficient record-keeping, and poor patient care. Staff regulations did not bind doctors who were not members of the staff, and members feared they would have no effective means of holding the other doctors to the same standards.[25] Likewise, a 1913 editorial in *Hospital World* argued, "[T]he open hospital sees many tragedies, trains internes and nurses badly, secures poor records and is lamentably deficient in its contributions to medical science."[26] Whether nuns allowed open staffing specifically to help doctors from different ethnic, racial, or religious backgrounds is unclear. Significantly, they did not restrict their medical staffs to Catholic physicians. Because Catholic hospitals did not function primarily to distinguish among doctors, perhaps open-staffing decisions were easier for nuns to make.

Concern over open-staffing policies rose in several hospitals, but sisters generally held their ground on the issue when pushed. In 1900, the doctors at St. Joseph's Infirmary, Fort Worth, proposed to limit the number of physicians joining the staff, but Mother St. Madeleine Chollet took a firm stand. She wrote Dr. W. A. Adams, one of a group of doctors who had issued circulars describing themselves as "Surgeons in Charge." She objected to this seeming exclusivity. She began in a tone of respect and humility: "We sincerely hope that you and your esteemed partner, may honor St. Joseph's with your patronage and that, on your part, dear Doctor, our relations may be as amicable as they were in the past."[27] She then proceeded to reaffirm their policy of opening St. Joseph's to all doctors, as they did at Santa Rosa Infirmary in San Antonio. In a letter to two other physicians involved in the incident, Doctors Thompson and Saunders, she used a similar style:

> With regard to the proposed changes, we must keep to our determination to let the public understand that St. Joseph's is open to all physicians. I thank you sincerely for suggesting not to get into difficulty again, by choosing a staff of a certain number; therefore we will omit all names and reserve the right to issue all circulars.

She then proceeded to offer specific hours just for them. She closed by graciously stating, "We regret that this has come up now, when everything was quiet, but you understand our position, dear Doctors, and sooner or later, this would have become a necessity."[28] Doctors Adams and Thompson had been with the hospital since its opening, and Dr. Saunders was a celebrated surgeon;[29] thus, it was important that she maintain their favor.

A principal theme in many hospital studies is the competition between medical staffs and well-established male executives over policy decisions, particularly those involving admissions. As noted previously, in the nineteenth-century voluntary hospital, most institutionalized patients did not pay for hospitalization. As the primary benefactors, a lay board of trustees controlled admissions by evaluating patients according to their worthiness of charity. Typically this meant being stable members of the community who were temporarily victims of circumstance. Trustees evaluated all applicants for admission, and physicians had to plead cases to the board for prospective admission candidates. Subscribers and contributors could also nominate patients for admission. Thus, hospitalization depended on the individual goodwill of the trustees as sponsors. By the 1870s, however, responsibility for admissions was shifting to medical men and their categories of clinical diagnoses.[30]

By contrast, Catholic hospitals' different funding patterns had distinct implications for control over admissions. Furthermore, much of the social function of Protestant hospital support did not apply in Catholic circumstances. Because of nuns' tight control over finances, especially in the early years, the sisters often had final say in admission decisions. Mother St. Pierre Cinquin, as superior at Santa Rosa Infirmary, reserved the right to approve the admission of full charity patients. In these situations, she worked primarily with physicians who had to petition her to get their patients admitted.[31] The nuns also wanted to insure that people who otherwise might go untreated would have hospital access. The Incarnate Word Sisters especially guarded this responsibility since their constitutions specified that they alone would have charge of the sick poor on the grounds that the patients would be "better cared for."[32]

Control over admissions, however, was a negotiated process. Sometimes doctors refused to admit patients because their illnesses were either not serious enough or were of a chronic or terminal nature, and sisters complied. At other times, nuns found ways to circumvent physicians' wishes. In 1889 at St. Joseph's, Fort Worth, a doctor refused to see an orphaned, sick Egyptian boy, arguing that he "had not the conditions requisite" for admission. The nuns disagreed, however, and devised their own way of caring for him by hiring him to do light labor under their watchful eye until he could get well.[33] Occasionally, sister-administrators banned certain doctors' patients from the hospital. In 1909 at Holy Cross Hospital, Sister Lidwina Butler had a running disagreement with the county physician and eventually forced him to remove all his patients.[34] Still, she worked to try to satisfy physicians' wishes. The previous year, she had spoken at a staff meeting, stating, "Our doors are always open to charity cases. Should such occur my action would be governed by the recommendations of your members."[35] Over time, medical men increasingly made decisions in Catholic hospitals but within the boundaries defined by the owners.

One way that doctors challenged hospital management was to criticize institutional costs and implicate hospitals in socialized medicine. In May 1903, at the Utah State Medical Association meeting, Dr. A. C. Maclean vehemently denounced the high prices that Salt Lake City institutions charged private patients. He also attacked doctors' contract practice at the hospitals. Physicians at this time were still beleaguered by too many practitioners in their own field and by hospitals that took their patients from them and deprived them of admitting privileges. Doctors particularly feared a form of socialized medicine, by which large, powerful organizations, either government or private, dictated doctors' income and practice conditions. Thus, physicians wanted to prevent any corporation from mediating between them and their private patients, and they worried about contract practice in which companies hired doctors to care for workers. From the physicians' views, this practice interfered with their right to give care and charge patients according to ability to pay.[36] Medical societies, for example, characterized the practice of payroll deductions for mining company doctors as exploitation, since company doctors would bid against each other and lower physicians' fees. Hence, Maclean argued that the miners' prepaid health insurance system was "an imposition upon the medical profession."[37]

Always watchful over the interests of Holy Cross Hospital, Sister Lidwina immediately wrote the local newspaper:

> You don't hear these doctors making any protest about their charges being too high. . . . They charge $200 or $300 for an operation that requires an hour or an hour and a half of their time. The sisters and nurses watch over these same patients day and night for two or three weeks. As the entire compensation for this care, for food, room and other attentions, the hospital charges only $10 to $25 per week, according to the kind of room the patient wants. . . . If these doctors who are objecting to the prices their patients pay only had the hospital bills to pay for a while, I do not think they would do so much objecting.

She concluded that the charges in Salt Lake City were much lower than in eastern hospitals, even though the cost of living in the West was higher. "Taking everything in consideration," she wrote, "I do not think the charges are any too much."[38] Maclean's censure did not result in any

FIGURE 7.2 Graduating nurses, the Sisters of Charity of the Incarnate Word, 1910. Dr. Ferdinand Herff is seated in front, and other physicians are in back row. (Photo # 69–8547. Courtesy University of Texas Institute of Texan Culture, San Antonio, TX)

obvious financial loss to the hospital, since donations for 1904 increased over previous years.[39]

Operating room policies also were sources of negotiation as doctors tried to exert authority over surgery. In Salt Lake City, Holy Cross Hospital doctors criticized the indiscriminate use of the operating room in 1904.[40] Other kinds of dissensions arose at Santa Rosa Infirmary when the Incarnate Word Sisters reserved a surgical suite and special instruments for surgeons of the Herff family. The nuns justified their policy based on the doctors' close association with the sisters since Santa Rosa's opening and because of the physicians' distinction in surgery. These special privileges led to complaints from other doctors.[41] For the most part, however, sisters knew that their hospitals would fail without physicians' support and often heeded doctors' wishes. In 1898, a physician refused to allow a doctor from another city to see a patient at Santa Rosa, and the sisters did not protest.[42] (See fig. 7.2.)

Nuns expected to have control over both sister-nurses and the secular nursing staff with a minimum of interference from physicians. Doctors could not directly discipline sister-nurses because their first loyalty was to the superior. Conflict over nursing, however, could and did occur. Fort

Worth was predominantly a Protestant city, and physicians worried that St. Joseph's Catholic identification might deter patients from coming. They made the contentious request that a policy guarantee that Protestant nurses would always be on staff. Mother St. Madeleine firmly resisted such a restriction, stating: "We could not bind ourselves to keep always in our service Protestant nurses. We have not the least objection to employ them because we never make religion a condition on which we engage nurses or others. . . . If they give satisfaction as to gentleness, capacity and good character, that is all we ask of them, be they Protestant or Catholic."[43]

POLITICS OF MODERNIZATION

By the early twentieth century, prerogatives of medical science were figuring prominently in physicians' arguments as they agitated for more hospital control.[44] In 1902, Dr. Harry Niles, gynecologist, surgeon, and staff member of Holy Cross Hospital, published an article in a professional journal in which he asked, "[D]o not our services justly entitle us to a voice in all professional questions in and out of the hospital . . . ?" He believed doctors should be second to no one, even to "those benevolent individuals, charitable organizations or religious societies that founded these institutions. . . . In view of the important relations our hospitals are destined to hold with progressive medicine, is it not about time the professional mind began to dominate in the control of these institutions?"[45] With his own situation in mind as a staff member of a Catholic hospital, Niles argued that hospital boards were content to measure their success and usefulness "by the number of patients treated, the lives saved, and sufferings mitigated in a given period," and they saw no reason to change their methods or purposes. This stance was inadequate to Niles, who measured success in terms of scientific advances. The hospital's power was "as a promoter of medical progress . . . in the cultivation of a spirit of scientific investigation and in furthering the efforts of good men to advance medicine."[46]

Led by Niles, in 1903 doctors at Holy Cross Hospital tried to recast the institution to fit their own professional goals. They specifically wanted the hospital to be distinguished as a scientific institution that would rival the Mayo Clinic in Minnesota. They discussed printing a bulletin to advertise their work: "There is a selfish motive in all this. . . . The bulletin would show the outside world that scientific work is done here—not all mercenary and when they receive that impression it will redound to our and the Institution's benefit." Hinting at possible objections to their move by the superior, they continued, "Not that there would be any immediate results," but they should "agitate" for these matters and "report and suggest from meeting to meeting."[47]

Some doctors felt threatened by newer institutions in the local community. In 1897, doctors at St. Joseph's Infirmary in Fort Worth feared competition from a new Catholic hospital being built in nearby Dallas, one that might attract patients from Fort Worth if St. Joseph's did not have similar facilities. Dr. W. A. Adams wrote Mother St. Madeleine:

> No doubt you have heard of the elegant infirmary which is being constructed in Dallas by the Sisters of Chicago. It is a fact . . . that our hospital here is very inferior, especially that feature which lacks to the comfort of private patients. . . . [W]e would dislike very much to have it said that Dallas had a superior hospital to Fort Worth.[48]

These statements hint at the sisters' resistance to the costs of modernizing their hospital facilities. They worked hard and long to develop their operational budgets, so it was important for them to foresee a clear return on each new capital investment. Since they believed patients already were being well served with the existing equipment and facilities, they needed to be convinced by local medical authorities of the need to update and modernize. Not long afterward, to maintain their competitive edge with other hospitals, the Incarnate Word Sisters did add more private rooms and updated facilities to St. Joseph's. And sisters at Holy Cross Hospital and elsewhere spent hundreds of thousands of dollars to renovate their buildings and bring them into line with scientific standards. Complications arose if doctors emphasized only medical and scientific functions and dismissed nuns' religious frames.

When Holy Cross Hospital superior, Sister Lidwina Butler, died in 1913, the outpouring of support at her funeral was a broad affirmation not only of her status in the community but also with physicians. Despite previous conflicts, eight doctors served as pallbearers.[49]

Negotiation Strategies

In their letters and dealings with physicians and businessmen, many sister-superiors clearly saw themselves as equal partners and deserving of respect. Whether writing to get the lowest rates for railroad passages or working with physicians, their letters reveal confidence. In 1901, Mother

St. Madeleine of the Incarnate Word Sisters had the self-confidence to insist on autonomy for her sister-nurses when they negotiated a contract to work as nurses in another hospital in St. Louis, Missouri. Unlike the sisters' own hospitals, the St. Louis facility was a physicians' project. Rather than inviting doctors to join the staff, as the nuns had done at Santa Rosa, the sisters found an organization and staff already in place. To their dismay, the sisters did not have any control over admissions or price setting. After being informed that a board of directors had to approve any decision taken by the sisters in setting fees, Mother St. Madeleine wrote the physician in charge:

> Must we infer from this that for every patient admitted we must ask the board to agree with us as to the compensation to be given the hospital? If so the Sisters would have no freedom, and it would be very difficult to manage matters. However, we rather think that your meaning is to agree with us as to general prices, but that you will leave the Sisters free to make the financial arrangement with patients in what concerns the hospital services, exclusive of the Physicians' account.

She wanted the freedom to admit patients that physicians might not approve, because "it occurs to us that cases might come up which we would find it hard to refuse."[50] Apparently she was able to make her point, because in a later letter she wrote, "[W]e are pleased to know that we misunderstood you as regards the first point. Concerning the second, I think we will have no trouble."[51]

Four years later, however, Mother St. Madeleine disagreed with a physician over his management of the sisters, and she promptly pulled them out of the Missouri hospital. She wrote:

> We are perfectly willing that our Sisters devote themselves to the care of the sick and suffering, but it is our duty to see that [the sisters] are treated with justice and respect.... It is not reasonable that they be interfered with by other officers, in a manner to prevent them from getting the necessaries for food, etc. for the patients.

She then chastised the physician for refusing the sisters any paid vacation time: "Must our Sisters be treated as mere mercenaries?" She hastened to add, "It is not for the paltry amount that we claim redress, but for the principle." She based her decision to remove the sister-nurses on the ground that "their services are asked for in many other places where they will receive the respect and deference due their calling."[52] Mother St.

Madeleine built her argument in a way that reinforced the sisters' religious vocational status. When she began, she acknowledged the sisters' willingness to devote themselves to the care of the sick, but she clearly expected them to be treated with the respect they deserved. Their services were always in demand in other dioceses.

At other times, superiors simply dictated their wishes to physicians, knowing that they would be respected. Regarding another hospital, Mother St. Madeleine wrote to Dr. C. A. Smith: "We do not consider that our Sisters receive sufficient remuneration for their services as nurses.... You will certainly agree with us, dear Doctor, that the Sisters should at least receive more than ordinary workmen."[53] This quality of decisiveness defied gender stereotypes of appropriate models for females.

Still, nuns had to deal with tensions between the independence they exerted in administering hospitals and the traditional beliefs of women's subordinate position in church and society. In interacting with the non-Catholic and male communities, nuns were in a weaker position. To cope with these tensions, sisters often downplayed their achievements or presented them as motivated by self-denial and self-abnegation. Sometimes this involved presenting a humble, composed demeanor that was very much in line with religious prescriptions for their behavior. In their communications with others, they often used traditionally "feminine" means such as humility and politeness. Father Dennis Kiely of Salt Lake City recalled that Sister M. Holy Cross Welsh's "humility would disarm criticism. She was patient beyond endurance."[54] And sisters used the weapon of tact, particularly in their efforts to break down anti-Catholic fears. Other tactics complicated gendered depictions of communication strategies. While sisters often sounded very polite and avoided inflicting their mind or views on others, at other times they imposed their claims on physicians and obtained agreement on issues of hospital policy.[55]

Some may interpret nuns' actions as manipulative, with sisters feigning charm to garner favors. Others may see superiors' letters as "linguistic marks of subordination," a term used by James C. Scott in his analysis of power conflicts between dominant and subordinate groups. Manners can be an expression of power. Subordinates may appear deferential and amiable, but in reality they are actively resisting power and appropriating flattery and deference to achieve their own ends.[56] Evidence suggests that power was inherent in sisters' manners and humble discourse. Despite its apparently benign appearance, this power was extremely effective in fashioning sisters' identities and behaviors.[57] As they drew on their religious roles, they conveyed a mode of selfless decision making. Had others seen sisters as asking favors for themselves alone, they likely would not have obtained them. As humble and gracious nuns, they could obtain certain courtesies or refuse secular direction without being seen as prideful or rebellious.

For example, in 1900, Mother St. Madeleine wrote a railroad executive: "We ask this in the name of charity and love for suffering humanity, as you are aware, kind sir, that our only resources are the labor of our hands in the service of the sick and the care of the poor."[58] Thanks in large part to their gracious attitudes, sisters often received reduced rates for railroad travel, or they obtained rebates to ship freight for hospital construction. Indeed, by projecting an image of self-sacrifice and humility, they were less threatening to males and thus able to accomplish more. The notion of power through meekness was a strategy that Catholic women in active religious communities successfully employed throughout the nineteenth and early twentieth centuries. Still, they conceived of their work not in terms of power but of service. In caring for the sick, they were doing God's work rather than their own. Thus, even though it involved authority and power, to the sisters it was a ministry.

RELATIONS WITH BISHOPS AND PRIESTS

The fact that the sisters and clergy were all Catholic should not obscure the drama of sisters' means of resistance to hierarchical authority. In 1901, a Salt Lake City newspaper article reported "that the independence of the Holy Cross [Hospital] has been emphasized at various times, causing the bishop to feel that its management does not wish to be identified with and subordinate to the local church authorities."[59] The bishop in question was Lawrence Scanlan, quoted at the beginning of this chapter. His lack of appreciation of the Holy Cross Sisters' show of independence was based on the hierarchical organization of the Catholic Church over women who were mere nuns. The Irish-born Scanlan epitomized the authoritarian cleric who had been empowered by the increased centralization of the church in Rome since the mid-nineteenth century. Furthermore, edicts dating back to the sixteenth century and the Council of Trent had given bishops the right to sanction enterprises in their dioceses. What proved problematic for Scanlan was that the sisters' congregation in South Bend, Indiana, owned Holy Cross Hospital, making it outside his jurisdiction. Furthermore, the sisters had constitutions with papal approval and legal contracts that protected them from the diocesan administrator's control. Bishop Scanlan also objected to the fact that most of the medical staff consisted of Protestants and Mormons. Hence, he favored a second

Catholic hospital, one that would be more responsive to his authority.[60]

In 1910, Bishop Scanlan helped establish Judge Memorial Home and Hospital, a Catholic institution run by the Sisters of Mercy. This women's order had been founded in Ireland in the 1840s and was not centralized. The sisters worked for local dioceses, leading bishops and priests particularly to favor them. Their facility in Salt Lake City served not only as a home for aged and infirm miners but also as a place where patients could receive medical and surgical treatment. The hospital closed, however, in 1915 due to a lack of patients and the realization that Holy Cross Hospital was adequately serving the community.[61] As this example shows, nuns' hospital administrative roles sometimes brought them into conflict with ecclesiastical superiors, even though women religious were supposed to be models of obedience and unassertiveness. Feminine qualities, which the Catholic Church cultivated, made nuns the ideal teachers and nurses. When their activities involved administrative functions, however, which were male roles, clashes with the hierarchy were more apt to ensue.[62]

The paternalism of the Catholic Church limited sisters in how much influence they had over church policies. Specific religious practices and obligations, including hearing confessions and saying Mass on Sunday, required a priest, and the local bishop chose the chaplains. Many sisters learned how to use this relationship with the bishop to their advantage.[63] While the church hierarchy had ultimate authority in appointing chaplains to the hospital, sisters could circumvent episcopal choices by providing room and board for visiting priests whom they respected, in exchange for Mass and confessions. Sisters often utilized the services of visiting clergymen, or even patients who were priests, to augment their spiritual lives. In May 1896, Father E. J. P. Schmidt said Mass for the sisters at Santa Rosa Infirmary. After spending some time there as a patient, he returned to his home in Indiana, prompting several sisters to write him to return for a visit. Sister M. Gabriel wrote, "It is needless to tell you that Rev. Mother and all would give you a hearty welcome."[64] Thus, encouraging visiting clergy to call on the sisters and stay in their hospital was a means of obtaining priests of their own choosing.[65] Other records reveal a more complicated relationship with priests and bishops than these examples of resistance show. Some sisters showed heightened concern over episcopal approval, while others had very positive relationships with the clergy.

Even though nuns served as hospital administrators and trustees and operated from a position of power and autonomy, in later years many ecclesiastical leaders still maintained that sisters represented the feminine ideal. In 1928, Father Edward Garesche, founder of the International

Catholic Federation of Nurses, described the sister-administrator as radiating "sweetness and charity," whose "associates work with her in charming concord."[66] While Father Garesche was bestowing this lavish praise, sister-administrators were quietly and efficiently exercising their sizeable administrative authority, no doubt aided by their comforting feminine attributes.

Nuns' work as nurses and hospital administrators shows the interplay of religion, gender, and power. Their status as women religious gave them legitimacy and a pivotal role in hospital activities. Furthermore, sisters' papally approved constitutions protected them from diocesan religious leaders' control. While compromise was the solution to most of their problems, nuns also organized and collectively resisted the authority of both physicians and clergy who tried to limit their activities. For their part, physicians and priests usually respected the sisters' authority.

Because church and societal prescriptions imposed constraints on women, nuns often used the language of obedience, humility, and self-effacement to fashion a public presentation of themselves. This positioned them within more acceptable cultural norms and convinced physicians and ecclesiastical superiors that their work was beyond reproach.[67] The picture drawn here is a complex one of nuns who were not only demure and submissive but also decisive, capable, and even stubborn at times. Those who employed such bold strategies successfully, however, had to follow two unspoken guidelines. First, when they stepped beyond traditional gender roles, they had to do so, not for self-serving purposes, but to ensure that just and humanitarian causes were upheld. Secondly, they had to have earned the right to be assertive by having lived the lives of proper and well-respected nuns.[68]

8

Addressing the Times:

NUNS AND THE STANDARDIZATION MOVEMENT

> We cannot help asking where now are the faithful nuns, those "angels of the battlefield" who taught the world how to nurse.... So much maligned, yes, even by some of our nursing journals....[1]
>
> A Sister of St. Francis
> February 1907

In this letter to the editor of a secular nursing journal, a sister protested the disrespect many felt in the early decades of the twentieth century. Rather than relying solely on their own autonomy to set up and manage their hospitals, nuns had to deal with external factors such as the professionalization of nursing, the Flexner Report, and the American College of Surgeons. Sisters carried an additional burden. They were religious women who were unfamiliar to many people when they first arrived on the American scene. Their gender traditions differed from Protestants: nuns had voluntarily taken the religious vow of chastity, and they wore habits that were distinctive to a woman's religious order. One layman voiced a common view that they lived "more or less secluded lives, quite apart from the world and under conditions quite peculiar to themselves—lives of service given almost solely to the care and comfort of the sick and ailing."[2] Sisters also were part of a Catholic tradition still trying to earn respectability. Added to perceptions about them was the growing anti-Catholicism that had resurfaced in the 1890s. Though their nursing during the Civil War helped lessen prejudice against them, hostility toward Catholicism had increased when immigrants from southern and eastern Europe poured into the country. Many Americans saw sisters as representatives of the immigrants' church. These images, along with the widespread idea that Catholics were a threat to democratic institutions, set nuns apart as "outsiders."[3] This "outsider" status influenced their adaptation to changes in nursing and medicine.

THE CATHOLIC HOSPITAL ASSOCIATION: A SISTERS' ORGANIZATION

The most important influence, however, was the hospital standardization movement. The American College of Surgeons (ACS) organized in 1913, and by 1917 it had adopted minimum standards for hospital approval. Hospitals had to have an organized medical staff with monthly meetings to discuss cases, a sufficient laboratory for proper diagnosis, and a sophisticated system for record keeping. It was at this point that physicians obtained more authority in hospital decision making, particularly those involving staffing.

To keep pace with the hospital reform movement, fourteen Sisters of St. Joseph of Carondelet met with Father Charles B. Moulinier, regent at Marquette University Medical School, in Minneapolis in 1914 to discuss plans for a Catholic organization that would ensure the highest hospital standards. The Catholic Hospital Association (CHA) was formed the following year, with Father Moulinier as president. At the first CHA convention in June 1915, two hundred sisters, physicians, and lay nurses representing forty-three hospitals attended.[4] The CHA was a powerful constituency in supporting the ACS's efforts at standardization,[5] and in 1918 it approved the ACS's plan for Catholic hospitals. The ACS began inspecting hospitals that year, and by the early 1920s it had approved most of the institutions represented in this book. Some hospitals, such as St. Mary's, Cairo, and St. Joseph's, Fort Worth, did not receive approval until the sisters constructed new buildings. New standards determined by a secular agency threatened nuns' control over their hospitals.[6] Neither they nor other Catholic leaders had helped formulate the ACS plan. On the other hand, because Father Moulinier was a member of the ACS standardization committee, which involved actual hospital inspections, Catholic hospitals could be protected from any strong secular control and generally were.[7]

Father Moulinier favored a sister for president of the CHA, but conservative bishops and priests opposed him and prohibited nuns' appointments as full-time officers. Priests held the highest leadership positions until the 1960s. Sisters, however, served on the executive board, headed committees, participated in conventions, and set standards for Catholic nursing education.[8] Two members of the Sisters of St. Joseph of Carondelet especially were active. Sister Esperance Finn, superior at St. Mary's Hospital, Minneapolis, was one of the founding members of the CHA and served as second vice-president from 1916 to 1919. Sister Madeleine Lyons was a member of the national executive board from 1921 to 1924 and became the first president of the CHA's Minnesota-North Dakota Conference.[9]

At the 1916 CHA convention, Sister Esperance presented a paper on the nuns' contributions to team work in Catholic hospitals. Emphasizing cooperation, she focused on their relationships with physicians and hospital chaplains. The physician was the "director of our team-work" whose medical orders should be supported. The chaplain held the highest honor, however, since he stood for the patient's "spiritual interests, which we sisters are eager to promote."[10] With typical humility, she did not discuss the nuns' authority in hospital management, but Father Moulinier did. He pointed out that nuns had an advantage over other hospitals because of their "closer control of the situation. It lies entirely in the hands of sisters of Catholic hospitals to manage" their institutions' affairs independent of any managerial boards.[11] In his President's Address at the 1918 convention, he affirmed that the CHA was the sisters' organization. He clarified, "It is not the clergy's; it is not the doctor's. I am going to say it is not even the hierarchy's."[12]

Not all agreed with Father Moulinier's identification with the ACS. A conflict occurred at the 1921 CHA convention when a group of physicians tried to separate the Catholic organization from the ACS. They claimed that the college was determining policies for Catholic hospitals as well as for physicians. To avert this challenge, Father Moulinier supported an amendment to the constitution, proposed by a sister, that the voting power for conducting the business of the CHA be left to the institutional membership. By this amendment, the religious communities holding the votes for each member hospital obtained control. The structure allowed sisters to circulate the issues they thought important. Nuns also dominated the committee membership and chair positions. By 1921 the individual membership in the CHA totaled 1,290, with sisters holding sovereignty.[13] (See fig. 8.1.)

Nevertheless, the ACS's standardization plans called for greater physician control over medical staffs, and by the 1920s internal redistributions of power were beginning to take place. Doctors wrote constitutions and bylaws spelling out the relationship between the medical staff and hospital

FIGURE 8.1 Meeting of the Catholic Hospital Association in St. Paul, MN, 1920. This is the right end and middle section of the official photograph. Father Charles Moulinier is in front row, second from left, holding hat. (Courtesy Archives of the Congregation of the Sisters of St. Joseph of Carondelet, St. Paul, MN)

administration and specifying procedures for staff selection. At Catholic hospitals, physicians established boards of governors and other committees to advise sister-superiors in these matters. While doctors obtained some power to select their own colleagues, superiors still had final approval of all recommendations from medical staff committees. By 1919 physicians at St. Joseph's Hospital in St. Paul had formed an advisory board. According to its 1921 constitution, the superior made all staff appointments from names recommended by the board. In this case, the board considered itself an executive committee to be "consulted on all matters of general policy in respect to the conduct of the affairs of the Hospital and Staff." The St. Joseph Hospital Corporation, however, reserved the right to make final decisions in all such matters. Other Catholic hospitals had similar policies.[14] Sisters continued to comprise their own boards of directors through their hospital corporations, and it was not until the 1960s that lay boards were appointed.[15]

FIGURE 8.2 The Sisters of the Holy Cross and the Poor Sisters of St. Francis Seraph of the Perpetual Adoration at the Indiana State Conference of the CHA, St. Elizabeth's Hospital, Lafayette, IN, 1922. (Courtesy Sisters of St. Francis of the Perpetual Adoration, Mishawaka, IN)

In 1929, the superior at Holy Cross Hospital in Salt Lake City was still a full participant at physicians' staff meetings. On April 1, she reported that a physician had performed gallbladder surgery on a patient without proper diagnostic foundation. The patient had been admitted with angina and a positive Wasserman test. The superior and the governing board together decided that the physician should be reprimanded and supervised until further notice. She also chastised some doctors for their negligence in completing their charts.[16] In doing so, she was acting under the authority given her by the CHA in 1918 when it approved the ACS's standardization plan. The CHA had stipulated that member hospitals establish an adequate case record system with a sister in charge. She was to have full authority to demand careful cooperation among physicians, interns, and nurses.[17] Hence, the superior at Holy Cross Hospital instructed the secretary of the board of governors to write to two doctors in particular that "they should complete their charts at once."[18] The physicians complied.

Case records, particularly patient histories, were often problematic due to physicians' time constraints. To deal with these matters, sister-superiors shared ideas at roundtable discussions at national and state CHA conventions. (See fig. 8.2.) Rather than "spanking the doctors into line," as one superior put it, she had a nun trained to take histories while physicians did the physical examinations. Other superiors invited representatives from the ACS to talk to staff physicians.[19]

Transitions to the new system were not always smooth. A conflict relating to the standardization movement occurred between physicians and the Congregation of the Poor Sisters of St. Francis Seraph of the Perpetual Adoration at St. Anthony's Hospital, Terre Haute, Indiana, which the sisters had established in 1882. In 1920, the nuns hired Dr. J. J. Moorhead from Chicago as chief of staff to bring the hospital into line with ACS standards. His changes were problematic for some of the other staff doctors, and twenty-six threatened to resign if the sisters did not remove Moorhead. The hospital superior made it clear that Moorhead would be retained as chief for one more year, prompting the physicians' mass resignations on January 1, 1921. Only eight doctors remained on staff. Notably, the hospital received the ACS approval later that year.[20] Over the next several months, the sisters encouraged the physicians to return, but they would agree only if they could elect their own chief. The acting hospital superior, Sister Ida Theno, supported the existing head, chosen by the physicians who currently comprised the staff. Newspapers referred to her as "a fighter from Fightersville" and said that "fear of physicians, individually or collectively, is unknown to Sister Ida." The superior general of the congregation traveled from Lafayette to Terre Haute to mediate the dispute, heard the different stories, and affirmed that the insurgents would not be recognized as a group. She allowed them to return as individuals rather than as a body, which they refused to do. The hospital suffered significantly because of the small number of doctors, and it was not until 1925 that a new superior successfully reorganized the medical staff.[21]

THE ATTRACTION OF SCIENTIFIC MEDICINE

Despite the tendency to see medical science and religion as mutually exclusive, an early goal of the CHA was to synthesize the two models. One way they sought to maintain economic leverage in the hospital market was to identify their institutions with scientific practices.[22] Scientific medicine influenced the demand for medical services, and after 1900, hospitals throughout the country began marketing themselves in terms of scientific fashions of the times. Trade journals for physicians and hospital administrators provide interesting illustrations of these concerns. Reflecting the theory that germs transmitted disease, hospital supply firms suggested that hidden dangers could be found in furniture, bedding, and floors. One ad stated that in hospitals, "where sanitation is one of the principal problems, every crack in a floor is a lair for a mass of death-dealing microbes." Thus, they needed wood floors specially treated that left the floor impenetrable to germs and "perfectly sanitary."[23] Henry B. Platt advertised his disinfectants to both Catholic and non-Catholic hospitals by featuring pictures of secular nurses as well as sister-nurses.[24]

Antisepsis and eventually asepsis decreased hospital mortality significantly, especially for surgical patients, and in the late nineteenth century, physicians began to perform aseptic operations in increasing numbers. To gain the trust of surgeons and paying patients, sisters' institutions had to provide reassurances of their safety and success. Thus, advertisements guaranteed physicians, prospective patients, and visiting committees that hospital personnel would practice scientific medicine.

Like other administrators, nuns fostered the image of science and technology in their hospitals by having pictures of operating rooms, laboratories, sterilizers, and other equipment as illustrations in their annual reports. In the early years, physicians often donated the equipment.[25] Such celebratory publications usually showed the idealized version.[26] Advertisements emphasized gleaming tiled walls, sanitary operating rooms, and the newest x-ray equipment. A 1914 newspaper in Salt Lake City described Holy Cross Hospital's most recent addition that included "the very latest in the most advanced systems." It had an entire floor devoted to an operating room, sterilizing and recovery rooms, x-ray department, and laboratory, all with the "highest type of sanitary arrangement and furnishing."[27] By the early twentieth century, pharmacies had also enlarged and modernized. (See fig. 8.3.) Annual reports also touted new services and equipment. The 1912 annual report for St. Joseph's Hospital in St. Paul pictured two white-clad nurses with physicians in dress suits leaning over a patient on the floor, and a Draeger pulmotor prominently displayed. The report noted the lifesaving benefits of this new technology: it was for "resuscitation in accidents in the latter stages of gas poisoning and asphyxia of the new born."[28]

In smaller communities, similar developments occurred. In 1890, Dr. W. W. Stevenson of Cairo, Illinois, proudly described St. Mary's Infirmary as a first-class hospital that had the "comforts of a home." Revealing the juxtaposition of science and homelike comforts in this period, in 1910 newspapers also proclaimed St. Mary's "superior advantages in the way of modern improvements, medical and surgical attendance." It had an x-ray room, "perfectly equipped operating room," and laboratory.[29]

Headlines also noted world-renowned doctors doing surgery in Catholic hospitals. For example, in 1902, the *Salt Lake Tribune* announced that Professor Adolph Lorenz from Austria had performed surgery at Holy Cross Hospital on a patient with congenital hip dislocation using

FIGURE 8.3 Holy Cross Hospital Pharmacy, Salt Lake City, UT, 1908. (Courtesy Utah State Historical Society, photo # 22385)

the "knifeless" method of reduction.[30] This statement assumed that prospective patients would be impressed not only with the surgical procedure but also with a European physician.

Leaders in the CHA were particularly interested in Catholic hospitals becoming advanced in medical science and education. Among the purposes of the organization, stated in the constitution adopted in 1915, was to promote "scientific efficiency and economy in hospital management."[31] Complying with ACS standards, nuns added pathologists, laboratory specialists, and radiologists to their hospital staffs. After William Roentgen's discovery of x-rays in 1895, x-ray departments were essential for any hospital caring for acutely ill or injured patients, and physicians often donated the initial machines. But just who was going to control the machine became a central question both inside and outside hospitals.[32] Sisters received training as x-ray technicians and headed their own departments. After Dr. W. S. Hamilton started the x-ray department at Santa Rosa Infirmary in 1912, Sister Clara Kalbfleisch obtained certification as a technician and operated the machine.[33] By 1924, a survey of over a hundred Catholic hospitals revealed that eighty-two had a sister in charge of the department, while seventy-eight had a "physician roentgenologist" who read and interpreted the films. In other hospitals, patients' individual physicians did this task.[34]

What sisters actually thought about this increasingly technical aspect of medical care can be inferred from Father Moulinier's President's Address to the 1918 CHA convention. Using both scientific and service rhetoric, he stated, "We never lost sight of the great fundamental, ethical principle that the patient has a right to all the most enlightened, self-sacrificing, scientific, philanthropic, and conscientious religious service that body, mind, and soul of man . . . has a right to." Significantly, he added, "We repudiated any such thought that the hospital is a mere boarding-house, a place where the surgeon merely operates, where the internist merely prescribes medicine or treatment . . . ."[35] Rather, it was their sacred obligation to provide the best possible service to the sick. Hence, while they accepted scientific advances, hospital leaders tried to prevent an emphasis on technology from being the overriding factor in their work.

Regardless of such admonition to keep the human element a vital aspect of hospital service, scientific procedures and technologies continued to advance. And to keep pace with those developments, Catholic hospitals expanded their clinical teaching facilities. As part of that instruction, physicians campaigned among sisters and CHA leaders for the opportunity to do autopsies. In many ways, the nursing sisters, with their spiritual identities clearly established, stood in direct contrast to the impersonal nature of medical technology. It was pivotal, then, that to promote the importance of scientific advances to the general public, the sisters themselves join in that promotion. In a 1923 *Hospital Progress* article, Dr. Charles A Gordon tried to convince them of that marketing strategy by arguing that the "Great Physician" gave authority for scientific research. He also used the language of competition: the time "has come when we must make a determined effort to increase our autopsy efficiency or fall behind in the hospital race." In getting family acceptance of autopsies, Gordon stressed that a "tactful Sister or two, well armed with information, may solve the problem; their apparent disinterestedness may carry the day."[36] During the 1920s, at least some Catholic hospitals complied. Fort Worth's St. Joseph's Infirmary, for example, had the entire fifth floor reserved for operating suites, treatment rooms, and an autopsy room (morgue) (fig. 8.4). The 1927 *Souvenir Book* published upon the dedication of the new addition noted that the autopsy room was "an important aid to scientific research."[37]

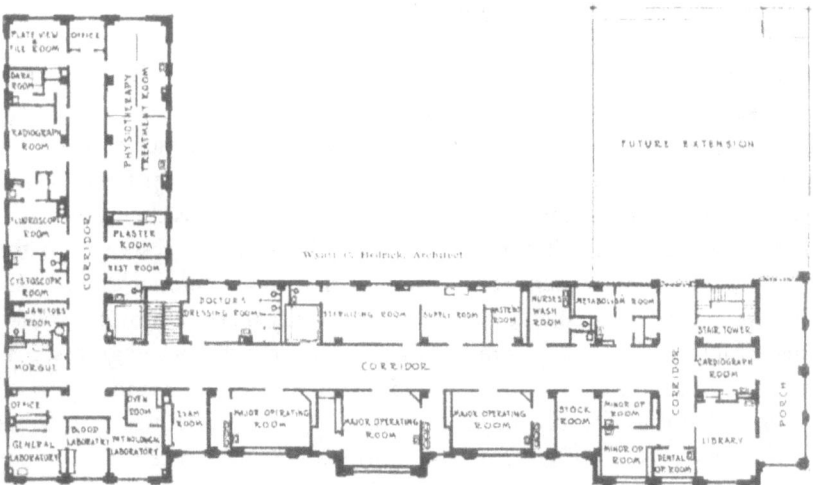

FIGURE 8.4 Fifth Floor "Scientific Department," St. Joseph's Infirmary, Fort Worth, TX, in *Souvenir Book: Dedication Day*, June 1927. (Courtesy Archives, Motherhouse of the Incarnate Word, San Antonio, TX)

New Standards in Nursing

While some women's religious congregations resisted modernization and attacked ACS standards, other communities supported them and pushed for more education in both nursing and hospital administration. Premodern nursing before 1870 consisted of administration of simple medications, maintaining cleanliness and safety, providing nourishment, and giving spiritual care, but after the turn of the century sisters specialized in one kind of work. Some nursed at the bedside or had charge of the surgical supply departments and medical and surgical floors, while others trained in pharmacology. Sister Cuthberta Chawke of the Sisters of St. Joseph registered as a pharmacist in Minnesota in 1915; and in 1918, Sister Cordelia Gahagan of the Sisters of the Holy Cross was the first woman to become a registered pharmacist in Utah.[38]

Particularly significant for nuns was nursing leaders' crusade to separate the trained from the untrained nurse. As nursing evolved from a service to a trained practice and scientific and technological advances developed, a good nurse came to be measured not only by her character but also by her technical competencies, knowledge of disease prevention, discipline, and organization. Nuns responded to these challenges and updated their practice through establishing their own nursing schools that emphasized scientific knowledge and expert training.[39]

After the turn of the century, sisters began adapting their clothing to meet scientific standards, although this created considerable controversy. The religious habit represented a nun's devotion to her particular order, and any changes had to be approved by either the bishop for diocesan orders or the Vatican for papally approved congregations. For many, this change in habit did not come about until the 1920s in response to the standardization movement. Discussion at that time centered around sisters wearing white washable habits while on duty instead of black woolen ones which, in the eyes of some medical authorities, harbored germs. Sisters addressed the issue at special CHA conferences. One nun expressed concern that they would compromise their religious identities and "think less of our habit if not given to us so often. When we received this religious habit, we were so happy. . . ."[40] Yet, another sister wrote, "[T]here was in these controversies a surprising display of lack of common sense and a superabundance of rule," and she called for modification of community rules.[41] Often, sisters wore the full black habit and a white gown over it, while others wore white habits only in certain instances. In all cases, nuns maintained their religious distinctiveness by wearing symbols such as crosses.

Some nursing orders began adapting their religious habits earlier. In November 1897, sisters at Santa Rosa wore white veils for the first time during an operation and had white caps made for the doctors.[42] In figure 8.5, a newspaper photograph taken in the early 1900s at Santa Rosa, sisters are wearing white aprons and sleeves over their black habits.[43] A nun who entered training at St. Mary's Hospital, Minneapolis, in 1910 became a surgical nurse and designed her own uniform: she pinned up her black skirt and sleeves under a white doctor's gown and wore a white outer veil over the black one.

Figure 8.5 is conspicuous for another reason: it shows the presence of sisters standing in the operating room as if they were overseeing the procedure. The photo appeared in the local San Antonio newspaper, and the message conveyed seems clear: that the nuns were an integral part of the hospital's professional services. Indeed, the feature that distinguished Catholic hospitals from their non-Catholic counterparts lay not in their identification with scientific medicine but in the hospital's sanction by women religious.

At the same time, some physicians, such as the Protestant S. Weir Mitchell, publicly criticized sisters' lack of training, and even Catholics expressed concerns.[44] Speakers at CHA conventions—priests, nuns, and

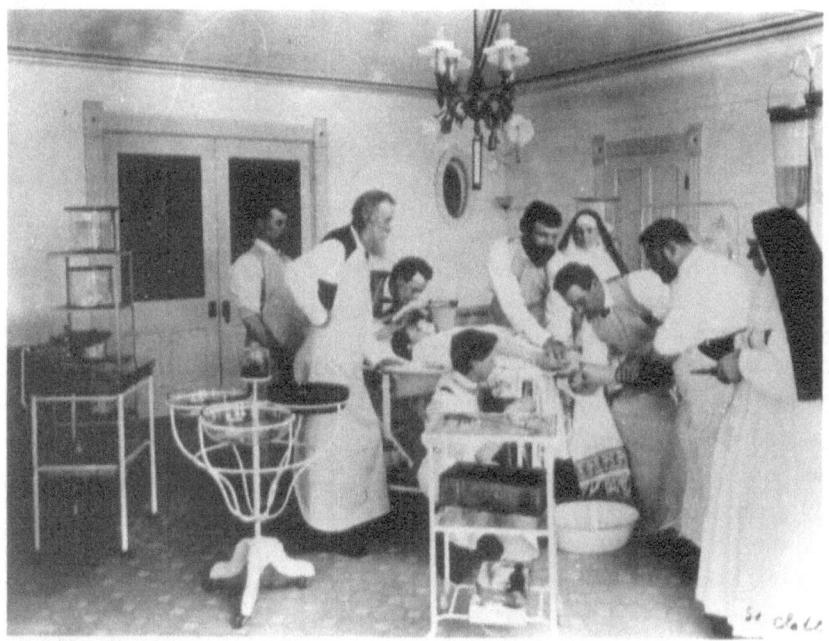

FIGURE 8.5 Operating Room, Santa Rosa Infirmary. Dr. Ferdinand Herff and son, Dr. Adolph Herff, are operating on a patient. Other medical personnel, including nuns, also attend (early 1900s). (Photo #69–8541. Courtesy University of Texas Institute of Texan Cultures at San Antonio)

physicians alike—extolled the need for more training. In 1923 Father Moulinier lamented that, in religious communities where both teaching and hospital work were done, the teaching sisters had preference in education because of the Catholic Educational Association's influence. This resulted in less education for hospital sisters. He noted that with few exceptions, sister-nurses were eager for education, but often hospital superiors could not spare them to give them the education they needed.[45]

Still, the constitution of the CHA reiterated principles espousing higher education for nurses, and sisters became leaders in the association's education movement.[46] Two members of the Sisters of St. Joseph from St. Mary's Hospital, Minneapolis, did postgraduate work in nursing education and administration at Columbia University in 1915. Another, Sister Conchessa Burbidge, a registered pharmacist and administrator, was instrumental in helping to establish a summer school at Marquette University, which offered seven different courses. Sixty-nine sisters from different congregations attended in 1916.[47] By the 1930s, some nuns were taking graduate courses at Catholic University's School of Nursing Education and at Marquette's Hospital College, one of the country's earliest academic hospital administration programs.[48]

More Tensions with Physicians and Clergy

Conflicts over Nursing Education

Sisters' work in hospital administration countered male dominance in that field, and their training schools solidified their authority with students. These factors also enhanced nuns' influence with physicians. In many non-Catholic hospitals, doctors formed schools of nursing to meet their own objectives, thus undermining the nursing superintendent's control.[49] By contrast, nuns kept control over financial management and student training in their own schools. The superintendent of the nursing school, a sister, was responsible to the hospital superior, not to a nonnursing board of trustees.

The training schools did not function entirely independent of physicians. Doctors supported nursing education and, in fact, became presidents at Santa Rosa, San Antonio; St. Joseph's, Fort Worth; and St. Joseph's, St. Paul. A 1905 constitution for the Santa Rosa Training School listed committees of physicians who, along with the sister-superintendent and hospital superior, established entrance and graduation requirements, selected faculty members, and determined course work. The doctors, however, had to apply for the privilege of teaching the students. If they missed three lectures, the superintendent of the training school informed them of their dismissal from the faculty. One of the first graduates of the Santa Rosa Training School was Sister Robert O'Dea (fig. 8.6). In 1919, when she became hospital superior and superintendent of nurses at Santa Rosa, she curtailed some of the doctors' control of the training school by insisting that the dean, a physician, consult with her before presenting any problems to the medical faculty. She also required physicians' applications for and resignations from the faculty to first come to her. Physicians protested, believing that peer review should be their prerogative. Undeterred, she continued with her plan.[50] By 1920, a few sisters from other congregations were advocating for secular boards for their training schools, but only if the hospital superior approved the membership. Efficiency would be improved, they felt, but board members should not conflict with the obedience due superiors.[51]

FIGURE 8.6 Left to right, Incarnate Word Sisters Philip Neri Neville, de Sales Keegan, and Robert O'Dea were among the first graduates of the Santa Rosa Training School for Nurses in 1906. (Courtesy Archives, Motherhouse of the Incarnate Word, San Antonio, TX)

In training young sisters and secular nurses for their work, most nuns saw themselves as the very best instructors. They asserted that, along with theoretical work and practical training, the teaching of moral and religious instruction should be characteristic of all Catholic nursing programs. This was difficult due to competition with other training schools, many of which the sisters considered too lax. Likewise, the "pleasure-seeking tendency" of the time was problematic. With nuns' good example, the religious atmosphere of the Catholic hospital, and a daily routine, however, sisters did not doubt their eventual success.[52]

While nuns held a measure of authority in their training schools, some church leaders hampered their autonomy. In the CHA, priests preoccupied themselves with concerns over whether sisters should attend professional meetings, take courses in secular institutions, obtain obstetrics training, and join secular nurse accrediting agencies such as the National League for Nursing Education (NLNE).[53] Religious rules forbade some sisters from serving in secular organizations, but other nuns were not so restricted, and they were both members and officers in state and national associations. By the early 1930s, more than three hundred sister-educators had joined the NLNE. They formed the Sisters' Committee within the league to enhance cooperation and to provide a Catholic influence. Yet some CHA leaders doubted the NLNE's neutrality in accrediting sisters' programs. Father Alphonse Schwitalla believed in "the sacred character of the hospital . . . and the inherently conventlike" atmosphere of Catholic nursing schools, which "precluded a secular agency's evaluation of Catholic nursing education." Eventually the CHA formed its own organization, the Council on Nursing Education, which began accrediting Catholic agencies in 1934. This was a contested issue among nuns, however, as some chafed at the association's separatist stance.[54]

Sister Conchessa Burbidge was a moderate on the NLNE issue. She articulated the sisters' majority opinion: the CHA accreditation plan guaranteed "that we shall be free to teach and to practice our own Catholic doctrine and follow principles with which we are heartily in accord." This translated into a safeguarding of Catholic attitudes in the education of nurses. Sisters could carefully guide students according to their own understandings of what nursing should be.[55]

Conflicts over Nursing Practice

In their 1907 history of nursing, Adelaide Nutting and Lavinia Dock asserted that European nursing sisters' practices "gradually declined" after the early nineteenth century, in that they "have not been allowed to share in the advance of medical science." The authors blamed clerics for hampering sisters' education by preventing them from witnessing childbirth or caring for parturient women. Nutting and Dock had less harsh words for sisterhoods in the United States, who more readily adapted to modern medicine.[56] Yet, even nuns in this country had to engage in subtle negotiations when taking on nursing services in troublesome areas. Some religious prescriptives that forbade nuns to nurse in operating or delivery rooms created a particularly problematic situation. This likely was related to the modesty requirement for chaste women.[57] In seventeenth-century France, Vincent de Paul worried that scandal would occur if sisters were involved with laboring women and warned them not to care for women in childbirth. At that time, nuns were excluding pregnant women and nursing mothers from their hospitals in order to uphold the moral integrity of their communities. Women who typically delivered babies in hospitals were unwed mothers or those without decent homes. Sisters worried that opening their hospitals to such women could hurt the institution's reputation and could cause problems with other potential admissions and with benefactors. Furthermore, women who delivered in hospitals rather than homes might be infected with venereal disease.[58]

In Revolutionary France in the late eighteenth and early nineteenth centuries, well-trained midwives delivered babies in hospitals such as Paris's Hotel-Dieu, where Augustinian nuns were the nurses. Immediately after birth, the mothers would return to the general wards. In 1814, at the time of the first Restoration in France, the nuns took over more control of hospital administration and insisted on separating maternity services from infant services, on the grounds that "innocent babies" should be separated from their "sinful mothers." Then, in 1901, the papal document *Normae* forbade sisters to work with maternity cases. While it was not formally promulgated until that year, it represented ideas that were widely held prior to that time.[59]

Other factors had to be considered in America in the nineteenth and early twentieth centuries. Catholic sisterhoods were not spared vitriolic contempt from nativism. Both priests and sisters were extremely sensitive to anticonvent discourse that included shocking tales of "unrestrained sexuality" within convent walls. Some critics considered the idea of autonomous women avoiding their procreative duties as dangerous to the natural, patriarchal order.[60] These threatening perceptions persisted in spite of the fact that nuns' nursing and teaching actually conformed to traditional domestic ideologies of the times.

Orders founded in the United States during the nineteenth century or those that had separated from European motherhouses were more likely to adopt modern methods of nursing. An 1899 textbook for sister-nurses, written by a priest for the sisters at St. John's Hospital in Springfield, Illinois, detailed the nuns' responsibilities while assisting physicians in the operating room, giving anesthesia, caring for wounds, assisting with pelvic examinations, inserting urinary catheters, giving massages, and caring for patients after gynecological surgery. It alluded to the problem sisters faced: during operations, the sister-nurse must especially guard "her eyes, avoiding everything that she is not obliged to see and by all means preserve her dignity and modesty." She may assist with a bladder operation for male patients, "but only when the doctors are extremely careful."[61]

In 1908, Vatican officials wrote superiors of nursing orders in the United States to express their concerns about nuns working in operating rooms and caring for men "in things not altogether becoming to virgins dedicated to God."[62] A superior of the Sisters of St. Joseph in St. Paul responded that the sisters admitted both men and women in their hospitals but did not give massages to patients of either sex or baths to males. Furthermore, sisters took "no part in operations performed... leaving the whole work of attendance on the operating surgeons to trained nurses and secular women." But she discreetly added, "At times Sisters may be found in the vicinity of the operating rooms, so as to see that whatever is needed is duly provided: but in all this nothing is done or allowed that could conflict with the strictest rules of religious modesty."[63]

Ultimately, the solution that sisters in the United States devised was a careful negotiation of their roles and sometimes even a circumvention of religious prescriptions. And it appears that, at least for the Sisters of St. Joseph, Sisters of the Holy Cross, and Incarnate Word Sisters, American bishops did not strictly enforce *Normae*. There is no recorded incidence in which they sent priests into hospitals to impose it. Some conservative bishops seemed more concerned with nuns wearing white habits instead of black ones in the operating room, fearing the sisters would appear more secular.[64] Despite Rome's statements, some of the sisters assisted in surgical procedures, although they likely tried to "guard their eyes." They also prepared dressings and supervised and maintained aseptic procedures. Early chronicles at Santa Rosa and Fort Worth's St. Joseph's Infirmaries indicate that two Incarnate Word Sisters regularly assisted surgeons in the operating room, and a sister often administered anesthesia.[65] Other hospitals revealed similar findings.

Nuns circumvented the surgery ban, probably because surgery was such a prominent aspect of their hospitals. Maternity care was more troublesome territory. At that time, midwifery was a complex issue in the United States, and in many places only physicians could work in that capacity. Because of a dual attraction of scientific medicine and increased comfort, safety, and convenience, hospital births became increasingly attractive to middle-class women. For most women, childbirth moved from the home to the hospital between 1910 and 1930.[66] As a result, doctors began agitating for more hospital space for obstetrical cases, and sisters responded.

While Holy Cross Hospital in Salt Lake City recorded only nine maternity cases in 1891, in 1908 the superior agreed to the doctors' request to receive more obstetrical cases, although she maintained that the women should have special nurses rather than sister-nurses.[67] The nuns recorded forty births in 1908, sixty-three in 1912, and 171 in 1915. The hospital opened a maternity ward in 1916 under the charge of Ella Mae Wicklund, a secular nurse and one of Holy Cross Training School's top graduates. When she resigned in 1917 to become secretary of the State Board of Nurse Examiners, a sister-nurse who had just completed her training succeeded Wicklund as head nurse.[68] Catholic hospitals eventually opened separate obstetrical wards, typically after World War I, and expanded hospital delivery rooms.[69]

Before the expansion of maternity services, the Incarnate Word Sisters simply adapted to the moment, which often meant ignoring religious stipulations. In 1890, nuns at both Santa Rosa and St. Joseph's Infirmaries delivered babies when no doctor was present.[70] The sisters did, in fact, obtain the authority to ignore their rules if necessary as early as 1872 in their constitution.[71] By 1906, they had added to their *Directory* that, although sisters should not attend obstetric cases, "this should not be taken in the extreme, as in many places and cases, circumstances are such that this cannot be avoided."[72]

Other issues were at stake. In 1913, the sister-superior at Holy Cross Hospital met with physicians to discuss operating room procedures. She expressed her willingness to do whatever she could to satisfy the staff's wishes, especially with reference to scheduling procedures. But she emphasized that she would not permit "criminal operations" to take place.[73] Other historians have explored the dilemma of obstetric surgery in Catholic hospitals. Joseph G. Ryan has effectively argued that one reason nursing sisters moved into operating and delivery rooms was to assure that the Catholic Church's sanctions against abortion and the destructive surgery of infant craniotomy would be observed in their hospitals.[74] Indeed, at the 1921 CHA convention, Dr. Emerson Root from Holy Cross Hospital in Salt Lake City posed the question, "How long would a doctor last in a hospital" if he did anything the Catholic Church considered wrong? "There is every kind of check in the hospital. . . . We know that in the operating room the Sister in charge . . . is just as watchful as anybody could be."[75]

That same year, the CHA adopted a Surgical Code for Catholic Hospitals, taken from one stipulated by the Detroit diocese and printed in the first edition of *Hospital Progress*. Specifically, it prohibited operations involving the destruction of fetal life, including craniotomies of a living child, "curettment of the uterus" during pregnancy, induction of labor before the fetus was viable, and operations on a living fetus in extra-uterine pregnancies.[76] It also prohibited the removal of an undiseased ovary, uterus, and Fallopian tube. The code was revised in later years, and clearer positions on issues of birth control and contraception were delineated. But for the sisters in 1921, tensions over their professional roles continued. By then, more were participating in obstetric nursing. Their authority to nurse maternity patients was enhanced when state boards of nursing began requiring nurse training schools to offer a course in obstetrics to obtain board approval. Official approval did not come from the Vatican until 1936, however, when Propaganda Fide published *Constans et Sedula*, which lifted the ban on sisters performing surgical and obstetrical work.[77]

Not all nursing orders circumvented the interdiction. The Congregation of the Poor Sisters of St. Francis Seraph of the Perpetual Adoration in Lafayette, Indiana, a community with German roots, is a case in point. The Vatican's Sacred Congregation for Religious had prohibited obstetrical nursing in Germany.[78] Although the first major operation was performed at the sisters' St. Elizabeth's Hospital in 1895, obstetric patients were not admitted until forty years later after the publication of *Constans et Sedula*. This same congregation had established a nurse training school for sisters in 1897 but did not admit laywomen until 1937.[79]

Thus, conflicts occurred over sisters' adaptations to twentieth-century changes in nursing and medicine, and sometimes nuns broke with Vatican prescriptions. It is doubtful that these circumventions were open acts of rebellion, however. Rather, nuns' actions were pragmatic adaptations that they made to maintain their hospitals and carry out their health-care missions.

The standardization movement drew Catholic hospitals toward common goals with non-Catholic institutions. Sisters and church leaders adapted their hospitals and nursing to bring them into line with secular society by keeping up with modern scientific standards, establishing their own professional organizations, and forming schools of nursing. This legitimized their practice and enhanced their influence with students, physicians, and hospital standardization organizations. Up to 1925, nuns were prepared in technical skills, and they had the authority to teach these skills to their students. Later writings reveal, however, that by the late 1930s and 1940s, when nursing education programs began moving into universities, nuns became increasingly self-conscious about their relative lack of education as more professionally and technically trained employees staffed the hospitals. It was not until 1948 that sisters began the Sister Formation Conference to work for higher education and professionalization of teachers and sister-nurses.⁸⁰ On the other hand, the nuns' sovereignty in the CHA, their separate professional organizations, Father Moulinier's influence with the ACS, and the obstacles sisters faced later, such as the Roman Catholic clergy's attempt to control nursing practice and evaluation processes, indicate a distinct approach to standardization and modernization for sisters and their hospitals.

Conclusion

By 1922, statistics from the Catholic Hospital Association (CHA) showed that approximately twenty thousand sisters were caring for the sick in the United States and Canada. From the time of their inception, 675 Catholic hospitals, run mainly by nuns, had cared for four million patients.[1] Catholic sisters were leaders in the CHA and held the voting power. This book set out to more closely examine how this came about. One of the major themes has been the complex ways in which religious women participated in a market economy. By the late nineteenth century, a more urban and industrial era had come of age. In that context, Catholic sisters entered a capitalistic medical marketplace that had developed as immigration brought diverse cultures and religions across the United States. An entrepreneurial ethos emerged among nuns, influencing them to build their congregations and establish, market, finance, and administer complex hospital networks. In the process, they worked with architects, supply companies, contractors, bankers, industrial owners, physicians, and clergy. Sisters' efficient administration of hospital corporate structures showed that women could be as successful as men in a growing medical marketplace. The leadership and authority of women such as Sister Lidwina Butler, along with scores of other hospital administrators, defied the stereotype of nuns as passive religious women.

Limited endowments meant that Catholic hospitals had to depend on patient fees from the very beginning to carry out their work. Thus, because of economic realities, they were never strictly charity institutions. To maintain financial viability, nuns themselves provided the labor in the early years, although they increasingly transferred nursing care to lay student nurses who worked in exchange for their education. Sisters also established bonds with individuals, church leaders, business groups, and local governments. They forged these links because they believed that their nursing and hospitals were integral to the Catholic Church's ministry. Indeed, institutions had more power to reach people than did individuals. By 1925, all seven hospitals had tremendously expanded their purchasing power. At the same time, questions about hospitals' reputations, either from the local community or from physicians, could decrease public support, which, considering the competitive medical marketplace, could carry devastating consequences. Indeed, not all sisters' hospitals were successful. Failures were linked to numerous factors, which included poor planning, unrealistic visions, changing local markets, lack of physicians' support, or inadequate governmental and public backing.

In the late nineteenth and early twentieth centuries, Catholic hospitals in the Midwest, Texas, and Utah followed much of the standard patterns as those in the East. They expanded in response to social and medical needs, ideas about the germ theory, antiseptic and aseptic surgery, and new technology. In other ways, however, geographic location seems to have accounted for some differences. The Catholic hospitals represented here followed a pattern suggested by Paul Starr.[2] Compared to elite eastern voluntary hospitals that preferred closed medical staffs, Catholic hospitals in the Midwest, Texas, and Utah were open to many qualified physicians. Most of these hospitals also had fewer close ties to large university medical schools. They were more likely to admit patients from diverse backgrounds, including those with tuberculosis, alcoholism, and mental disorders. However, while one might easily conclude that frontier conditions in the Midwest and Trans-Mississippi West allowed sisters greater hospital autonomy, Kathleen Joyce found similar situations in eastern hospitals in which sisters exerted unusual authority.[3]

A second theme of this book has involved the place of gender and religion as frames of reference for understanding sisters' participation in the hospital marketplace. These were single women who lived in a communal relationship with each other. Through their vow of chastity, they distanced themselves from other women, thereby claiming the respect due them as Roman Catholic sisters. By professing religious vocations, they left behind many of the traditional gender restraints experienced by secular women, and they expanded their activities in the public arena. An important ingredient in their success in dealing with others was their religious image, which included the language they used. When making business proposals or asking for special considerations, they emphasized spiritual aims rather than their own. Even though nuns' vows called for anonymity, they were able to use their religious identities to good advantage as they negotiated within and outside hospital walls. Indeed, their religious mantle afforded them special respect and status, and this implicit authority helped them secure higher spiritual and economic returns for their work. Also, those same factors persuaded medical staffs that were accustomed to acting independently to share authority with the sisters.

Ethnic identity also intersected with sisters' marketplace roles. All three orders originated in France, and the French influence was particularly strong in the Congregation of the Sisters of Charity of the Incarnate Word. French women controlled leadership positions throughout this sixty-year period. Mother St. Pierre Cinquin often relied on spiritual sustenance from the Lyons order. After their arrival in the United States, however, all three congregations assimilated women from Ireland, Germany, Canada, Mexico, and the United States. Religious, economic, and social motives drew entrants to these congregations. With few other occupational choices in their own country, Irish women were especially numerous. Convents served as training grounds not only for Irish nurses but also for congregational leaders and hospital administrators. With a strong sense of economic self-sufficiency, Irish women had major roles to play in the establishment and management of Catholic hospitals across the United States. Many obtained their early training on farms in Ireland. Although some came from poorer families, others did not, and they brought with them the skills they had developed in working in their families' farming business—bartering, buying land or cattle, and raising money. Sisters also relied on their ethnic bases for financial backing. After the turn of the century, a rising prosperity among Catholic laity, particularly Irish and German, resulted in increased economic support for hospital expansions.

Nuns' social and economic contributions to their local and regional communities have been another theme of this book. As they purchased goods for hospital construction projects, repair work, and operational supplies, they helped expand local and regional economies. The economies also were aided by the sisters' successful efforts to bring medical and nursing services to mining and railroad establishments. Sisters started nursing schools and trained many women to work in the region. And Catholic hospitals provided scores of immigrant and American-born women the opportunity for meaningful work. At the same time, nuns' nursing was a powerful means of spreading religious devotion to patients, and by extension, to the surrounding area. Finally, while sisters increasingly relied on physicians to bring in private patients, their hospitals also provided doctors a vehicle for practice.

Catholic hospitals provided services to a diverse populace with no special regard to religious persuasions. However, Catholic immigrants found in sisters' institutions a common religious and ethnic identity. This was especially true in Indiana and Texas, where Protestantism shaped much of mainstream society. In western states, however, immigrants brought diverse faiths. A pattern of religious pluralism developed and prevented some of the contentious competition that existed in hospitals farther east. Additionally, sister's work with diverse groups of people helped break down the walls of separation that had isolated Catholics from the rest of society.

Nuns' interaction with scientific medicine and the professionalization movement, key indicators of modernity, has been another integrating theme. As hospital owners, sisters had to keep their institutions financially solvent. Yet, they measured their success and usefulness by the number of patients treated, lives and souls saved, and sufferings mitigated. Because they were reluctant to change their methods or purposes as long as those goals were being met, they sometimes needed convincing by local medical authorities of the need to update and modernize. After the hospital standardization movement got underway in the early twentieth century, Catholic hospitals were drawn toward common goals with secular institutions. Through the CHA, nuns had a forum for addressing ways to keep pace with the hospital reform movement. They modernized by admitting secular students to their training programs, hiring secular nurses, and obtaining nursing licensure.

Still, sisters held firmly to their mission of Catholic service. In that regard, they viewed themselves as stewards of the hospital's resources and bound by their faith to reapply them to aid the sick. This included investments to expand technology, surgery, nursing services, and outpatient facilities that became part of the modern hospital. Improvements in diagnosis and surgery attracted more people who, in years past, would have remained inaccessible to nursing sisters. And as hospitals evolved into curative institutions and mortality rates fell, nuns demonstrated that they could offer substantial opportunities not only for religious salvation and spiritual comfort but also for physical survival and comfort. Well-equipped facilities and competent medical and nursing staffs certainly helped in building public confidence in Catholic hospitals, which in turn influenced admissions and generated income. Also, the sisters' evolving skills in public relations and marketing endeavors added to the hospitals' successes. While these successes kindled public trust in hospitals, they also inspired confidence in the nuns' competence, skill, and spiritual commitment.

Importantly, then, there was no clear dichotomy between charity and marketplace roles for Catholic sister-nurses. Their hospital activities revealed complex relationships that included interactions of gender, religion, and economic realities. That reality frames the last major theme of this book: how nuns interwove market values with the sacred. One of their most important reasons for raising funds was to provide institutions that integrated medical and religious values. Regardless of geographic location, these hospitals maintained a Catholic identity. Architecture, religious icons, light shining through stained-glass windows, and distinctive ceremonies provided a rich tapestry that reflected the hospital's Catholic identity. Even the presence of death provided spiritual opportunities for the sisters. Catholic hospitals were places where the dying could make peace with God and organize their spiritual affairs before leaving earthly life. The fact that hospital nursing involved intercession in human death gave great significance to the sisters' service identities. While providing aid and comfort to the dying, nuns could be mediators to the divine.

Sisters' spiritual personas were observable as they advertised, raised money, and participated in public religious celebrations. When people entered Catholic hospitals and paid for their care, they bought more than antiseptic conditions, competent doctors, and modern equipment. They also purchased the sisters' spirituality. Ill persons who suffered, died, or recovered did so in a spiritual environment within the caring presence of sister-nurses. Their attendance, along with the availability of the sacraments, could have as much significance to patients as competent surgeons in safe operating rooms.

Over time, the sisters developed an appreciation of the interrelationship between business and spiritual objectives. They understood that the more financially stable the hospital, and the larger number of people helped, the greater the social and spiritual returns for their work. The end purpose of their entrepreneurship, then, was not to expand profits and market share but rather to advance Catholic spirituality.

Because of the dearth of information heretofore published about nursing sisters, they have been almost invisible in the history of health care and the modern hospital. Perhaps one factor in that omission is simply the fact that, in spite of their religious identities, they still were regarded as women who in their nursing roles were merely doing what has long been assumed to be "women's work." Another factor to consider is that hospitals, even those owned by Catholic sisters, are not often thought of as religious institutions. The nuns, of course, did not share that view. As they looked at medical problems and attended to the care of the body, they simultaneously saw spiritual souls. Because their views of suffering, illness, and death were based upon long-standing and deeply held spiritual convictions, it stands to reason that their justification for establishing hospitals was much deeper than the simple commitment to acts of charity. Catholic hospitals provided sisters opportunities to nurse the sick and dying, placing nuns in situations that linked the worldly and the divine. Illness and suffering also awakened compassion in nursing sisters and presented them with opportunities for healing and relieving the suffering of others. For the nuns, this certainly included sound medical care but also works of mercy and, at times, divine intervention.

Importantly, medical history has begun to challenge an exclusively somatic conception of illness. Many recent studies have questioned the boundaries between the somatic and psychological. It is logical to expect that such a research movement will now evolve into a deeper study of the spiritual components of health care and medical practice. To assume that illness is exclusively a biological event and that institutions that respond to illness are preeminently secular institutions is shortsighted and narrow. A primary argument of this book has been that, to understand what nuns were doing, the notion of hospitals as inevitably and uniquely medical must be discarded. In reality, Catholic sisters' hospitals were both medical and religious institutions. By recognizing this broader definition of hospitals, conceptions of health and disease must be reevaluated. Indeed, when considering the roles that Catholic sisters played in the hospital marketplace, one must rethink the very meaning of health care. Acknowledging, from the view of history, that the hospital has only recently become a uniquely medical institution invites further studies of why and how people are establishing hospitals.

Finally, this book has addressed the dynamic years of Catholic hospital establishment when sisters' autonomy and influence within the medical marketplace reached their peak. As the twentieth century advanced and pressures to professionalize increased, nuns' religious lives became more regimented and their autonomy more challenged. Additionally, governmental regulations increased, limiting sisters' sovereignty even more. All of these changes affected the identities and business practices of Catholic hospitals. This transition process, its modern outcomes, and its future implications for gender and religious influences upon American health-care institutions call for further study. Among the questions such a study would need to address is whether the forces of economics, governmental control, and professional standardization are inevitably forcing Catholic hospitals to become bland, culturally benign institutions that are virtually indistinguishable from nonsectarian hospitals. If that were, in fact, the future portrait of the American Catholic hospital, then the spiritual components of health care and healing, as emphasized by the nuns in this book, would surely be endangered.

Epilogue

This book has depicted the early historical tensions that Catholic hospitals faced while striving to retain their religious identities in an increasingly competitive secular marketplace. It is abundantly clear that these issues continue to be played out in Catholic nursing congregations throughout the country. As sisters compete for patients, staff, and reimbursements in today's hospital marketplace, some fear they are getting away from their original purpose of helping those most in need. To that end, many nursing congregations are getting out of the hospital business altogether, while others redirect their health care into new services.[1]

The Sisters of Charity of the Incarnate Word have continued medical and nursing services in Texas, across the United States, and Mexico. Change was in the air in the 1980s, which brought a revolution in hospital reimbursement as health-care expenditures took on a greater percentage of the Gross Domestic Product. In response, the federal government and private insurance payers began capping hospital reimbursements. Due to increasing costs, duplication of services, and a large debt, in 1991 the Incarnate Word Sisters sold St. Joseph's Hospital in Fort Worth to the Daughters of Charity Health System-West Central, after over a hundred years of service.[2] In 1999, the Incarnate Word Health System merged with the Sisters of Charity Health Care System to become CHRISTUS Health. It now includes more than forty hospitals and facilities in five American states and Mexico, with assets of more than $3.4 billion. As a component of that system, Santa Rosa Hospital in San Antonio, the city's first private hospital, is now a 400-plus bed general acute-care facility and is still located in the heart of the city.[3]

In 1987, the Sisters of St. Joseph of Carondelet merged St. Joseph's

Hospital in St. Paul into the Health East System, along with two Lutheran facilities and one Baptist hospital. Then in 1991, the sisters sold St. Mary's Hospital in Minneapolis to Fairview Health System. The nuns could no longer obtain the financial resources needed to keep St. Mary's a "state of the art" institution that would meet demand for a broader array of services in Minnesota's competitive environment. These decisions caused dissension among the sisters, their congregational leadership, and the local residents.[4]

But the women had other health-care ministries in mind. In the 1990s, they began a system of clinics that served those who could not afford health insurance and who did not qualify for subsidized government health programs.

In 1973, the Sisters of the Holy Cross withdrew sponsorship from St. Mary's Hospital in Cairo, Illinois. The racial situation had always been tense, and the charged atmosphere did not improve during the civil rights movement in the 1960s. Fiery crosses burned on the hospital lawn after the sisters ended the century-long segregation of hospital wards, a decision that the medical staff opposed. By 1972, the hospital was in dire financial straits, and the sisters could not get assistance from the state or the city. Some members of the media blamed the hospital's closing on the attitudes of local city officials and their continued discrimination against African Americans. The mayor blamed "fiscal mismanagement over the past ten years." Other sources attributed the closing to the shortage of physicians. Once again, however, the sisters did not measure their successes in monetary value alone. One historian of the congregation stated, "Not only did the Sisters work hard in the hospital, bringing healing to the sick and dying. They also brought lost Catholics back to the Church, [and] baptized countless babies and adults when they were at death's door."[5]

On October 4, 1993, the *Wall Street Journal* announced the intent of the Sisters of the Holy Cross to sell Holy Cross Hospital in Salt Lake City to HealthTrust, Inc., a for-profit company that operated hospitals in twenty-one states.[6] Church law required the sale of Catholic facilities valued at greater than $3 million to be approved by the Vatican, based on the local bishop's recommendation. Bishop William Weigand of Salt Lake City made the required recommendation at the sisters' request, but only with the understanding that they would do everything possible to find a Catholic buyer. After the October announcement, the bishop learned that another Catholic health system had been interested in buying Holy Cross Hospital, and he tried to persuade the sisters' president and general council to reconsider. But the binding and exclusive letter of intent between the two parties prevented them from doing so. The nuns were beginning a new ministry to the undocumented and underserved sick, giving priority to women, children, and the elderly. They could no longer bear the $80 million hospital debt and still meet the demand for a broader array of services in Utah's competitive marketplace. The hospital's sale to HealthTrust, Inc., would enable a more comprehensive and integrated network of delivery for the Utah community.[7]

But the bishop disagreed, since the sale would leave Utah without a Catholic hospital. Many local residents were saddened, as well, and one even accused the sisters of being "corporate raiders, selling to the highest bidder."[8] Others objected to a hospital run "strictly as a business, without the strong mission spirit and option for the poor" that Holy Cross Hospital had.[9] Bishop Weigand traveled to Rome to ask the Vatican to block the pending sale, but after months of negotiation, he was unsuccessful.[10] The sisters persisted with their plan and, in fact, did sell the facility to the company of their choice. They held tenaciously to their rights to protect the integrity of their community and to determine the type of work appropriate to their particular order.

Then on June 29, 1999, officials of Holy Cross Health System, sponsored by the Sisters of the Holy Cross, announced that they would merge with Mercy Health Services based in Farmington Hills, Michigan. Both are not-for-profit Catholic health systems with hospitals, clinics, nursing homes, and home-health agencies. The resulting merger is the third-largest Catholic health-care system in the United States and the ninth-largest overall, with forty-seven hospitals and other facilities in seven states.[11] As part of this network, Trinity Health, the Sisters of the Holy Cross have continued to sponsor St. Joseph's Hospital in South Bend, now a 288-bed acute-care facility known as St. Joseph Regional Medical Center. The sisters use its resources to support other services, including clinics for underserved populations. Recently, the hospital announced plans to move to a new site and build "from the bottom up." As of this writing, deliberations are still underway about the future use of the current campus.[12]

In his paper on Catholic social theory and late-twentieth-century Catholic institutional life, Clark E. Cochran asserts: "Never have Catholic health care institutions been more vibrant. They are the dominant institutions in the United States not-for-profit hospital sector. They are among the most financially stable and the most active in mergers and acquisitions."[13] In these hospitals, foundational values have not changed. A 1994 editorial in *Health Progress* entitled "How to Approach Catholic Identity in Changing Times" lists them as including: (1) Health care is viewed as a service and never strictly a commodity to be exchanged for profit; (2) Every person has intrinsic spiritual worth, at every stage of development, and is the subject of human dignity with a right to health care; (3) Particular commitment is to the needs of the poor and disenfranchised; and (4) Stewardship requires that natural and social resources be prudently used.[14]

These values have been grounded in a historical tradition of health care embodied in Catholic sisters of the past. In the late nineteenth and early twentieth centuries, a hospital's Catholic identity was never in question because of the nuns' presence. Yet their numbers have significantly declined today, and their diminished presence has been felt deeply by former patients, physicians, and employees. When Holy Cross Hospital was sold, one admirer summed up the nuns' work and unknowingly reinforced the major theme of this book: "I sincerely hope that the Holy Cross ... sisters will be able to serve a function at the hospitals because their presence has always been an important element in health care here."[15] Likewise, in 1991 when the Incarnate Word Sisters sold St. Joseph's Hospital in Fort Worth, a former employee noted, "Saint Joseph was different from all the other hospitals in the city, when the nuns were here." And according to a doctor, "Fort Worth always recognized Saint Joseph as the hospital with a heart, a Christian, charitable institution, and that was because of the presence of the sisters.... Their presence had an invaluable influence."[16] Such spoken sentiments call for continued study of the richness and complexity of sisters' roles in the Catholic hospital movement.

Notes

Preface

1. Mary Douglas, *How Institutions Think* (Syracuse, NY: Syracuse University Press, 1986), 4.
2. Cynthia Smith, Cathy Cowan, Art Sensenig, Aaron Catlin, and the Health Accounts Team, "Trends: Health and Spending Growth Slows in 2003," *Health Affairs* 24, no. 1 (January–February 2005): 185–89.
3. James C. Scott, *Weapons of the Weak: Everyday Forms of Peasant Resistance* (New Haven: Yale University Press, 1985). For further discussion, see Michel Foucault, "Truth and Power," in, *Power/Knowledge*, ed. Colin Gordon (New York: Pantheon, 1980), 109–33; and Mario Biagioli, *Galileo, Courtier: The Practice of Science in the Culture of Absolutism* (Chicago and London: University of Chicago Press, 1993), 2.

Introduction

1. Although the word "nun" specifically refers to a member of a cloistered religious order, it is popularly used today and will be used interchangeably with "sister" and "women religious."
2. "Record of Apostolic Service, Lidwina Butler," Congregation of the Sisters of the Holy Cross, Saint Mary's, Notre Dame, IN (hereafter cited as CSC).
3. "Facts About the Catholic Health Association of the United States" (St. Louis, MO: Catholic Health Association, November 29, 2000).
4. Christopher J. Kauffman, *Ministry and Meaning: A Religious History of Catholic Health Care in the United States* (New York: Crossroad, 1995), 193.
5. Two exceptions are Mary J. Oates, *The Catholic Philanthropic Tradition in America* (Bloomington: Indiana University Press, 1995); and Angelyn Dries, OSF, *The Missionary Movement in American Catholic History* (Maryknoll, NY: Orbis Books, 1998).
6. See, for example, Renate Wilson, *Pious Traders in Medicine: A German Pharmaceutical Network in Eighteenth-Century North America* (University Park: Pennsylvania State University Press, 2000).

7. This high intake of Irish sisters was typical when compared to entrants in English, Welsh, and Australian religious communities. See Sioban Nelson, *Say Little, Do Much: Nursing, Nuns, and Hospitals in the Nineteenth Century* (Philadelphia: University of Pennsylvania Press, 2001); and Barbara Walsh, *Roman Catholic Nuns in England and Wales, 1800–1937: A Social History* (Dublin and Portland, OR: Irish Academic Press, 2002).

8. Hasia R. Diner, *Erin's Daughters in America: Irish Immigrant Women in the Nineteenth Century* (Baltimore and London: Johns Hopkins University Press, 1983), 120–21, 152 (for quotation).

9. John O'Grady, *Catholic Charities in the United States: History and Problems* (Washington, DC: National Conference of Catholic Charities, 1930; repr., New York: Arno Press, 1971), 195–96; "The Chronological Development of the Catholic Hospital of the United States and Canada," *Hospital Progress* 21 (April 1940): 122–33; and Ursula Stepsis, CSA, and Dolores Liptak, RSM, eds., *Pioneer Healers: The History of Women Religious in American Health Care* (New York: Crossroad, 1989), 287.

10. See Barbra Mann Wall, "Healthcare as Product: Catholic Sisters Confront Charity and the Hospital Marketplace, 1865–1925," in *Commodifying Everything: Relationships of the Market*, ed. Susan Strasser (New York: Routledge, 2003), 143–68.

11. For sources on Protestant women, see Nancy F. Cott, *The Bonds of Womanhood: "Woman's Sphere" in New England, 1780–1835* (New Haven: Yale University Press, 1977); Peggy Pascoe, *Relations of Rescue: The Search for Female Moral Authority in the American West, 1874–1939* (New York: Oxford University Press, 1990); Evelyn Brooks Higginbotham, *Righteous Discontent: The Women's Movement in the Black Baptist Church, 1880–1920* (Cambridge: Harvard University Press, 1993); and Ruth Bordin, *Women and Temperance: The Quest for Power and Liberty, 1873–1900* (New Brunswick, NJ: Rutgers University Press, 1990).

12. Walsh, *Roman Catholic Nuns;* Suellen Hoy, "The Journey Out: The Recruitment and Emigration of Irish Religious Women in the United States, 1812–1914," *Journal of Women's History* 6 and 7 (Winter/Spring 1995): 63–98; Jo Ann Kay McNamara, *Sisters in Arms: Catholic Nuns through Two Millennia* (Cambridge, MA and London: Harvard University Press, 1996); Carol K. Coburn and Martha Smith, *Spirited Lives: How Nuns Shaped Catholic Culture and American Life, 1836–1920* (Chapel Hill and London: University of North Carolina Press, 1999); Margaret Susan Thompson, "Sisterhood and Power: Class, Culture, and Ethnicity in the American Convent," *Colby Library Quarterly* 25 (1989): 149–75; and Patricia Wittberg, *The Rise and Fall of Catholic Religious Orders: A Social Movement Perspective* (Albany: State University of New York Press, 1994).

13. Kauffmann, *Ministry and Meaning;* and Kathleen M. Joyce, "Science and the Saints: American Catholics and Health Care, 1880–1930" (PhD diss., Princeton University, 1995), 119.

14. Nelson, *Say Little, Do Much.* For an earlier study on Irish nuns, see Mary Patricia Tarbox, "The Origins of Nursing by the Sisters of Mercy in the United States: 1843–1910" (EdD diss., Columbia University Teacher's College, 1986).

15. Bernadette McCauley, " 'Who Shall Take Care of Our Sick?': Roman Catholic Sisterhoods and Their Hospitals, New York City, 1850–1930" (PhD diss., Columbia University, 1992).

16. Morris J. Vogel, *The Invention of the Modern Hospital: Boston, 1870–1930* (Chicago: University of Chicago Press, 1980); David Rosner, *A Once Charitable Enter-*

prise: Hospitals and Health Care in Brooklyn and New York, 1885–1915 (Cambridge: Cambridge University Press, 1982); Erwin H. Ackerknecht, *A Short History of Medicine*, rev. ed. (Baltimore and London: Johns Hopkins University Press, 1982); Paul Starr, *The Social Transformation of American Medicine: The Rise of a Sovereign Profession and the Making of a Vast Industry* (New York: Basic Books, 1982); and Charles E. Rosenberg, *The Care of Strangers: The Rise of America's Hospital System* (Baltimore and London: Johns Hopkins University Press, 1987). Exceptions are Joan Lynaugh, *The Community Hospitals of Kansas City, Missouri, 1870–1915* (New York and London: Garland Publishing, 1989); and Kauffman, *Ministry and Meaning*.

17. Guenter B. Risse, *Mending Bodies, Saving Souls: A History of Hospitals* (New York and Oxford: Oxford University Press, 1999).

18. Stevens shows that government funds to private, "charitable" hospitals have a long history. See Rosemary Stevens, *In Sickness and in Wealth: American Hospitals in the Twentieth Century* (New York: Basic Books, 1989).

19. Barbara Melosh, *The Physician's Hand: Work Culture and Conflict in American Nursing* (Philadelphia: Temple University Press, 1982); Susan M. Reverby, *Ordered to Care: The Dilemma of American Nursing, 1850–1945* (Cambridge: Cambridge University Press, 1987).

20. Marvin R. O'Connell, "The Roman Catholic Tradition since 1545," in *Caring and Curing: Health and Medicine in the Western Religious Traditions*, ed. Ronald L. Numbers and Darrel W. Amundsen (New York: Macmillan Publishing Co., 1986), 108–45. Beginning as a response to the Protestant Reformation, a general council of bishops at Trent met from 1545 to 1563 in an effort to secure a uniform religious expression for Catholics throughout the world. Against Luther, bishops upheld the divine validity of the seven sacraments, the church's hierarchical nature, the divine institution of the priesthood, and the sacrificial character of the Mass.

21. It was not until 1900 that Pope Leo XIII issued *Conditae a Christo* which fully recognized active communities. See Lynn Marie Jarrell, "The Development of Legal Structures for Women Religious between 1500 and 1900: A Study of Selected Institutes of Religious Life for Women" (PhD diss., Catholic University of America, 1984), 28, 280.

22. Wittberg, *Rise and Fall*, 63.

23. Coburn and Smith, *Spirited Lives*, 13; Wittberg, *Rise and Fall*, 38; and Raymond Deville, *The French School of Spirituality: An Introduction and Reader*, trans. Agnes Cunningham (Pittsburgh: Duquesne University Press, 1994), 215.

24. Mary Ewens, OP, "Women in the Convent," in *American Catholic Women: A Historical Exploration*, ed. Karen Kennelly, CSJ (New York: Macmillan Publishing Company, 1989), 25.

25. Andrew Abbott, *The System of Professions: An Essay on the Division of Expert Labor* (Chicago: University of Chicago Press, 1988); Harold L. Wilensky, "The Professionalization of Everyone?" *American Journal of Sociology* 70 (September 1964): 137–58; Eliot Freidson, *Profession of Medicine: A Study of the Sociology of Applied Knowledge* (New York: Harper & Row, 1970); Eliot Freidson, "Are Professions Necessary?" in *The Authority of Experts: Studies in History and Theory*, ed. Thomas L. Haskell (Bloomington: Indiana University Press, 1984), 3–27; and Magali Sarfatti Larson, *The Rise of Professionalism: A Sociological Analysis* (Berkeley: University of California Press, 1977). Lori Ginzberg, in *Women and the Work of Benevolence: Morality, Politics, and Class in the Nineteenth-Century United States* (New Haven: Yale University

Press, 1990), also addresses professionalism, giving special emphasis to issues of gender and social class.

26. Abbott, *System of Professions*, 71.

CHAPTER 1

1. John Gordon Morrison, *Civil War Diary*, July 17 and 20, 1862. Used with permission from Lt. Col. James Owens. This excerpt is from his great-grandfather's diary, the original being located in the library of the Naval Museum at the Washington, DC, Naval Yard. Morrison subsequently won the Medal of Honor.

2. Sister Mary Denis Maher, *To Bind Up the Wounds: Catholic Sister Nurses in the U.S. Civil War* (Baton Rouge: Louisiana State University Press, 1989); and Ellen Ryan Jolly, LLD, *Nuns of the Battlefield* (Providence, RI: Providence Visitor Press, 1927).

3. Jay P. Dolan, *The American Catholic Experience: A History from Colonial Times to the Present* (Notre Dame and London: University of Notre Dame Press, 1992), 127–57; Kerby A. Miller, *Emigrants and Exiles: Ireland and the Irish Exodus to North America* (New York: Oxford University Press, 1985), 193–99, 291–93.

4. Starr, *Social Transformation*, 201, 315–20; Joyce, "Science and the Saints," 62.

5. Dolan, *American Catholic Experience*, 321–26.

6. Wittberg, *Rise and Fall*, 133.

7. In the seventeenth century, members of "contemplative" religious orders were descendants of the early medieval monastics. They were called "nuns" and took solemn, or perpetual, vows; exercised strict rules of cloister; and devoted their lives to prayer and contemplation. Members of "active" congregations, called "sisters," took simple vows that they renewed every year, had modified rules of enclosure, and performed works of charity in addition to focusing on prayer. A group who took solemn vows was called an "order." The terms "community" or "congregation" were used for sisters with simple vows. For the purposes of this paper, these terms will be used interchangeably, as they are in the 1983 revised Code of Canon Law.

8. Elizabeth Rapley, *The Devotes: Women and Church in Seventeenth-Century France* (Montreal: McGill-Queen's University Press, 1990); Wilson, *Pious Traders in Medicine*, 31; and Penelope Johnson, *Equal in Monastic Profession: Religious Women in Medieval France* (Chicago and London: University of Chicago Press, 1991).

9. Nelson, *Say Little, Do Much*; and Colin Jones, *The Charitable Imperative: Hospitals and Nursing in Ancien Regime and Revolutionary France* (London and New York: Routledge, 1989).

10. Reverby, *Ordered to Care*, 11–16.

11. Barbra Mann Wall, "Called to a Mission of Charity: The Sisters of St. Joseph in the Civil War," *Nursing History Review* 6 (1998): 86–113.

12. Dolan, *American Catholic Experience*, 101–24, 158–61, 221–40; and Jay P. Dolan, *In Search of an American Catholicism: A History of Religion and Culture in Tension* (New York and Oxford: Oxford University Press, 2002), 71–126.

13. Once a religious community received preliminary status as a recognized religious order within the Roman Catholic Church, a group or its founder wrote a constitution to establish guidelines for living the religious life. Ultimately, the community had to submit the constitution to the Sacred Congregation of Religious and Secular Institutes in Rome for approval. In usage today, "Rules" and "Constitutions" are used inter-

changeably. See Florence Jean Deacon, "Handmaids or Autonomous Women: The Charitable Activities, Institution Building and Communal Relationships of Catholic Sisters in Nineteenth-Century Wisconsin" (Ph.D. diss., University of Wisconsin, Madison, 1989), 218–20.

14. Deacon, "Handmaids or Autonomous Women," 219, 234–35. Papal approval also signified that a congregation had been fully recognized by the Catholic Church.

15. The following data on nursing communities are taken from Suzy Farren, *A Call to Care: The Women Who Built Catholic Healthcare in America* (St. Louis: Catholic Health Association of the United States, 1996); Ann Doyle, "Nursing by Religious Orders in the United States," Parts 1–4, *American Journal of Nursing* 29, no. 7 (July 1929): 775–86; 29, no. 8 (August 1929): 959–69; 29, no. 9 (September 1929): 1085–95; 29, no. 10 (October 1929): 1197–1207; Barbara Misner, SCSC, *"Highly Respectable and Accomplished Ladies": Catholic Women Religious in America, 1790–1850* (New York and London: 1988), 211–34; Stepsis and Liptak, *Pioneer Healers;* O'Grady, *Catholic Charities;* Maher, *To Bind Up the Wounds,* 27–43; and Kauffman, *Ministry and Meaning.*

16. Diane Batts Morrow, *Persons of Color and Religious at the Same Time: The Oblate Sisters of Providence, 1828–1860* (Chapel Hill and London: University of North Carolina Press, 2002), 71–72, 147–49; Kauffman, *Ministry and Meaning,* 55–56, 79.

17. Dolan, *American Catholic Experience;* and Mary Ewens, *The Role of the Nun in Nineteenth Century America* (1971; repr. Salem, NH: Ayer Company, Publishers, Inc., 1984).

18. This topic is addressed in Barbra Mann Wall, "Called to a Mission of Charity," 86.

19. Doyle, "Nursing by Religious Orders," 779, 959; Maher, *To Bind Up the Wounds,* 34; and Stepsis and Liptak, *Pioneer Healers,* 30–33, 287; O'Grady, *Catholic Charities,* 194–96; "Chronological Development of the Catholic Hospital," 122–33.

20. Coburn and Smith, *Spirited Lives,* 190–91; and Mary Lucinda Savage, *The Congregation of St. Joseph of Carondelet: A Brief Account of Its Origin and Its Work in the United States, 1650–1922* (St. Louis: Herder Book Co., 1923), 100–102.

21. Joy Clough, RSM, "Chicago's Sisters of Mercy," *Chicago History* 32, no. 1 (Summer 2003): 42–55; and Tarbox, "The Origins of Nursing by the Sisters of Mercy," 197–200.

22. Sister Mary Paulinus Oakes, *Angels of Mercy: An Eyewitness Account of the Civil War and Yellow Fever by a Sister of Mercy* (Baltimore: Cathedral Foundation Press, 1998).

23. Stepsis and Liptak, *Pioneer Healers,* 31–33; Doyle, "Nursing by Religious Orders," 960.

24. Maher, *To Bind Up the Wounds,* 1; and Barbra Mann Wall, "Grace under Pressure: The Nursing Sisters of the Holy Cross, 1861–1865," *Nursing History Review* 1 (1993): 71–87.

25. Susan Carol Peterson and Courtney Ann Vaughn-Roberson, *Women with Vision: The Presentation Sisters of South Dakota, 1880–1985* (Urbana: University of Illinois Press, 1988); Todd L. Savitt and Janice Willms, "Sisters' Hospital: The Sisters of Providence and St. Patrick Hospital, Missoula, Montana, 1873–1890," *Montana: The Magazine of Western History* 53, no. 1 (Spring 2003): 28–43; and Kauffman, *Ministry and Meaning,* 99–105.

26. Kaufman, *Ministry and Meaning,* 131–38.

27. Stepsis and Liptak, *Pioneer Healers*, 287.

28. "The History of the Medical Center," copy presented to author from Philip C. Haughey, Boston, MA. This hospital has recently been named one of the top twenty-five in the country, in the teaching hospital category, in caring for individuals with heart disease. See "A Network for Heart Health," *Boston Globe*, October 30, 2002.

29. Anita Specht, "The Power of Ethnicity in a Community of Women Religious: The Poor Handmaids of Jesus Christ in the United States, 1868–1930," *U. S. Catholic Historian* 19 (Winter 2001): 53–64.

30. Fortieth Anniversary of the Saint Francis Hospital, 1889–1929, Wichita, KS; 1887–1937 Golden Jubilee, St. Margaret's Hospital, Kansas City, KS; and Fiftieth Year Golden Jubilee, Annual Report of St. Mary's Hospital, Quincy, IL, PINS, Box 20, University of Notre Dame Archives (hereafter cited as UNDA).

31. Kauffman, *Ministry and Meaning*, 131–38, 145–48, 256–57; and *Golden Jubilee, 1897–1947, St. Vincent's Hospital School of Nursing*, PINS 19/13, UNDA.

32. Barbra Mann Wall, "Courage to Care: The Sisters of the Holy Cross in the Spanish-American War," *Nursing History Review* 3 (1995): 55–77.

33. "Chronological Development of the Catholic Hospital," 122; and US Bureau of the Census, *Benevolent Institutions, 1910* (Washington, DC: Government Printing Office, 1913), 68; and O'Grady, *Catholic Charities*, 195–210.

34. Doyle, "Nursing by Religious Orders in the United States, Part 4—Lutheran Deaconesses, 1849–1928," *American Journal of Nursing* 29, no. 10 (October 1929): 1197–1207; Nelson, *Say Little, Do Much*; Elaine Shaw Sorensen, " 'For Zion's Sake': The Emergence of Mormon Nursing," *Nursing History Review* 6 (1998): 51–69.

35. Patricia Byrne, CSJ, "Sisters of St. Joseph: The Americanization of a French Tradition," *U. S. Catholic Historian* 5 (1986): 243.

36. Ibid., 246; and Thomas Bokenkotter, *A Concise History of the Catholic Church* (New York: Image Books, Doubleday, 1990), 248.

37. Ibid., 241–72.

38. Ibid., 248–60, 272; Sister Dolorita Marie Dougherty, CSJ, et al., *Sisters of St. Joseph of Carondelet* (St. Louis: B. Herder Book Co., 1966), 368; and Carol K. Coburn and Martha Smith, " 'Pray for Your Wanderers': Women Religious on the Colorado Mining Frontier, 1877–1917," *Frontiers* 15 (1995): 27–52.

39. Sister Ignatius Loyola Cox, "Notes on the Early History of the Sisters of St. Joseph in Minnesota," *Acta et Dicta* 3 (July 1914): 253. Sister Ignatius wrote this in 1897.

40. *The (Official) Catholic Directory and Almanac* (Milwaukee: M. H. Wiltzius & Co., 1900); Sister Helen Angela Hurley, *On Good Ground: The Story of the Sisters of St. Joseph in St. Paul* (Minneapolis: University of Minnesota Press, 1951), 10–20, 173.

41. Edward Sorin to Father Moreau, December 5, 1842, vol. 1, *Circular Letters of the Very Reverend Basil Anthony Moreau*, trans. Edward L. Heston (Notre Dame, IN: Ave Maria Press, 1943), 61.

42. *Rules of the Sisters of the Holy Cross* (Notre Dame, IN: Ave Maria Steam Press, 1871), CSC.

43. Sister M. Georgia Costin, CSC, *Priceless Spirit: A History of the Sisters of the Holy Cross, 1841–1893* (Notre Dame, IN: University of Notre Dame Press, 1994).

44. Sister Mary Immaculate Creek, CSC, *A Panorama: 1847–1977, Saint Mary's College, Notre Dame, Indiana* (Notre Dame, IN: Saint Mary's College, 1977), 17–19; and Sister M. Campion Kuhn, CSC, "Americanization," vol. 1, *Fruits of the Tree:*

Sesquicentennial Chronicles, Sisters of the Holy Cross (Notre Dame, IN: Ave Maria Press, 1988), 73–99.

45. Moreau to Brothers in Christ, Circular Letter No. 14, September 1, 1841, in *Circular Letters*, 39.

46. Wall, "Grace under Pressure," 71–87. For their work on the USS *Red Rover*, they were named the "first Navy nurses."

47. Membership Roster, CSC.

48. John M. Lozano, *Jeanne Chezard de Matel and the Sisters of the Incarnate Word* (Chicago: Claret Center for Resources in Spirituality, 1983).

49. Sister Margaret Patrice Slattery, CCVI, *Historical Development from 1869 to 1994*, vol. 1, *Promises to Keep: A History of the Sisters of Charity of the Incarnate Word, San Antonio, Texas* (San Antonio: private printing, 1995), 72–73.

50. 1885 *Constitution of the Sisters of Charity of the Incarnate Word*, Archives, Motherhouse of the Incarnate Word (hereafter cited as AMIW).

51. Slattery, *Historical Studies of Hospitals, Schools in Mexico, and Incarnate Word College*, vol. 2, *Promises to Keep*, chapters 3–7.

52. Slattery, *Historical Development*, 25–27.

53. *Benevolent Institutions, 1910*, 68. See also Frances Stuart Hanckel, "American Hospitals in 1910" (Doctor of Science diss., School of Hygiene and Public Health of the Johns Hopkins University, 1985), 358.

54. Hoy, "The Journey Out," 63–98; Diner, *Erin's Daughters;* and Coburn and Smith, *Spirited Lives*.

55. Kuhn, "Americanization," 81.

56. Jolly, *Nuns of the Battlefield*, 155.

57. Hoy, "The Journey Out," 69–75. Irish nuns in the nineteenth century had studied history, literature, mathematics, French, music, and geography either in pay schools in Ireland, with private tutors, or in schools abroad.

58. Quoted in Emmet Larkin, "The Devotional Revolution in Ireland, 1850–75," *American Historical Review* 77 (June 1972): 651n 45.

59. Matriculation Records, CSC.

60. Hoy, "The Journey Out," 84.

61. Ibid., 63–98 (quotation on p. 75); Walsh, *Roman Catholic Nuns*, 137–49; Miller, *Emigrants and Exiles*, 349–53.

62. See personnel records, AMIW; and Hoy, "The Journey Out," 79–81.

63. Slattery, *Historical Development*, 112–13. See also "Irish Postulants Arrive on 'Republic,'" *New World*, November 29, 1929.

64. David Fitzpatrick, "The Modernisation of the Irish Female," in *Rural Ireland 1600–1900: Modernisation and Change*, ed. Patrick O'Flanagen, Paul Ferguson, and Kevin Whelan (Cork, Ireland: Cork University Press, 1987), 166.

65. Walsh, *Roman Catholic Nuns*, 7.

66. Diner, *Erin's Daughters*, 29 (quotation), 159.

67. David R. Roediger, *The Wages of Whiteness: Race and the Making of the American Working Class* (London and New York: Verson, 1991, rev. 1999); Noel Ignatiev, *How the Irish Became White* (New York: Routledge, 1995).

68. Sister M. Francis de Sales, "A Holy Cross Sister in Peace and in War," *Holy Cross Courier* 4 (1930): 5.

69. Costin, *Priceless Spirit*, 149–50; Byrne, "Sisters of St. Joseph," 265.

70. One articulation of a national self-understanding was an interpretation labeled

"Americanization" that included how the Catholic Church and its many immigrants should adjust to the novel environment of the United States. See Philip Gleason, "American Identity and Americanization," in *Harvard Encyclopedia of American Ethnic Groups*, ed. Stephen Thernstrom (Cambridge, MA: Belknap Press, 1980), 31–57.

71. Coburn and Smith, *Spirited Lives*, 53.

72. Margaret Susan Thompson, "Philemon's Dilemma: Nuns and the Black Community in Nineteenth-Century America: Some Findings," *Records of the American Catholic Historical Society of Philadelphia* 96 (1986): 3–18.

73. Marvin R. O'Connell, *John Ireland and the American Catholic Church* (St. Paul: Minnesota Historical Society Press, 1988). Ireland was bishop of St. Paul from 1875 to 1888 and archbishop until his death in 1918.

74. Slattery, *Historical Studies*, 121, 161, 250–52.

75. Byrne, "Sisters of St. Joseph," 249, 271.

76. Mother St. Pierre Cinquin to Rt. Rev. A. N. Gallagher, February 7, 1889; and p. 315, Letters of Mother St. Pierre Cinquin, trans. Sister Kathleen Garvey (hereafter cited as LSPC), AMIW; Slattery, *Historical Development*, 106–7.

Chapter 2

1. Mother St. Pierre Cinquin to Beloved Sisters, December 18, 1889, LSPC, AMIW.

2. McNamara, *Sisters in Arms*, 2.

3. Wittberg, *Rise and Fall*, 23; and William A. Gamson, "The Social Psychology of Collective Action," in *Frontiers in Social Movement Theory*, ed. Aldon D. Morris and Carol McClurg Mueller (New Haven and London: Yale University Press, 1992), 60.

4. For example, see "Questions of the Postulant Miss Amanda Anderson [future Mother Augusta], Entered June 9, 1852"; and "Queries," of Mary Anne Wilson [future Mother Perpetua], CSC.

5. Barbara Welter, "The Cult of True Womanhood, 1820–1860," *American Quarterly* 18 (Summer 1966): 151–57.

6. Darlene Clark Hine, *Black Women in White: Racial Conflict and Cooperation in the Nursing Profession, 1890–1950* (Bloomington and Indianapolis: Indiana University Press, 1989), 3; Deborah Gray White, *Ar'n't I a Woman? Female Slaves in the Plantation South* (New York: Norton, 1985); Jacqueline Jones, *Labor of Love, Labor of Sorrow: Black Women, Work, and the Family, From Slavery to the Present* (New York: Vintage Books, 1985); Sarah Deutsch, *No Separate Refuge: Culture, Class, and Gender on an Anglo-Hispanic Frontier in the American Southwest, 1880–1940* (New York: Oxford University Press, 1987); Christine Stansell, *City of Women: Sex and Class in New York, 1789–1860* (New York: Alfred A. Knopf, 1986); and Jeanne Boydston, *Home and Work: Housework, Wages, and the Ideology of Labor in the Early Republic* (New York: Oxford University Press, 1990).

7. Rev. Bernard O'Reilly, LD, *The Mirror of True Womanhood: A Book of Instruction for Women in the World* (New York: Peter. F. Collier, Publisher, 1879), 226–28. See also James Cardinal Gibbons, *Discourses and Sermons for Every Sunday and the Principal Festivals of the Year* (Baltimore and New York: John Murphy Company, 1908), 484; Colleen McDannell, *The Christian Home in Victorian America, 1840–1900* (Bloomington: Indiana University Press, 1986).

8. Mary A. Dowd, "The Public Rights of Women," *Catholic World* 59 (June 1894): 312–20; Oates, *Catholic Philanthropic Tradition;* Orestes Brownson, "The Woman Question," in vol. 18, *The Works of Orestes A. Brownson, Collected and Arranged by Henry F. Brownson*, 381–417 (Detroit: Thorndike Nourse, Publisher, 1885). See Kathleen Sprows Cummings, " 'Not the New Woman?': Irish American Women and the Creation of a Usable Past, 1890–1900," *U. S. Catholic Historian* 19 (Winter 2001): 37–52 for an analysis of Irish women's alternative version of the "new woman."

9. Marta Danylewycz, *Taking the Veil: An Alternative to Marriage, Motherhood, and Spinsterhood in Quebec, 1840–1920* (Toronto: McClelland and Stewart, 1987), 39–42; and James J. Kenneally, "Eve, Mary, and the Historians: American Catholicism and Women," in *Women in American Religion*, ed. Janet Wilson James (Philadelphia: University of Pennsylvania Press, 1980), 191–206.

10. Karen Kennelly, CSJ, "Ideals of American Catholic Womanhood," chap. 1 in *American Catholic Women—A Historical Exploration* (New York: Macmillan Publishing Co., 1989). Cummings, in "Not the New Woman?" argues that middle-class Catholic women both defended and challenged this ideology.

11. Cynthia Eagle Russett, *Sexual Science: The Victorian Construction of Womanhood* (Cambridge, MA and London: Harvard University Press, 1989); Ann Douglas Wood, " 'The Fashionable Diseases': Women's Complaints and Their Treatment in Nineteenth-Century America," in *Women and Health in America: Historical Readings*, ed. Judith Walzer Leavitt (Madison: University of Wisconsin Press, 1984), 222–38.

12. Hoy, "The Journey Out," 63–98. Quotation is on p. 82; and Nelson, *Say Little, Do Much.*

13. Walsh, *Roman Catholic Nuns*, 125–56; Diner, *Erin's Daughters*, 1–29, 130–38; Catriona Clear, *Nuns in Nineteenth-Century Ireland* (Washington, DC: Catholic University of America Press, 1987), 136–38; Hoy, "The Journey Out," 71–72; and Mary Peckham Magray, *The Transforming Power of the Nuns: Women, Religion, and Cultural Change in Ireland, 1750–1900* (New York and Oxford: Oxford University Press, 1998), 3–13.

14. Danylewycz, *Taking the Veil*, 96; Margaret Susan Thompson, "Discovering Foremothers: Sisters, Society, and the American Catholic Experience," *U. S. Catholic Historian* 5 (Summer/Fall, 1986): 275.

15. Sister Mary Helen, "Mother M. Perpetua," vol. 2, *Superior Generals—Centenary Chronicles of the Sisters of the Holy Cross* (Paterson, NJ: Saint Anthony Guild Press, 1941), 139–52; Sister M. Francesca, "Mother Annunciata," *Superior Generals*, 111–36.

16. Assignments, Holy Cross Hospital, Salt Lake City, UT, CSC. Sister Lydia was born in Ireland in 1841 and entered the Sisters of the Holy Cross in 1859.

17. Ginzburg, *Women and the Work of Benevolence.*

18. Clear, *Nuns*, 135. See also Wittberg, *Rise and Fall*, 61–2.

19. Larkin, "The Devotional Revolution," 625–52. Quotation is on p. 649.

20. Wittberg, *Rise and Fall*, 63; Rapley, *The Devotes*, 5.

21. To the Sisters of the Holy Cross, First Conference, "On the Religious State," October 6, 1896, CFIT box 2, folder 4, UNDA.

22. Quotation is in "Corner Stone Laid," *South Bend Weekly Tribune*, May 2, 1903, 1–2. See also Fifteenth Conference, "Piety and Devotion," May 4, 1897, CFIT, box 2, folder 12, UNDA.

23. See St. Augustine, Letter 37, *Select Letters*, trans. James Houston Baxter (London: William Heinemann Ltd.; and New York: G. P. Putnam's Sons, 1930), 269–73;

Kari Elisabeth Borresen, *Subordination and Equivalence: The Nature and Role of Woman in Augustine and Thomas Aquinas,* trans. Charles H. Talbot (Washington, DC: University Press of America, 1981).

24. Rev. William Stang, *Pastoral Theology* (New York: Bensiger Brothers, 1897), 269.

25. Rosemary Radford Ruether, "Misogynism and Virginal Feminism in the Fathers of the Church," in *Religion and Sexism: Images of Woman in the Jewish and Christian Traditions,* ed. Rosemary Radford Ruether (New York: Simon and Schuster, 1974), 150–79; and Richard L. Camp, "From Passive Subordination to Complementary Partnership: The Papal Conception of a Woman's Place in Church and Society since 1878," *Catholic Historical Review* 76 (July 1990): 506–25.

26. "Conferences on Suffering, 1897–98," CFIT box 2, folder 7, p. 5, UNDA.

27. Ruth P. Liebowitz, "Virgins in the Service of Christ: The Dispute over an Active Apostolate for Women during the Counter-Reformation," in *Women of Spirit: Female Leadership in the Jewish and Christian Traditions,* ed. Rosemary Ruether and Eleanor McLaughlin, (New York: Simon and Schuster, 1979), 133–34; McNamara, *Sisters in Arms,* 4–5.

28. Wittberg, *Rise and Fall,* 49–50, 118–28; and Peter Brown, *The Body and Society: Men, Women, and Sexual Renunciation in Early Christianity* (New York: Columbia University Press, 1988), 66–67.

29. Eighth Conference, "The Vow of Chastity," January 19, 1898, CFIT, box 2, folder 10, UNDA.

30. McNamara, *Sisters in Arms,* 1; and Wittberg, *Rise and Fall,* 119.

31. Penelope Johnson refers to a "psychological space" by which medieval nuns defined themselves by their spiritual and social activities. See *Equal in Monastic Profession,* 246.

32. Coburn and Smith, *Spirited Lives,* 82–83; Mary Ewens, "Removing the Veil: The Liberated American Nun," in Ruether and McLaughlin, *Women of Spirit,* 156–58.

33. Johnson, *Equal in Monastic Profession,* x; Coburn and Smith, " 'Pray for Your Wanderers,' " 27–52; and Coburn and Smith, *Spirited Lives,* 4, 82, 94–95.

34. Mother Mary Annunciata to Sisters, September 20, 1896, CSC.

35. Sister Liguori McNamara to Mother, October 13, 1898, Archives of the Congregation of the Sisters of St. Joseph of Carondelet, St. Louis (hereafter cited as ACSJC-SL).

36. Mother St. Pierre Cinquin to Sister Alphonse, February 5, 1889, LSPC, AMIW.

37. Carol K. Coburn and Martha Smith, CSJ, "Creating Community and Identity: Exploring Religious and Gender Ideology in the Lives of American Women Religious, 1836–1920," *U. S. Catholic Historian* 14 (Winter 1996): 94–97; Coburn and Smith, *Spirited Lives;* and Sioban Nelson, "Hybrid Space: Vowed Nineteenth Century Women and Nursing," presented at Breaking Boundaries: Eleventh Berkshire Conference on the History of Women, University of Rochester, June 4–6, 1999.

38. Kuhn, "Americanization," 92.

39. Rosabeth Moss Kanter, *Commitment and Community: Communes and Utopias in Sociological Perspective* (Cambridge, MA: Harvard University Press, 1972), 103; Wittberg, *Rise and Fall,* 29.

40. Father Sorin to Sisters, November 5, 1879, CSCS, box 1, UNDA.

41. See, for example, Mother St. Pierre to Sisters, September 14, 1889, LSPC, AMIW.
42. See O'Connell, "The Roman Catholic Tradition," 121.
43. Mother St. Pierre to Sister of the Assumption, May 11, 1885. Quotation in Mother St. Pierre to Gabbie, n.d., probably January 15, 1889, LSPC, AMIW.
44. See Rapley, *The Devotes*, 146; Sioban Nelson, "Entering the Professional Domain: The Making of the Modern Nurse in 17th Century France," *Nursing History Review* 7 (1999): 181; and Nelson, "Hybrid Space," 5.
45. "Rules Given to Our First Mothers on Leaving France 1869 [1867]," trans. Sister Kathleen Garvey, AMIW.
46. Nelson, "Hybrid Space," 5–7; copy of "Mother M. de Chantal Keating Papers, 1857–1917," Archives, St. Joseph Convent, Brentwood, NY; and Wall, "Called to a Mission of Charity," 85–113.

Chapter 3

1. *San Antonio Weekly Express*, March 11, 1869, 6.
2. Rosenberg, *Care of Strangers*, 110, 121; Starr, *Social Transformation*, 170–71.
3. Starr, *Social Transformation*; and Rosenberg, *Care of Strangers*.
4. These conditions indicated questionable morality and therefore were sent to public institutions. See Rosenberg, *Care of Strangers; Vogel, Invention of the Modern Hospital;* and *Once Charitable Enterprise*. For an analysis of the twentieth century, see Stevens, *In Sickness and in Wealth*.
5. See "Annals of St. Mary's Hospital, Cairo, Illinois" (hereafter cited as "Annals-C"); and typed copy of narrative, Flint Bondurant, MD, n.d., CSC. See also Remark Book, Santa Rosa Infirmary, San Antonio, TX (hereafter cited as RBSR), AMIW; Forty-Third Annual Report of St. Joseph's Hospital for the Year 1895–96, and Forty-Fourth Annual Report of St. Joseph's Hospital for the Year 1896–97, 200.2–1, box 2, folder 10, Archives of the Sisters of St. Joseph of Carondelet, St. Paul Province, St. Paul, MN (hereafter cited as ACSJC-SP). Later, each congregation opened separate tuberculosis institutions.
6. Slattery, *Historical Studies*, 100.
7. McCauley, "'Who Shall Take Care of Our Sick?'" 134.
8. *Manual of Decrees, Sisters of St. Joseph of Carondelet*, 114, ACSJC- SL.
9. Copy of Warranty Deed, Henry M. Rice, Wife, & Fr. Joseph Cretin, February 8, 1853, ACSJC-SP. A hospital history notes that the bishop donated his own money to construct the building. See *History of St. Joseph's Hospital, 1853–1978* (St. Paul, MN: St. Joseph's Hospital, 1979).
10. "The Catholic Hospital," *Daily Minnesota Pioneer*, January 26, 1855, 3; and John M. Culligan and Harold J. Prendergast, "St. Joseph's Hospital in St. Paul," *Acta et Dicta* 6 (October 1934): 199.
11. "St. Joseph's Hospital," *St. Paul Daily Dispatch*, December 29, 1876, 1, ACSJC-SP.
12. "Editorial," *Northwestern Medical and Surgical Journal* 1 (March 1871), 305–6. See Starr, *Social Transformation*, 157, for a discussion on "kitchen surgery."
13. Conflicting dates are given for their establishments. See *Benevolent Institutions*, 1910, 306; and "Twenty-five Years' Growth of the Hospital Field," *National Hospital Record* 7 (September 1903): 25.

14. The administrator of the hospital was also the head of the religious community. Mother Jane's responsibilities included not only hospital administration but also the activities of the religious community housed at the hospital.

15. Rosner, *Once Charitable Enterprise*, 62–93; Rosenberg, *Care of Strangers*, 288–309.

16. "Twenty-five Years' Growth," 26. According to this source, the first hospital in Texas was the State Lunatic Asylum in Austin, established in 1857.

17. Slattery, *Historical Studies*, 375.

18. US Bureau of the Census, *Ninth Census*, vol. 1, *The Statistics of the Population of the United States* (Washington, DC: Government Printing Office, 1872), 63.

19. Bishop Claude Marie Dubuis, CM, succeeded Jean Marie Odin, CM, as bishop of the diocese of Galveston 1862. It included all of Texas at that time.

20. Rose of Lima was a Peruvian mystic who was named patron saint of South America and the Philippines. See *The Harper Collins Encyclopedia of Catholicism*, ed. Richard P. McBrien (San Francisco: Harper Collins Publishers, 1995), 1:138.

21. *San Antonio Weekly Express*, November 25, 1869.

22. Ibid., April 8, 1869.

23. Ibid., July 22, 1869.

24. Slattery, *Historical Development*, 26; and *Historical Studies*, 3–5, 46, 376. Santa Rosa Infirmary served as both motherhouse and novitiate for the Incarnate Word Sisters. Mother St. Pierre assumed both the hospital administrative position and mother superior of the order. In 1900, the sisters moved the motherhouse to the Brackenridge estate at the headwaters of the San Antonio River. At that time, the offices of the superior general of the congregation and the administrator of Santa Rosa Infirmary separated.

25. Slattery, *Historical Studies*, 4.

26. LSPC, 185–87, AMIW.

27. Catholic belief held that the Holy Spirit in the "Communion of Saints" unites believers in heaven, earth, and purgatory. See *The Catechism of the Council of Trent* (New York: Joseph F. Wagner, 1934), 109.

28. Mother St. Pierre Cinquin, "Prayer to St. Joseph," n.d., LSPC; and "Devotions to St. Joseph," *Manual of Prayers for the Sisters of Charity of the Incarnate Word* (San Antonio, TX: n.p., 1933), 117–20, AMIW.

29. Slattery, *Historical Studies*, 4–5.

30. *Cairo Business Mirror and City Directory for 1864–65* (Cairo: Daily Democrat Job Rooms, 1864); and Sister M. Campion Kuhn, "The First Hospital: Saint Mary's Infirmary," paper presented at the 1996 Conference on the History of the Congregations of Holy Cross, King's College, Wilkes-Barre, PA, June 14–16, 1996; and "Annals-C."

31. US Bureau of the Census, *A Compendium of the Ninth Census (June 1, 1870)* (Washington, DC: Government Printing Office, 1872), 606–8. See also E. H. L. Corwin, *The American Hospital* (New York: Commonwealth Fund, 1946), 32–33.

32. Contract between the St. Mary's Infirmary of Cairo and the United States, December 21, 1867, CSC. The Treasury Department approved the contract on January 2, 1868. Box 5G, 2.1, CSC. See also *Archives Book of St. Mary's Infirmary* (hereafter cited as *ABSMI*), 1868, by Sister M. Angela, Superior; and Kuhn, "First Hospital," 1–2, CSC.

33. "Annals-C," 1868; and Kuhn, "First Hospital," 2, CSC.

34. Sister M. Angela to Hon. Mr. Bontwell, Secretary of Treasury, July 8, 1872. See also "Annals-C," 1885, CSC.

35. Financial Records, St. Mary's Infirmary, Cairo, IL, CSC.

36. Typed copy of Denis Kiely to Archbishop [Alemany], February 22, 1875, CSC. Immigrants located in mining camps that typically held from 100 to 1,500 inhabitants. For population statistics in mining areas, see US Bureau of the Census, *Tenth Census of the United States, 1880*, vol. 1, *Population* (Washington, DC: Government Printing Office, 1880), 81–82, 351–53.

37. Copy, letters to Archbishop Alemany from Rev. Lawrence Scanlan and Rev. Denis Kiely, February 22, 1875. See also Helen Zeese Papanikolas, *Peoples of Utah* (Salt Lake City: Utah State Historical Society, 1976); and Thomas G. Alexander, *Utah, The Right Place: The Official Centennial History* (Salt Lake City: Gibbs-Smith Publisher, 1995).

38. Sister Augusta Anderson to Father Edward Sorin, September 3, 1875, Indiana Province Center Archives, Notre Dame, IN.

39. *Archive Book, Holy Cross Hospital,* Salt Lake City, UT (hereafter cited as *ABHCH*), CSC. For a discussion of Paulist priests, see Jay P. Dolan, *Catholic Revivalism: The American Experience, 1830–1900* (Notre Dame, IN and London: University of Notre Dame Press, 1978).

40. Sister M. of the Holy Cross to Father Sorin, September 19, [1875], MCIS 1.078–180, M 31, #1, UNDA.

41. *ABHCH*, CSC.

42. "Assignments, Holy Cross Hospital, Salt Lake City, Utah," CSC.

43. Newspaper article of 1884 entitled, "Mirth and Music at the Hospital," quoted in "Dr. M. A. Hughes Wrote Prophetic Words on Holy Cross in 1907," *Intermountain Catholic Register*, February 3, 1956, 2.

44. Kiely to Archbishop, CSC.

45. "Assignments, Holy Cross Hospital, Salt Lake City, Utah"; and *ABHCH*, CSC.

46. Keith L. Bryant Jr., "Entering the Global Economy," in *The Oxford History of the American West*, ed. Clyde A. Milner II, Carol A. O'Connor, and Martha A. Sandweiss (New York: Oxford University Press, 1994), 195–235.

47. Sister Euphrosine Pepin to Father Sorin, August 7, 1879, MCIS 1.078–180, M 31, #1, UNDA.

48. Mark A. Pendleton, "Memories of Silver Reef," *Utah Historical Quarterly* 3 (October 1930): 100–101.

49. Sister M. Febronia to Father Sorin, March 13, 1881, CSC.

50. Brother Franklin Cullen, CSC, "Holy Cross in the Black Hills: The Dakota Apostolates, 1878–1897," in vol. 2 of *Fruits of the Tree: Sesquicentennial Chronicles, Sisters of the Holy Cross* (Notre Dame, IN: Ave Maria Press, 1989), 154; and Sister M. Claudia Duratschek, OSB, *Builders of God's Kingdom: The History of the Catholic Church in South Dakota* (Yankton, SD: Benedictine Sisters of Sacred Heart Convent, 1985), copy of excerpts located in CSC.

51. Quoted in Cullen, "Holy Cross in the Black Hills," 157.

52. "Sisters' Hospital," *Black Hills Daily Times*, August 22, 1878.

53. "The Hospital Benefit," *Black Hills Daily Times*, August 30, 1878.

54. Copy of Father John Toohey to Superior, December 16, 1879, CSC.

55. Annual Account of St. Edward's Hospital, July 1, 1879 to July 1, 1880, CSC.

56. Duratschek, *Builders of God's Kingdom*.

57. Duratschek, *Builders of God's Kingdom*; Sister Edward Murphy to Mother Charles, July 17, 1880; and copy of Father Gleeson to Father General, August 27, 1880, CSC.

58. Bishop Martin Marty to Father Colovin, May 5, 1881, James Gleeson Letters Received, CZAJ, UNDA.

59. Mother M. Perpetua to Rev. J. Stariha, May 13, 1904, CSC.

60. Sister Eugenia Logan, SP, vol. 2, *History of the Sisters of Providence of Saint Mary-of-the-Woods, Indiana* (Terre Haute, IN: Moore-Langen Printing Company, 1978), 1–7; and Sister Mary Roger Madden, SP, vol. 3, T*he Path Marked Out: History of the Sisters of Providence of Saint Mary-of-the-Woods* (Terre Haute, IN: Office of Congregational Advancement–Sisters of Providence), 113–19.

61. *Ninth Census*, 1:537.

62. Madden, *Path Marked Out*, 5–10; Logan, *History*, 61.

63. Extracts from "Diary of Mother Mary Cecilia," May 15, 1861, Sisters of Providence Archives, Saint Mary-of-the-Woods, IN (hereafter cited as ASMW).

64. "Notes from the Necrology," ASMW.

65. "Extracts from Annals of the Sisters of Providence, Saint Mary-of-the-Woods," ASMW; *Indianapolis Daily Journal*, July 23, 1861; "Diary of Mother Mary Cecilia," ASMW; and Logan, *History*, 60–78.

66. "St. John's Home for Invalids," excerpt from the *Indianapolis Sentinel*, October 10, 1865, typed copy in ASMW; and Logan, *History*, 75–7.

67. Logan, *History*, 135–6. Population statistics are in *Ninth Census*, vol. 1.

68. Typed copy of announcement of cornerstone placement, ASMW.

69. "Contract, Sisters of Providence of Saint Mary's, Vigo County, and Snapp and Haynes," August 25, 1870, ASMW.

70. Logan, *History*, 136, 172; and Mary Roger Madden, SP, "Letter to the Editor," "SPs, Chauncey Rose Gave City First Hospital," copy of newspaper article (n.d.) in ASMW.

71. *Terre Haute Express*, June 26, 1872.

72. Ibid., June 29, 1872; and Logan, *History*, 177.

73. "Providence Hospital, Dedication Services Yesterday, Immense Assemblage of the People," *Terre Haute Weekly Express*, July 1, 1872, Terre Haute, IN. In 1879, Parvin was elected president of the American Medical Association. See Charles N. Combs, MD, typescript of *The History of Medicine in Vigo County, Indiana, 1818–1951* (1951), 138, Vigo County Public Library, Terre Haute, IN.

74. "Providence Hospital Dedication Services."

75. Sisters of Providence, "Providence Hospital," *Terre Haute Express*, July 6, 1872, 4.

76. *Terre Haute Express*, September 28, 1872, 4.

77. "Register of Invalids, Providence Hospital," ASMW.

78. Ibid., November 26, 1873; and September 1874, ASMW.

79. Logan, *History*, 157, 187; and Historian and Archivist to Paul G. Fox, May 13, 1960, ASMW.

80. Combs, *History of Medicine*, 138, 256, 420; and Logan, *History*, 178–82.

81. *Terre Haute Express*, December 7, 1873, 4.

82. Logan, *History*, 184, 201–5; "Community Diary," September 30, 1874; and Madden, "Letter to the Editor," ASMW.

83. *Ninth Census*, 1:353.

84. Logan, *History*, 182.

85. Ibid., 185–90.

Chapter 4

1. "Corner Stone Laid," *South Bend Times,* April 21, 1903, CSC.
2. These questions are also addressed in Barbra Mann Wall, "The Pin-striped Habit: Balancing Charity and Business in Catholic Hospitals, 1865–1915," *Nursing Research* 51 (January/February 2002): 50–58.
3. Rosenberg, *Care of Strangers;* Starr, *Social Transformation.*
4. *Benevolent Institutions, 1910,* 68. These included hospitals and sanitariums, not homes for adults or institutions for children. Charles P. Emerson, "The American Hospital Field," in *Hospital Management,* ed. Charlotte A. Aikens (Philadelphia and London: W. B. Saunders Co., 1911), reports 5,034 hospitals. Emerson cites these figures from Polk's "Medical Register and Directory," 11th ed., 1910.
5. Rosenberg, *Care of Strangers,* 166–89; Nelson, *Say Little, Do Much,* 45.
6. Rosenberg, *Care of Strangers,* 142–65.
7. *Mortality Statistics, Tenth U.S. Census* (Washington, DC: Government Printing Office, 1882). See also *Statistics and Technology of the Precious Metals* (Washington, DC: Government Printing Office, 1885), 173–77. Similar statistics are reported in J. D. Hackett, *Health Maintenance in Industry* (Chicago and New York: A. W. Shaw Company, 1925), 17–19.
8. The ICC recorded injuries that were minor as well as fatal. See *Report on the Agencies of Transportation in the United States* (Washington, DC: Government Printing Office, 1883), 13; *Third Annual Report of the Interstate Commerce Commission* (Washington, DC: Government Printing Office, 1889), 84; *Fifteenth Annual Report of the Interstate Commerce Commission* (Washington, DC: Government Printing Office, 1902), 58; *Twenty-Fifth Annual Report of the Interstate Commerce Commission* (Washington, DC: Government Printing Office, 1912), 77. Mining figures were even higher.
9. For sources on the railroad industry, see Starr, *Social Transformation,* 201; and C. A. Smith, "The Medical and Surgical Department of a Railway System: What It Is and What It Tries to Accomplish," *Texas State Journal of Medicine* 1 (July 1905): 13–14.
10. Starr, *Social Transformation,* 30–92, 163; and Rosenberg, *Care of Strangers,* 202–6.
11. Starr, *Social Transformation,* 163.
12. See letter to father, November 14, 1891, 200.2-1, box 1, folder 4, ACSJC-SP.
13. US Bureau of the Census, *Compendium of the Eleventh Census: 1890, Part I—Population* (Washington, DC: Government Printing Office, 1892), 434; and *Report of Statistics of Churches of the United States* (Washington, DC: Government Printing Office, 1894); and *Report on the Social Statistics of Cities, Part II, South and Western States, 1880 Census* (Washington, DC: Government Printing Office, 1887). St. Paul became an archdiocese in 1888. Of the foreign-born population, 44 percent were from Ireland, 1 percent from Germany, 1 percent from Canada, 6 percent from Sweden, 5 percent from England, and 4 percent from Norway. See "Number of Patients Admitted Per Month, St. Joseph's Hospital, 1876–1901," 200.2-1, box 1, folder 4; and "Place of Patients' Birth, St. Joseph's Hospital, 1876–1883," 200.2-1, box 2, folder 10, ACSJC-SP.
14. After 1917, a new Code of Canon Law stated that a person could be superior only six years. Thereafter, hospital administration changed every six years. Mother Bernardine was born to a farming family in Canada in 1853 and entered the convent in 1871. See "Personal File," ACSJC-SP.

15. "Yearly Admissions to St. Joseph's Hospital, 1883–1962," 200.2–1, box 2, folder 10; "Number of Patients Admitted per Month, St. Joseph's Hospital, 1876–1901," 200.2–1, box 1, folder 4; "St. Joseph's Hospital in 125 Years"; *Forty-Third Annual Report of St. Joseph's Hospital for the Year 1895–96,* 200.2–1, box 1; and *Sixty-Fifth Annual Report for St. Joseph's Hospital for the Year 1919,* 200.2–1, box 2, folder 10, ACSJC-SP. The original structure was torn down in 1895.

16. *Forty-Third Annual Report,* ACSJC-SP; Culligan and Prendergast, "St. Joseph's Hospital in St. Paul," 202–203; and "Partial Listings of the Milestones of St. Joseph's Hospital," personal copy of Sister Marie de Paul Rochester.

17. Culligan and Prendergast, "St. Joseph's Hospital in St. Paul," 195–211; *History of St. Joseph's Hospital,* 13, 17; and "Home Notes," *Northwestern Medical and Surgical Journal* 1 (November 1870): 187. Other pioneering physicians included Doctors James D. Goodrich, Albert C. Brisbine, O. P. Marsh; Charles E. Smith, J. H. Stewart, D. W. Hand, and S. Flagg. See *American Medical Directory, 1916, A Register of Legally Qualified Physicians of the United States* (Chicago: American Medical Association, 1916), 837–39.

18. See Charles E. Rea, "The First Cholecystectomy in America," reprinted from *Minnesota Medicine* 23 (September 1940): 658. O'Hage published his feat in the *Medical News* in 1887.

19. See *Forty-Third Annual Report; Fifty-Fifth Report, St. Joseph's Hospital for the Years 1907–1908;* and *Fifty-Eighth Report, St. Joseph's Hospital for the Year 1912,* ACSJC-SP. These figures can be compared to both large and small hospitals in the East. See Rosenberg, *Care of Strangers,* 149; and "New England Notes," *National Hospital Record* 6 (February 1903): 68.

20. US Bureau of the Census, *Eleventh Census, 1890, Part I;* and *Part II: Vital and Social Statistics—Foreign Born Population* (Washington, DC: Government Printing Office, 1894), 643–44.

21. See Coburn and Smith, *Spirited Lives,* 195, for a discussion of religious, ethnic, and linguistic factors affecting Catholic charities.

22. See "Assignments" of three insurance policies turned over to Bishop Ireland by the Sisters of Mercy, ACSJC-SP. See also Kathleen O'Brien, RSM, *Journeys: A Pre-Amalgamation History of the Sisters of Mercy Omaha Province* (Omaha: private printing, 1987), 398–99.

23. Cox, "Notes on the Early History of the Sisters of St. Joseph, 253–69; Cox, "Additional Notes on the Mission of the Sisters of St. Joseph in St. Paul," *Acta et Dicta* 3 (July 1914): 270–75; and Sister Ann Thomasine Sampson, CSJ, *Care with Prayer: The History of St. Mary's Hospital & Rehabilitation Center, Minneapolis, Minnesota, 1887–1987* (Minneapolis: St. Mary's Hospital & Rehabilitation Center, 1987), 4.

24. "St. Mary's Hospital," *Irish Standard,* October 22, 1887, 4. Dunn graduated from Rush Medical College in Chicago in 1878. For an account of the early physicians at St. Mary's, see Sister Anita Marie Chamberlain, "The First Seventy-Five Years at St. Mary's Hospital," 220.2–2, box 1, ACSJC-SP; and Sampson, *Care with Prayer,* 3–4.

25. "St. Mary's Hospital," *American Medical Directory* (Chicago: American Medical Association, 1916), 829–32.

26. "The History of St. Mary's Hospital: The First 90 Years, 1887–1977," 200.2–2, box 1, ACSJC-SP. See also Sampson, *Care with Prayer,* 5–6. Patient numbers are noted on advertisement card, St. Mary's Hospital, Minneapolis, MN, ACSJC-SP.

27. 1887 Ledger for St. Mary's Hospital. See also personal records of sisters, ACSJC-SP.

28. *Annual Report of Saint Mary's Hospital, Minneapolis, Minnesota, 1920*, 200.2–2, box 1, ACSJC-SP. In 1890, the percentage of foreign-born whites in the urban areas of Minnesota totaled 37.7 percent of the total. By 1910, this percentage had dropped to 28.8 percent. US Bureau of the Census, *Thirteenth Census Taken in the Year 1910: Population* (Washington, DC: Government Printing Office, 1913); and vol. 1, *Census Reports, Twelfth Census of the United States, Taken in the Year 1900* (Washington, DC: Government Printing Office, 1901).

29. Mother Jane was born in Savoy, France, in 1841 and entered the convent in 1861. Sister Esperance was born in Oswego, New York, and entered the community in 1885. Sister Esperance had been in charge of two boarding schools before her assignment at St. Mary's. See personal records, ACSJC-SL.

30. *American Medical Directory*, 829–30; Sampson, *Care with Prayer*, 9–19; and Chamberlain, "The First Seventy-Five Years," ACSJC-SP. Dr. Hill was president of the Hennepin Medical Society and, in 1912, served in the same capacity for the Minnesota State Medical Association.

31. Quoted in Sampson, *Care with Prayer*, 19. These financial papers are in Sister Esperance's personal file, ACSJC-SP.

32. After Sister Madeleine left St. Mary's, she assumed a similar position at a hospital in Lewiston, Idaho, and returned later to St. Mary's for another term. See Sampson, *Care with Prayer*, 21–25; and *Annual Report, 1920*, ACSJC-SP.

33. Abraham Flexner, *Medical Education in the United States and Canada: A Report to the Carnegie Foundation for the Advancement of Teaching, Bulletin # 4* (New York: Carnegie Foundation, 1910).

34. *History of St. Joseph's Hospital*, 18–20; and Sampson, *Care with Prayer*, 12. By 1909, the University of Minnesota College of Medicine and Surgery had absorbed all other state medical schools.

35. Flexner, *Medical Education*, 248.

36. "Attractions of Cairo, Illinois," issued by Dr. W. W. Stevenson, noted in *Cairo Evening Citizen*, December 11, 1890. See also *ABSMI*; "Aged Nun Dies at Infirmary," September 7, 1908, *Cairo News*, copy in "Annals-C," 61; and Kuhn, "The First Hospital," 5, CSC.

37. St. Mary's Infirmary to Dr. C. Smith, May 21, 1887, CSC. The weekly fee of $5 was lower than the $11.38 average full-time weekly earnings for railroad workers in 1890. See Bureau of the Census and Social Science Research Council, *Historical Statistics of the United States, Colonial Times to 1957* (Washington, DC: US Department of Commerce, 1957), 91. Sister Adela was born in 1831 in County Mayo, Ireland, and entered the community in 1856. Her past nursing experience included service on the naval ship *Red Rover* during the Civil War. See Wall, "Grace under Pressure," 71–87.

38. "Annals-C"; Circular, St. Mary's Infirmary (n.d.); typed copy of Dr. W. W. Stevenson, "St. Mary's Infirmary," *Cairo Evening Citizen*, December 11, 1890, CSC; *American Medical Directory*, 413.

39. Circular, "St. Mary's Infirmary," 1901, CSC.

40. The number of Catholics admitted was 140, compared to 305 Protestants, 12 Greek Orthodox, 30 Jewish patients, and 840 with no religious preference.

41. "Annals-C," CSC; and *Cairo Evening Citizen and Bulletin*, November 2, 1938.

42. *Daily Tribune,* February 9, February 12, and February 14, 1884.

43. "Hospital of the Holy Cross, Salt Lake City, Utah," 1875; "Sisters' Hospital," *Salt Lake Daily Tribune,* October 22, 1875; *ABHCH; Holy Cross Hospital Record Book, 1875–1920* (hereafter cited as *HCHRB*), Salt Lake City, UT, CSC. See also *Sadlier's Catholic Directory, Almanac and Ordo* (New York: D. & J. Sadlier & Co., 1895).

44. "Twenty-five Years' Growth," 25–26. According to this source, the first hospital in Salt Lake City was Fort Douglass Military Hospital, established in 1862.

45. See Ralph T. Richards, *Of Medicine, Hospitals, and Doctors* (Salt Lake City: University of Utah Press, 1953), 24–31, 229–43; "Home Also a Hospital," *Salt Lake Tribune,* December 10, 1901; and *Salt Lake Tribune,* July 21, 1871.

46. Sister Beniti was born in Ireland in 1864 and entered the community in 1888. See "Personal File of Sister Biniti O'Connor"; Sister Virginia, "History of Holy Cross Hospital," noted in Richards, *Of Medicine,* 54–55; *ABHCH*; and Jack Goodman, "Holy Cross Hospital's Chapel Adds Old-World Charm to Young S.L.," copy of newspaper article (n.d.), CSC.

47. *Journal of Admissions by Physicians, 1908–1915,* ACCN #588, box 3, Manuscript Division, University of Utah Libraries (hereafter cited as MDU); *Holy Cross Hospital, Salt Lake City, Utah, Budgets and Annual Accounts from 1892 to Date* (hereafter cited as *HCHBAA*), CSC. In 1870, 41 percent of the population of Salt Lake County, Utah, was foreign born. This had diminished to 24 percent by 1900. See vol. 1, *Ninth Census: Population;* and *Twelfth Census, 1900.*

48. *ABHCH;* typed copy, M. A. Hughes, MD, "Historical Sketch of Holy Cross Hospital," 1907, CSC; and Richards, *Of Medicine,* 29, 51–72. In 1899, after graduation at the University of Michigan and two years of European study in pathology and surgery, Dr. Andrew Hosmer was appointed to the staff; and William Tyndale joined in 1904 after graduation from Rush Medical College and eighteen months of study in Berlin and Vienna. Dr. Root later became president of the Utah State Medical Association. See *American Medical Directory,* 1524.

49. Flexner, *Medical Education,* 313.

50. Franklin A. Meacham, "A Synopsis of Clinical Surgery During the Service of Samuel H. Pinkerton, M.D., Surgeon to the Holy Cross Hospital, by Franklin A. Meacham, A.B., M.D., Assistant Surgeon to the Holy Cross Hospital, Salt Lake City, Utah, For the Year 1892," reprinted in Richards, *Of Medicine,* 220–23. See also *ABHCH,* CSC; and "Journal of Admissions by Physicians, Holy Cross Hospital, 1908–1915," ACCN #588, box 3, MDA.

51. Fitz published his paper in the *American Journal of Medical Science* 92 (1886): 32. See Howard A. Kelly, *Appendicitis and Other Diseases of the Vermiform Appendix* (Philadelphia and London: J. B. Lippincott Company, 1905), 114; and Hyman Morrison, "The Chapter on Appendicitis in a Biography of Reginald Heber Fitz," *Bulletin of the History of Medicine* 20 (July 1946): 259–69.

52. Richards, *Of Medicine,* 66–67, 204–5; and August Schachner, *Ephraim McDowell, "Father of Ovariotomy" and Founder of Abdominal Surgery* (Philadelphia and London: J. B. Lippincott Company, 1921). For critiques, see Wood, "The Fashionable Diseases," 224; Lawrence D. Longo, "The Rise and Fall of Battey's Operation: A Fashion in Surgery," in *Women and Health in America,* 270–84.

53. According to one hospital history, accident cases routinely went to the county farm or jail before St. Joseph's was built. See *Saint Joseph's Medical Center: A Century of Caring* (South Bend, IN: private printing, 1982), 8; and John W. Stamper, *City of*

South Bend Summary Report: Indiana Historic Sites and Structures Inventory (n.p., 1981). For population statistics, see US Bureau of the Census, *1880 Census—Report on the Social Statistics of Cities, Part II: South and Western States* (Washington, DC: Government Printing Office, 1887). For statistics on religious denominations, see Department of the Interior, Census Office, *Report on Statistics of Churches in the United States at the Eleventh Census: 1890* (Washington, DC: Government Printing Office, 1894).

54. Sister Edward was born in Ireland in 1834 and entered the convent in 1854. See "Personal File," CSC.

55. *South Bend Evening Register,* July 27, 1882.

56. *Archive Book, St. Joseph's Hospital, South Bend, Indiana* (hereafter cited as *ABSJH-SB*) for 1897, CSC.

57. Ibid., 1901, CSC.

58. See "St. Joseph Hospital to Have Charity Wards," *South Bend Tribune,* December 10, 1913.

59. *ABSJH-SB,* CSC; and "From Humble Beginnings, to Medical Center," *South Bend Tribune,* October 29, 1982.

60. Daugherty was president of the Indiana State Medical Society in 1893. See *American Medical Directory,* 542; Logan Esarey, vol. 3, *History of Indiana from Its Exploration to 1922* (Dayton, OH: Dayton Historical Publishing Co., 1923), 73–75; and Fred P. Eastman, MD, "Early History of the St. Joseph County Medical Society," unpublished manuscript, South Bend Medical Foundation, South Bend, IN.

61. These included Doctors Berteling, Cassidy, Hager, Daugherty, Stolz, Borley, Dugdale, Hill, Greene, Holtzendorff, Dresch, and Wood. See *ABSJH-SB,* 1902–1903; Essary, *History of Indiana,* 73–76; and *Saint Joseph's Medical Center,* 13.

62. US Bureau of the Census, *Special Reports, Religious Bodies: 1906, Part I* (Washington, DC: Government Printing Office, 1910).

63. *South Bend Saturday Tribune,* October 21, 1882.

64. *ABSJH-SB,* 1905–1906, CSC.

65. Ibid.

66. Ibid., 1904–1905, 25, CSC; and "Minutes of Epworth Hospital and Training School Board of Directors," May 22, 1905, Memorial Hospital Archives Project, South Bend, IN.

67. *ABSJH-SB,* 1896–97, 1905–1907, 1914–1915, 1923, CSC.

68. Ibid.

69. Rosenberg, *Care of Strangers,* 147.

70. *RBSR,* January 10, January 11, January 12, and January 13, 1899, AMIW.

71. See *RBSR* for 1888; Mother St. Madeleine per Sister M. Gabriel, sec., to Dr. B. E. Hadra, City Physician, June 7, 1897, AMIW; and Slattery, *Historical Studies,* 8–15.

72. US Bureau of the Census, *Benevolent Institutions, 1904* (Washington, DC: Government Printing Office, 1905), 210–11. Many of the patients came to the southwestern part of the United States for treatment of tuberculosis.

73. Many Mexican Americans came to the Dallas-Fort Worth area in the late nineteenth and early twentieth centuries to meet labor needs. See James Talmadge Moore, *Through Fire and Flood: The Catholic Church in Frontier Texas, 1836–1900* (College Station, TX: Texas A&M University Press, 1992), 166–83; 222–38; and Jay P. Dolan and Gilberto M. Hinojosa, *Mexican Americans and the Catholic Church, 1900–1965* (Notre Dame and London: University of Notre Dame Press, 1994), 71–75. See also

Slattery, *Historical Studies,* 85; and Mother St. Pierre Cinquin to Sister of the Assumption, May 8, 1885, LSPC, AMIW.

74. Slattery, *Historical Studies,* 24–25. For statistics on patient admissions, see *Benevolent Institutions,* 1910, 356–57.

75. From January to April 1884, Santa Rosa Infirmary received 105 patients, 58 of whom were private and the others charity. See "Santa Rosa Hospital," *San Antonio Daily Times,* April 8, 1884, box 90; *RBSR;* and *Diary, Santa Rosa Infirmary,* 1884–1895; Sister M. Gabriel Wheelahan for Rev. Mother Madeleine Chollet, to Dr. B. E. Hadra, June 7, 1897; and *1922 Annual Report, Santa Rosa Infirmary, San Antonio, Texas,* box 91, #10. All of these sources are in AMIW.

76. Flexner, *Medical Education,* 312.

77. *American Medical Directory,* 1509–10; Slattery, *Historical Studies,* 7–23; *Men of Texas: Collection of Portraits* (Houston: Houston Post, 1903), 418; and "Much of City History Blended around Pioneer Doctor's Life" [Dr. Adolph Herff], copy in Texas Medical Association Library, Austin, TX. My thanks to Elizabeth Borst White, who helped me obtain this information at the Historical Research Center, HAM-TMC Library, Houston, TX; and Patty Mullens at the Texas Medical Association Library in Austin, TX.

78. Laura L. Barber, ed., *The Doctors Herff: A Three-Generation Memoir By Ferdinand Peter Herff* (San Antonio: Trinity University Press, 1973), 78.

79. For population statistics, see *Tenth Census.*

80. See Sr. St. Gabriel, Sec., for Mother St. Pierre Cinquin to Rev. N. A. Gallagher, February 27, 1885; and Mother St. Pierre Cinquin to Reverend Mother Marie de Salome, March 9, 1885, LSPC, AMIW. Salaries included $15 per month for nurses, cooks, and other helpers, and $20 a month for the superior. See also Slattery, *Historical Studies,* 84.

81. Slattery, *Historical Studies,* 84–88; and *Historical Development,* 53. See also Mother St. Pierre Cinquin to Mother St. Marie de Jesus, March 17, 1885; and to Sister Alphonse, February 5, 1889, LSPC, AMIW.

82. Doctor circular. In the 1930s, the Incarnate Word Sisters changed St. Joseph and Santa Rosa's names from "Infirmaries" to "Hospitals."

83. *Remark Book, St. Joseph's Hospital,* Fort Worth, Texas (hereafter cited as *RBSJ*), April 24, April 29, and April 30, 1889; and entries for July 1890, AMIW. See also Slattery, *Historical Studies,* 91.

84. Slattery, *Historical Studies,* 97; and *RBSJ,* December 15, 1890. See also letters to Farrar's brother, Dr. Miles C. Farrar to Rev. Mother St. Pierre, December 24, 1888; and Mother St. Pierre to M. C. Farrar, January 8, 1889, LSPC, AMIW.

85. See *American Medical Directory,* 1489–90; and George Plunkett Red, *The Medicine Man in Texas* (n.p., 1930), 311–13.

86. *RBSR,* 1892, 1895, 1896–1898; *RBSJ,* AMIW. Exact numbers are unavailable for these early years. By contrast, in 1922 at Santa Rosa, surgeons performed over 600 procedures on the ear, nose, or throat, over 300 appendectomies, 400 gynecological surgical procedures, and 100 genitourinary operations. See the *1922 Annual Report, Santa Rosa Infirmary,* 28–39.

87. For example, in the 1920s, the average woman visited the physician 2.4 times per year compared to males' visits of 1.8 times per year. Edward Shorter argues that women became the "keystone of modern medical practice." See Edward Shorter, *Doctors and Their Patients: A Social History* (New Brunswick, NJ, and London: Transaction Publishers, 1991), 110–11. Quotation is on p. 110.

88. Walter Nugent, *Into the West: The Story of Its People* (New York: Vintage Books, 1999); and Nugent, *Crossings: The Great Transatlantic Migrations, 1870–1914* (Bloomington and Indianapolis: Indiana University Press, 1995), 49–54; and David M. Emmons, *The Butte Irish: Class and Ethnicity in an American Mining Town* (Urbana and Chicago: University of Illinois Press, 1989). In 1880, Daly bought the Anaconda Mine in Butte, Montana.

89. Mother St. Pierre Cinquin to Mother Marie de Salome, March 9, 1885, LSPC, AMIW.

90. Cyprian Davis, OSB. *The History of Black Catholics in the United States* (New York: Crossroad, 1991), 116–30.

91. See *Ninth Census, 1870*; and *Thirteenth Census, 1910*. For a discussion of the health and welfare services for blacks after the Civil War, see Howard N. Rabinowitz, *Race Relations in the Urban South, 1865–1890* (Urbana: University of Illinois Press, 1980), 128–51. For a discussion of African American health problems, see Vanessa Northington Gamble, ed., *Germs Have No Color Line: Blacks and American Medicine, 1900–1940* (New York: Garland Publishing, 1989); and Gamble, "Roots of the Black Hospital Reform Movement," in *Sickness and Health in America: Readings in the History of Medicine and Public Health*, ed. Judith Walzer Leavitt and Ronald L. Numbers (Madison: University of Wisconsin Press, 1997), 371. See also "Annals-C"; and "St. Mary's Infirmary Was Founded Here Three Years after Close of Civil War," *Cairo Evening Citizen and Bulletin*, November 2, 1938, CSC.

92. According to Slattery, for many years, St. Joseph's was the only private hospital in Fort Worth that admitted African American patients and accepted African American physicians on staff. See *Historical Studies*, 23, 93,105–6.

93. Kuhn, "First Hospital," 7–9.

94. Ignatiev, *How the Irish Became White*; and Roediger, *The Wages of Whiteness*, 133–63.

95. Thompson, "Philemon's Dilemma," 3–18, esp. 14–15.

96. *Statutes and Constitutions of the Sisters of Charity of the Incarnate Word*, 1872, Part First, Chapter XII, Article 8; and 1906 *Directory of the Sisters of Charity of the Incarnate Word*, 207, AMIW.

97. *Benevolent Institutions, 1904*; and Stevens, *In Sickness and in Wealth*, 24.

98. Emerson, "The American Hospital Field," 22.

99. See William A. Glaser, *Social Settings and Medical Organization: A Cross-National Study of the Hospital* (New York: Atherton Press, 1970), 35.

100. Ferenc Szasz and Margaret Connell Szasz, "Religion and Spirituality," in *The Oxford History of the American West*, ed. Clyde A. Milner II et al. (New York: Oxford University Press, 1994), 360–70.

CHAPTER 5

1. Mother St. Pierre Cinquin to Reverend Mother, December 15, 1885, LSPC, AMIW.

2. See Deacon, "Handmaids or Autonomous Women," 277. The sisters in each order took a simple vow of poverty, which allowed them to own their own personal property but not use it without the superior general's permission.

3. Portions of this chapter have been adapted from the author's "The Pin-striped Habit," 50–58.

4. Rev. Lawrence Scanlan to Archbishop Alemany, February 22, 1875; *ABHCH; ABSJH-SB*, CSC. See also Oates, *The Catholic Philanthropic Tradition* for a discussion of sisters' begging.

5. *RBSJ* and *RBSR*, AMIW; "Register of Patients, St. Mary's Hospital," 200.2–2, box 1, ACSJC-SP; *ABHCH, ABSJH-SB*, and "Annals-C," CSC; and Corwin, *The American Hospital*, 30–35.

6. "St. Joseph's Hospital," *St. Paul Daily Minnesotian*, October 22, 1857.

7. "Annals-C," CSC; and Logan, *History*, 184.

8. Copy of Agreement between Mutual Hospital Aid Association and Holy Cross Hospital, September 29, 1886, CSC.

9. Slattery, *Historical Studies*, 106.

10. Sisters instigated this plan in the 1890s, during an era of droughts and economic panics. See Sampson, *Care with Prayer*, 12.

11. Advertisement for St. Mary's Hospital, late 1880s, ACSJC-SP.

12. *RBSR*, 1896, AMIW.

13. During a sixty-hour workweek, the average worker in both farming and industrial work earned approximately $8.42 in 1890. For railroad workers, it was slightly higher, $10.76. See Census, *Historical Statistics of the United States, Colonial Times to 1957*, 92. Thus, for about one-half of their weekly pay, railroad workers on a ward at Santa Rosa received room, board, nursing care, and medicines for a week in the hospital. Hospitalization for nonrailroad workers at both Santa Rosa and St. Mary's, Minneapolis, cost approximately three-fourths of their weekly pay. Hospital rooms in larger secular facilities in the East were slightly higher.

14. "St. Mary's Hospital," Pamphlet, CSC. See also *Fifty-Fifth Report, St. Joseph's Hospital*, ACSJC-SP.

15. Numerous examples are in *RBSR*, AMIW.

16. Sister Superior to Doctors E. W. Whitney and H. N. Mayo, Committee of Staff, Holy Cross Hospital, attached to Minutes of a Meeting of the Medical Staff of the Holy Cross Hospital, December 7, 1908. See also Sister M. Beniti to Staff of Holy Cross Hospital, November 6, 1916, MDU.

17. *Diary, Santa Rosa Hospital; RBSR*, AMIW; and Slattery, *Historical Studies*, 4. See also Financial Records for Holy Cross Hospital, St. Joseph's Hospital, and St. Mary's Infirmary, CSC.

18. Mother St. Madeleine to Rev. P. Kaenders, March 11, 1903, AMIW.

19. *RBSR*, February 4, 1896; *RBSJ*, February 11, 1890 and January 22, 1892; and "Wiped Out an Old Account," *San Antonio Express*, August 1, 1899, box 90, AMIW.

20. See Starr, *Social Transformation*, 201–2; Smith, "The Medical and Surgical Department of a Railway System," 13; Rosenberg, *Care of Strangers*, 113–14; and Pierce Williams, *The Purchase of Medical Care through Fixed Periodic Payment* (New York: National Bureau of Economic Research, 1932), 196–201.

21. The relationship between the amount of money coming into the company from deductions and the expenditures to the hospital are unknown, so that whether deductions were reasonable or not is also unknown. Depending on the degree of injury or illness in the workforce, companies might even make a profit from running insurance plans.

22. Joyce, "Science and the Saints," 50, 63; Starr, *Social Transformation*, 201; Smith, "Medical and Surgical Department"; Mark Aldrich, "Train Wrecks to Typhoid Fever:

Notes to Chapter Five 219

The Development of Railroad Medicine Organizations, 1850 to World War I," *Bulletin of the History of Medicine* 75 (Summer 2001): 254–89; and Wall, "The Pin-striped Habit," 53.

23. Mother St. Pierre Cinquin to Rev. Mother St. Marie de Salome, March 9, 1885, LSPC, AMIW.

24. *Quarterly Accounts of the Hospital of Holy Cross* (hereafter cited as *Quarterly Accounts*), CSC. Utah miners' monthly contributions of $1 to a hospital fund were comparable to those in other parts of the country. See Jerome L. Schwartz, "Early History of Prepaid Medical Care Plans," *Bulletin of the History of Medicine* 39 (September–October 1965): 456; and Stuart D. Brandes, *American Welfare Capitalism, 1880–1940* (Chicago and London: University of Chicago Press, 1976), 93.

25. *ABHCH;* and *HCHRB*, CSC.

26. *ABSJH-SB*, CSC.

27. *RBSJ*, April 11, 1890, AMIW.

28. Sisters of the Holy Cross General Council Minutes, January 7, 1881, CSC.

29. "Reflecting on a Journey toward Tomorrow," undated brochure on Epworth Hospital; and "History of Epworth Hospital," Memorial Hospital Archives Project, South Bend, IN.

30. Stevens, *In Sickness and in Wealth*, 17–51.

31. See, for example, Sister Seraphine to Sister Ira, June 29, 1914, 2.1–12, folder 20.8, Correspondence and Reports of Sister Seraphine Ireland, ACSJC-SP.

32. "The Catholic Fair," *Daily Tribune*, December 12, December 15, December 18, December 19, December 20, and December 22, 1883, copies in Holy Cross Hospital Scrapbook; "A Great Success," January 22, 1902; "St. Mary's Hospital, Cairo, Illinois; Clippings, 1902–1967," 32; *Saint Joseph's Medical Center;* and *ABSJH-SB*, CSC. In 1909, local women founded the St. Joseph's Hospital Aid Society in South Bend.

33. "Annals-C," CSC. See also newspaper clipping, February 18, 1902, in Scrapbook of St. Mary's Infirmary, Cairo, IL, CSC. For a discussion of Catholic laywomen's philanthropic efforts, see Oates, *Catholic Philanthropic Tradition*.

34. *ABHCH;* and *HCHRB*, CSC; and Diner, *Erin's Daughters*, 137–38.

35. Newspaper clipping, "'Tag' or Be Tagged," 22; and information for years 1914–1915, *ABSJH-SB*, CSC. In this event, women and men sold tags to individuals identifying them as donors to the hospital fund.

36. Financial Reports of St. Mary's Hospital, 1906–1915, ACSJC-SP. The sisters included bequest forms in their annual reports. See *Forty-Fourth Annual Report;* and *Fifty-Eighth Report, St. Joseph's Hospital, St. Paul*.

37. *ABSJH-SB*, CSC. See also Slattery, *Historical Studies*, 8.

38. See "Certificate of Authority to Indorse Draft," to Mother Jane Francis Bouchet as Treasurer of St. Mary's Hospital Corporation; "Old Accounts of St. Mary's Hospital," found in hospital safe by Sister Ann Thomasine Sampson, CSJ, in 1988; and archive note by Sister Ann Thomasine, November 19, 1988, ACSJC-SP. On the back of the account list is marked the words "All Paid."

39. *ABSJH-SB*, CSC. For information on interest rates, see Bureau of the Census, *Report on Real Estate Mortgages in the United States at the Eleventh Census: 1890* (Washington, DC: Government Printing Office, 1895), 248.

40. Mother St. Pierre Cinquin to Reverend and Good Mother, December 15, 1885, LSPC, AMIW.

41. Margaret Susan Thompson makes this point also in "Women, Feminism, and

the New Religious History," in *Belief and Behavior: Essays in the New Religious History*, ed. Philip R. Vandermeer and Robert P Swierenga (New Brunswick, NJ: Rutgers University Press, 1991), 147.

42. "Articles of Incorporation of the Sisters of Charity of the Incarnate Word, San Antonio, Texas," July 23, 1881; and "Charter of Saint Joseph's Infirmary, Articles of Incorporation," March 6, 1917, Office of the Secretary of State, Corporations Section, Austin, TX.

43. "Articles of Incorporation, St. Mary's Hospital," February 28, 1894, 200.2-2, box 1; "Articles of Incorporation, St. Joseph's Hospital," St. Paul, Minnesota, April 16, 1895, 200.2-1, box 1, folder 4; and "Extract from Minutes of Consultors Meeting, [St. Joseph's Hospital]," April 22, 1895, 200.2-1, box 2, folder 10, ACSJC-SP.

44. "Extract from Minutes of Consultors' Meeting [St. Joseph's Hospital] of 22 April 1895"; and "Certificate of Authority to Indorse Draft, [St. Mary's Hospital]," March 27, 1908, 200.2-2, box 1, ACSJC-SP.

45. "Articles of Incorporation of the Sisters of the Holy Cross Hospital Association," filed March 20, 1903, CSC. The association owned and conducted hospitals in South Bend, IN; Columbus, OH; Anderson, IN; and Salt Lake City, UT.

46. Copy, M. L. Ritchie to Sister M. Lidwina, February 19, 1903, CSC. See also Articles 3 and 4, "Articles of Association of the Sisters of the Holy Cross Hospital Association," filed March 20, 1903; and copy, "Evolution of Governance in Holy Cross," CSC.

47. Ginzburg, *Women and the Work of Benevolence*, 48, 50–52. See also Deacon, "Handmaids or Autonomous Women" ; and Janet Margaret Welsh, OP, "Where the Spirit Dwells: Catholic and Protestant Women and the Development of Christianity in the Upper Mississippi River Valley Lead Region, 1830–1870" (PhD diss., University of Notre Dame, 1995).

48. See, for example, *ABHCH*, 1881 and *ABSJH-SB*, CSC; *RBSJ*, June 23, 1889 and July 20, 1889, AMIW.

49. Sisters of the Holy Cross General Council Minutes, September 11, 1875, CSC.

50. Sister Augusta to Father Sorin, September 3, 1875, and Sister Augusta to Father General, October 14, 1875, Province Archives Center, Notre Dame, IN.

51. Sisters of the Holy Cross General Council Minutes, September 11, 1875, and December 28, 1880, CSC.

52. Sisters of the Holy Cross General Council Minutes, April 28, 1881, CSC.

53. Slattery, *Historical Studies*, 92–99.

54. National banks charged 11 percent interest for loans in 1894 and 10 percent in 1899. *Annual Report of the U. S. Comptroller of the Currency to the First Session of the Fifty-Sixth Congress of the United States*, vol. 1 (Washington, DC: Government Printing Office, 1899), 485.

55. See, for example, Sisters of the Holy Cross General Council Minutes, May 13, 1902 and March 17, 1903, CSC; and "Extract from Minutes of Consultors' Meeting [St. Joseph's Hospital]," April 22, 1895, ACSJC-SP.

56. Typed copy, "Cost of 1902 Building, Holy Cross Hospital," and "Annals-Salt Lake City," for the years 1902–1903, CSC. This was at the same time that Bishop Scanlan borrowed $60,000 at 5 percent interest for a new cathedral in Salt Lake City. See Bernice Maher Mooney and Monsignor Jerome C. Stoffel, eds., *Salt of the Earth: The History of the Catholic Diocese of Salt Lake City, 1776–1987* (Salt Lake City: Catholic Diocese, 1987), 100.

57. *ABHCH*, CSC.
58. *ABSJH-SB*, 1903, 34–35, CSC.
59. Copy of loan to Sisters of the Holy Cross Hospital Association by the Massachusetts Mutual Life Insurance Company, November 12, 1904, CSC. By contrast, New York Hospital's floating debt was $650,000 in 1901. See Rosner, *Once Charitable Enterprise*, 47–48. The board of governors paid $26,000 a year in interest charges alone. Thus, sisters were not alone in going into debt to meet hospital construction expenses.
60. "Reflecting on a Journey toward Tomorrow," undated brochure on Epworth Hospital; and "History of Epworth Hospital," Memorial Hospital Archives Project, South Bend, IN.
61. *ABSJH-SB*, CSC.
62. My conversation with Sister Florence Deacon, OSF, May 20, 1999, and Sister Kathryn Callahan, CSC, August 18, 1999, confirms this conclusion.
63. For example, see *RBSJ*, July 6, October 3, and October 14, 1889, AMIW.
64. See Chester Arthur Phillips, *Bank Credit: A Study of the Principles and Factors Underlying Advances Made by Banks to Borrowers* (New York: Macmillan Company, 1924), 165–69.
65. *ABHCH*, CSC; and *Benevolent Institutions, 1910*, 357.
66. As a contrast, Deacon reports that the Franciscan Sisters in Milwaukee helped finance institutions of other women and men's religious congregations, parish churches, and a cemetery. In 1884, they generated over $3,000 from interest, typically charging 4 percent interest on their loans. See Florence Deacon, OSF, "More Than Just a Shoe String and a Prayer: How Women Religious Helped Finance the Nineteenth-Century Social Fabric," *U. S. Catholic Historian* 14 (Winter 1996): 76.
67. *ABSJH-SB*, 1913–1914, CSC.
68. "Financial Accounts, St. Mark's Hospital," MDU.
69. McCauley, "'Who Shall Take Care of Our sick?'" 189. See also William Glaser, *Paying the Hospital: The Organization, Dynamics, and Effects of Differing Financial Arrangements* (San Francisco and London: Jossey-Bass Publishers, 1987), 24. As non-Catholic hospitals began to use nursing student labor for little pay, personnel budgets lowered.
70. *Fifty-Fifth Report, St. Joseph's Hospital*, ACSJC-SP.
71. *Fifty-Second Annual Report, St. Joseph's Hospital, Saint Paul, Minnesota, for the Year Ending June 30, 1905*, 200.2-1, box 2, folder 10, ACSJC-SP.
72. Advertisement, "Hospital of the Holy Cross," October 25, 1875, CSC.
73. Copy in ACSJC-SP.
74. Quoted in Slattery, *Historical Studies*, 88.
75. Frederick Law Olmsted to Henry Whitney Bellows, September 25, 1861, quoted in Jane Turner Censer, ed., *The Papers of Frederick Law Olmsted*, vol. 4, *Defending the Union: The Civil War and the U.S. Sanitary Commission, 1861–1863* (Baltimore: Johns Hopkins University Press, 1986), 202–3.
76. See, for example, Frank Larimore to Sister M. Frances De Sales O'Neill, March 10, 1916, CSC.
77. "St. Mary's Infirmary, Cairo, Illinois," written approximately between 1900 and 1905, CSC.
78. Brochure, "St. Mary's Infirmary, Cairo, Illinois," 1901, CSC.
79. "St. Mary's Hospital Addition," *Irish Standard*, April 26, 1890, 4.

80. See *The Catholic Heritage: Martyrs, Ascetics, Humanists, Activists, Outsiders, and Saints* (New York: Crossroad, 1983), 128–46; and Ryan K. Smith, "The Cross: Church Symbol and Contest in Nineteenth-Century America," *Church History* 70 (December 2001): 716–17. "Sacred space" is discussed in Mircea Eliade, *The Sacred and the Profane* (New York: Harcourt, Brace and World, 1959), 20–65; and Ellen Skerrett, "Creating Sacred Space in an Early Chicago Neighborhood," in *At the Crossroads: Old Saint Patrick's and the Chicago Irish*, ed. Skerrett (Chicago: Loyola Press and Wild Onion Books, 1997), 21–38.

81. *Salt Lake Tribune*, June 3, 1883. See also William Schaefers, "Catholic Hospital Atmosphere," *Hospital Progress* 11 (1930): 400.

82. "History of Holy Cross Hospital," CSC. The chapel is listed in the National Register of Historic Buildings. See Jack Goodman, "Holy Cross Hospital's Chapel Adds Old-World Charm to Young S.L.," *Salt Lake Tribune*, n.d., *ABHCH*, CSC.

83. "St. Mary's New Hospital," *Catholic Bulletin* (September 7, 1918).

84. Pius IX declared St. Joseph as the patron of the Catholic Church in 1870, and devotions to St. Joseph were frequent thereafter. See McBrien, *Harper Collins Encyclopedia of Catholicism*, 718–19.

85. *RBSJ*, April 23 and April 30, 1889, AMIW. In the stained-glass panels, a cross encircled by a Crown of Thorns symbolized Christ's suffering and death, through which he won redemption and eternal life for others. The Pelican-in-Her-Piety symbolized Christ's atonement. The Lamb of God (*Agnus Dei*) lying upon the Book of Seven Seals denoted the Eucharist and Jesus' sacrificial death. The Crown noted Christ's kingly office and eternal life. See F. R. Webber, *Church Symbolism* (Cleveland, OH: J. H. Jansen, 1938), 57–63; and Apostolos-Cappodona, *Dictionary of Christian Art* (New York: Continuum, 1994), 91, 203–4, 275.

86. Glaser, in *Paying the Hospital*, 37, notes that this procedure was typical of hospitals in Europe and Canada.

87. *HCHRB*, and *Quarterly Accounts*, CSC; and "Financial Reports of St. Mary's, Hospital," 1915, Archives Room, ACSJC-SP.

88. *Quarterly Accounts*, CSC. For comparison, see Lynaugh, *Community Hospitals*, 112. She found that, in 1915 at Kansas City's St. Luke's Hospital, operating room charges equaled 15 percent of earnings. Copy of Patient's Bill, St. Joseph's Hospital, November 4, 1909, ACSJC-SP:

> Board and Attendance for Oct. 27–Nov. 4 at $12/week: $13.70
> Supplies for operation: 3.00
> Medicine and Sterile Dressings: 1.85
> Extra Board: 1.00
> Total: 19.55

89. "Financial Reports of St. Mary's Hospital," 1914, ACSJC-SP. Sisters did not document whom the special nurses tended.

90. This income source represented approximately half the budgets of nonsectarian private hospitals and nearly three-fourths that of ecclesiastical institutions. See Stevens, *In Sickness and in Wealth*, 23–24; and *Benevolent Institutions, 1904*. Hospital administrators began to accept payment "in principle," having become convinced that regulating charges according to a patient's economic condition, rather than giving away free services, was desirable. See Henry M. Lyman, "On Paying Patients in Hospitals," in *Hospitals, Dispensaries, and Nursing, Papers and Discussions in the Interna-

tional Congress of Charities, Corrections and Philanthropy, Section III, ed. John S. Billings and Henry M. Hurd (Baltimore: Johns Hopkins Press, and London: Scientific Press, Limited, 1894), 124–28; James S. Knowles, "A Few Reasons Why Hospitals Show Such a Small Earning Power," *National Hospital Record* 2 (November 1898): 1–2; and John N. Elliott Brown and Edward Fletcher Stevens, "A General Hospital for One Hundred Patients," in *Hospital Management*, 125.

91. Secular hospitals did so, as well. See Charles E. Rosenberg, "Community and Communities: The Evolution of the American Hospital," in *The American General Hospital: Communities and Social Contexts*, ed. Diana Elizabeth Long and Janet Golden (Ithaca, NY and London: Cornell University Press, 1989), 15; Stevens, *In Sickness and in Wealth*, 38–39; Rosner, *Once Charitable Enterprise;* and Risse, *Mending Bodies, Saving Souls*, 557.

92. Editorial, *The Northwestern Medical and Surgical Journal* 1 (March 1871), 41.

93. H. Sweetser, "Financial Support of Hospitals, "*Hospital Progress* 1, no. 6 (1920): 232.

94. Advertisement, *Hospital Progress* 1 (1920): xiv.

CHAPTER 6

1. *RBSR,* January 18, 1898, AMIW.

2. Colleen McDannell, *Material Christianity: Religion and Popular Culture in America* (New Haven, CT and London: Yale University Press, 1995), 135; and Ruth Harris, *Lourdes: Body and Spirit in the Secular Age* (New York: Viking, 1999). These miracles do not appear to be as common in the United States as they were in traditionally Catholic countries such as France or Ireland. Nevertheless, after the mid-nineteenth century, interest in miraculous cures became more widespread in this country and Europe among both Protestants and Catholics. See Ann Taves, *The Household of Faith: Roman Catholic Devotions in Mid-Nineteenth-Century America* (Notre Dame, IN: University of Notre Dame Press, 1986), 56–58; and Thomas Kselman, *Miracles and Prophesies in 19th-Century France* (New Brunswick, NJ: Rutgers University Press, 1983), 12–35.

3. *RBSJ,* November 24, 1889, AMIW.

4. On the place of medicine and healing in the early church, see Darrel W. Amundsen,
Medicine, Society, and Faith in the Ancient and Medieval Worlds (Baltimore: Johns Hopkins University Press, 1996); and Gary B. Ferngren, "Early Christianity as a Religion of Healing," *Bulletin of the History of Medicine* 66 (1992): 1–15; 40–64. For the nineteenth century, see O'Connell, "The Roman Catholic Tradition," 108–45.

5. Pain and suffering did not disappear among the general population, despite the introduction of anesthesia and new painkillers in the middle and late nineteenth centuries. See Martin S. Pernick, *A Calculus of Suffering: Pain, Professionalism, and Anesthesia in Nineteenth-Century America* (New York: Columbia University Press, 1985); and Roselyne Rey, *The History of Pain* (Cambridge, MA: Harvard University Press, 1995).

6. *Manual of Decrees, Customs and Observances, For the Use of the Congregation of the Religious of St. Joseph of Carondelet* (St. Louis: Ev. E. Carreras, Steam Printer and Binder, 1888), 114, ACSJC-SL.

7. James Cardinal Gibbons, "Sickness a Season of Divine Mercy," in *Discourses and Sermons for Every Sunday and the Principal Festivals of the Year*, ed. Gibbons (Baltimore and New York: John Murphy Company, 1908), 482.

8. Ibid., 481–85.

9. Coburn and Smith, "Creating Community," 91–108; and Coburn and Smith, *Spirited Lives*, 79.

10. For further discussion on this topic, see Sioban Nelson, "Reading Nursing History," *Nursing Inquiry* 4 (1997): 229–36; and Maher, *To Bind Up the Wounds*, 37.

11. See *Directory of the Sisters of Charity of the Incarnate Word*, 1906, 207, AMIW; and
Rules of the Congregation of the Sisters of the Holy Cross, 1895, 142, CSC.

12. Copy of "Instructions on the Care of the Sick," Marillac Provincial House, Daughters of Charity of St. Vincent de Paul, St. Louis, MO (hereafter cited as MPH). Hereafter, this source will be cited as Clark, "Instructions." These "Instructions" reflect the teachings of Vincent de Paul in vol. 1–4, *The Conferences of St. Vincent de Paul to the Sisters of Charity*, trans. Joseph Leonard, CM (Westminster, MD: Newman Press, 1952).

13. Clark, "Instructions," 2nd, MPH. (Instructions rather than pages are numbered.) See also Sister Daniel Hannefin, DC, *Daughters of the Church: A Popular History of the Daughters of Charity in the United States, 1809–1987* (New York: New City Press, 1989); and Kauffman, *Ministry and Meaning*, 37.

14. Clark, "Instructions," 5th, 13th (quotation), 15th, MPH.

15. Ibid., "Instructions," 16th, MPH.

16. Clark, "Instructions," 4th–9th, 11th, 16th, MPH. An 1899 text emphasized similar messages. See Rev. L. Hinssen, *The Nursing Sister: A Manual for Candidates and Novices of Hospital Communities* (Springfield, IL: H. W. Rokker Co., 1899), chapters 14, 18, 19.

17. Translation, *Rules Given to Our First Mothers on Leaving France, 1869 [1867]*, trans. Sister Kathleen Garvey, AMIW.

18. See Ralph Gibson, *A Social History of French Catholicism* (London and New York: Routledge, 1989), 158–92; Larkin, "Devotional Revolution," 644–45; and Dolan, *American Catholic Experience*, 229–33. Taves asserts, "Veneration of the Blessed Sacrament was a devotional reflection of the Catholic doctrine of the real presence" of Christ. The forty hours devotion focused on the Blessed Sacrament and involved a period of forty hours' adoration "in memory of the forty hours Jesus' body spent in the sepulchre." See Taves, *Household of Faith*, 30.

19. See, for example, *RBSJ* March 25, 1892; *RBSR* February 17 and August 15, 1896, January 18 and February 20, 1898, AMIW.

20. In June 1892, the Incarnate Word Sisters celebrated the Feasts of the Pentecost, Corpus Christi, John the Baptist, and St. Peter and St. Paul. In July, they celebrated five more feasts. See *RBSR* June 5, June 16, June 24, June 29, 1892; July 2, July 16, July 19, July 22, and July 31, 1892; August 15, 1896, AMIW.

21. Barbra Mann Wall and Sioban Nelson, " 'Our Heels Are Praying Very Hard All Day': The Working Prayer of the 19th-Century Religious Nurse," *Holistic Nursing Practice* (2003): 4.

22. *RBSR*, January 6 and October 27, 1897, AMIW.

23. Mother Angela Gillespie to Orestes Brownson, March 19, 1862, O. A, Brownson Letters Received, I-4-b, UNDA.

24. *Manual of Decrees*, 114, ACSJC-SL.
25. Sister Augusta Anderson to Father Sorin, July 13, 1875, CSC.
26. Sister Liguori to Reverend Mother, October 31 and December 1, 1898, ACSJC-SL. For a discussion of scapulars, see McDannell, *Material Christianity*, 22–23.
27. O'Connell, "The Roman Catholic Tradition," 113–17, 134–35. For information on the Council of Trent, see Bokenkotter, *A Concise History of the Catholic Church*, 215–18, 223.
28. O'Connell, "The Roman Catholic Tradition," 115–17. The term *sacrament* comes from the Latin *sacramentum*. By the fifth century, the term *sacramentum* included a broad definition as any symbol or ceremony that was a "sign of a sacred reality." Christians restricted its usage in later times, however, and by the twelfth century, the term referred to the seven formal sacraments. These sacraments were the principal ways that people could gain access to the supernatural. The seven sacraments include baptism, confirmation, the Eucharist, reconciliation, anointing, marriage, and ordination. See Joseph Martos, *Doors to the Sacred: A Historical Introduction to the Sacraments in the Catholic Church* (Liguori, MO: Triumph Books, 1991).
29. O'Connell, "The Roman Catholic Tradition," 117.
30. Martos, *Doors to the Sacred*, 3–5. Quotation is on page 5. See also McBrien, *Harper Collins Encyclopedia*; and Eliade, *Sacred and the Profane*, 20–115.
31. Clarke E. Cochran, "Thinking Sacramentally: A Perspective on Catholic Social Theory, with Reference to Healthcare Policy," 20–21, presented at the University of Notre Dame, Notre Dame, IN, Spring 1999. Quoted with author's permission.
32. Martos, *Doors to the Sacred*, 5. See also Patricia Wittberg, "Ties That No Longer Bind," *America* (September 26, 1998): 10–14.
33. Gibbons, *Discourses and Sermons*, 480–81. See also Thomas Dwight, "The Training-Schools for Nurses of the Sisters of Charity," *Catholic World* 61 (May 1895): 191.
34. "Instructions on the Care of the Sick," pt. 1, MPH.
35. Sister Mary Helena Finck, *The Congregation of the Sisters of Charity of the Incarnate Word of San Antonio, Texas: A Brief Account of its Origin and Its Work* (Washington, DC: Catholic University of America, 1925), 119.
36. Clark, "Instructions," 17th, MPH.
37. 1885 *Constitutions of the Sisters of Charity of the Incarnate Word*, Part Fifth, Chapter III, Article 3, AMIW. For a source on the twentieth century, see Berenice Beck, OSF, *Handmaid of the Divine Physician* (Milwaukee, WI: Bruce Publishing Co., 1952).
38. See, for example, *RBSR*, April 8 and November 23, 1896, AMIW. Some Catholic Church leaders criticized "secret societies," such as the Masons, with their secret rituals of initiation. They feared the societies would become "substitutes for the church." In the late nineteenth century, Masons also were known to be anti-Catholic. See Dolan, *American Catholic Experience*, 312–13.
39. *RBSR*, 1896, AMIW.
40. "Copy of a Letter from Mother St. John Fournier to the Superior General of the Sisters of St. Joseph in Lyons [1873]," in Sister Maria Kostka Logue, *Sisters of St. Joseph of Philadelphia: A Century of Growth and Development, 1847–1947* (Westminster, MD: Newman Press, 1950), 336–37.
41. See, for example, Carl Capellmann, *Pastoral Medicine* (New York and Cincinnati: Fr. Pustet, 1879), 137–54; and Canon John Fletcher, *Notes for Catholic Nurses* (London: Catholic Truth Society, 1912), 21–24.

42. Slattery, *Historical Studies*, 13; and *RBSR*, October 24, 1896, AMIW.

43. Michael Sappol, *A Traffic of Dead Bodies: Anatomy and Embodied Social Identity in Nineteenth-Century America* (Princeton, NJ: Princeton University Press, 2002); Ruth Richardson, *Death, Dissection and the Destitute* (London: Penguin, 1989); and Rey, *The History of Pain*.

44. Thompson. "Philemon's Dilemma," 14; and Dolan, *American Catholic Experience*, 325.

45. *RBSR* , 1896, AMIW.

46. *St. Mary's Infirmary Archives, 1915–1941*, for the year 1925, CSC.

47. Peter Brown, *The Cult of the Saints: Its Rise and Function in Latin Christianity* (Chicago: University of Chicago Press, 1981), 69–70; and Darrel W. Amundsen and Gary B. Ferngren, "The Early Christian Tradition," in *Caring and Curing: Health and Medicine in the Western Religious Traditions*, ed. Ronald L. Numbers and Darrel W. Amundsen, 40–64 (New York: Macmillan, 1986).

48. Philippe Aries, *The Hour of Our Death*, trans. Helen Weaver (New York: Alfred A. Knopf, 1981), 99–124. Aries attributes these changes to fears brought about by the plague, and to missionaries' attempts to impress people by using powerful images of death. See also Amanda Porterfield, "Healing in the History of Christianity–Presidential Address, January 2002, American Society of Church History," *Church History: Studies in Christianity and Culture* 71, no. 2 (June 2002): 228–31.

49. Aries, *Hour of Our Death*, 108. See also Aries, "The Reversal of Death: Changes in Attitudes toward Death in Western Societies," in *Death in America*, ed. David E. Stannard (Philadelphia: University of Pennsylvania Press, 1975), 134–58.

50. Jean Baptiste Marie Vianney, *Sermons for the Sundays and Feasts of the Year* (New York: Joseph F. Wagner, 1901), 33. These sermons were originally preached in the 1850s.

51. Kathryn Norberg, "The Counter Reformation and Women: Religious and Lay," in vol. 2, *Catholicism in Early Modern History: A Guide to Research*, ed. John W. O'Malley, SJ (Ann Arbor, MI: Edwards Brothers, 1988), 138–39. See also Wittberg, "Ties That No Longer Bind."

52. Geoffrey Gorer, in *Death, Grief, and Mourning* (New York: Arno Press, 1977), 195, argues that today's society denies death. His article "The Pornography of Death" was first published in *Encounter*, October 1955. See also Philippe Aries, *Western Attitudes toward Death: From the Middle Ages to the Present* (Baltimore and London: Johns Hopkins University Press, 1974), 92; Aries, *Hour of Our Death*; Aries, "The Reversal of Death," 134–58; and Ivan Illich, *Medical Nemesis: The Expropriation of Health* (New York: Pantheon Books, 1976), 174–208.

53. *Manual of Decrees*, 114–15, ACSJC-SL.

54. 1872 *Constitutions of the Sisters of Charity of the Incarnate Word*, Part First, Chapter XII, # 9, AMIW.

55. Most of what is known about nursing care comes from the sisters' writings and from texts and annual reports. See, for example, "The History of St. Joseph's Hospital School of Nursing," AMIW; Hinssen, *The Nursing Sister*, chaps. 13–23, 40–48; H. J. O'Brien, *Medical and Surgical Nursing* (New York and London: G. P. Putnam's Sons, 1900), 26–79; and *Annual Reports*, St. Joseph Hospital, St. Paul, MN.

56. Quoted in George Carmack, "Dr. Cayo First San Antonio Orthopedic Surgeon," *San Antonio Express*, May 26, 1976, 11 A.

57. Richards, *Of Medicine*, 59.

58. Richard Dunlop, *Doctors of the American Frontier* (New York: Ballantine Books, 1965), 118.

59. See, for example, *RBSJ*, August 6, 1890; *RBSR*, October 18, 1895, and April 13 and 20, 1897, AMIW. Doctors operated on the child with the obstructed larynx, but despite all efforts, the child died.

60. *RBSJ*, September 3 and September 14, and June 24, 1889; *RBSR*, April 24, May 4, May 6, June 17, and November 13, 1896, AMIW.

61. See Nancy Tomes, "The Great Restraint Controversy: A Comparative Perspective on Anglo-American Psychiatry in the Nineteenth Century," in *The Anatomy of Madness: Essays in the History of Psychiatry*, ed. W. F. Bynum, Roy Porter, and Michael Shephard (London and New York: Routledge, 1988), 190–225; and Neville E. Strumpf and Nancy Tomes, "Restraining the Troublesome Patient: A Historical Perspective on a Contemporary Debate," *Nursing History Review* 1 (1993): 3–24.

62. *RBSJ*, September 4, 1889, AMIW.

63. *RBSJ*, January 16 and February 1, 1892; and *RBSR*, November 13 and 14, 1896, AMIW.

64. *RBSJ*, June 10, 1889, AMIW.

65. Quotations are in Florence Nightingale, *Notes on Nursing* (D. Appleton and Co., 1860; repr. London: Longman, Green, and Roberts, 1869), 184, 187.

66. Quoted in Jo Ann Widerquist, "Called to Serve," *Christian Nurse International* 11, no. 1 (1995): 5.

67. Nelson, *Say Little, Do Much*, 62–64; Wall and Nelson, " 'Our Heels Are Praying,' " 326.

68. Dwight, "Training-Schools for Nurses," 191. He admittedly based his allegations on personal experience with only one hospital.

69. Vogel, *Invention of the Modern Hospital;* and Michel Foucault, *The Birth of the Clinic: An Archeology of Medical Perception* (Paris: Presses Universitaires de France, 1963; repr. New York: Vintage Books, 1994). Foucault criticized the changes brought about in hospitals during the French Revolution as patients became objects of study and subject to a controlling "clinical gaze" for scientific advancement.

70. Robert A. Orsi, *Thank You, St. Jude: Women's Devotion to the Patron Saint of Hopeless Causes* (New Haven, CT and London: Yale University Press, 1996), 147–66; and Kauffman, *Ministry and Meaning*, 212.

71. Dolan, *American Catholic Experience*, 325

72. For community health nursing by secular women, see Diane Hamilton, "Constructing the Mind of Nursing," *Nursing History Review* 2 (1994): 3–28; Karen Buhler-Wilkerson, *False Dawn: The Rise and Decline of Public Health Nursing, 1900–1930* (New York: Garland Publishing Co., 1989); and Buhler-Wilkerson, *No Place Like Home: A History of Nursing and Home Care in the United States* (Baltimore and London: Johns Hopkins University Press, 2001).

73. *Constitutions of the Sisters of Charity of the Incarnate Word*, 1872, Part First, Chapter XII, Article 11; and *RBSJ*, March 31, 1890, AMIW. See also Slattery, *Historical Studies*, 7.

74. Suellen Hoy, "Caring for Chicago's Women and Girls: The Sisters of the Good Shepherd, 1859–1911," *Journal of Urban History* 23 (March 1997): 260–94; and Hoy, "Walking Nuns: Chicago's Irish Sisters of Mercy," in *At the Crossroads*, 39–51.

75. Orsi, *Thank You, St. Jude*, 167.

CHAPTER 7

1. Quoted in Lawrence Scanlan, "Annual Report of the State of Catholicity in the Territory of Utah, United States of America, to the Society for the Propagation of the Faith, France," October 12, 1876, in *Utah Historical Quarterly* 29 (October 1961): 339.

2. Welter, "Cult of True Womanhood," 151–57; and Kauffman, *Ministry and Meaning*, 112.

3. Joyce, "Science and the Saints," 119.

4. Quoted in Slattery, *Historical Studies*, 3.

5. *Rules Given to Our First Mothers on Leaving France 1869* [1867], trans. Sister Kathleen Garvey, AMIW.

6. *Diary, Santa Rosa Hospital, 1869–1946*, AMIW.

7. Barber, *The Doctors Herff*, 476–77.

8. "Minutes of the Meeting of the Staff, Holy Cross Hospital," November 12, 1903, ACCN #588, box 5, MDU.

9. "Minutes of the Meeting of the Staff," December 17, 1903, MDU. Sister Lidwina Butler was superior at Holy Cross Hospital for eighteen years, from 1895 to 1913. See "Record of Apostolic Service, Sister M. Lidwina Butler," CSC.

10. Starr, *Social Transformation*, bk. 1; and Edward Cowles, "The Relations of the Medical Staff to the Governing Bodies in Hospitals," in *Hospitals, Dispensaries and Nursing: Papers and Discussions in the International Congress of Charities, Correction and Philanthropy, Section III, Chicago, June 12th to 17th, 1893*, ed. John S. Billings and Henry M. Hurd (Baltimore: Johns Hopkins Press; and London: Scientific Press, Limited, 1894), 69–76.

11. Wittberg, *Rise and Fall*, 63; and Glaser, *Social Settings*, 50–56.

12. Thomas M. Gannon, SJ, "Catholic Religious Orders in Sociological Perspective," in *American Denominational Organization: A Sociological View*, ed. Ross P. Scherer (Pasadena: William Carey Library, 1980), 172.

13. Glaser, *Social Settings*, 56–57.

14. See, for example, *Statutes and Constitutions of the Congregation of the Sisters of Charity of the Incarnate Word*, 1872, Part First, Chapter XII, pp. 27–28, AMIW.

15. Medical societies of the day criticized doctors for advertising in newspapers to secure patients. See Bayard Holmes, MD, "The Hospital Problem," *Journal of the American Medical Association* 47 (August 4, 1906): 319.

16. "Internes' Rules and Regulations," n.d., St. Joseph's Hospital, St. Paul, MN, 200.2–1, box 1, folder 4, ACSJC-SP.

17. "Internes' Rules," St. Joseph's; and "St. Mary's Hospital, Minneapolis, Minn., Internes' Rules and Regulations," n.d. [presumably around 1920], Archives Room, ACSJC-SP. Apparently, a Committee on Interns wrote the Rules.

18. "Internes' Rules," St. Mary's, ACSJC-SP.

19. S. M. Marguerite S. to Sister Madeleine Lyons, n.d. Located in Sister Madeleine Lyons' personal folder, ACSJC-SP. S. was a sister to the intern and wrote Mother St. Madeleine of her brothers' remembrance of St. Mary's Hospital.

20. See, for example, "Weekly Meetings of the Administration of Holy Cross Hospital, Salt Lake City, Utah," for the year 1886, CSC.

21. See application letters by W. D. Donoher to Sister Superior, September 23, 1915; L. F. Hummer to Sisters and Staff, May 20, 1916; and T. A. Flood to Sister M. Beniti, June 2, 1916; and "Minutes of the Meeting of the Staff," December 7, 1908, MDU.

22. *ABHCH,* April 12, 1909, CSC. This may have been in 1913, according to records at MDU.
23. Quoted in Starr, *Social Transformation,* 165 (first quotation), and 166 (second quotation).
24. Ibid., 165–66.
25. "Minutes of the Meeting of the Staff," November 12, 1903 and January 21, 1904, MDU.
26. Editorial, *Hospital World* 3 (February 1913): 76.
27. Mother St. Madeleine to Dr. W. A. Adams, January 28, 1900, AMIW.
28. Sister M. Gabriel for Mother St. Madeleine to Doctors Thompson and Saunders, January 28, 1900, AMIW.
29. Slattery, *Historical Studies,* 97.
30. Rosner, *Once Charitable Enterprise,* 22, and chap. 4; Charles E. Rosenberg, "Inward Vision & Outward Glance: The Shaping of the American Hospital, 1880–1914," *Bulletin of the History of Medicine* 53 (Fall 1979): 357–60; and William Glaser, "American and Foreign Hospitals: Some Sociological Comparisons," in *The Hospital in Modern Society,* ed. Eliot Freidson (London: Free Press of Glencoe, Collier-Macmillan Limited, 1963), 37–72.
31. See, for example, *RBSR,* July 9, 1897; and *RBSJ,* June 29, 1890, AMIW.
32. 1872 *Constitutions,* Part First, Chapter XII, #14, AMIW.
33. *RBSJ,* June 9, 1889, AMIW.
34. *ABHCH,* March 9, 1909, CSC.
35. "Minutes of the Meeting of the Staff," December 7, 1908, MDU.
36. Starr, *Social Transformation,* 198–99, 235–36.
37. Newspaper clipping, May 16, 1903, "Doctors Are Greedy," Holy Cross Hospital Scrapbook, Salt Lake City, UT, 1875–July 1920, CSC. See also Starr, *Social Transformation,* 203.
38. "Doctors Are Greedy."
39. *HCHBAA 1892 to July 1941,* for the year 1904, CSC.
40. "Minutes of the Meeting of the Staff," November 12, 1903, January 21, 1904, MDU.
41. Barber, *The Doctors Herff,* 334; and Slattery, *Historical Studies,* 23.
42. *RBSR,* February 2, 1898, AMIW.
43. Sister M. Gabriel Wheelahan for Rev. Mother St. Madeleine Chollet to Doctors Thompson and Saunders [day and month not given], 1901, AMIW.
44. Starr, *Social Transformation,* 17–21, 79–179; Rosenberg, "Inward Vision & Outward Glance," 357–60.
45. H. D. Niles, MD, "Our Hospitals," *Journal of the American Medical Association* 38 (March 22, 1902): 761.
46. Ibid., 759–60.
47. "Minutes of the Meeting of the Staff," November 12, 1903, MDU.
48. Quotation in Slattery, *Historical Studies,* 95.
49. "Many Mourn for Sister Lidwina," *Salt Lake City Tribune,* February 17, 1913, 12.
50. Sister M. Gabriel Wheelahan for Mother St. Madeleine Chollet to Dr. T. Lutz, (no month) 1901, AMIW.
51. Sister M. Gabriel Wheelahan for Mother St. Madeleine Chollet to Dr. T. Lutz, June 30, 1901, AMIW. The letter from Dr. Lutz to Mother St. Madeleine is not available.

52. Mother St. Madeleine Chollet to Dr. C. A. Smith, Chief Surgeon, August 9, 1905, AMIW. Mother St. Madeleine no doubt recalled her constitution, which instructed that in hospitals, sisters were not to be treated as "mercenaries" but as respected "daughters." See 1872 *Constitutions,* Part First, Chapter XII, #15, AMIW.

53. Mother St. Madeleine to D. C. A. Smith, 1903, AMIW.

54. Quoted in Marilyn C. Barker and R. P. Morris, *The Early Holy Cross Hospital and Salt Lake City* (Salt Lake City: n.p., 1975), 16, CSC.

55. See Robin Lakoff, *Language and Woman's Place* (New York: Harper & Row Publishers, 1975), 18; and Carole Spitzack and Kathryn Carter, "Women in Communication Studies: A Typology for Revision," *Quarterly Journal of Speech* 73 (November 1987): 401–23.

56. Scott, *Weapons of the Weak,* 30–5. Quotation is on page 30.

57. For further discussion of this point, see Michel Foucault, "Truth and Power," in *Power/Knowledge,* ed. Colin Gordon (New York: Pantheon, 1980), 109–33. For another example, see Mario Biagioli, *Galileo, Courtier: The Practice of Science in the Culture of Absolutism* (Chicago and London: University of Chicago Press, 1993), 2.

58. Sister M. Gabriel Wheelahan for Mother St. Madeleine Chollet to Mr. H. A. Jones, August 21, 1900, AMIW. See also Gail Porter Mandell, *Madeleva: A Biography* (Albany: State University of New York Press, 1997), for an insightful interpretation of similar strategies used by Sister Madeleva Wolff of the Sisters of the Holy Cross.

59. "Home Also a Hospital," *Salt Lake Tribune,* December 10, 1901, Holy Cross Hospital Scrapbook, Salt Lake City, UT, CSC.

60. Ibid. See also Mooney and Stoffel, *Salt of the Earth,* 96.

61. Mooney and Stoffel, *Salt of the Earth,* 115; Rev. Louis J. Fries, STB, *One Hundred and Fifty Years of Catholicity in Utah* (Salt Lake City: Intermountain Catholic Press, 1926), 128–31; and Richards, *Of Medicine,* 236. These sources indicated the Sisters of Mercy converted the building to a school. However, Judge Mercy Hospital is listed in the *Salt Lake City Directory for 1925* (Salt Lake City: R. L. Polk Publisher, 1925), 210.

62. Kenneally, "Eve, Mary, and the Historians," 197–98.

63. Byrne, "Sisters of St. Joseph," 271.

64. Sister M. Gabriel to Rev. E. Schmitt, July 12, 1896. See also Sister M. of the Holy Ghost to Rev. Father E. J. P. Schmitt, August 25, 1896, CSCT 5/03, UNDA. Magray, in *Transforming Power,* 113–16, notes similar examples in her sample of nuns in Ireland.

65. Magray, *Transforming Power,* 113–15.

66. Quotation in Kauffman, *Ministry and Meaning,* 217.

67. This builds on Joyce's conclusion in "Science and the Saints," 132–33.

68. Wall, "Called to a Mission of Charity," 102.

Chapter 8

1. A Sister of St. Francis, "Admission to Our Training Schools," Letter to the Editor, *Trained Nurse and Hospital Review* 38 (February 1907): 122–24.

2. John T. Bottomley, "The Right Limitations to Privilege of Practice in Hospitals in the Scheme of Hospital Standardization," *Hospital Progress,* 1, no. 1 (May 1920): 5.

3. Philip Gleason, *Keeping the Faith: American Catholicism Past and Present* (Notre

Dame, IN: University of Notre Dame Press), 63; and R. L. Moore, *Religious Outsiders and the Making of Americans* (New York: Oxford University Press, 1986).

4. Today this organization is known as the Catholic Health Association. See Christopher J. Kauffman, "The Push for Standardization: The Origins of the Catholic Hospital Association, 1914–1920," *Health Progress* 71 (January–February 1990): 64; and Kauffman, *Ministry and Meaning*, 168–92.

5. Stevens, *In Sickness and in Wealth*, 115. Stevens notes that it was "the association's pledge to bring six hundred Catholic hospitals into the standardization program that got the ACS's program moving." See 384n24 for quotation.

6. *Bulletin of the American College of Surgeons* 4 (1919), 11; 5 (1920); 6 (1921); and 7 (1922); Stevens, *In Sickness and in Wealth*, 384n24; and Kauffman, *Ministry and Meaning*, 182.

7. Christopher J. Kauffman, "The Leadership of Father Moulinier: The Catholic Hospital Association Comes of Age, 1921–1928," *Health Progress* 71 (March 1990): 42; Stevens, *In Sickness and in Wealth*, 115; and Kauffman, *Ministry and Meaning*, 177.

8. "Official Actions of the Catholic Hospital Association with Reference to Nursing Education," Archives of the Catholic Health Association, St. Louis, MO (hereafter cited as CHA); and Kauffman, *Ministry and Meaning*, 171.

9. "The Catholic Health Association and Its Roots in Minneapolis, Minnesota"; "Minutes of 1st Meeting of the Minnesota Conference of the Catholic Hospital Association," May 23, 1922, folder, Sister Madeleine Lyons, ACSJC-SP.

10. Mother Esperance Finn, "What the Sisters Should Contribute to the Team-Work," in *Transactions of the Second Annual Meeting of the Catholic Hospital Association*, Milwaukee, WI, June 7–9, 1918. Quotations are on pages 66, 71, and 72, CHA.

11. Father Moulinier, in response Sister Esperance's comments in *Transactions of the Second Annual Meeting*, 73–74.

12. Rev. Charles B. Moulinier, SJ, "President's Address," *Transactions of the Third Annual Meeting of the Catholic Hospital Association, Held at Chicago, Illinois, 18–20 June 1918*, p. 7, CHA.

13. Editorial, "Sisters' Hospitals," *Hospital Progress* 2 (September 1921): 350–51; and Kauffman, *Ministry and Meaning*, 180–89.

14. *Constitution and By-Laws of the St. Joseph Hospital of St. Paul, Minnesota*, revised 1921; and Minutes of Staff Meetings, St. Joseph's Hospital, St. Paul, MN, 200.2–1, box 1, folder 4, ACSJC-SP. See also *Constitution By-Laws and Rules of the Staff and Diagnostic Department*, St. Mary's Hospital, Minneapolis, MN, 1920, ACSJC-SP; and *Constitution and By-Laws of the Staff of the Holy Cross Hospital of Salt Lake City, Utah*, Article VI, [1923], MDU.

15. See Lynaugh, *Community Hospitals*, 150–51, for similar findings at St. Joseph's Hospital in that city.

16. "Minutes of the Meeting of the Staff," April 1, 1929, MDU.

17. Noted in *Bulletin of the American College of Surgeons*, 12.

18. "Minutes of the Meeting of the Staff," April 1, 1929, MDU.

19. "The Round Table Conferences: Conference of Mothers Provincial and Superior, and Superintendents," *Hospital Progress* 1, no. 5 (September 1920): 203–7.

20. "Hospital Staff Quits," *Tribune*, Terre Haute, IN, January 4, 1921. Also in *Miscellaneous Proceedings of the Vigo County Medical Society, 1902–1954*, Scrapbook, microfilm, Vigo County Public Library, Terre Haute, IN.

21. Newspaper clippings in Vigo County Public Library; and Sister M. Rosanna

Peters, "The History of the Poor Sisters of St. Francis Seraph of the Perpetual Adoration, 1875–1940" (PhD diss., Indiana University, 1944), 59–60. Sister Augustina Dirkmann was hospital administrator but apparently was ill during part of this struggle.

22. See Barbra Mann Wall, "Science and Ritual: The Hospital as Medical and Sacred Space, 1865–1920," *Nursing History Review* 11(2003): 51–68.

23. *Hospital World* 3 (April 1913): xxxviii.

24. *Medical Examiner* 8 (February 1898): 64; (May 1898): 160; and (September 1898): 288.

25. For example, Dr. Harry O'Brien donated an ambulance in 1902 to St. Joseph's, St. Paul. At St. Joseph's Hospital, South Bend, Dr. Olney, who performed most of the surgery, donated $1,200 for a new operating table. See *ABSJH-SB*, CSC.

26. Rima Apple, "Picturing the Hospital: Photographs in the History of an Institution," in *The American General Hospital: Communities and Social Contexts*, ed. Diana Elizabeth Long and Janet Golden (Ithaca, NY and London: Cornell University Press, 1989), 76.

27. Typed copy of newspaper, *Salt Lake Tribune*, May 13, 1914, CSC.

28. *Fifty-Eighth Report, St. Joseph's Hospital, 1912.*

29. W. W. Stevenson, "Attractions of Cairo, Illinois," October 1890; newspaper clipping December 5, 1906 and July 5, 1910, Scrapbook, St. Mary's Infirmary, Cairo, IL, CSC.

30. *Salt Lake Tribune*, October 31, 1902.

31. Article II–Object, sec. 1, *Constitution and By-Laws*, CHA.

32. Joel D. Howell, *Technology in the Hospital: Transforming Patient Care in the Early Twentieth Century* (Baltimore and London: Johns Hopkins University Press, 1995), 157–63.

33. Slattery, *Historical Studies*, 22.

34. "Conference Reports Relate Initial Activities of [CHA] Committees in Assembling Statistical Data," *Hospital Progress* 5 (October 1924): 406.

35. Moulinier, "President's Address" [1918], 4–5, CHA.

36. Charles A. Gordon, MD, "Autopsies," *Hospital Progress* 3, no. 10 (October 1922): 399–401 (quotations on pages 399 and 401).

37. *Benevolent Institutions, 1910*, 356–57. See also Slattery, *Historical Studies*, 92–99. The 1916 *American Medical Directory*, 1469–70, lists a fifty-bed public general hospital that was founded in 1903, and several sanitariums founded before 1910. Information on the Incarnate Word Sisters' training schools was supplied by the Texas Board of Nurse Examiners. My thanks to Cheryl Rosenthal. See also Slattery, *Historical Studies*, 92–100. Quotation is on page 99.

38. See *RBSR*, May 10, 1889 and August 16, 1890. See also "Santa Rosa Hospital" booklet, box 90, AMIW; Sister Cuthberta Chawke, "Personal File," ACSJC-SP.

39. Isabel H. Robb, *Educational Standards for Nurses, with Other Addresses on Nursing Subjects* (1907; repr. New York: Garland Publishing, 1985); Reverby, *Ordered to Care*; M. E. Smith, "Nursing as a Vocation," *Trained Nurse and Hospital Review* 29 (1902): 329; Ewens, *Role of the Nun*, 272–73; and Barbra Mann Wall, " 'Definite Lines of Influence': Catholic Sisters and Nurse Training Schools, 1890–1920," *Nursing Research* 50 (September–October 2001): 314–21.

40. "The Round Table Conferences," 204.

41. Sister Mary Benedict, "Rule and Common Sense," *Hospital Progress* 2, no. 1 (January 1921): 21.

42. *RBSR,* November 20, 1897, AMIW.

43. Aseptic conditions did not yet prevail. The physicians are wearing aprons but no gloves or caps.

44. S. W. Mitchell, "Nurses and their Education," *American Journal of Nursing* 2 (August 1902): 90; and Dwight, "The Training Schools of the Sisters of Charity," 187–92.

45. "Round Table Discussion: The Priest and Vocations to the Sisterhoods," *Hospital Progress* 4, no. 12 (December 1923): 476.

46. Article II, *Constitution and By-Laws,* CHA. See also Robert J. Shanahan, SJ, *The History of the Catholic Hospital Association, 1915–1965, Fifty Years of Progress* (St. Louis: Catholic Hospital Association of the United States and Canada, 1965); and Kauffman, *Ministry and Meaning,* chap. 8, for analysis of the Catholic Hospital Association's efforts toward this end.

47. "The Catholic Health Association and Its Roots in Minneapolis, Minnesota," ACSJC-SP. See also Kauffman, "The Push for Standardization," 62–63; and Sampson, *Care with Prayer,* 17.

48. Kauffman, *Ministry and Meaning,* 181–92, 230–44; and Kauffman, "Leadership of Father Moulinier," 45. He reports the opening of the Marquette College in 1924. Stevens describes the first graduate program in hospital administration at the University of Chicago in 1934. See Stevens, *In Sickness,* 157–58.

49. Reverby, *Ordered to Care,* 62, 72–76; and Melosh, *The Physician's Hand,* 32.

50. Sister Charles Marie Frank, CCVI, "The Story of One Collegiate School of Nursing, Division of Nursing, Incarnate Word College, San Antonio, Texas, Its Evolution, Growth, and Contribution to Health Services, 1903–1976," 9–16; and Minutes of the Meeting of the Staff, Santa Rosa Infirmary, September 12, 1905, September 19, 1910, September 24, 1911, and September 29, 1911, box 1900, AMIW.

51. Sister M. Veronica, "The Internal Organization of Training Schools," *Hospital Progress* 1 (September 1920): 193.

52. Sister Magdalene, OSF, "The Training of the Nurse," *Hospital Progress* 2, no. 7 (July 1921): 268–69; Sister Zoe, "Nursing Problems," *Hospital Progress* 4, no. 1 (January 1923): 28–29.

53. "Official Actions of the Catholic Hospital Association with Reference to Nursing Education," CHA. See also Coburn and Smith, *Spirited Lives,* 202 and 295n47; and Kauffman, *Ministry and Meaning,* 171.

54. Kauffman, *Ministry and Meaning,* 230–39. Quotation is on page 232. Sister Olivia Gowan, OSB, who became dean of the Catholic University School of Nursing, fought against this separatist stance. She chaired the Sisters' Committee within the National League for Nursing Education. See "Sister M. Olivia Gowan, OSB," in Stepsis and Liptak, *Pioneer Healers,* 226–27.

55. Kauffman, *Ministry and Meaning,* 231–33. Quotation is on page 233. See also Wall, "Definite Lines of Influence," 319.

56. Adelaide Nutting and Lavinia Dock, *A History of Nursing* (New York and London: G. P. Putnam's Sons, 1907, 1912), 1:318, 437–38; 2:245–46; 3:187–93, 289–90. These strict prohibitions were especially significant in France, where they likely arose because of prevailing Jansenistic notions about the evil inclinations of material things, especially the human body. Jansenism started as a seventeenth-century movement in France that marked the excesses of the French spirituality school by emphasizing a rigorist sexual doctrine, strict asceticism, and a pessimism about human nature without

God's grace. Bordering on heresy, Jansenism resembled Calvinism which emphasized human nature's radical corruption. Among those opposed to Jansenism were the Jesuits who had a more optimistic view of human nature. This particular spirituality was known for its austerity, contemplative life, and studious environment and became the center for a spiritual and intellectual elite in Paris. See Jordan Aumann, *Christian Spirituality in the Catholic Tradition* (San Francisco: Ignatius Press, 1985), 228–32; Jean Delumeau, *Sin and Fear: The Emergence of a Western Guilt Culture 13th–18th Centuries*, trans. Eric Nicholson (New York: St. Martin's Press, 1990), 258; and McBrien, *Encyclopedia of Catholicism*, 687.

57. Dries, *The Missionary Movement*, 105. It also may have been an extension of prohibitions on priests. The Fourth Lateran Council of 1215 had forbidden priests to "shed blood." See McBrien, *Encyclopedia of Catholicism*, 752; and Darrel W. Amundsen, "The Medieval Catholic Tradition," in Numbers and Amundsen, *Caring and Curing*, 85.

58. Jones, *The Charitable Imperative*, 43, 68, 144, 190; and Laurence Brockliss and Colin Jones, *The Medical World of Early Modern France* (Oxford, UK: Clarendon Press, 1997), 272.

59. Dora Weiner, *The Citizen-Patient in Revolutionary and Imperial Paris* (Baltimore and London: Johns Hopkins University Press, 1993), 86, 102–27. Quotation is on page 126. The *Normae* dealt with vows, the cloistered lifestyle, and the approbation process of active women's institutes. See Jarrell, "The Development of Legal Structures for Women Religious," 286–88; and Ewens, *Role of the Nun*, 265–74.

60. The classic anticonvent tale was "Maria Monk's" *Awful Disclosures of the Hotel Dieu Nunnery* (New York: Howe and Bates, 1836). See also J. T. Christian, *America or Rome, Which?* (Louisville, KY: Baptist Book Concern, 1895), PANT, 6/05; and "The American Protective Association," *The Forum* (July 1894), PANT 4/06, UNDA. For an account on the antebellum period, see Joseph G. Mannard, "Maternity . . . of the Spirit: Nuns and Domesticity in Antebellum America," *U.S. Catholic Historian* 5 (1996): 305–24.

61. Hinssen, *The Nursing Sister*, 66–8, 112–13, 187–216. Quotations are on pages 68 and 202.

62. Apostolic Delegation, United States of America, No. 3422, to Reverend and Dear Mother, November 10, 1909, ACSJC-SL.

63. Letter from superior at St. Paul [Mother Seraphine Ireland] to "Excellency," December 12, 1909, box 2.1–12, folder 20.8, "Correspondence and Reports S. Seraphine Ireland," ACSJC-SP.

64. Kauffman, *Ministry and Meaning*, 181–84.

65. *RBSR*, January 19, 1897, December 10, 1897, December 17, 1897; and *RBSJ*, March 31, 1890, AMIW.

66. Judith Walzer Leavitt, *Brought to Bed: Childbearing in America, 1750–1950* (New York and Oxford, UK: Oxford University Press, 1986), 82, 171–95. This move occurred as more middle-class women entered hospitals because of the image of what science could offer.

67. Sister Superior to Doctors E. W. Whitney and H. N. Mayo, attached to "Minutes of Medical Staff," December 7, 1908, MDU. The building constructed at Holy Cross Hospital in 1914 contained a separate obstetrical department. See *ABHCH*, October 27, 1916, CSC.

68. "Admissions," Holy Cross Hospital; *ABHCH*, for year 1917; and "Holy Cross

Hospital School of Nursing from Beginning to End, 1901–1973," CSC. This sister-nurse probably was Sister Alfreda Nagel. Records refer to her only as "Sister Alfreda."

69. See Slattery, *Historical Studies*, 22. St. Paul's St. Joseph's Hospital mentions a maternity ward in the 1919 *Annual Report*. See *Sixty-Fifth Report of St. Joseph's Hospital, St. Paul*.

70. *RBSR*, October 8, 1897; and *RBSJ*, March 2, 1890, AMIW. See also *ABHCH*, CSC; and typed note cards on the early sisters, located in ACSJC-SP.

71. The 1872 *Constitution of the Sisters of Charity of the Incarnate Word*, Part First, Chapter XII, Number 5, stated that sisters were prohibited from "assistance in operations contrary to modesty," and "the bandaging of wounds of such genre even on women." Number 6 prohibited them from performing midwifery. Yet Number 7 stated that if it was impossible to get others to perform the tasks, the "Sisters may overrun these rules."

72. 1906 *Directory of the Sisters of Charity of the Incarnate Word*, 211, AMIW.

73. "Minutes of a Regular Meeting of the Medical Staff of the Holy Cross Hospital, 5 May 1913," MDU.

74. Joseph G. Ryan, "The Chapel and the Operating Room: The Struggle of Roman Catholic Clergy, Physicians, and Believers with the Dilemmas of Obstetric Surgery, 1800–1900," *Bulletin of the History of Medicine* 76 (Fall 2002): 492.

75. "Discussions of the First Day's Papers" [discussion by Dr. E. R. Root], *Hospital Progress* 2 (August 1921): 293.

76. "Brief Articles on Practical Topics–A Surgical Code," *Hospital Progress* 1, no. 1 (May 1920): 36.

77. Dries, *Missionary Movement*, 105. Vatican approval was influenced by the work of Dr. Anna Dengel, one of the founders of the Society of Catholic Medical Missionaries, the first Roman Catholic women's religious congregation to engage in work as surgeons, obstetricians, and physicians.

78. Kauffman, *Ministry and Meaning*, 182.

79. *Historical Review*, "Our First One Hundred Years," (n.d.), St. Elizabeth's Hospital, Lafayette, IN.

80. Mother Judith, "Contemporary Needs in the Formation of the Sister for Hospital Work," *Sister Formation Bulletin* 7 (Winter 1960–61): 246; Alma S. Woolley, "Nuns and GUNS: Holy Wars at Georgetown, 1903–1947," *Nursing History Review* 11 (2003): 69–87; and Kauffman, *Ministry and Meaning*, 250.

Conclusion

1. Rev. C. B. Moulinier, "The President's Address," *Hospital Progress* 3 (August 1922): 300. The Catholic Hospital Association represented Canada as well.

2. Starr, *Social Transformation*, 170–73.

3. Joyce, "Science and the Saints," 132–33.

Notes to Epilogue

1. Wittberg, "Ties That No Longer Bind," 10–14.

2. Slattery, *Historical Studies*, 116–17.

3. http://www.christussantarosa.org and http://www.christushealth.org. Last visited November 23, 2003.

4. Sisters of St. Joseph of Carondelet, St. Paul Province, *Eyes Open on a World: The Challenges of Change* (St. Cloud, MN: North Star Press of St. Cloud, 2001), 148–49.

5. Kuhn, "The First Hospital," 9–10. Quotation is on page 10. See also Letter from Sister M. Louis et al. to Sisters, September 17, 1973, CSC.

6. "Operator of 3 Utah Hospitals to Be Purchased by Firm," *Wall Street Journal*, October 4, 1993. Holy Cross Health Services of Utah operated three hospitals in the state in 1993.

7. President and General Council of the Sisters of the Holy Cross, "A Message to the Community from the Sisters of the Holy Cross," CSC. See also Barbara Stinson Lee, "Holy Cross Sale to Leave Utah without Catholic Hospital," *Today's Catholic*, October 17, 1993.

8. M. Pagliaro, "Junk-bond Sisters," *Our Sunday Visitor*, December 19, 1993.

9. "Barbara Stinson Lee, "Utahns Sad, Disappointed at News of Health System Sale," *Intermountain Catholic*, November 5, 1993.

10. Barbara Stinson Lee, "Bishop Calls for Healing after Efforts to Block Hospital Sale," *Today's Catholic*, December 3, 1993.

11. David Rumbach, "Holy Cross, Mercy Health Systems to Merge," *South Bend Tribune*, June 29, 1999. Data confirmed by Holy Cross Heath System Corporation.

12. http://www.sjmed.com. Last visited November 23, 2003.

13. Clarke E. Cochran, "Sacramental Theology, Catholic Political Thought, and the Crisis of Institutions," presented at the American Religion Seminar, University of Notre Dame, February 17, 1999; and Cochran, "Sacrament and Solidarity: Catholic Social Thought and Health Care Policy Reform," *Journal of Church and State* 41, no. 3 (Summer 1999): 475–99.

14. Editorial, "How to Approach Catholic Identity in Changing Times," *Health Progress* (April 1994).

15. Lee, "Utahns Sad."

16. Quotations in Slattery, *Historical Studies*, 117.

Bibliography

ARCHIVES

The most significant primary sources for this book were the nuns' letters, journals, and constitutions housed in the Archives of the Sisters of the Holy Cross, Saint Mary's, Notre Dame, Indiana; Archives, Motherhouse of the Incarnate Word, San Antonio, Texas; Archives of the Sisters of St. Joseph of Carondelet, St. Louis, Missouri, and St. Paul, Minnesota; and Sisters of Providence Archives, Saint Mary-of-the-Woods, Indiana. These repositories contain data on individual nuns, including dates of entrance to the community, places of birth, records of deaths, and lists of work assignments. Particularly important sources are "annals," or chronicles of events in sisters' congregations. For example, the Sisters of Charity of the Incarnate Word kept chronicles or "remark books" of hospital events in the late nineteenth century for both Santa Rosa and St. Joseph's infirmaries. And the Sisters of the Holy Cross maintained "annals" or "archive books" of monthly events for each of the three hospitals represented in this study: St. Mary's Hospital, Cairo, Illinois; Holy Cross Hospital, Salt Lake City, Utah; and St. Joseph's Hospital, South Bend, Indiana. Because of the many authors, these "annals" vary in detail. Catholic sisters often did not sign their names to their writings, reflecting their attempts to avoid calling attention to themselves. Such was the case with their "annals." Other congregational records include Rules and constitutions, directories, council minutes, hospital annual reports, and chapter books, the Chapter being the elected legislative body of the congregation.

Primary sources also include letters by mothers superior and superior generals. For example, Sister Kathleen Garvey translated the letters of Mother Pierre Cinquin of the Sisters of Charity of the Incarnate Word in San Antonio. These documents are part of an extensive collection that also includes letters that Sister Gabriel Wheelahan wrote for Mother Madeleine Chollet. The papers of Mother M. de Chantal Keating are located in the Archives of St. Joseph Convent, Brentwood, New York. Unfortunately, letters by Mother Angela Gillespie of the Sisters of the Holy Cross and Mother Seraphine Ireland of the Sisters of St. Joseph were destroyed years ago. Other superiors' letters, however, are located in the sisters' archives.

Nuns' letters and documents of wartime nursing are also readily available in the sisters' archives. In 1894, Mother Augusta Anderson of the Holy Cross order sent a questionnaire to the surviving Civil War nurses. It asked them when and where they served during the war, with whom they served, who was in charge, and how long they stayed. She also asked them to recall any memorable incidents that occurred during their wartime service. Sister Emerentiana Nowlan was one of twelve Holy Cross Sisters who worked in army camps during the Spanish-American War. She asked the sisters to keep diaries and then maintained them in a large ledger. In addition to the diaries, her collections include nuns' letters, photographs, and newspaper clippings pertaining to the war camps and the war itself. A series of letters written by the Sisters of St. Joseph during the Spanish-American War to the St. Louis motherhouse are located in the archives there. The group's superior, Mother Liguori McNamara, wrote most of them.

Anniversary issues of hospitals, physicians' letters, conferences, and letters by priest superiors of women's orders are located in university archives. For example, retreat records for the Sisters of the Holy Cross and letters from Father Edward Sorin, CSC, to the sisters are located in the Archives of the University of Notre Dame and in the Indiana Province Center Archives, South Bend, Indiana. The University of Utah in Salt Lake City houses minutes of physicians' meetings that took place at Holy Cross Hospital in the early twentieth century. I obtained other records on hospitals at the Taubman Library at the University of Michigan, Ann Arbor; the Utah State Historical Society, Salt Lake City; Vigo County Library, Terre Haute, Indiana; the Memorial Hospital Archives Project, South Bend, Indiana; the Catholic Health Association in St. Louis, Missouri; and the Marillac Provincial House of the Daughters of Charity of St. Vincent de Paul, St. Louis, Missouri.

Census Records

Annual Report of the U. S. Comptroller of the Currency to the First Session of the Fifty-Sixth Congress of the United States. Vol. 1. Washington, DC: Government Printing Office, 1899.

Department of the Interior, Census Office. *Report on Statistics of Churches in the United States at the Eleventh Census: 1890.* Washington, DC: Government Printing Office, 1894.

Fifteenth Annual Report of the Interstate Commerce Commission. Washington, DC: Government Printing Office, 1902.

Report on the Agencies of Transportation in the United States. Washington, DC: Government Printing Office, 1883.

Third Annual Report of the Interstate Commerce Commission. Washington, DC: Government Printing Office, 1889.

Twenty-Fifth Annual Report of the Interstate Commerce Commission. Washington, DC: Government Printing Office, 1912.

US Bureau of the Census. *A Compendium of the Ninth Census (June 1, 1870).* Washington, DC: Government Printing Office, 1872.

———. *1880 Census—Report on the Social Statistics of Cities.* Pt.2, *South and Western States.* Washington, DC: Government Printing Office, 1887.

———. *A Compendium of the Eleventh Census: 1890.* Pt. 1, *Population.* Washington, DC: Government Printing Office, 1892.

———. *Benevolent Institutions, 1904*. Washington, DC: Government Printing Office, 1905.

———. *Benevolent Institutions, 1910*. Washington, DC: Government Printing Office, 1913.

———. *Census Reports*. Vol. 1, *Twelfth Census of the United States, Taken in the Year 1900*. Washington, DC: Government Printing Office, 1901.

———. *Eleventh Census, 1890*, pt. 1; and pt. 2, *Vital and Social Statistics—Foreign Born Population*. Washington, DC: Government Printing Office, 1894.

———. *Mortality Statistics, Tenth U.S. Census*. Washington, DC: Government Printing Office, 1882.

———. *Ninth Census*. Vol. 1, *The Statistics of the Population of the United States*. Washington, DC: Government Printing Office, 1872

———. *Report of Statistics of Churches of the United States*. Washington, DC: Government Printing Office, 1894.

———. *Report on Real Estate Mortgages in the United States at the Eleventh Census: 1890*. Washington, DC: Government Printing Office, 1895.

———. *Report on the Social Statistics of Cities*. Pt. 2, *South and Western States, 1880 Census*. Washington, DC: Government Printing Office, 1887.

———. *Special Reports, Religious Bodies: 1906*, pt. 1. Washington, DC: Government Printing Office, 1910.

———. *Statistics and Technology of the Precious Metals*. Washington, DC: Government Printing Office, 1885.

———. *Tenth Census of the United States, 1880*. Vol. 1, *Population*. Washington, DC: Government Printing Office, 1880.

———. *Thirteenth Census Taken in the Year 1910: Population*. Washington, DC: Government Printing Office, 1913.

US Bureau of the Census and Social Science Research Council. *Historical Statistics of the United States, Colonial Times to 1957*. Washington, DC: US Department of Commerce, 1957.

Newspapers

Black Hills Daily Times
Boston Globe
Cairo Evening Citizen
Cairo Evening Citizen and Bulletin
Cairo News
Daily Minnesota Pioneer
Daily Tribune
Indianapolis Daily Journal
Indianapolis Sentinel
Intermountain Catholic
Intermountain Catholic Register
Irish Standard
Our Sunday Visitor
Salt Lake Daily Tribune
Salt Lake City Tribune

Salt Lake Tribune
San Antonio Daily Times
San Antonio Express
San Antonio Weekly Express
South Bend Evening Register
South Bend Saturday Tribune
South Bend Times
South Bend Tribune
South Bend Weekly Tribune
St. Paul Daily Minnesotian
Terre Haute Express
Today's Catholic
Wall Street Journal

Unpublished Sources

Cochran, Clarke E. "Sacramental Theology, Catholic Political Thought, and the Crisis of Institutions." Presented at the American Religion Seminar, University of Notre Dame, February 17, 1999.

———. "Thinking Sacramentally: A Perspective on Catholic Social Theory, with Reference to Healthcare Policy." Presented at the University of Notre Dame, Notre Dame, IN, Spring 1999.

Deacon, Florence Jean. "Handmaids or Autonomous Women: The Charitable Activities, Institution Building and Communal Relationships of Catholic Sisters in Nineteenth Century Wisconsin." PhD diss., University of Wisconsin, Madison, 1989.

Dunlop, Richard. *Doctors of the American Frontier.* New York: Ballantine Books, 1965.

"Facts about the Catholic Health Association of the United States." St. Louis, MO: Catholic Health Association, November 29, 2000.

Hanckel, Frances Stuart. "American Hospitals in 1910." Doctor of Science diss., School of Hygiene and Public Health of the Johns Hopkins University, 1985.

Kuhn, Sister M. Campion. "The First Hospital: Saint Mary's Infirmary." Presented at the 1996 Conference on the History of the Congregation of Holy Cross, King's College, Wilkes-Barre, PA, June 14–16, 1996.

Jarrell, Lynn Marie. "The Development of Legal Structures for Women Religious Between 1500 and 1900: A Study of Selected Institutes of Religious Life for Women." PhD diss., Catholic University of America, 1984.

Joyce, Kathleen M. "Science and the Saints: American Catholics and Health Care, 1880–1930." PhD diss., Princeton University, 1995.

Nelson, Sioban. "Hybrid Space: Vowed Nineteenth Century Women and Nursing." Presented at Breaking Boundaries: Eleventh Berkshire Conference on the History of Women, University of Rochester, June 4–6, 1999.

McCauley, Bernadette. " 'Who Shall Take Care of Our Sick?': Roman Catholic Sisterhoods and Their Hospitals, New York City, 1850–1930." PhD diss., Columbia University, 1992.

Morrison, John Gordon. *Civil War Diary*, July 17 and July 20, 1862. Original in the library of the Naval Museum at the Washington, DC, Naval Yard.

Peters, Sister M. Rosanna. "The History of the Poor Sisters of St. Francis Seraph of the Perpetual Adoration, 1875–1940." PhD diss., Indiana University, 1944.

Tarbox, Mary Patricia. "The Origins of Nursing by the Sisters of Mercy in the United States: 1843–1910." EdD diss., Columbia University Teacher's College, 1986.

Welsh, Janet Margaret, OP. "Where the Spirit Dwells: Catholic and Protestant Women and the Development of Christianity in the Upper Mississippi River Valley Lead Region, 1830–1870." PhD diss., University of Notre Dame, 1995.

Electronic Sources

Centers for Medicare and Medicaid, http://cms.hhs.gov/statistics/nhe/projections-2002/proj2002.pdfandhttp://www.cms.hhs.gov/statistics/nhe/historical/t5.asp
http://healthaffairs.org
http://www.christushealth.org.
http://www.christussantarosa.org/Downtownhospital.html
http://www.sjmed.com/expansion

Published Sources

Books

Abbott, Andrew. *The System of Professions: An Essay on the Division of Expert Labor.* Chicago: University of Chicago Press, 1988.

Ackerknecht, Erwin H. *A Short History of Medicine,* rev. ed. Baltimore and London: Johns Hopkins University Press, 1982.

Alexander, Thomas G. *Utah, the Right Place: The Official Centennial History.* Salt Lake City: Gibbs-Smith Publisher, 1995.

American Medical Directory, 1916, A Register of Legally Qualified Physicians of the United States. Chicago: American Medical Association, 1916.

Amundsen, Darrel W. *Medicine, Society, and Faith in the Ancient and Medieval Worlds.* Baltimore: Johns Hopkins University Press, 1996.

Apostolos-Cappodona. *Dictionary of Christian Art.* New York: Continuum, 1994.

Aries, Philippe. *Western Attitudes toward Death: From the Middle Ages to the Present.* Baltimore and London: Johns Hopkins University Press, 1974.

———. *The Hour of Our Death.* Translated by Helen Weaver. New York: Alfred A. Knopf, 1981.

Aumann, Jordan. *Christian Spirituality in the Catholic Tradition.* San Francisco: Ignatius Press, 1985.

Barber, Laura L., ed. *The Doctors Herff: A Three-Generation Memoir by Ferdinand Peter Herff.* San Antonio: Trinity University Press, 1973.

Barker, Marilyn C., and R. P. Morris. *The Early Holy Cross Hospital and Salt Lake City.* Salt Lake City: n.p., 1975.

Beck, Berenice, OSF. *Handmaid of the Divine Physician.* Milwaukee: Bruce Publishing Co., 1952.

Biagioli, Mario. *Galileo, Courtier: The Practice of Science in the Culture of Absolutism.* Chicago and London: University of Chicago Press, 1993.
Bokenkotter, Thomas. *A Concise History of the Catholic Church.* New York: Image Books, Doubleday, 1990.
Bordin, Ruth. *Women and Temperance: The Quest for Power and Liberty, 1873–1900.* New Brunswick, NJ: Rutgers University Press, 1990.
Borresen, Kari Elisabeth. *Subordination and Equivalence: The Nature and Role of Woman in Augustine and Thomas Aquinas.* Translated by Charles H. Talbot. Washington, DC: University Press of America, 1981.
Boydston, Jeanne. *Home and Work: Housework, Wages, and the Ideology of Labor in the Early Republic.* New York: Oxford University Press, 1990.
Brandes, Stuart D. *American Welfare Capitalism, 1880–1940.* Chicago and London: University of Chicago Press, 1976.
Brockliss, Laurence, and Colin Jones. *The Medical World of Early Modern France.* Oxford: Clarendon Press, 1997.
Brown, Peter. *The Cult of the Saints: Its Rise and Function in Latin Christianity.* Chicago: University of Chicago Press, 1981.
———. *The Body and Society: Men, Women, and Sexual Renunciation in Early Christianity.* New York: Columbia University Press, 1988.
Brownson, Orestes. "The Woman Question." In vol. 18, *The Works of Orestes A. Brownson, Collected and Arranged by Henry F. Brownson,* 381–417. Detroit: Thorndike Nourse, Publisher, 1885.
Buhler-Wilkerson, Karen. *False Dawn: The Rise and Decline of Public Health Nursing,* New York: Garland Publishing Co., 1989.
———. *No Place Like Home: A History of Nursing and Home Care in the United States.* Baltimore and London: Johns Hopkins University Press, 2001.
Capellmann, Carl. *Pastoral Medicine.* New York and Cincinnati: Fr. Pustet, 1879.
Censer, Jane Turner, ed. *The Papers of Frederick Law Olmsted.* Vol. 4, *Defending the Union: The Civil War and the U.S. Sanitary Commission, 1861–1863.* Baltimore: Johns Hopkins University Press, 1986.
Christian. J. T. *America or Rome, Which?* Louisville, KY: Baptist Book Concern, 1895.
Clear, Catriona. *Nuns in Nineteenth-Century Ireland.* Washington, DC: Catholic University of America Press, 1987.
Coburn, Carol K., and Martha Smith. *Spirited Lives: How Nuns Shaped Catholic Culture and American Life, 1836–1920.* Chapel Hill and London: University of North Carolina Press, 1999.
Combs, Charles N., MD. Typescript of *The History of Medicine in Vigo County, Indiana, 1818–1951.* Vigo County Public Library, Terre Haute, IN, 1951.
Corwin, E. H. L. *The American Hospital.* New York: Commonwealth Fund, 1946.
Creek, Sister Mary Immaculate, CSC. *A Panorama: 1847–1977, Saint Mary's College, Notre Dame, Indiana.* Notre Dame, IN: Saint Mary's College, 1977.
Costin, Sister M. Georgia, CSC. *Priceless Spirit: A History of the Sisters of the Holy Cross, 1841–1893.* Notre Dame, IN: University of Notre Dame Press, 1994.
Cott, Nancy F. *The Bonds of Womanhood: "Woman's Sphere" in New England, 1780–1835.* New Haven, CT: Yale University Press, 1977.
Danylewycz, Marta. *Taking the Veil: An Alternative to Marriage, Motherhood, and Spinsterhood in Quebec, 1840–1920.* Toronto: McClelland and Stewart, 1987.

Davis, Cyprian, OSB. *The History of Black Catholics in the United States.* New York: Crossword, 1991.

Delumeau, Jean. *Sin and Fear: The Emergence of a Western Guilt Culture 13th–18th Centuries.* Translated by Eric Nicholson. New York: St. Martin's Press, 1990.

de Paul, Vincent. *The Conferences of St. Vincent de Paul to the Sisters of Charity.* Translated by Joseph Leonard, CM. 4 vols. Westminster, MD: Newman Press, 1952.

Deutsch, Sarah. *No Separate Refuge: Culture, Class, and Gender on an Anglo-Hispanic Frontier in the American Southwest, 1880–1940.* New York: Oxford University Press, 1987.

Deville, Raymond. *The French School of Spirituality: An Introduction and Reader.* Translated by Agnes Cunningham. Pittsburgh, PA: Duquesne University Press, 1994.

Diner, Hasia R. *Erin's Daughters in America: Irish Immigrant Women in the Nineteenth Century.* Baltimore and London: Johns Hopkins University Press, 1983.

Dolan, Jay P. *Catholic Revivalism: The American Experience, 1830–1900.* Notre Dame, IN and London: University of Notre Dame Press, 1978.

———. *The American Catholic Experience: A History from Colonial Times to the Present.* Notre Dame, IN and London: University of Notre Dame Press, 1992.

———, and Gilberto M. Hinojosa. *Mexican Americans and the Catholic Church, 1900–1965.* Notre Dame, IN and London: University of Notre Dame Press, 1994.

———. *In Search of an American Catholicism: A History of Religion and Culture in Tension.* New York and Oxford: Oxford University Press, 2002.

Dougherty, Sister Dolorita Marie, CSJ, et al. *Sisters of St. Joseph of Carondelet.* St. Louis: B. Herder Book Co., 1966.

Douglas, Mary. *How Institutions Think.* Syracuse, NY: Syracuse University Press, 1986.

Dries, Angelyn, OSF. *The Missionary Movement in American Catholic History.* Maryknoll, NY: Orbis Books, 1998.

Duratschek, Sister M. Claudia, OSB. *Builders of God's Kingdom: The History of the Catholic Church in South Dakota.* Yankton, SD: Benedictine Sisters of Sacred Heart Convent, 1985.

Eliade, Mircea. *The Sacred and the Profane.* New York: Harcourt, Brace and World, 1959.

Emmons, David M. *The Butte Irish: Class and Ethnicity in an American Mining Town.* Urbana and Chicago: University of Illinois Press, 1989.

Esarey, Logan. *History of Indiana from Its Exploration to 1922.* Vol. 3. Dayton, OH: Dayton Historical Publishing Co., 1923.

Ewens, Mary. *The Role of the Nun in Nineteenth Century America.* 1971. Reprint, Salem, NH: Ayer Company, Publishers, Inc., 1984.

Farren, Suzy. *A Call to Care: The Women Who Built Catholic Healthcare in America.* St. Louis: Catholic Health Association of the United States, 1996.

Finck, Sister Mary Helena. *The Congregation of the Sisters of Charity of the Incarnate Word of San Antonio, Texas: A Brief Account of Its Origin and Its Work.* Washington, DC: Catholic University of America, 1925.

Fletcher, Canon John. *Notes for Catholic Nurses.* London: Catholic Truth Society, 1912.

Flexner, Abraham. *Medical Education in the United States and Canada: A Report to the Carnegie Foundation for the Advancement of Teaching, Bulletin # 4.* New York: Carnegie Foundation, 1910.

Foucault, Michel. *The Birth of the Clinic: An Archeology of Medical Perception.* New

York: Vintage Books, 1994. First published 1963 by Presses Universitaires de France.

Freidson, Eliot. *Profession of Medicine: A Study of the Sociology of Applied Knowledge.* New York: Harper & Row, 1970.

Fries, Rev. Louis J., STB. *One Hundred and Fifty Years of Catholicity in Utah.* Salt Lake City: Intermountain Catholic Press, 1926.

Gamble, Vanessa Northington, ed. *Germs Have No Color Line: Blacks and American Medicine, 1900–1940.* New York: Garland Publishing, 1989.

Gibbons, James Cardinal. In *Discourses and Sermons for Every Sunday and the Principal Festivals of the Year,* edited by Gibbons, 480–85. Baltimore and New York: John Murphy Company, 1908.

Gibson, Ralph. *A Social History of French Catholicism.* London and New York: Routledge, 1989.

Ginzberg, Lori. *Women and the Work of Benevolence: Morality, Politics, and Class in the Nineteenth-Century United States.* New Haven, CT: Yale University Press, 1990.

Glaser, William A. *Social Settings and Medical Organization: A Cross-National Study of the Hospital.* New York: Atherton Press, 1970.

———. *Paying the Hospital: The Organization, Dynamics, and Effects of Differing Financial Arrangements.* San Francisco and London: Jossey-Bass Publishers, 1987.

Gleason, Philip. *Keeping the Faith: American Catholicism Past and Present.* Notre Dame, IN: University of Notre Dame Press.

Gorer, Geoffrey. *Death, Grief, and Mourning.* New York: Arno Press, 1977.

Hackett, J. D. *Health Maintenance in Industry.* Chicago and New York: A. W. Shaw Company, 1925.

Hannefin, Sister Daniel, DC. *Daughters of the Church: A Popular History of the Daughters of Charity in the United States, 1809–1987.* New York: New City Press, 1989.

Harris, Ruth. *Lourdes: Body and Spirit in the Secular Age.* New York: Viking, 1999.

Hinssen, Rev. L. *The Nursing Sister: A Manual for Candidates and Novices of Hospital Communities.* Springfield, IL: H. W. Rokker Co., 1899.

Higginbotham, Evelyn Brooks. *Righteous Discontent: The Women's Movement in the Black Baptist Church, 1880–1920.* Cambridge: Harvard University Press, 1993.

Hine, Darlene Clark. *Black Women in White: Racial Conflict and Cooperation in the Nursing Profession, 1890–1950.* Bloomington and Indianapolis: Indiana University Press, 1989.

History of St. Joseph's Hospital, 1853–1978. St. Paul, MN: St. Joseph's Hospital, 1979.

Howell, Joel D. *Technology in the Hospital: Transforming Patient Care in the Early Twentieth Century.* Baltimore and London: Johns Hopkins University Press, 1995.

Hurley, Sister Helen Angela. *On Good Ground: The Story of the Sisters of St. Joseph in St. Paul.* Minneapolis: University of Minnesota Press, 1951.

Ignatiev, Noel. *How the Irish Became White.* New York: Routledge, 1995.

Illich, Ivan. *Medical Nemesis: The Expropriation of Health.* New York: Pantheon Books, 1976.

Johnson, Penelope. *Equal in Monastic Profession: Religious Women in Medieval France.* Chicago and London: University of Chicago Press, 1991.

Jolly, Ellen Ryan, LLD. *Nuns of the Battlefield.* Providence, RI: Providence Visitor Press, 1927.

Jones, Colin. *The Charitable Imperative: Hospitals and Nursing in Ancien Regime and Revolutionary France.* London and New York: Routledge, 1989.

Jones, Jacqueline. *Labor of Love, Labor of Sorrow: Black Women, Work, and the Family, from Slavery to the Present.* New York: Vintage Books, 1985.

Kanter, Rosabeth Moss. *Commitment and Community: Communes and Utopias in Sociological Perspective.* Cambridge, MA: Harvard University Press, 1972.

Kauffman, Christopher J. *Ministry and Meaning: A Religious History of Catholic Health Care in the United States.* New York: Crossroad, 1995.

Kelly, Howard A. *Appendicitis and Other Diseases of the Vermiform Appendix.* Philadelphia and London: J. B. Lippincott Company, 1905.

Kselman, Thomas. *Miracles and Prophesies in 19th-Century France.* New Brunswick, NJ: Rutgers University Press, 1983.

Lakoff, Robin. *Language and Woman's Place.* New York: Harper & Row Publishers, 1975.

Larson, Magali Sarfatti. *The Rise of Professionalism: A Sociological Analysis.* Berkeley: University of California Press, 1977.

Leavitt, Judith Walzer. *Brought to Bed: Childbearing in America, 1750–1950.* New York and Oxford: Oxford University Press, 1986

Logan, Sister Eugenia, SP. *History of the Sisters of Providence of Saint Mary-of-the-Woods, Indiana.* Vol. 2. Terre Haute, IN: Moore-Langen Printing Company, 1978.

Logue, Sister Maria Kostka. *Sisters of St. Joseph of Philadelphia: A Century of Growth and Development, 1847–1947.* Westminster, MD: Newman Press, 1950.

Lozano, John M. *Jeanne Chezard de Matel and the Sisters of the Incarnate Word.* Chicago: Claret Center for Resources in Spirituality, 1983.

Lynaugh, Joan. *The Community Hospitals of Kansas City, Missouri, 1870–1915.* New York and London: Garland Publishing, Inc., 1989.

Madden, Sister Mary Roger, SP. *The Path Marked Out: History of the Sisters of Providence of Saint Mary-of-the-Woods.* Vol. 3. Terre Haute, IN: Office of Congregational Advancement–Sisters of Providence.

Magray, Mary Peckham. *The Transforming Power of the Nuns: Women, Religion, and Cultural Change in Ireland, 1750–1900.* New York and Oxford: Oxford University Press, 1998.

Maher, Sister Mary Denis. *To Bind Up the Wounds: Catholic Sister Nurses in the U.S. Civil War.* Baton Rouge: Louisiana State University Press, 1989.

Mandell, Gail Porter. *Madeleva: A Biography.* Albany: State University of New York Press, 1997.

Martos, Joseph. *Doors to the Sacred: A Historical Introduction to the Sacraments in the Catholic Church.* Liguori, MO: Triumph Books, 1991.

McBrien, Richard P., ed. *The Harper Collins Encyclopedia of Catholicism.* San Francisco: Harper Collins Publishers, 1989.

McDannell, Colleen. *The Christian Home in Victorian America, 1840–1900.* Bloomington: Indiana University Press, 1986.

———. *Material Christianity: Religion and Popular Culture in America.* New Haven and London: Yale University Press, 1995.

McNamara, Jo Ann Kay. *Sisters in Arms: Catholic Nuns through Two Millennia.* Cambridge, MA and London: Harvard University Press, 1996.

Melosh, Barbara. *The Physician's Hand: Work Culture and Conflict in American Nursing.* Philadelphia: Temple University Press, 1982.

Men of Texas: Collection of Portraits. Houston, TX: Houston Post, 1903.

Miller, Kerby A. *Emigrants and Exiles: Ireland and the Irish Exodus to North America.* New York: Oxford University Press, 1985.

Misner, Barbara SCSC. *Highly Respectable and Accomplished Ladies: Catholic Women Religious in America, 1790–1850.* New York and London: 1988.

Moreau, Basil Anthony. *Circular Letters of the Very Reverend Basil Anthony Moreau.* Trans. Edward L. Heston. 2 vols. Notre Dame, IN: Ave Maria Press, 1943.

Moore, R. L. *Religious Outsiders and the Making of Americans.* New York: Oxford University Press, 1986.

"Monk, Maria." *Awful Disclosures of the Hotel Dieu Nunnery.* New York: Howe and Bates, 1836.

Mooney, Bernice Maher, and Monsignor Jerome C. Stoffel, ed. *Salt of the Earth: The History of the Catholic Diocese of Salt Lake City, 1776–1987.* Salt Lake City: Catholic Diocese, 1987.

Moore, James Talmadge. *Through Fire and Flood: The Catholic Church in Frontier Texas, 1836–1900.* College Station, TX: Texas A&M University Press, 1992.

Morrow, Diane Batts. *Persons of Color and Religious at the Same Time: The Oblate Sisters of Providence, 1828–1860.* Chapel Hill and London: University of North Carolina Press, 2002.

Nelson, Sioban. *Say Little, Do Much: Nursing, Nuns, and Hospitals in the Nineteenth Century.* Philadelphia: University of Pennsylvania Press, 2001.

Nightingale, Florence. *Notes on Nursing.* London: Longman, Green, and Roberts, 1869. First published 1860 by D. Appleton and Co.

Nugent, Walter. *Crossings: The Great Transatlantic Migrations, 1870–1914.* Bloomington and Indianapolis: Indiana University Press, 1995.

——— . *Into the West: The Story of Its People.* New York: Vintage Books, 1999.

Nutting, Adelaide, and Lavinia Dock. *A History of Nursing.* 3 vols. New York and London: G. P. Putnam's Sons, 1907, 1912.

Oakes, Sister Mary Paulinus. *Angels of Mercy: An Eyewitness Account of the Civil War and Yellow Fever by a Sister of Mercy.* Baltimore: Cathedral Foundation Press, 1998.

Oates, Mary J. *The Catholic Philanthropic Tradition in America.* Bloomington, IN: Indiana University Press, 1995.

O'Brien, H. J. *Medical and Surgical Nursing.* New York and London: G. P. Putnam's Sons, 1900.

O'Brien, Kathleen, RSM. *Journeys: A Pre-Amalgamation History of the Sisters of Mercy Omaha Province.* Omaha, NE: private printing, 1987.

O'Connell, Marvin R. *John Ireland and the American Catholic Church.* St. Paul: Minnesota Historical Society Press, 1988.

Official Catholic Directory. Milwaukee: M. H. Wiltzius and Co., 1901, 1910.

O'Grady, John. *Catholic Charities in the United States: History and Problems.* New York: Arno Press, 1971. First published 1930 by National Conference of Catholic Charities.

Orsi, Robert A. *Thank You, St. Jude: Women's Devotion to the Patron Saint of Hopeless Causes.* New Haven, CT and London: Yale University Press, 1996.

Papanikolas, Helen Zeese. *Peoples of Utah.* Salt Lake City: Utah State Historical Society, 1976.

Pascoe, Peggy. *Relations of Rescue: The Search for Female Moral Authority in the American West, 1874–1939.* New York: Oxford University Press, 1990.

Pernick, Martin S. *A Calculus of Suffering: Pain, Professionalism, and Anesthesia in Nineteenth-Century America.* New York: Columbia University Press, 1985.

Peterson, Susan Carol, and Courtney Ann Vaughn-Roberson. *Women with Vision: The*

Presentation Sisters of South Dakota, 1880–1985. Urbana: University of Illinois Press, 1988.
Phillips, Chester Arthur. *Bank Credit: A Study of the Principles and Factors Underlying Advances Made by Banks to Borrowers*. New York: Macmillan Company, 1924.
Rabinowitz, Howard N. *Race Relations in the Urban South, 1865–1890*. Urbana: University of Illinois Press, 1980.
Rapley, Elizabeth. *The Devotes: Women and Church in Seventeenth-Century France*. Montreal: McGill-Queen's University Press, 1990.
Red, George Plunkett. *The Medicine Man in Texas*. N.p., 1930.
Reverby, Susan M. *Ordered to Care: The Dilemma of American Nursing, 1850–1945*. Cambridge: Cambridge University Press, 1987.
Rey, Roselyne. *The History of Pain*. Cambridge, MA: Harvard University Press, 1995.
Richards, Ralph T. *Of Medicine, Hospitals, and Doctors*. Salt Lake City: University of Utah Press, 1953.
Richardson, Ruth. *Death, Dissection and the Destitute*. London: Penguin, 1989.
Risse, Guenter B. *Mending Bodies, Saving Souls: A History of Hospitals*. New York and Oxford: Oxford University Press, 1999.
Robb, Isabel H. *Educational Standards for Nurses, with Other Addresses on Nursing Subjects*. 1907. Reprint, New York: Garland Publishing, 1985.
Roediger, David R. *The Wages of Whiteness: Race and the Making of the American Working Class*. Rev. ed. London and New York: Verson, 1999.
Rosenberg, Charles E. *The Care of Strangers: The Rise of America's Hospital System*. Baltimore and London: Johns Hopkins University Press, 1987.
Rosner, David. *A Once Charitable Enterprise: Hospitals and Health Care in Brooklyn and New York, 1885–1915*. Cambridge: Cambridge University Press, 1982.
Russett, Cynthia Eagle. *Sexual Science: The Victorian Construction of Womanhood*. Cambridge and London: Harvard University Press, 1989.
Sadlier's Catholic Directory, Almanac and Ordo. New York: D. & J. Sadlier & Co., 1885 and 1895.
Saint Joseph's Medical Center: A Century of Caring. South Bend, IN: private printing, 1982.
Salt Lake City Directory for 1925. Salt Lake City: R. L. Polk Publisher, 1925.
Sampson, Sister Ann Thomasine, CSJ. *Care with Prayer: The History of St. Mary's Hospital & Rehabilitation Center, Minneapolis, Minnesota, 1887–1987*. Minneapolis: St. Mary's Hospital & Rehabilitation Center, 1987.
Sappol, Michael. *A Traffic of Dead Bodies: Anatomy and Embodied Social Identity in Nineteenth-Century America*. Princeton, NJ: Princeton University Press, 2002.
Savage, Mary Lucinda. *The Congregation of St. Joseph of Carondelet: A Brief Account of Its Origin and Its Work in the United States, 1650–1922*. St. Louis: Herder Book Co., 1923.
Schachner, August. *Ephraim McDowell, "Father of Ovariotomy" and Founder of Abdominal Surgery*. Philadelphia and London: J. B. Lippincott Company, 1921.
Shanahan, Robert J. *The History of the Catholic Hospital Association, 1915–1965, Fifty Years of Progress*. St. Louis: Catholic Hospital Association of the United States and Canada, 1965.
Shorter, Edward. *Doctors and Their Patients: A Social History*. New Brunswick, NJ and London: Transaction Publishers, 1991.
Sisters of St. Joseph of Carondelet, St. Paul Province. *Eyes Open on a World: The Challenges of Change*. St. Cloud, MN: North Star Press of St. Cloud, 2001.

Slattery, Sister Margaret Patrice, CCVI. *Historical Development from 1869 to 1994.* Vol. 1, *Promises to Keep: A History of the Sisters of Charity of the Incarnate Word, San Antonio, Texas.* San Antonio: private printing, 1995.

———. *Historical Studies of Hospitals, Schools in Mexico, and Incarnate Word College.* Vol. 2, *Promises to Keep: A History of the Sisters of Charity of the Incarnate Word, San Antonio, Texas.* San Antonio: private printing, 1995.

Stamper, John W. *City of South Bend Summary Report: Indiana Historic Sites and Structures Inventory.* N.p., 1981.

Stang, Rev. William. *Pastoral Theology.* New York: Bensiger Brothers, 1897.

Starr, Paul. *The Social Transformation of American Medicine: The Rise of a Sovereign Profession and the Making of a Vast Industry.* New York: Basic Books, 1982.

Stepsis, Ursula, CSA, and Dolores Liptak, RSM, eds. *Pioneer Healers: The History of Women Religious in American Health Care.* New York: Crossroad, 1989.

Stevens, Rosemary. *In Sickness and in Wealth: American Hospitals in the Twentieth Century.* New York: Basic Books, 1989.

Taves, Ann. *The Household of Faith: Roman Catholic Devotions in Mid-Nineteenth-Century America.* Notre Dame, IN: University of Notre Dame Press, 1986.

The Catechism of the Council of Trent. New York: Joseph F. Wagner, Inc., 1934.

The Catholic Heritage: Martyrs, Ascetics, Humanists, Activists, Outsiders, and Saints. New York: Crossroad, 1983.

The (Official) Catholic Directory and Almanac. Milwaukee: M. H. Wiltzius & Co., 1900.

Vianney, Jean Baptiste Marie. *Sermons for the Sundays and Feasts of the Year.* New York: Joseph F. Wagner, 1901.

Vogel, Morris J. *The Invention of the Modern Hospital: Boston, 1870–1930.* Chicago: University of Chicago Press, 1980.

Webber, F. R. *Church Symbolism.* Cleveland: J. H. Jansen, 1938.

Weiner, Dora. *The Citizen-Patient in Revolutionary and Imperial Paris.* Baltimore and London: Johns Hopkins University Press, 1993.

White, Deborah Gray. *Ar'n't I a Woman? Female Slaves in the Plantation South.* New York: Norton, 1985.

Williams, Pierce. *The Purchase of Medical Care through Fixed Periodic Payment.* New York: National Bureau of Economic Research, 1932.

Wilson, Renate. *Pious Traders in Medicine: A German Pharmaceutical Network in Eighteenth-Century North America.* University Park: Pennsylvania State University Press, 2000.

Wittberg, Patricia. *The Rise and Fall of Catholic Religious Orders: A Social Movement Perspective.* Albany: State University of New York Press, 1994.

Articles

Advertisement. *Hospital Progress* 1 (1920): xiv.

Aldrich, Mark. "Train Wrecks to Typhoid Fever: The Development of Railroad Medicine Organizations, 1850 to World War I." *Bulletin of the History of Medicine* 75 (Summer 2001): 254–89.

"American Protective Association, The." *Forum.* July 1894.

Amundsen, Darrel W., and Gary B. Ferngren. "The Early Christian Tradition." In *Caring and Curing: Health and Medicine in the Western Religious Traditions,* edited by Ronald L. Numbers and Darrel W. Amundsen, 40–64. New York: Macmillan Publishing Co., 1986.

Aries, Philippe. "The Reversal of Death: Changes in Attitudes toward Death in Western Societies." In *Death in America*, edited by David E. Stannard, 134–58. Philadelphia: University of Pennsylvania Press, 1975.

Apple, Rima. "Picturing the Hospital: Photographs in the History of an Institution." In *The American General Hospital: Communities and Social Contexts*, edited by Diana Elizabeth Long and Janet Golden, 76. Ithaca and London: Cornell University Press, 1989.

A Sister of St. Francis. "Admission to Our Training Schools," Letter to the Editor. *Trained Nurse and Hospital Review* 38 (February 1907): 122–24.

Augustine, St. Letter 37. In *Select Letters*. Translated by James Houston Baxter. London: William Heinemann Ltd.; and New York: G. P. Putnam's Sons, 1930.

Benedict, Sister Mary. "Rule and Common Sense." *Hospital Progress* 2, no. 1 (January 1921): 21.

Bottomley, John T. "The Right Limitations to Privilege of Practice in Hospitals in the Scheme of Hospital Standardization." *Hospital Progress* 1, no. 1 (May 1920): 5.

"Brief Articles on Practical Topics—A Surgical Code." *Hospital Progress* 1, no. 1 (May 1920): 36.

Brown, John N. Elliott, and Edward Fletcher Stevens. "A General Hospital for One Hundred Patients." In *Hospital Management*, edited by Charlotte A. Aikens, 125. Philadelphia and London: W. B. Saunders Co., 1911.

Bryant, Keith L., Jr. "Entering the Global Economy." In *The Oxford History of the American West*, edited by Clyde A. Milner II, Carol A. O'Connor, and Martha A. Sandweiss, 195–235. New York: Oxford University Press, 1994.

Bulletin of the American College of Surgeons 4 (1919): 11; 5 (1920); 6 (1921); and 7 (1922).

Byrne, Patricia, CSJ. "Sisters of St. Joseph: The Americanization of a French Tradition." *U. S. Catholic Historian* 5 (1986): 241–72.

Camp, Richard L. "From Passive Subordination to Complementary Partnership: The Papal Conception of a Woman's Place in Church and Society Since 1878." *Catholic Historical Review* 76 (July 1990): 506–25.

"Catholic Hospital, The." *Daily Minnesota Pioneer*, January 26, 1855, 3.

Clough, Joy, RSM. "Chicago's Sisters of Mercy." *Chicago History* 32, no. 1 (Summer 2003): 42–55.

"Chronological Development of the Catholic Hospital of the United States and Canada, The." *Hospital Progress* 21 (April 1940): 122–33.

Coburn, Carol K., and Martha Smith, CSJ. "'Pray for Your Wanderers': Women Religious on the Colorado Mining Frontier, 1877–1917." *Frontiers* 15 (1995): 27–52.

——— . "Creating Community and Identity: Exploring Religious and Gender Ideology in the Lives of American Women Religious, 1836–1920." *U. S. Catholic Historian* 14 (Winter 1996): 94–100.

Cochran, Clarke E. "Sacrament and Solidarity: Catholic Social Thought and Health Care Policy Reform." *Journal of Church and State* 41, no. 3 (Summer 1999): 475–99.

"Conference Reports Relate Initial Activities of [CHA] Committees in Assembling Statistical Data." *Hospital Progress* 5 (October 1924): 406.

Cowles, Edward. "The Relations of the Medical Staff to the Governing Bodies in Hospitals." In *Hospitals, Dispensaries and Nursing: Papers and Discussions in the*

International Congress of Charities, Correction and Philanthropy, Section III, Chicago, June 12th to 17th 1894, edited by John S. Billings and Henry M. Hurd, 69–. Baltimore: Johns Hopkins Press; and London: Scientific Press, Limited, 1894.

Cox, Sister Ignatius Loyola. "Notes on the Early History of the Sisters of St. Joseph in Minnesota." *Acta et Dicta* 3 (July 1914): 253–69.

———."Additional Notes on the Mission of the Sisters of St. Joseph in St. Paul." *Acta et Dicta* 3 (July 1914): 270–75.

Cullen, Brother Franklin, CSC. "Holy Cross in the Black Hills: The Dakota Apostolates, 1878–1897." In *Fruits of the Tree: Sesquicentennial Chronicles, Sisters of the Holy Cross*, vol. 2, 149–95. Notre Dame, IN: Ave Maria Press, 1989.

Culligan, John M., and Harold J. Prendergast. "St. Joseph's Hospital in St. Paul." *Acta et Dicta* 6 (October 1934): 199.

Cummings, Kathleen Sprows. " 'Not the New Woman?': Irish American Women and the Creation of a Usable Past, 1890–1900." *U. S. Catholic Historian* 19 (Winter 2001): 37–52.

Deacon, Florence, OSF. "More Than Just a Shoe String and a Prayer: How Women Religious Helped Finance the Nineteenth-Century Social Fabric." *U. S. Catholic Historian* 14 (Winter 1996): 76.

de Sales, Sister M. Francis. "A Holy Cross Sister in Peace and in War." *Holy Cross Courier* 4 (1930): 5.

"Devotions to St. Joseph." *Manual of Prayers for the Sisters of Charity of the Incarnate Word.* San Antonio, TX: n.p., 1933.

"Discussions of the First Day's Papers." *Hospital Progress* 2 (August 1921): 293.

Dowd, Mary A. "The Public Rights of Women." *Catholic World* 59 (June 1894): 312–20.

Doyle, Ann. "Nursing by Religious Orders in the United States," pts. 1–4. *American Journal of Nursing* 29, no. 7 (July 1929): 775–86; 29, no. 8 (August 1929): 959–69; 29, no. 9 (September 1929): 1085–95; 29, no. 10 (October 1929): 1197–1207.

———. "Nursing by Religious Orders in the United States, Part 4—Lutheran Deaconesses, 1849–1928." *American Journal of Nursing* 29, no. 10 (October 1929): 1197–1207.

Dwight, Thomas. "The Training-Schools for Nurses of the Sisters of Charity." *Catholic World* 61 (May 1895): 191.

Editorial, "How to Approach Catholic Identity in Changing Times." *Health Progress* (April 1994).

"Editorial." *Northwestern Medical and Surgical Journal* 1 (March 1871): 41, 305–6.

Editorial, "Sisters' Hospitals." *Hospital Progress* 2 (September 1921): 350–51.

"Editorial." *Hospital World* 3 (February 1913): 76.

Emerson, Charles P. "The American Hospital Field." In *Hospital Management*, edited by Charlotte A. Aikens, 17–71. Philadelphia and London: W. B. Saunders Co., 1911.

Ewens, Mary, OP. "Women in the Convent." In *American Catholic Women: A Historical Exploration*, edited by Karen Kennelly, CSJ, 25. New York: Macmillan Publishing Company, 1989.

———. "Removing the Veil: The Liberated American Nun." In *Women of Spirit: Female Leadership in the Jewish and Christian Traditions*, edited by Rosemary Ruether and Eleanor McLaughlin, 156–58. New York: Simon and Schuster, 1979.

Ferngren, Gary B. "Early Christianity as a Religion of Healing." *Bulletin of the History of Medicine* 66 (1992): 1–15; 40–64.

Fitzpatrick, David. "The Modernisation of the Irish Female." In *Rural Ireland 1600–1900: Modernisation and Change*, edited by Patrick O'Flanagan, Paul Ferguson, and Kevin Whelan, 166. Cork, Ireland: Cork University Press, 1987.

Foucault, Michel. "Truth and Power." In *Power/Knowledge*, edited by Colin Gordon, 109–33. New York: Pantheon, 1980.

Francesca, Sister M. "Mother Annunciata." Vol. 2, *Superior Generals—Centenary Chronicles of the Sisters of the Holy Cross*. Paterson, NJ: Saint Anthony Guild Press, 1941.

Freidson, Eliot. "Are Professions Necessary?" In *The Authority of Experts: Studies in History and Theory*, edited by Thomas L. Haskell, 3–27. Bloomington: Indiana University Press, 1984.

Gamble, Vanessa Northington. "Roots of the Black Hospital Reform Movement." In *Sickness and Health in America: Readings in the History of Medicine and Public Health*, edited by Judith Walzer Leavitt and Ronald L. Numbers, 369–91. Madison: University of Wisconsin Press, 1997.

Gamson, William A. "The Social Psychology of Collective Action." In *Frontiers in Social Movement Theory*, edited by Aldon D. Morris and Carol McClurg Mueller, 60. New Haven, CT and London: Yale University Press, 1992.

Gannon, Thomas M., SJ. "Catholic Religious Orders in Sociological Perspective." In *American Denominational Organization: A Sociological View*, edited by Ross P. Scherer, 172. Pasadena: William Carey Library, 1980.

Gibbons, James Cardinal. "Sickness a Season of Divine Mercy." In *Discourses and Sermons for Every Sunday and the Principal Festivals of the Year*, edited by Gibbons, 481–85. Baltimore and New York: John Murphy Company, 1908.

Glaser, William. "American and Foreign Hospitals: Some Sociological Comparisons." In *The Hospital in Modern Society*, edited by Eliot Freidson, 37–72. London: Free Press of Glencoe, Collier-Macmillan Limited, 1963.

Gleason, Philip. "American Identity and Americanization." In *Harvard Encyclopedia of American Ethnic Groups*, edited by Stephen Thernstrom, 31–57. Cambridge, MA: Belknap Press, 1980.

Gordon, Charles A., MD. "Autopsies." *Hospital Progress* 3, no. 10 (October 1922): 399–401.

Hamilton, Diane. "Constructing the Mind of Nursing." *Nursing History Review* 2 (1994): 3–28.

Helen, Sister Mary. "Mother M. Perpetua." Vol. 2, *Superior Generals—Centenary Chronicles of the Sisters of the Holy Cross*. Paterson, NJ: Saint Anthony Guild Press, 1941.

"History of the Medical Center: A Network for Heart Health." *Boston Globe*, October 30, 2002.

Holmes, Bayard, MD. "The Hospital Problem." *Journal of the American Medical Association* 47 (August 4, 1906): 319.

"Home Notes." *Northwestern Medical and Surgical Journal* 1 (November 1870): 187.

Hoy, Suellen. "The Journey Out: The Recruitment and Emigration of Irish Religious Women in the United States, 1812–1914." *Journal of Women's History* 6–7 (Winter/Spring 1995): 63–98.

———. "Caring for Chicago's Women and Girls: The Sisters of the Good Shepherd, 1859–1911." *Journal of Urban History* 23 (March 1997): 260–94.

———. "Walking Nuns: Chicago's Irish Sisters of Mercy." In *At the Crossroads: Old Saint Patrick's and the Chicago Irish,* edited by Ellen Skerret, 39–51. Chicago: Loyola Press and Wild Onion Books, 1997.

Judith, Mother. "Contemporary Needs in the Formation of the Sister for Hospital Work." *Sister Formation Bulletin* 7 (Winter 1960–61): 246.

Kauffman, Christopher J. "The Leadership of Father Moulinier: The Catholic Hospital Association Comes of Age, 1921–1928." *Health Progress* 71 (March 1990): 42.

———. "The Push for Standardization: The Origins of the Catholic Hospital Association, 1914–1920." *Health Progress* 71 (January–February 1990): 64.

Kenneally, James J. "Eve, Mary, and the Historians: American Catholicism and Women." In *Women in American Religion,* edted by Janet Wilson James, 191–206. Philadelphia: University of Pennsylvania Press, 1980.

Kennelly, Karen, CSJ. "Ideals of American Catholic Womanhood." Chapter 1 in Karen Kennelly, *American Catholic Women—A Historical Exploration.* New York: Macmillan Publishing Co., 1989.

Knowles, James S. "A Few Reasons Why Hospitals Show Such a Small Earning Power." *National Hospital Record* 2 (November 1898): 1–2.

Kuhn, Sister M. Campion, CSC. "Americanization." Vol. 1, *Fruits of the Tree: Sesquicentennial Chronicles, Sisters of the Holy Cross,* 73–99. Notre Dame, IN: Ave Maria Press, 1988.

Larkin, Emmet. "The Devotional Revolution in Ireland, 1850–75." *American Historical Review* 77 (June 1972): 651.

Liebowitz, Ruth P. "Virgins in the Service of Christ: The Dispute over an Active Apostolate for Women during the Counter-Reformation." In *Women of Spirit: Female Leadership in the Jewish and Christian Traditions,* edited by Rosemary Ruether and Eleanor McLaughlin, 133–34. New York: Simon and Schuster, 1979.

Longo, Lawrence D. "The Rise and Fall of Battey's Operation: A Fashion in Surgery." In *Women and Health in America: Historical Readings,* edited by Judith Walzer Leavitt, 270–84. Madison: University of Wisconsin Press, 1984.

Lyman, Henry M. "On Paying Patients in Hospitals." In *Hospitals, Dispensaries, and Nursing, Papers and Discussions in the International Congress of Charities, Corrections and Philanthropy,* sec. 3, edited by John S. Billings and Henry M. Hurd. Baltimore: Johns Hopkins Press, and London: Scientific Press, Limited, 1894.

Magdalene, Sister, OSF. "The Training of the Nurse." *Hospital Progress* 2, no. 7 (July 1921): 268–69.

Mannard, Joseph G. "Maternity . . . of the Spirit: Nuns and Domesticity in Antebellum America." *U.S. Catholic Historian* 5 (1996): 305–24.

Mitchell, S. W. "Nurses and Their Education." *American Journal of Nursing* 2 (August 1902): 90.

Morrison, Hyman. "The Chapter on Appendicitis in a Biography of Reginald Heber Fitz." *Bulletin of the History of Medicine* 20 (July 1946): 259–69.

Moulinier, Rev. C. B. "The President's Address." *Hospital Progress* 3 (August 1922): 300.

Nelson, Sioban. "Reading Nursing History." *Nursing Inquiry* 4 (1997): 229–36.

———. "Entering the Professional Domain: The Making of the Modern Nurse in 17th Century France." *Nursing History Review* 7 (1999): 171–87.

Niles, H. D., MD "Our Hospitals." *Journal of the American Medical Association* 38 (March 22, 1902): 761.

Norberg, Kathryn. "The Counter Reformation and Women: Religious and Lay." In *Catholicism in Early Modern History: A Guide to Research*, vol. 2, edited by John W. O'Malley, SJ, 138–39. Ann Arbor, MI: Edwards Brothers, 1988.

"New England Notes." *National Hospital Record* 6 (February 1903): 68.

O'Connell, Marvin R. "The Roman Catholic Tradition since 1545." In *Caring and Curing: Health and Medicine in the Western Religious Traditions*, edited by Ronald L. Numbers and Darrel W. Amundsen, 108–45. New York: Macmillan Publishing Co., 1986.

O'Reilly, Rev. Bernard, LD. *The Mirror of True Womanhood: A Book of Instruction for Women in the World*. New York: Peter. F. Collier, Publisher, 1879.

Pendleton, Mark A. "Memories of Silver Reef." *Utah Historical Quarterly* 3 (October 1930): 100–101.

Porterfield, Amanda. "Healing in the History of Christianity—Presidential Address, January 2002, American Society of Church History." *Church History: Studies in Christianity and Culture* 71, no. 2 (June 2002): 228–31.

Rea, Charles E. "The First Cholecystectomy in America." *Minnesota Medicine* 23 (September 1940): 658.

Rosenberg, Charles E. "Inward Vision & Outward Glance: The Shaping of the American Hospital, 1880–1914." *Bulletin of the History of Medicine* 53 (Fall 1979): 357–60.

———. "Community and Communities: The Evolution of the American Hospital." In *The American General Hospital: Communities and Social Contexts*, edited by Diana Elizabeth Long and Janet Golden, 3–17. Ithaca, NY and London: Cornell University Press, 1989.

"Round Table Conferences: Conference of Mothers Provincial and Superior, and Superintendents, The." *Hospital Progress* 1, no. 5 (September 1920): 203–7.

"Round Table Discussion: The Priest and Vocations to the Sisterhoods." *Hospital Progress* 4, no. 12 (December 1923): 476.

Ruether, Rosemary Radford. "Misogynism and Virginal Feminism in the Fathers of the Church." In *Religion and Sexism: Images of Woman in the Jewish and Christian Traditions*, edited by Rosemary Radford Ruether, 150–79. New York: Simon and Schuster, 1974.

Ryan, Joseph G. "The Chapel and the Operating Room: The Struggle of Roman Catholic Clergy, Physicians, and Believers with the Dilemmas of Obstetric Surgery, 1800–1900." *Bulletin of the History of Medicine* 76 (Fall 2002): 461–94.

Savitt, Todd L., and Janice Willms. "Sisters' Hospital: The Sisters of Providence and St. Patrick Hospital, Missoula, Montana, 1873–1890." *Montana: The Magazine of Western History* 53, no. 1 (Spring 2003): 28–43.

Scanlan, Lawrence. "Annual Report of the State of Catholicity in the Territory of Utah, United States of America, to the Society for the Propagation of the Faith, France," October 12, 1876. *Utah Historical Quarterly* 29 (October 1961): 339.

Schaefers, William. "Catholic Hospital Atmosphere." *Hospital Progress* 11 (1930): 400.

Schwartz, Jerome L. "Early History of Prepaid Medical Care Plans." *Bulletin of the History of Medicine* 39 (September–October 1965): 456.

Skerrett, Ellen. "Creating Sacred Space in an Early Chicago Neighborhood." In *At the Crossroads: Old Saint Patrick's and the Chicago Irish*, edited by Skerrett, 21–38. Chicago: Loyola Press and Wild Onion Books, 1997.

Smith, C. A. "The Medical and Surgical Department of a Railway System: What It

Is and What It Tries to Accomplish." *Texas State Journal of Medicine* 1 (July 1905): 13–14.

Smith, Cynthia, Cathy Cowan, Art Sensenig, Aaron Catlin, and The Health Accounts Team. "Trends: *Health Spending* Growth Slows in 2003." *Health Affairs* 24, no. 1 (January–February 2005): 185–89.

Smith, M. E. "Nursing as a Vocation." *Trained Nurse and Hospital Review* 29 (1902): 329.

Smith, Ryan K. "The Cross: Church Symbol and Contest in Nineteenth-Century America." *Church History* 70 (December 2001): 705–34.

"Sister M. Olivia Gowan, OSB." In *Pioneer Healers: The History of Women Religious in American Health Care,* edited by Ursual Stepsis, CSA, and Dolores Liptak, RSM, 226–27. New York: Crossroad, 1989.

Sorensen, Elaine Shaw. " 'For Zion's Sake': The Emergence of Mormon Nursing." *Nursing History Review* 6 (1998): 51–69.

Specht, Anita. "The Power of Ethnicity in a Community of Women Religious: The Poor Handmaids of Jesus Christ in the United States, 1868–1930." *U. S. Catholic Historian* 19 (Winter 2001): 53–64.

Spitzack, Carole, and Kathryn Carter. "Women in Communication Studies: A Typology for Revision." *Quarterly Journal of Speech* 73 (November 1987): 401–23.

"St. Mary's Hospital." *American Medical Directory.* Chicago: American Medical Association, 1916.

"St. Mary's New Hospital." *Catholic Bulletin* (September 7, 1918).

Strumpf, Neville E., and Nancy Tomes. "Restraining the Troublesome Patient: A Historical Perspective on a Contemporary Debate." *Nursing History Review* 1 (1993): 3–24.

Stansell, Christine. *City of Women: Sex and Class in New York, 1789–1860.* New York: Alfred A. Knopf, 1986.

Sweetser, H. "Financial Support of Hospitals. "*Hospital Progress* 1, no. 6 (1920): 232.

Szasz, Ferenc, and Margaret Connell Szasz. "Religion and Spirituality." In *The Oxford History of the American West,* edited by Clyde A. Milner II, Carol A. O'Connor, and Martha A. Sandweiss, 360–70. New York: Oxford University Press, 1994.

Thompson, Margaret Susan. "Philemon's Dilemma: Nuns and the Black Community in Nineteenth-Century America: Some Findings." *Records of the American Catholic Historical Society of Philadelphia* 96 (1986): 3–18.

———. "Discovering Foremothers: Sisters, Society, and the American Catholic Experience." *U. S. Catholic Historian* 5 (Summer/Fall 1986): 275.

———. "Sisterhood and Power: Class, Culture, and Ethnicity in the American Convent." *Colby Library Quarterly* 25 (1989): 149–75.

———. "Women, Feminism, and the New Religious History." In *Belief and Behavior: Essays in the New Religious History,* edited by Philip R. Vandermeer and Robert P Swierenga, 136–63. New Brunswick, NJ: Rutgers University Press, 1991.

Tomes, Nancy. "The Great Restraint Controversy: A Comparative Perspective on Anglo-American Psychiatry in the Nineteenth Century." In *The Anatomy of Madness: Essays in the History of Psychiatry,* edited by W. F. Bynum, Roy Porter, and Michael Shephard, 190–225. London and New York: Routledge, 1988.

"Twenty-five Years' Growth of the Hospital Field." *National Hospital Record* 7 (September 1903): 25.

Veronica, Sister M. "The Internal Organization of Training Schools." *Hospital Progress* 1 (September 1920): 193.

Wall, Barbra Mann. "Grace under Pressure: The Nursing Sisters of the Holy Cross, 1861–1865." *Nursing History Review* 1 (1993): 71–87.

———. "Courage to Care: The Sisters of the Holy Cross in the Spanish-American War." *Nursing History Review* 3 (1995): 55–77.

———. "Called to a Mission of Charity: The Sisters of St. Joseph in the Civil War." *Nursing History Review* 6 (1998): 86–113.

———. " 'Definite Lines of Influence': Catholic Sisters and Nurse Training Schools, 1890–1920." *Nursing Research* 50 (September–October 2001): 314–21.

———. "The Pin-striped Habit: Balancing Charity and Business in Catholic Hospitals, 1865–1915." *Nursing Research* 51 (January/February 2002): 50–58.

———. "Healthcare as Product: Catholic Sisters Confront Charity and the Hospital Marketplace, 1865–1925." In *Commodifying Everything: Relationships of the Market*, edited by Susan Strasser, 143–68. New York: Routledge, 2003.

——— "Science and Ritual: The Hospital as Medical and Sacred Space, 1865–1920." *Nursing History Review* 11 (2003): 51–68.

———, and Sioban Nelson. " 'Our Heels Are Praying Very Hard All Day.' " *Holistic Nursing Practice* 17, no. 6 (November/December 2003): 320–28.

Welter, Barbara. "The Cult of True Womanhood, 1820–1860." *American Quarterly* 18 (Summer 1966): 151–57.

Widerquist, Jo Ann. "Called to Serve." *Christian Nurse International* 11, no. 1 (1995): 5.

Wilensky, Harold L. "The Professionalization of Everyone?" *American Journal of Sociology* 70 (September 1964): 137–58.

Wittberg, Patricia. "Ties That No Longer Bind." *America*, September 26, 1998, 10–14.

Wood, Ann Douglas. " 'The Fashionable Diseases': Women's Complaints and Their Treatment in Nineteenth-Century America." In *Women and Health in America: Historical Readings*, edited by Judith Walzer Leavitt, 222–38. Madison: University of Wisconsin Press, 1984.

Woolley, Alma S. "Nuns and GUNS: Holy Wars at Georgetown, 1903–1947." *Nursing History Review* 11 (2003): 69–87.

Zoe, Sister. "Nursing Problems." *Hospital Progress* 4, no. 1 (January 1923): 28–29.

Index

Abbott, Andrew, 9, 189
abortion, 183
Adams, W. A., 96, 155, 160
admissions policies, 156–57
African Americans, 18, 32, 98–99, 154, 193, 217n92
aged, homes for, 27
Alderling, Bishop Herman J., 74
Alexian Brothers, 21
ambulance services, 142, *143*
American College of Surgeons (ACS), 166–71. *See also* doctors
Anderson, Sister Augusta, *40*, 57, 59, 60, 111–12
appendectomies, 90. *See also* surgery
Aransas Pass Railroad, 93
Aries, Philippe, 140
autopsies, 174

Baltimore Almshouse, 18
Baltimore Infirmary, 18
baptisms, 99, 135, 138, 139
Baty, John, 70
begging tours, 68, 72, 104
Berteling, J. B., 91
Bessonies, Father August, 66–67
bishops, 163–65, 182
boards, 78, 83, 151, 153–59, 169, 170, 178
Bouchet, Sister Jane Frances, *39*, 55, 84, 109, 213n29

Braunagel, Julius, 94
Brown, Mother Anastasie, 67, 68, 72
Brownson, Orestes, 135
Buisson, Sister Agnes, 27, 56
Burbidge, Sister Conchessa, 177, 180
Butler, Sister Lidwina, 1–2, 88, 89, 106, 150, 154, 157, 160

Cabrini, Mother Frances, 21
Cairo, Ill., 99, 100, 104, 108
Camp Bowie, 96
Camp Hamilton, Lexington, Ky., 21, 38
Carroll, Sister Julitta, *79*
Casey, Sister Benigna, *79*
Casey, Sister Paula, *45*
Catholic Church: authority of, 41–42; on death, 137–38; hierarchy of, 17, 23, 35–36, 163, 164; and hospital administration, 151; ideology of womanhood, 36–37, 148–50, 164; image of, 15, 19–20, 189; on maternity cases, 181–84; opposition to, 19, 70, 72; on segregation, 98; on sickness, 130–32; spiritual movement of, 76, 135
Catholic Counter-Reformation, 16, 140
Catholic Hospital Association (CHA), 167–71, *169, 170;* on charity, 124; on education, 177, 180; nuns' status

in, 186; on scientific medicine, 171, 173, 174, 189; statistics on care provided by nuns, 186; surgical code of, 183
Catholic University School of Nursing, 178
Cecilia, Mother Mary, 66
chapels, 121–22
chaplains, 168. See also priests
charity: and admissions policies, 156–57; de-emphasis of, 123–25; and early Christian nursing, 15–16; at Holy Cross Hospital, 88, *89;* in hospital work, 46; at Santa Rosa Infirmary, 56; of Sisters of Charity of the Incarnate Word, 27; at St. Joseph's Hospital (St. Paul), 80, *81;* at St. Mary's Hospital (Minneapolis), 153. See also poor
chastity, 42–43
Chawke, Sister Cuthberta, 175
Chollet, Sister St. Madeleine, 27, 28, *39,* 56, 112, 155, 159, 161–63, 213n32, 230n52
CHRISTUS Health, 192
churches, locations of, 77
Cinquin, Sister St. Pierre, *28;* on admissions policies, 156; autonomy of, 33; duties of, 208n24; establishment of Santa Rosa Infirmary, 27; and establishment of Sisters of Charity of the Incarnate Word, 28; on finances, 102, 110, 111; French influence on, 188; on Irish railroad patients, 107; marketing by, 118; on religious life, 35, 46; at St. Joseph's Infirmary (Fort Worth), 95, 96; at Santa Rosa Infirmary, 56, 57, 94; on spiritual mission, 98; on status of nuns, 44
Civil War, 13, 20, 23, 26, 31, 33, 44, 46, 66, 135–36
Clark, Mother Xavier, 133–34, 138
class status, 99, 104–5
Clifford, Sister Lydia, 21–22, 38, *38,* 40
Cochran, Clark E., 194

College and Academy of the Incarnate Word, 27
College of St. Catherine, 24
commitment mechanisms, 45
"community," 200n7
"congregation," 200n7
Constans et Sedula, 184
constitutions: on authority of nun-administrator, 151; and autonomy of nuns, 163; definition of, 41–42, 200n13; on doctor-nun relations, 149; on evangelical work, 136; modification of, 103; record of nuns' role in, 17; of Sisters of Charity of the Incarnate Word, 27, 183, 235n71
conversions, 136, 138, 140
Conway, Rose, 108
Council of Nursing Education, 180
Council of Trent, 5, 7, 136, 137, 163, 199n20
Cox, Sister Ignatius Loyola, 82, 84
Cretin, Bishop Joseph, 24, 54
Cupples, George, 94

Dallas, Tex., 160
Daly, Marcus, 59, 98
Darnell, Sister Bartholomew, 60
Daugherty, C. A., 91
Daughters of Charity, 16, 21, 138. See also Sisters of Charity (Emmitsburg, Md.)
Daughters of Charity Health System-West Central, 192
Daughters of Charity of St. Vincent De Paul, 133
Davis, Mary, 108
Deadwood, Dakota Territory, 63–65, 108
death, 137–41, 144–46, 190
Dengel, Anna, 235n77
De Paul, Vincent, 16, 181
Deseret Hospital, 88
devotions, 134–35
Diner, Hasia, 30
Dirkmann, Sister Augustina, 232n21
Dock, Lavinia, 180
doctors: on admissions policies, 156–57;

and advancement of medicine, 160;
authority of, 158–59, 167; and
emergencies, 144; hiring and firing
of, 100–101, 153–55; at Holy Cross
Hospital, 89; hospital privileges of,
77–78, 83, 89, 100; at Providence
Hospital, 70; relationship with
nuns, 9, 33–34, 75, 146–47,
149–53, 168, 178–85, 188; at St.
Edward's Hospital, 65; at St.
Joseph's Hospital (South Bend,
Ind.), 91–92, 114; at St. Joseph's
Hospital (St. Paul), 54–55, 81; at
St. Joseph's Infirmary (Fort Worth),
95, 96; at St. Mary's Hospital
(Minneapolis), 82–83; at St. Mary's
Infirmary (Cairo, Ill.), 59, 86; at
Santa Rosa Infirmary, 56, 94; on
socialized medicine, 157; in voluntary hospitals, 52. *See also* American
College of Surgeons (ACS)
Dougherty, Sister Irmina, *79*
Downs, Sister Florentia, *79*
Draeger pulmotor, 172
Drexel, Katherine, 21, 32
Dubuis, Bishop Claude, 26–27, 55–56, 110
Dunn, J. H., 82–83
Dunsmoor, Frederick A., 83
Dwight, Thomas, 145

economy, nuns' contributions to, 188
Electa, Sister (Charity), *45*
emergencies, 144
Emily, Sister, *79*
endowments for beds, 109
epidemics, 16, 18, 27, 54
Episcopalians, 22
Epworth Hospital and Training
School, 90, 91–93, 108, 109, 114
ethnicity, 4, *30*, 30–31, 72, 73, 97–98,
188–89. *See also* immigrants
evangelical work, 136

Fairview Health System, 193
Farrar, Francis, 96
Farr, Robert E., 84
fees, 55, 57, 59, 60, 70–71, 104–7,

157–58, 218n13, 222n88, 222n90
Ferguson, James, 81
Fidelis, Sister (Ursuline), *45*
Finn, Sister Esperance, *39*, 84, 168,
213n29
Fitzpatrick, Ellen, 108
Fitz, Reginald, 90
Flexner, Abraham, 85, 89, 94
Flexner Report, 166
Fogarty, Sister Athanasius, 66, 69–70
Fontbonne, Mother St. Jean, 23
Fort Wayne, Ind., 77
Fort Worth, Tex., 33, 98, 100, 106, 107
Foucault, Michel, 227n69
Fournier, Mother St. John, 24, 139
Fowler, Allen, 89
France, 9, 16, 23, 31, 66, 181, 188,
233n56
French immigrants, 66, 70–72

Gabriel, Sister M., 164
Gahagan, Sister Cordelia, 88, 175
Galveston, Tex., 27, 55
Garesche, Father Edward, 164–65
Gaven, Bridget, 108
Geary, Sister Aida, *79*
Geary, Sister Blandina, *79*
gender, 4–9, 36–37, 41–44, 47,
148–50, 162–65, 187–88
German immigrants, 15, 20, 21, 24,
30, 31, 71, 188
germ theory, 72, 93, 171–72, 187
Gibbons, Cardinal James, 131–32, 138
Gillespie, Mother Angela, *25*, 26, 29,
57–59, 103, 104, 111, 135–36
Ginzburg, Lori, 40
Glaser, William A., 100
Gleason, Sister Beatrice, *79*
Gordon, Charles A., 174
Gowan, Sister Olivia, 233n54
Graves, Amos, 94
Grinstead, W. F., 86
Guerin, Mother Theodore, 66
Guilbeau, Francisco, 56

Hamilton, W. S., 173
Hartnett, Matilda, 57
Hawaiian Islands, 20

health care, 4–5, 13–15
health care institutions, establishment of, 22
Health East System, 193
Health Trust, Inc., 193–94
Herff, Adolph, 93, 94, *177*, 216n77
Herff, Ferdinand, 94, *158, 177*
Herff, John, 94
Hill, Richard J., 84
Hiver, Mother Angelique, 55–56
Hogan, Sister Edith, *79*
Holmes, Bayard, 152
Holy Cross Health Services, 236n6
Holy Cross Health System, 194
Holy Cross Hospital Association, 111
Holy Cross Hospital (Salt Lake City), 61, *87*, 121–23; admissions policy at, 156; architecture of, *121, 122;* autonomy of, 163–64; census data on, *101;* establishment of, 26, 59–61; expansion of, 86–90, 113; fees at, 60, 157–58; financial management of, 104, 106–8, 111–12, *115*, 115–16, *117*, 123, *124;* hiring of doctors at, 154, 155; incorporation of, 111; interdenominational cooperation at, 101; marketing of, 118; maternity cases at, 183; modernization of, 160; nursing staff, *152;* patients at, 59–61, 86–88, *89*, 106, 107, 142; pharmacy, *173;* private room in, *105;* sale of, 193–95; scientific medicine at, 159–60, 172; Sister Lidwina Butler at, 1–2; standardization at, 170; surgery at, 88–90, 158
Holy Cross, Sister M., 91
Holy Cross priests, 109–10
holy water, 129
Homestake Mine, 63, 64
Hosmer, Andrew, 214n48
Hospital Progress, 124
hospitals: architecture of, 120–23, 190; attitudes toward Catholic, 189–90; budgets of, 115–16, *117;* competition among, 75, 87, 90–93, 100, 109, 114; demographics in Catholic, 97–99; establishment of, 4, 18–22; expansions of, 188; fees, 104–7; financial management of, 32, 51–52, 102–17, *115*, 123–25, *124;* functions of Catholic, 52–53, 191, 194–95; history of, 2–3, 6; incorporation of, 19, 110–12; locations of, *77;* market for, 29–34, 72–78, 190; marketing of, 106, 118–23, 171–72, 174; measurements of success of, 123–25; and medical schools, 85; modernization of, 159–60; patterns of, 100–101; as sacramental locations, 8; standardization of, 166–67, 176, 184, 189. *See also individual hospitals*

immigrants: Americanization of, 204n70; effect on health care, 14–15, 18–21; effect on nuns' work, 4, 167, 188–89; exclusion from employment, 154; financial support of hospitals, 73, 107–8; at Holy Cross Hospital, 88; in Minneapolis, 82, 213n28; racial division among, 98, 99; at St. Joseph's Infirmary (Fort Worth), 95; at St. Mary's Hospital (Minneapolis), 84; in St. Paul, Minn., 79; in Salt Lake County, Utah, 214n47; at Santa Rosa Infirmary, 93–94; and Sisters of Providence of Saint Mary-of-the-Woods (Indiana), 66; and Sisters of St. Joseph Carondelet, 15, 24; in South Bend, Ind., 90; in Terre Haute, Ind., 71. *See also* ethnicity; French immigrants; German immigrants; Irish immigrants
Incarnate Word Health System, 192
Incarnate Word Hospital (St. Louis), 27
Indiana, 24–25, 66, 112, 189
Indianapolis, Ind., 66–67, 70
injuries, 142
interns, 89, 142, 152–53
Interstate Commerce Commission (ICC), 76
Ireland, Archbishop John, 24, 32, 82, 103, 109, 110

Index

Ireland, Sister Seraphine, 24, 82, 111
Irish immigrants: advantages of religious life for, 37–38, 40–41; at Holy Cross Hospital, 61; in Indiana, 24; influx of, 14–15; as miners and railroad workers, 98; mortality rate of, 20–21; as nuns, 1, 19, 29–31, 61, 188, 203n57; provision of medical care for, 107; role in hospital field, 4; in Terre Haute, Ind., 71
Irish Standard, 120
Italian immigrants, 21

Jansenism, 233n56
Jesuits, 234n56
Jolly, Ellen Ryan, *45*
Joyce, Kathleen, 187
Judge Memorial Home, 164

Kalbfleisch, Sister Clara, 173
Kauffman, Christopher, 5
Keating, Mother de Chantal, 46
Keegan, Sister de Sales, *179*
Kelly, Sister Melanie, *79*
Kiely, Father Denis, 59, 61, 162
Kiernan, Sister Magdalen, 85

Larkin, Emmet, 41
Latter-day Saints Hospital, 88
laywomen, 108
Lead City, 63, 64
lead poisoning, 142
Lister, Joseph, 93
Little Sisters of the Poor, 70
Lorenz, Adolph, 172–73
Louisville, Ky., 18
Lutherans, 22
Lynch, Mother Joseph, 82
Lyons, Sister Madeline, *79*, 85, 168

Mackin, Father Bernard, 63
Maclean, A. C., 157–58
Maher, Sister Bernardine, *79*, 79–80, 211n14
Maloney, Sister Mary Louise, 66
Manica, Sister (Providence), *45*
Manual of Decrees and Customs, 53, 131, 136, 141
Marillac, Louise de, 16
marine hospitals, 58
Marquette University, 167, 177, 178, 233n48
Marty, Bishop Martin, 65
Mary of the Assumption, Sister, 95
Masons, 225n38
Mass, 134
Massachusetts Mutual Life Insurance Company, 113, 116
Matel, Jeanne Chezard de, 26
maternity cases, 75, 180–84
Mayo Clinic, 21, 159
McAuley, Catherine, 19
McCauley, Bernadette, 5–6
McDaniel, A. S., 94
McGolrick, Sister Elizabeth, *79*
McNamara, Sister John Baptist, *79*
McNamara, Sister Liguori, 43, 136
McNeill, Sister Christina, *79*
McSheffery, Annunciata, 38
Meacham, F. A., 89
Medaille, Jean Pierre, 23
medical schools, 85, 89
medical specialties, 75, 81–82, 173. *See also* surgery
medicine, 134, 159–60, 171–74, 180–81, 184, 187, 189
mental institutions, 22, 27, 54
Mercy Health Services, 194
Mercy Hospital, 19
Mexican Americans, 99, 215n73
Midwest, 2–3, 15, 19, 21, 26, 51, 66, 100, 187
Military Hospital (Indianapolis), 66
Miller, Arthur, 81
Mills, W. F., 91
miners, 76; and financial management of hospitals, 106–7; hospitals for, 59–60, 62–65, 87, 88, 98, 119–20, 142, 164, 188; payment for medical care, 157, 219n24
Miners' Hospital, 64–65
Minneapolis, Minn., 82, 84, 100, 213n28
Minnesota Hospital College, 83
miraculous cures, 223n2

Miriam, Sister (Mercy), *45*
The Mirror of True Womanhood (O'Reilly), 36
Missionary Sisters of the Sacred Heart, 21
Missouri Pacific Railroad Hospital (Fort Worth), 95, 123
Mitchell, S. Weir, 176–77
monasteries, 16
Moorhead, J. J., 171
Moran, Sister Adela, 85–86, 213n37
Moreau, Father Basil Anthony, 24, 26, 33
Mormons, 22, 87–88, 101, 163
Morrison, John Gordon, 13
Morton, Oliver, 66
Moulinier, Father Charles B., 167, 168, 174, 177
Mound City, Ill., 135
Murphy, Sister Edward, 63–65, 90, 112, 215n54
Murphy Mansion, 82, 83
Mutual Hospital Aid Association, 104

National League for Nursing Education (NLNE), 180
Native Americans, 24
Nelson, Sioban, 5
Neraz, Bishop John, 95
Neville, Sister Philip Neri, *179*
Nightingale, Florence, 144–45
Nightingale, William, 144
Niles, Harry, 90, 159–60
Normae (1901), 181–82, 234n59
nun-administrators: authority of, 151, 153–59; negotiation strategies of, 160–63; relationship with bishops and priests, 163–65; relationship with doctors, 149–53
nuns: Americanization of, 31–32, 204n70; authority of, 167–68, 170, 180, 187, 188; autonomy of, 32–33, 161–64, 178, 180, 191; central government of, 111; clothing of, 176, 182; commitment to health care, 13–14; criticism of, 144–47, 166–67; demand for respect, 161–62; early nursing tradition of, 16–17; entrepreneurship of, 8, 33–34, 38–40, 75, 102–14, 186–87, 190; expectations of, 41–42; factors influencing success of, 29–34; image of, 181–82; meaning of term, 200n7; modesty of, 180–82; recruitment of, 29–31, 61; religious identities of, 15, 36, 42–47, 132, 162, 174, 176, 187–88, 190; role in shaping modern hospital, 3–9, 189–90; status of, 7–8, 37–38, 42–44, 130, 151, 188; work histories of, *39–40*. *See also* nun-administrators
nurses, secular, 158–59
nurses, special, 123
nursing: early Christian, 15–16; historical studies of, 5–9; and ideology of womanhood, 36–37, 148–49; modern standards in, 175–78; practices of, 141–44, 180–85; spirituality of, 27, 46–47
nursing schools: conflicts over, 178–85; establishment of, 176, 188; growth of, 100; obstetrics courses at, 184; at St. Joseph's Hospital (South Bend, Ind.), 91, 92; at St. Joseph's Hospital (St. Paul), 80; at St. Joseph's Infirmary (Fort Worth), 96; at St. Mary's Infirmary (Cairo, Ill.), 86; at Santa Rosa Infirmary, 94; of Sisters of Charity of the Incarnate Word, 232n37; superintendents of, 151. *See also* nursing training
nursing training, 132–34, 173–74, 177–78, 180–82. *See also* nursing schools
Nutting, Adelaide, 180

Oblate Sisters of Providence, 18
O'Brien, Harry J., 80, 232n25
O'Dea, Sister Robert, *39*, 94, 178, *179*
O'Donnell, Sister Cornelia, *79*
O'Hage, Justus, 81
Olmsted, Frederick Law, 118–19
Olney, Thomas, 92, 232n25
O'Neill, Sister de Sales, 31

open-staffing, 154–55
"order," 200n7
Order of the Incarnate Word and Blessed Sacrament, 9, 26. *See also* Sisters of Charity of the Incarnate Word
O'Reilly, Bernard, 36
O'Shaughnessy, Mother Mary John, 30
Outten, W. B., 95

Pariseau, Mother Joseph, 20
Parvin, Theophilus, 68–69
patients: admissions policies for, 156–57; at Catholic hospitals, 100–101, 187; competition for, 87, 90–93, 100, 114, 158–59, 189; difficulty in dealing with, 142–44; discipline of, 145; diversity of, 97–98; histories of, 170; at Holy Cross Hospital, 59–61, 86–88, *89*, 106–7, 142; male, 182; at Providence Hospital, 70; recruitment of, 75; reliance on paying, 123–25; at St. Edward's hospital, 64; at St. Joseph's Hospital (South Bend, Ind.), 91–92, *113*, 114; at St. Joseph's Hospital (St. Paul), 80, *81;* at St. Joseph's Infirmary (Fort Worth), 95–96, 143; at St. Mary's Hospital (Minneapolis), 84; at St. Mary's Infirmary (Cairo, Ill.), 58–59, 85–86, 99, 104, 105; at Santa Rosa Infirmary, 93–94, 142, 144, 216n75. *See also* miners; poor; railroad workers; veterans
Patricia, Sister (St. Joseph), *45*
Pepin, Sister Euphrosine, 62
Pericoloso, 7
pharmacies, 172, *173*
pharmacists, 175
Platt, Henry B., 172
Pommerel, Mother Celestine, 24
poor, 67, 70–71, 91, 96, 104–6, 146. *See also* charity
Poor Handmaids of Jesus Christ, 21, 217n2
Poor Sisters of St. Francis Seraph of the Perpetual Adoration, 21, *170*, 171, 184
prayer, 135
Presbyterian Hospital (Chicago), *115*, 116, *117*
Presentation Sisters, 20
priests, 109–10, 163–65, 167–68, 180
Propaganda Fide, 184
Protestants: competition for patients, 87, 90–93, 100, 114, 158–59, 189; and death, 140; hospitals of, 52; as hospital workers, 101, 163; identity in Ireland, 40; in Minneapolis, 82; objection to dedication of Providence Hospital, 68–69; response to immigration, 18–19, 71; spiritual ministry to, 136, 138; support of St. Mary's Infirmary, 108
Providence Hospital (Terre Haute, Ind.), 65–73, 104

racial tension. *See* segregation
railroad workers, 76; and financial management of hospitals, 106–7; at Holy Cross Hospital, 86–88; hospitals for, 98, 120, 142, 188; payment for medical care, 163, 218n13; at St. Joseph's Infirmary (Fort Worth), 95–96; at St. Mary's Infirmary (Cairo, Ill.), 86; at Santa Rosa Infirmary, 93, 94
Red Rover, USS, 13, 26, 231n37
Reid, James D., 91
religious life, 35–44, 46
Remigius, Sister, 93
Risse, Guenter, 6
Rooney, Sister M. Sophia, 90–91
Root, Emerson F., 89, 183, 214n48
Rosati, Bishop Joseph, 23
Rose, Chauncey, 67, 69
Rule (1867), 46, 134
Russell, Mother Baptist, 19
Ryan, Sister Anatolia, *79*
Ryan, Joseph G., 183

sacraments, 134–38, 190, 224n18, 225n28
St. Anthony's Hospital (Terre Haute,

Ind.), 171
St. Edwards Hospital (Deadwood, Dakota Territory), 63–65
St. Elizabeth's Hospital for Women (Boston), 21
St. Elizabeth's Hospital (Lafayette, Ind.), 21, 184
St. John's Home for Invalids, 66–67
St. John's Hospital (Silver Reef, Utah), 62–63
St. John's Hospital (Springfield, Ill.), 21, 181
St. Joseph, 57, 222n84
St. Joseph Regional Medical Center, 194
St. Joseph's Hospital (Cleveland, Ohio), 19
St. Joseph's Hospital Corporation, 169
St. Joseph's Hospital (Fort Worth), 192, 195
St. Joseph's Hospital (Philadelphia), 19
St. Joseph's Hospital (South Bend, Ind.): celebration of addition to, 74; census data on, *101,* 114; establishment of, 26; expansion of, 90–93, 113–14; financial management of, 108–10, 112, *113;* operation of, 194
St. Joseph's Hospital (St. Paul, Minn.), *80;* administration of, 84; census data on, *101;* establishment of, 19, 23, 54–55; expansion of, 78–82; financial management of, 109; incorporation of, 110–11; marketing of, 118; merger with Health East System, 193; nursing education at, 178; payment policies at, 105; scientific medicine at, 172; staff appointments at, 169; as teaching hospital, 85, 153
St. Joseph's Hospital Training School for Nurses, 80
St. Joseph's Infirmary (Fort Worth), *97;* admissions policy at, 156; ambulance service of, *143;* autopsies at, 174; census data on, *101;* competition of, 160; emergencies at, 144; expansion of, 95–97; financial management of, 104, 112, 114; hiring of doctors at, 155; and hospital standardization, 167; incorporation of, 110; maternity cases at, 183; mission of, 77; naming of, 122–23; nursing education at, 178; patients at, 95–96, 143; Scientific Department, *175;* spiritual practices at, 130; surgery at, 97, 182
St. Lawrence Hospital, 1
St. Louis, Arkansas, and Texas Railroad, 86
St. Louis, Mo., 23, 27, 33, 161
St. Luke's Hospital (Kansas City), 222n88
St. Luke's Hospital (San Francisco), *115,* 116, *117*
St. Mark's Hospital, 87, 88, 89, 116
Saint Mary's Academy, 25, 26
Saint Mary's College, 25, 26
Saint Mary's (Holy Cross motherhouse), 112
St. Mary's Hospital (Cairo, Ill.), 193
St. Mary's Hospital Corporation, 110
St. Mary's Hospital (Minneapolis, Minn.), *83;* administration of, 24; census data on, *101;* chapel at, 122; clothing of nuns at, 176; expansion of, 82–85; fees at, 218n13; financial management of, 104, 109, *115,* 116, *117,* 123, *124;* interns at, 153; marketing of, 118, *119;* payment policies at, 105; sale of, 193
St. Mary's Hospital (Rochester, Minn.), 21
St. Mary's Hospital (San Francisco), 19
St. Mary's Infirmary (Cairo, Ill.): census data on, 100, *101;* deaths at, 139–40; establishment of, 26, 57–59; expansion of, 85–86; financial support of, 108; and hospital standardization, 167; marketing of, 120; patients at, 58–59, 85–86, 99, 104, 105; scientific medicine at, 172
St. Mary's Infirmary (Galveston), 27

Saint Mary's Institute, 66
Saint-Palais, Bishop Maurice de, 67, 71
St. Patrick's Hospital (Missoula, Mont.), 20
St. Paul Medical School, 85
St. Paul, Minn., 24, 54–55, 77, 79, 100, 104
St. Paul School of Medical Instruction, 85
saints, 134, 135
St. Vincent's Charity Hospital (Cleveland, Ohio), 19
St. Vincent's Hospital (Indianapolis), 21
St. Vincent's Hospital (Santa Fe), 20
Salt Lake City, Utah, 77, 87, 101, 112, 157, 163–64
Salt Lake County, Utah, 214n47
San Antonio, 27–28, 30, 55, 77, 100
Santa Rosa Hospital (San Antonio), 192
Santa Rosa Infirmary (San Antonio), 58; admissions policy at, 156; census data on, 100, 101; clothing of nuns at, 176; community support of, 51; death at, 139; doctor-nun relations at, 149–50; establishment of, 27, 55–57; expansion of, 93–94; fees at, 218n13; financial management of, 102, 106; incorporation of, 110; maternity cases at, 183; as motherhouse and novitiate, 208n24; patients at, 93–94, 142, 144, 216n75; payment policies at, 105; spiritual practices at, 135; surgery at, 99, 150, 158, 177, 182, 216n86; training school at, 178; visiting clergy at, 164; x-ray department at, 173
Saunders, Bacon, 96, 155
Scanlan, Father Lawrence, 59, 62, 104, 148, 163–64
Schmidt, Father E. J. P., 164
Schwitalla, Father Alphonse, 180
Scott, James C., 162
segregation, 98–99, 193
Servatius, Sister, 45

Shea, Sister Aubin, 38
Sherlock, Sister Gertrude, 69
sickness, 130–32, 137, 191
Silver Reef, Utah, 62–63
Sister Formation Conference, 184–85
"sisters," 200n7
Sisters of Charity, 20, 133, 145. *See also* Daughters of Charity
Sisters of Charity (Emmitsburg, Md.), 18, 22
Sisters of Charity Health Care System, 192
Sisters of Charity of Leavenworth, Kans., 20
Sisters of Charity of Nazareth, 18, 20
Sisters of Charity of Our Lady of Mercy, 18
Sisters of Charity of St. Augustine, 19
Sisters of Charity of the Incarnate Word, 2, 192; admissions policy of, 156; and advantages of religious life, 35; autonomy of, 32; beginning of health care work, 20; class distinctions in, 38; competence of, 147; and death, 138, 139; establishment of hospital in St. Louis, 33; ethnic backgrounds of, 30; feasts celebrated by, 224n20; financial management by, 105, 106, 108, 110, 112, 114; foundation of, 26–29; French influence on, 31, 188; graduating nurses, 158; and immigration, 15; mission and duties of, 46, 99, 134, 235n71; modernization efforts of, 160; motherhouse of, 208n24; nursing practices of, 141, 142, 144, 158, 182, 183; nursing training of, 133, 232n37; recruitment of, 30–31; relationship with doctors, 149–50; at St. Joseph's Hospital (Fort Worth), 195; at St. Joseph's Infirmary (Fort Worth), 77, 95–97, 122–23; at Santa Rosa Infirmary (San Antonio), 55–57, 93–94; service to poor, 146; spiritual practices of, 129, 130, 135
Sisters of Mercy, 19, 20, 82, 109, 145,

164
Sisters of Providence (French-Canadian), 20
Sisters of Providence of Saint Mary-of-the-Woods (Indiana), 20, 65–73
Sisters of St. Francis of Our Lady of Lourdes, 21
Sisters of St. Joseph of Carondelet, 2, 79, 192–93; charity work of, 124, 146; class distinctions in, 38; closure of hospitals, 29; on death and dying, 139; entrepreneurship of, 103; establishment of, 9; establishment of hospitals, 19; evangelical work of, 136; financial management by, 32, 104, 110; and formation of Catholic Hospital Association, 167, 168; foundation of, 23–24; and immigration, 15, 24; independence from French motherhouse, 31; Irish women in, 29; mission of, 33; nursing practices of, 141, 182; recruitment of surgeons, 54–55; at St. Joseph's Hospital (St. Paul, Minn.), 78–82; at St. Mary's Hospital (Minneapolis), 82–85, 109; on sickness, 131; spiritual instruction of patients, 53; work during Spanish-American War, 21–22
Sisters of the Blessed Sacrament for Indians and Colored People, 21
Sisters of the Holy Cross, 2, 170, 193; administration of St. John's Hospital (Silver Reef, Utah), 62; autonomy of, 32–33, 163–64; beginning of health care work, 20; Sister Lidwina Butler with, 1; in Civil War, 13, 135; class distinctions in, 38; closure of hospitals, 29; entrepreneurship of, 103; establishment of, 9; establishment of hospitals, 57–65; financial management by, 104, 108–14, 116; foundation of, 24–26; at Holy Cross Hospital (Salt Lake City), 86–90; and immigration, 15; independence from French motherhouse, 31; influence in Salt Lake City, 101; Irish women in, 29, 37–38; marketing by, 118; modernization efforts of, 160, 182; nursing training of, 133; praise of, 148; relationship with Cairo, Ill. community, 99; religious identity of, 44, 46; and religious life, 36; at St. Joseph's Hospital (South Bend, Ind.), 90–93; at St. Mary's Infirmary (Cairo, Ill.), 85–86; sale of Holy Cross Hospital, 195; in Spanish-American War, 21–22
Sisters of the Holy Family, 18
Sisters of the Poor of St. Francis, 20
Sisters of the Sorrowful Mother, 21
Sisters of the Third Franciscan Order, Minor Conventuals, 20
Sisters of the Third Order of St. Francis, 20, 21
"Sisters' Tickets," 104
Smith, C. A., 162
socialized medicine, 157–58
Sorin, Father Edward, 24–26, 46, 111–12
South Bend, Ind., 90
South Dakota, 112
Southern Pacific Railroad, 93
Spalding, Mother Catherine, 18
Spanish-American War, 21–22, 23, 31, 33, 38, 43, 136
spirituality: and criticism of nun-nurses, 144–47; emphasis on, 124–25; of Irish, 41; marketing of, 118–23; and meaning of sickness, 130–32; as mission of Catholic hospitals, 3, 27, 53, 75, 76, 92, 99, 132–41, 188, 190; practices of, 129–30, 134–35; and religious identity, 44–47; of religious life, 35, 36, 41–43. See also sacraments
Stang, Father William, 42
Starr, Paul, 187
Stevenson, W. W., 86, 172
Stevens, Rosemary, 6
Studebaker, Clem, 108, 114
suffering, 46, 47, 131, 141, 146, 190–91

surgery: advances in, 172–73; authority over, 158; at Catholic hospitals, 75; cost of, 123; at Holy Cross Hospital, 88–90, 158; nuns' assistance with, 143, 181–84; at St. Joseph's Hospital (South Bend, Ind.), 91–93; at St. Joseph's Hospital (St. Paul), 54, 81–82; at St. Joseph's Infirmary (Fort Worth), 97, 182; at St. Mary's Hospital (Minneapolis), 82–85; at Santa Rosa Infirmary, 99, 150, 158, *177*, 182, 216n86
Sweetser, H. B., 83

"Tag Day," 109
Tarrant County, Tex., 95
technology, 75
Terre Haute, Ind., 67–73
Texas, 3, 15, 19, 26–27, 30, 31, 51, 187, 189, 192
Theno, Sister Ida, 171
Thompson, F. D., 96, 155
Thompson, Margaret Susan, 99
Toohey, Father John, 64
Trinity Health, 194
Troeger, Sister Isidore, *79*

tuberculosis institutions, 22
Twohig, John, 56
Tyndale, William, 214n48
typhoid fever, 142

University of Minnesota Medical School, 83, 85
University of Notre Dame, 25, 109–10
University of Utah Medical Department, 89
Urrutia, Aureliano, 94, 99
US Treasury Department, 58, 72
Utah: availability of medical care in, 100; Catholic population in, 19, 60; history of Catholic hospitals in, 3; hospital patterns in, 187; hospitals in, 22, 26, 51, 59–63, 194; immigrant population in, 15; mining deaths in, 76

Vasey, Sister Loretta, *79*
veterans, 66–67
Vincennes, Bishop of, 66
Vincennes, Ind., 66
Volker, R. C., 95

WOMEN, GENDER, AND HEALTH
Susan L. Smith and Nancy Tomes, Series Editors

This series focuses on the history of women and health, but also includes studies that address gender and masculinity. Works in the series examine the history of sickness, health, and healing in relation to health workers, activists, and patients. They also explore the ways in which issues of gender, race, ethnicity, and health have reflected and shaped beliefs, values, and power dynamics in society.

Beyond the Reproductive Body: The Politics of Women's Health and Work in Early Victorian England
Marjorie Levine-Clark

Handling the Sick: The Women of St. Luke's and the Nature of Nursing, 1892-1937
Tom Olson and Eileen Walsh

Any Friend of the Movement: Networking for Birth Control, 1920-1940
Jimmy Elaine Wilkinson Meyer

Reproductive Health, Reproductive Rights: Reformers and the Politics of Maternal Welfare, 1917-1940
Robyn L. Rosen

Sexual Borderlands: Constructing an American Sexual Past
Edited by Kathleen Kennedy and Sharon Ullman

Don't Kill Your Baby: Public Health and the Decline of Breastfeeding in the Nineteenth and Twentieth Centuries
Jacqueline H. Wolf

A Social History of Wet Nursing in America: From Breast to Bottle
Janet Golden

Motherhood in Bondage
Margaret Sanger

Women in Labor: Mothers, Medicine, and Occupational Health in the United States, 1890-1980
Allison L. Hepler

Bodies of Technology: Women's Involvement with Reproductive Medicine
Edited by Ann R. Saetnan, Nelly Oudshoorn, and Marta Kirejczyk

Travels with the Wolf: A Story of Chronic Illness
Melissa Anne Goldstein

Modern Mothers in the Heartland: Gender, Health, and Progress in Illinois, 1900-1930
Lynne Curry

Crack Mothers: Pregnancy, Drugs, and the Media
Drew Humphries

Women's Health: Complexities and Differences
Edited by Sheryl Burt Ruzek, Virginia L. Olesen, and Adele E. Clarke

Mothers and Motherhood: Readings in American History
Edited by Rima D. Apple and Janet Golden

Making Midwives Legal: Childbirth, Medicine, and the Law, 2nd Edition
Raymond G. DeVries

Listen to Me Good: The Life Story of an Alabama Midwife
Margaret Charles Smith and Linda Janet Holmes

The Selling of Contraception: The Dalkon Shield Case, Sexuality, and Women's Autonomy
Nicole J. Grant

www.ingramcontent.com/pod-product-compliance
Lightning Source LLC
Chambersburg PA
CBHW020943230426
43666CB00005B/148